The Philosophy of the *Mòzǐ*

The Philosophy of the Mòzǐ

The First Consequentialists

CHRIS FRASER

COLUMBIA UNIVERSITY PRESS
NEW YORK

Columbia University Press
Publishers Since 1893
New York   Chichester, West Sussex
cup.columbia.edu
Copyright © 2016 Columbia University Press
All rights reserved

Library of Congress Cataloging-in-Publication Data
Names: Fraser, Chris, author.
Title: The philosophy of the Mòzi : the first consequentialists / Chris Fraser.
Description: New York : Columbia University Press, 2016. | Includes bibliographical
    references and index.
Identifiers: LCCN 2015038566 | ISBN 9780231149266 (cloth : alk. paper) |
    ISBN 9780231149273 (pbk.) | ISBN 9780231520591 (electronic)
Subjects: LCSH: Moism.
Classification: LCC B127.M65 F73 2016 | DDC 181/.115—dc23
LC record available at http://lccn.loc.gov/2015038566

Columbia University Press books are printed on permanent
and durable acid-free paper.
This book is printed on paper with recycled content.
Printed in the United States of America

c 10 9 8 7 6 5 4 3 2 1
p 10 9 8 7 6 5 4 3 2 1

COVER DESIGN: Lisa Hamm
COVER IMAGE: © Watchrra Teartsin/Shutterstock

References to websites (URLs) were accurate at the time of writing.
Neither the author nor Columbia University Press is responsible for URLs
that may have expired or changed since the manuscript was prepared.

For my family

CONTENTS

Preface ix
Acknowledgments xvii

INTRODUCTION 1
1. ORDER, OBJECTIVITY, AND EFFICACY 27
2. EPISTEMOLOGY AND LOGIC: DRAWING DISTINCTIONS 49
3. POLITICAL THEORY: ORDER THROUGH SHARED NORMS 77
4. HEAVEN: THE HIGHEST ETHICAL MODEL 104
5. ETHICS: THE BENEFIT OF ALL 129
6. INCLUSIVE CARE: FOR OTHERS AS FOR ONESELF 158
7. MOTIVATION: CHANGING PEOPLE IN A GENERATION 185
8. WAR AND ECONOMICS 203
EPILOGUE 232

Glossary 237
Notes 243
Bibliography 273
Index 281

PREFACE

HISTORY HAS NOT been kind to Mòzǐ and the social and intellectual movement he founded. The Mohists were tremendously influential grassroots social reformers and one of the most prominent and respected schools of thought in preimperial China. They were instrumental in setting the early Chinese philosophical agenda, and their theories and arguments represent a quantum leap in clarity and rigor over anything that preceded them. In texts from the early imperial era, Mòzǐ is regularly paired with Confucius (Kǒngzǐ) as one of the two great moral teachers of the past.[1] Central Mohist concepts such as all-inclusive care for the welfare of others and the importance of clear, objective models for action strongly influenced Ruist (Confucian) thinkers such as Mencius (Mèngzǐ) and Xúnzǐ. The Mohist ideal of inclusive care appears ultimately to have been absorbed into Ruism itself.[2] During the Western Hàn dynasty (206 B.C.E.–8 C.E.), however, the Mohist movement faded away, probably largely because changing social, political, and economic factors in first-century B.C.E. China eliminated much of its intellectual appeal and sociopolitical relevance. With the exception of their dialectics, the Mohists' philosophy no longer attracted much attention, and their texts fell into neglect. Throughout Chinese history, classical texts have been sustained as living, comprehensible intellectual resources through a lively commentarial tradition. But the only significant ancient commentary on the Mòzǐ was the now-lost work of Lǔ Shèng (fl. 300 C.E.), which covered only the dialectical chapters.

During the seventh century C.E., chance events contrived to prevent Mohist philosophy from receiving serious consideration from Chinese intellectuals for nearly a millennium. The unabridged text of the Mòzǐ was gradually pushed out of circulation by the publication of an abbreviated version comprising only the first thirteen of the seventy-one chapters. This truncated version was the edition read by Táng- (618–907) and Sòng-dynasty (960–1279) scholars such as Hán Yù (768–824) and Chéng Yí (1033–1107), whose remarks on Mòzǐ indicate that they never laid eyes on the essays expounding inclusive care or condemning the Rú (Confucians, Erudites). Fortunately, the unabridged text was preserved in the Dào Zàng (the Daoist Patrology scriptures), from which it was eventually recovered during the Míng dynasty and published again whole in 1552.[3] Had the text not been included in this vast Daoist collection, many details of Mohist thought, including the main expositions of Mohist ethics and all the Mohist dialectical writings, might have been lost forever.[4]

With the development of rigorous philology in the Qīng dynasty, scholars set out to clarify or emend the many obscure or corrupt graphs in the Mòzǐ, explain its often peculiar grammar, and reconstruct the damaged, misarranged, and corrupt dialectical chapters. This work began with the pioneering efforts of Bì Yuán (1730–1797) and Sūn Xīngyǎn (1753–1818) and culminated in the comprehensive commentary of Sūn Yíràng published in 1894.

The Qīng philologists provided would-be readers of the Mòzǐ with a legible, intelligible text. But the availability of such a text does not ensure that it will be understood or appreciated. By and large, the Mòzǐ has fared badly at the hands of philosophical interpreters during the modern era. To be sure, the Mòzǐ found appreciative readers during the early decades of the twentieth century, when prominent public intellectuals such as Hú Shì and Liáng Qǐchāo turned to Mohism to explore alternatives to Ruism in the Chinese intellectual tradition. Chinese Marxists in the mid-twentieth century admired Mohism for its egalitarian and communitarian tendencies and its concern for the welfare of the common people. Some Chinese Christians felt Mohist religious beliefs resonated with their own.

But the general trend in both Chinese and international scholarship has been deeply uncharitable toward Mohism. Indeed, few philosophers in any tradition have been the victims of such bad press. The Mohists are regularly the targets of an implicit prejudice that casts Ruist views and practices as norms from which Mohist positions are deviations—even when the practice at stake is deeply questionable, such as the three-year mourning custom, and opposition to it surely reasonable. All too often, Mòzǐ is treated as a dull, misguided foil against which to contrast favored Ruist views, particularly those of Mencius, a self-described arch-opponent of Mohism. Mohist ideas are routinely misconstrued and frequently twisted into implausible caricatures wildly counter to common sense. Mencius himself called Mòzǐ a "beast" for advocating all-inclusive moral care, which Mencius equated with denying one's father (*Me* 6.9). A related line of interpretation was taken up by the influential twentieth-century Ruist Táng Jūnyì, who suggested that on the Mohist conception of mind, agents lack any way of conceptualizing or caring about the particular, concrete man who is their father, as distinct from the entire set of men who together constitute the kind *fathers*.[5] Another prominent twentieth-century Ruist, Móu Zōngsān, claimed that Mohism fails to recognize any source of genuinely moral motivation.[6] Among Western interpreters, David Nivison attributes to Mòzǐ a bizarre form of voluntarism, on which agents can simply choose, easily and immediately, to feel an emotion or believe a claim, just as they can choose to move their limbs.[7] Benjamin Schwartz claims that the Mohists saw all people as fundamentally unloving and self-interested.[8] David Wong calls Mohist arguments defending inclusive care "wishes masquerading as arguments."[9] He charges the Mohists with advocating a "wholly outer-directed" ethics focused on mere behavioral conformity rather than "ensuring that one has the right motives for acting correctly."[10] Bryan Van Norden takes the Mohists to assume that "the structure of human motivations and dispositions is almost infinitely malleable."[11] Most notorious of all is the curt, uninformed dismissal of Mohism by Wing-tsit Chan, dean of an earlier generation of scholars of Chinese thought: "One thing is certain, and that is, philosophically Mohism is shallow and unimportant."[12] As this book will show, all these characterizations of Mohist thought are unjustified.

Among scholars publishing in English, defenders of the intellectual importance of the Mohists have been few and far between. I have already mentioned Hú Shì, who assigned the Mohists a prominent place in his pioneering 1922 work *The Development of the Logical Method in Ancient China*. Another important early advocate of the Mohists' importance was Yi-Pao Mei, author of the earliest monograph on Mòzǐ in English, who rightly called the Mohist doctrine of inclusive care "one of the epoch-making discoveries in the evolution of human relations."[13] In the preface to Mei's book appear these remarks, happily less accurate today than when he wrote them in 1934 but still pertinent:

> The growing conviction through the work is that Confucianism is not the only valuable way of life that China has ever possessed and can offer, that that system has won its place of supremacy by accidental circumstances as well as intrinsic worth, and that Western attention in Chinese systems of thought has been led to distribute itself unjustly—a large amount to Confucius, only a little to Laotse, and none to speak of to Motse, to mention only the three most original thinkers. (ix)

Mei described his project as "a positive endeavor to remedy the situation by presenting the much neglected author to the public" (ix). Two important more recent contributors to this endeavor have been A. C. Graham and Chad Hansen.[14] Graham's 1978 *Later Mohist Logic, Ethics and Science* recognized the pivotal role of the Mohists in the development of classical Chinese thought and showed how a detailed account of Mohist dialectics was crucial to fully understanding the ethics, philosophy of language, epistemology, and psychology of early Ruist, Daoist, and other thinkers. Hansen's 1992 *A Daoist Theory of Chinese Thought* went further in articulating the Mohists' role as a driving force—perhaps the single most influential driving force—in classical Chinese intellectual discourse. He identified numerous presuppositions common to Confucius and Mohism and showed how the early Mohists articulated much of the shared conceptual framework of preimperial thought. Hansen was probably the first to point out that, by our contemporary understanding of what philosophy is—not merely ethical instruction but a process of critically questioning values, concepts, and beliefs while seeking answers supported by good arguments—it is Mòzǐ, not Confucius, who deserves the title of China's first philosopher.[15]

This book is intended as a contribution to what Hansen called the philosophical "rehabilitation" of Mohism.[16] It does not aim to establish that Mohist positions in any particular area are correct—I myself disagree with many aspects of Mohist ethics—but to show that, properly understood, numerous features of Mohist thought are interesting, instructive, and worthy of attention. As Franklin Perkins remarks in an introduction to a recent collection of essays on Mohism, "in a global philosophical dialogue, the *Mòzǐ* has valuable things to say."[17] One aim of this book is to help us see more clearly what some of those things might be.

In particular, I hope to elucidate the Mohist ethical theory—notable as history's first version of consequentialism and perhaps the earliest systematic normative theory of any kind—and to show that it is both more plausible than it is typically taken to be and deeply instructive as to the shape a convincing normative theory might take. It does not, as often suggested, have the unappealing consequence that we have an equal moral obligation to promote the well-being of all persons, regardless of their relation to us.[18] To the contrary, it emphasizes the central place of special kinship and political relationships in human life while also systematically developing the fundamental moral insight that the right way to live must take into account not only those with whom we share such relationships but also those with whom we have no personal or political relationship at all. An especially significant achievement of Mohist ethics, which I will explore at length, is their discovery of the centrality of impartiality—and, indirectly, universalizability—in ethical theory. Despite their tremendous contributions on this point, however, the Mohists' approach to articulating impartiality constitutes a major flaw in their ethics. I will examine this issue in detail and argue that the Mohists' mishandling of impartiality is among the most instructive features of their ethical theory.

A second topic to which I will devote special attention is the Mohists' fascinating nonmentalistic, nonsubjectivist psychology, which permeates their epistemology, political theory, and ethics. The Mohists regard perception, inference, and action as based not on an innate capacity to form inner, mental representations or to grasp logical relations between propositions but on the public, often socially acquired ability to distinguish different kinds of things and respond to each kind in a consistent way. This model is the basis for a plausible philosophy of mind and action intriguingly different from the familiar individualist, subjectivist, and representationalist picture that has come down to us from the Judeo-Christian tradition and Enlightenment conceptualism. It is valuable both for its inherent interest and as a potential inspiration for contemporary philosophy of psychology. The failure to recognize the place of this model in Mohist thought is among the main factors driving the pervasive misunderstanding of their moral psychology.[19]

This book seeks to fill a gap in the literature on early Chinese thought by providing an extended, in-depth discussion of Mohism from a philosophical perspective. To my knowledge, it is one of only a handful of monographs on the Mohists in English and the first by a philosopher.[20] It is intended as a philosophical study, not a work of intellectual history. Hence I devote only limited attention to the Mohists' historical background, to philological issues, and to relations between the Mohists and other thinkers. The content is deliberately imbalanced, in that the book devotes much attention to aspects of Mohist thought I find philosophically rich while touching only briefly on, or sometimes passing over entirely, other features that, despite their historical or anthropological value, seem philosophically less interesting. A further imbalance is that to address Mohist ethical and political thought in the detail it deserves, I have had to forgo an originally planned chapter on later Mohist philosophy of language, epistemology, and logic. This seems a reasonable trade-off, since I have previously published an easily accessible chapter-length account of later Mohist thought, which readers are invited to consult.[21]

I have tried to write the book to appeal to a broad audience, so that it will have something to offer university undergraduates and general readers as well as specialists. As a result, in a few places professional scholars may find the exposition too elementary, while in others general readers may find it too technical. Overall, however, I hope to have maintained a satisfactory balance between accessibility and depth.

Throughout the book, all translations from Chinese sources are my own. To complement this philosophical study, I have also completed a new, abridged translation of the *Mòzǐ*, which is forthcoming. Readers may wish to consult previous English translations of Mohist ethical and political writings as well. These include Yi-Pao Mei, trans., *The Ethical and Political Works of Motse*, which can be accessed online at Ctext.org, a rich electronic resource created by Donald Sturgeon; Ian Johnston, trans., *The Mozi*; and John Knoblock and Jeffrey Riegel, trans., *Mozi: A Study and Translation of the Ethical and Political Writings*. Partial translations are available in Burton Watson, trans., *Mo Tzu: Basic Writings*, and Philip J. Ivanhoe and Bryan W. Van Norden, eds., *Readings in Classical Chinese Philosophy*. Readers will find that my renderings of key Mohist philosophical terms often diverge from those of previous writers, such as my use of "inclusive care" where most translations have "universal love" or "impartial love." These interpretive choices are explained in the relevant chapters that follow.

I have rendered all Chinese terms in the Hànyǔ Pīnyīn romanization system. The correct pronunciation of Hànyǔ Pīnyīn is typically not obvious to speakers of English, so I encourage readers to consult one of the many useful pronunciation guides available online. The Chinese characters for key terms are included at their first appearance in each chapter, and characters for all Chinese terms and names appear in a glossary at the end.

CITATIONS TO CLASSICAL TEXTS

Citations to ancient Chinese texts use the following abbreviations and editions.

Hnz	Hé Níng 何寧, ed., 淮南子集釋 [Collected explications of the *Huáinánzǐ*] (Běijīng: Zhōnghuá, 1998).
HS	Bān Gù 班固, 漢書 [*Hàn shū*, history of the Former Han], ed. Yán Shīgǔ 顏師古 (Běijīng: Zhōnghuá, 1962).
LH	D. C. Lau and Chen Fong Ching, eds., *A Concordance to the "Lunheng"* (Hong Kong: Commercial Press, 1996).
LSCQ	John Knoblock and Jeffrey Riegel, *The Annals of Lü Buwei* (Stanford: Stanford University Press, 2000). Citations are to section numbers.
LY	D. C. Lau et al., eds., *A Concordance to the "Lunyu"* (Hong Kong: Commercial Press, 1995). Citations give section numbers.
MB	A. C. Graham, *Later Mohist Logic, Ethics and Science* (Hong Kong: Chinese University Press, 1978). References to the Mohist "Dialectics" (*Mò biàn*) cite canon or section numbers in this edition.

Me	D. C. Lau et al., eds., *A Concordance to the "Mengzi"* (Hong Kong: Commercial Press, 1995). Citations give section numbers.
Mz	William Hung, ed., *A Concordance to Mo Tzu*, Harvard-Yenching Institute Sinological Index Series, supplement no. 21 (reprint) (Shànghǎi: Shànghǎi gǔjí, 1986). Citations give chapter and line numbers.
SJ	Sīmǎ Qiān 司馬遷, 史記 [*Shǐjì*, records of the grand historian] (Běijīng: Zhōnghuá, 1959).
Xz	William Hung, ed., *A Concordance to Hsun Tzu*, Harvard-Yenching Institute Sinological Index Series, supplement no. 22 (reprint) (Shànghǎi: Shànghǎi gǔjí, 1986). Citations give chapter and line numbers.
Zz	William Hung, ed., *A Concordance to Chuang Tzu*, Harvard-Yenching Institute Sinological Index Series, supplement no. 20 (reprint) (Shànghǎi: Shànghǎi gǔjí, 1986). Citations give chapter and line numbers.

ACKNOWLEDGMENTS

ALL ACADEMIC AUTHORS owe a vast debt to family, friends, colleagues, and teachers for support and encouragement and for inspiring the ideas and formulations in their work. My understanding of the Mohists has benefited greatly from discussions with many people. I am particularly grateful to Chad Hansen, Dan Robins, Franklin Perkins, Kai Yee Wong, Hon Lam Li, Jiwei Ci, William Haines, Kwok Wai Lee, and the many thoughtful and enthusiastic students who have attended my courses on Mohist thought and Chinese ethics. I also thank Hui-chieh Loy, Franklin Perkins, Carine Defoort, and Karen Desmet for sharing with me their work in progress on various aspects of Mohism. Chad Hansen, Hui-chieh Loy, Franklin Perkins, William Haines, Dan Robins, Timothy O'Leary, P. J. Ivanhoe, and Carine Defoort all offered helpful comments on material later incorporated into the book, as did three anonymous readers for Columbia University Press, who saved me from several errors.

I am singularly indebted to Hansen for kindling my interest in the Mòzǐ in the first place through his book *A Daoist Theory of Chinese Thought*, which I read in 1994. A similarly important debt is to A. C. Graham, whose *Later Mohist Logic, Ethics and Science* has been an indispensable resource. Yet another influence has been Taeko Brooks, from whose model I learned much about how to read the Mòzǐ.

I am grateful to colleagues in the Department of Philosophy at the Chinese University of Hong Kong for providing a hospitable working environment and for their warm support during a health crisis while the book was in preparation. I also thank colleagues in the Department of Philosophy of the University of Hong Kong, my current institution, for a congenial, supportive climate.

I thank my wife, Flora Chi, for her enthusiastic encouragement through the final stages of the project.

Earlier versions of some of the material in this book have appeared in the *Stanford Encyclopedia of Philosophy*, the *Journal of Chinese Philosophy*, and three edited anthologies, *Ethics in Early China* (Hong Kong University Press, 2011), edited by myself, Dan Robins, and Timothy O'Leary; *The "Mozi" as an Evolving Text: Different Voices in Early Chinese Thought* (Brill, 2013), edited by Carine Defoort and Nicolas Standaert; and *Chinese Metaphysics and Its Problems* (Cambridge University Press, 2014), edited by Chenyang Li and Franklin Perkins. I thank the editors of the *Stanford Encyclopedia of Philosophy* and of the *Journal of Chinese Philosophy*, the International Society for Chinese Philosophy, Blackwell Publishing, Hong Kong University Press, Brill, and Cambridge University Press for permission to use this material.

Finally, I am grateful to Wendy Lochner, Christine Dunbar, Mike Ashby, Amber Morena, and the production staff at Columbia University Press for their wonderful support and assistance.

The Philosophy of the *Mòzǐ*

INTRODUCTION

IMAGINE LIVING IN an ancient society in which you are a successful, self-reliant craftsman—a carpenter, say—admired for your sturdy, useful products. Your diligence, skill, and integrity have won a demand for your services, ensuring that you have enough income to support your family. Your forebears were farmers and laborers, and most people in your society still work the land. Their lives are difficult, the threat of poverty and hunger never far off. But economic development and population growth have enabled you to make a decent living from your craft. You have even been fortunate enough to receive a rudimentary education, so that, unlike your ancestors, you can read and write, though haltingly. In your society, the class of partly literate, hardworking, urban middle-income people like yourself—artisans, merchants, teachers, civil servants—is growing rapidly. Unlike earlier times, there are real opportunities for advancement open to you and your peers in business, trade, government service, or the military.

Politically, though, you are nearly powerless. Your state, like others, is governed by a hereditary lord and his cronies. These aristocrats control the military, courts, and police, collect taxes, and provide limited public services—in the best cases, defense and security forces, public works, and famine relief. Fundamentally, you don't object to rule by an elite few. It is the only system you know, and as a craftsman you think the best system of leadership, whether for a construction project or a community, is to put competent experts in charge. Long ago, people say, competent, honest leaders really did run things. The system worked, society flourished, and people were well-off. These days, however, many of those at the top are anything but effective and honest. They mismanage the government and economy. They appoint inept relatives and lackeys to run the courts and public works. Worst of all, many aristocrats are simply warmongering bullies who hardly care about building a stable, prosperous society. Infatuated with military glory, they dream of conquering the world and winning fame like that of the legendary kings of old. Heedless of the harm to people, property, and even their own interests, they raise massive armies and set off to plunder the treasure and enslave the residents of other lands.

> Now the rulers of the great states say, without scruples, "Dwelling in a great state without attacking small states, how am I great?" Hence they muster their sharpest soldiers and assemble their boat and chariot forces to attack an innocent state. Entering the state's borders, they mow down its crops, fell its trees, raze its city walls, filling its moats with the rubble, burn its ancestral shrines, and slaughter its sacrificial animals. People who resist are beheaded; those who don't resist are brought back in chains, the men to labor in stables and on chain gangs, the women to thresh grain.
>
> The warlike rulers don't know this is unbenevolent and unrighteous. They announce it to the lords of neighboring states, saying, "I attacked a state, defeated an army, and killed such-and-such many generals." The rulers of the neighboring states don't know this is unbenevolent and unrighteous, either. Some prepare furs and coins, opening their treasuries, and send envoys to offer gifts and congratulations.... The warlike rulers don't know this is unbenevolent and unrighteous, the rulers of neighboring states don't know this is unbenevolent and unrighteous, and hence the aggression goes on for generation after generation without cease.[1] (Mz 28/46–55)

You yourself have seen or heard of numerous states that were extinguished in unprovoked attacks, often at great cost to both sides in lives and wealth. Ultimately even the victors would have been better off had they never gone to war.

Beyond the direct costs of aggression, the rulers' belligerent mentality percolates down through society, breeding a general atmosphere of selfishness and lawlessness. Not everyone disregards others, but enough people do that crime and disorder leave you deeply worried.

> Now the various lords know only to care about their state and don't care about others' states, and hence they don't hesitate to deploy their state to attack others' states. Now the heads of clans know only to care about their clan and don't care about others' clans, and hence they don't hesitate to deploy their clan to subvert others' clans. Now people know only to care about themselves and don't

care about others, and hence they don't hesitate to deploy themselves to injure others' selves.

Thus the various lords not caring about each other, they inevitably go to war; the heads of clans not caring about each other, they inevitably subvert each other; people not caring about each other, they inevitably injure each other; rulers and subjects not caring about each other, they are not generous and loyal; fathers and sons not caring about each other, they are not paternally kind or filially devoted; elder and younger brothers not caring about each other, they are not peaceful and harmonious. The people of the world all not caring about each other, the strong inevitably oppress the weak, the wealthy inevitably humiliate the poor, the noble are inevitably contemptuous of the common, and the cunning inevitably deceive the ignorant. (Mz 15/4–9)

The self-centered aristocracy taxes their subjects heavily to fund lives of luxury for themselves. Among their most conspicuous displays of wealth are huge musical extravaganzas. A single massive set of bells for one of their court orchestras can be as large as a house and cost more than you and all your neighbors will earn in your lives. These shows are part of elaborate state ceremonies, over which preside another prominent elite group, who call themselves the Erudites. The Erudites wear peculiar, old-fashioned robes and hats, speak in a pretentious, archaic idiom, and spend their time studying ancient scrolls, practicing ceremonies and dances, and chanting poetry to music. Obsessed with ancient ways, they favor tradition over innovation. Despite fussing incessantly about virtue, they seem to do little to improve things. They claim, for instance, that a gentleman doesn't take the initiative to dissuade his ruler from a bad policy. In any case, they hold, everything that happens is fated, so activism is pointless.

Even worse, as experts in funeral rites, the Erudites promote the wasteful custom of bizarrely protracted mourning rituals and extravagant burials. At the death of a lord of a state, the public treasury may be emptied to build an immense tomb filled with treasure, weapons, furniture, carts, and horses. Dozens of human victims might be sacrificed to accompany their deceased ruler in death. Under the prevailing custom of packing tombs with burial goods, even commoners' deaths are likely to exhaust their families' wealth. Meanwhile, mourners are expected to withdraw from normal life, live in a rough hut, sleep on the ground, wear thin, sackcloth robes, and eat only porridge, so that they appear suitably cold, hungry, weak, and miserable. The Erudites hold that such mourning practices should continue for more than two years after the death of a sovereign, parent, wife, or eldest son; one year after the death of uncles, brothers, or other sons; five months after the death of other close relatives; and several months for distant relatives.²

These political and social circumstances would provoke frustration or outrage in many of us. But what would we do about them? What I have been describing was roughly the situation faced some twenty-five hundred years ago by residents of several of the "Central States" that were later united to form the Chinese empire. Many people reluctantly accepted the status quo and hoped a wise, virtuous leader might emerge to improve things. Confucius, China's first great moral teacher and a leader among the Erudites,³ advocated a return to the ways of the glorious Zhōu dynasty, whose decline precipitated the rampant interstate warfare. In the meantime, he is reported to have endorsed withdrawal from public service when the Dào 道—the right social, political, and moral Way—did not prevail in the world (*LY* 8.13). (Other remarks attributed to him, especially in later textual strata, suggest the early Erudites disagreed among themselves over whether to take up or avoid service in a corrupt government.⁴) The writers of texts we now associate with the Daoist tradition—specifically, the *Dàodéjīng* and the *Zhuāngzǐ*—tended to recommend avoiding political activity and government service, if practical. Some went so far as to advocate leaving civil society behind and moving out to the wilderness.

By contrast, a charismatic artisan named Mò Dí 墨翟, who lived in the middle of the fifth century B.C.E., thought the only defensible response to these problems was public activism. He condemned cruel, immoral rulers and customs, defended the interests of the poor and weak, and campaigned to reform society according to objective moral standards—as he saw it, the same sort of objective, reliable, publicly verifiable standards that a carpenter uses to saw a straight line or a wheelwright uses to shape a wheel. He traveled from state to state trying to persuade rulers and officials to adopt a platform of policies intended to end warfare, alleviate poverty, and promote the welfare of all. In the process, he became the first real philosopher in Chinese history, developing systematic ethical, political, and epistemological theories and giving clear, logical arguments to justify his views. A magnetic leader, he attracted a following that grew into one of the most influential social and intellectual movements in preimperial China. He and his school of followers—the Mohists—played a pivotal role in shaping and articulating the conceptual framework of early Chinese thought. Members of his school wrote a large collection of texts presenting, developing, and extending the ideas of their founder, whom they called *Mòzǐ* 墨子, or Master Mò.⁵ By the Hàn dynasty (206 B.C.E.–220 C.E.), these texts had been collated into an anthology called the *Mòzǐ*, the major source for our knowledge of Mohist thought. (In the older, Wade-Giles romanization, *Mòzǐ* is written *Mo-tzu* or *Mo Tzu*.)

This book explores the thought of Mò Dí and his school. As a first step toward understanding that thought, it is crucial to keep in mind the roots from which Mohism arose: opposition to the inhumanity and immorality of warmongering rulers, parasitic aristocrats, wasteful, senseless customs, and people with no regard for others—especially for the poor and powerless, the farmers, laborers, and artisans struggling to keep their families clothed and fed. Mohism was above all a social and political program aimed at overcoming war, strife, crime, and poverty. In some places, the Mohists' rhetoric may exaggerate or their arguments oversimplify. But their aim was not pieces of argumentation fit to publish in a contemporary journal of analytic philosophy. It was to lead people—particularly the rich and powerful—to show concern for the interests of others—particularly the poor and defenseless—and to alleviate poverty, eliminate crime and feuding, and end meaningless warfare. To the extent that their rhetoric led a few merchants to donate food to the destitute or a warlike ruler to call off an invasion, their project was already partly successful. Just how successful they were is impossible to gauge—we have no way of counting the wars their activism might have prevented, for example. What we can say is that the Mohists helped change the tenor of classical Chinese moral and political culture, making the justification of war and the welfare of the common people issues no one could ignore. Above all, they spread the idea that conduct should be judged by objective moral standards, not just prevailing customs, and that concern for others is central to the ethical life.

The Mohists' motivation and the nature of their project render some of their views deeply compelling, for often they are in effect arguing on behalf of basic decency and against utter disregard for others. Their motives and aims naturally evoke respect and appreciation. Mòzǐ and his followers were driven by a profound concern for other people and a desire to right the world's wrongs. They were China's first real social critics and political activists, who identified various problems in society, developed a theory to explain them, and set out to change things. At the same time, however, understanding their motivation can help us pinpoint some of Mohism's weaknesses. As responses to perceived social, economic, and moral crises, Mohist ethical and political doctrines are infused with a sense of moral urgency that in most people's lives—at least in more stable times—may be unnecessary or inappropriate. This air of crisis helps explain why the Mohists' political philosophy places order and unity above all else and why their economic program is aimed solely at surviving hard times, without an inkling that spending on nonessentials might improve people's quality of life or contribute to economic growth. Above all, as we will see, it tends to turn Mohism into an ethics for saints and heroes, not ordinary people.

THE WARRING STATES ERA

Mòzǐ and his followers flourished during the Warring States era (481 B.C.E.–221 B.C.E.), historians' term for the latter centuries of the long, gradual disintegration of the once-grand Zhōu dynasty (1045 B.C.E.–256 B.C.E.). By the Mohists' time, the Zhōu was effectively powerless. An emperor, or "Son of Heaven," still occupied the imperial throne at Luòyáng, and various fiefdoms and states remained nominally his vassals. But de facto power lay in the hands of the hereditary lords of roughly a dozen states, which had incorporated most of the small fiefdoms, and the non-Zhōu states of Chǔ, Wú, and Yuè in the south. By the Mohists' time, these dozen-odd states had evolved into a system of rival powers linked by shifting alliances. A handful were particularly large, powerful, and aggressive, each aspiring to conquer the others and unify them under its rule.

By all accounts, this was a period of great social change and economic expansion. The decline of the old feudal and clan system led to an increase in social mobility and economic opportunity. Growth in cultivated land area and improvements in agricultural productivity sparked a rapid increase in population. Technological innovations and large-scale manufacturing led to greater occupational specialization and an expansion in trade. Reliable interstate transportation and stable trade relations facilitated the emergence of a class of prosperous merchants, some of whom eventually rivaled the aristocracy in wealth and power. Literacy became more widespread, and opportunities opened up for educated, capable commoners to reach positions of influence in government administration.[6]

Despite these positive developments, the Warring States was also an era of violent upheaval and perceived cultural decline. The larger states competed relentlessly for power, land, population, and wealth, frequently instigating wars of conquest against weaker neighbors. These conflicts were not the brief, small-scale skirmishes of earlier times but prolonged battles between massive infantry armies. Able-bodied men were regularly conscripted for military service or work gangs, while a steady stream of war captives were seized from their homes and enslaved. People were subjected to heavy taxes to pay for the grand palaces and luxuries enjoyed by despotic rulers. Landless peasants, frustrated in their attempts to make a living, formed roving bands of robbers who terrorized travelers and villages. Many rulers of states and fiefs were seen as ineffectual or immoral. The Zhōu social and political order was crumbling, and a new regime inspiring the same level of respect and loyalty was nowhere in sight. Teachers and scholars perceived the era as dissolute—the traditional order had been lost, the Dào (Way) had fallen into neglect.

Ironically, many of those who lamented the decline of the Dào probably owed their livelihood to the very social and economic factors that undermined the Zhōu order. For these also enabled the rise of a class of nonaristocratic statesmen, counselors, and scholars, or "officers" (shì 士). These men—as far as we know, they were all male—typically made their living as either government administrators, political advisers and retainers, or teachers and mentors to young protégés eager to move into government service themselves. Confucius and Mòzǐ are the first such teachers whose names have come down to us. They and their successors rarely succeeded in placing students in high office, but they seem regularly to have helped them find middle- or lower-level posts. Like Mòzǐ, many of these teachers and advisers devoted themselves to social and political advocacy, seeking to persuade rulers to adopt their policy recommendations, which were usually but not always humanitarian.

Such teachers and advisers also benefited from state patronage, as prestige-hungry rulers competed to attract brilliant or renowned figures to their retinue. Many of them fell into a class that became known as the disputers or dialecticians (biàn zhě 辯者). They debated philosophical and political issues among themselves and in the courts of the various lords, competing to attract adherents and win social and political influence. Despite the purported degeneracy of the era, it was actually among the most intellectually dynamic and fertile periods in Chinese history. Later scholars dubbed it the age of the "hundred schools" of thought. This is the intellectual milieu in which Mòzǐ exerted an early, formative influence and his later followers thrived, down through the unification of China under the Qín dynasty in 221 B.C.E. and well into the first century of the Hàn.

MÒ DÍ AND THE MOHISTS

History has preserved little biographical information about Mò Dí or the members of his school. The Hàn-dynasty *Shǐjì* (Records of the grand historian) tells us he was an official in the state of Sòng who lived either at the same time as or after Confucius (d. 479 B.C.E.), with whom Hàn texts pair him as the two great moral teachers of the Warring States era (SJ 74, 2350). However, nothing in the *Mòzǐ* supports the claim that he held office in Sòng, or anywhere else.[7] He could have been from Qí, as several anecdotes place him there and one has him traveling from Qí to see the King of Chǔ. But a stronger hypothesis is that, like Confucius, he was from Lǔ (in modern Shāndōng), which by triangulation seems the implicit point of origin for many of his reported journeys.[8] The Mohist "Dialogues" (books 46–50 of the *Mòzǐ*) repeatedly mention him traveling to other states but only from, never to, Lǔ. Lǔ figures prominently in the "Dialogues," is mentioned in the title of one, the "Questions of Lǔ," and was the home state of Wūmǎzǐ, one of Mòzǐ's frequent interlocutors (*Mz* 46/52–55). So it is the most likely candidate for Mòzǐ's home state.

Given the dates of several kings and battles mentioned in the *Mòzǐ*, it seems probable that Mò Dí flourished during the middle to late decades of the fifth century B.C.E., roughly contemporaneous with Socrates in Greece. Mò 墨, the Chinese word for "ink," is an unusual surname. Hence scholars have speculated that it may have been an epithet given Mòzǐ because he had the dark skin of a laborer or the facial tattoos of a slave or convict. It is hard to imagine Mò Dí committing a crime, however. One passage in the *Mòzǐ* quotes a fortune-teller commenting on his dark skin (*Mz* 47/49–53), though this is insufficient evidence to draw any conclusions. If in fact Mò was a sobriquet of some kind, its origin and meaning are probably lost.

Though the *Mòzǐ* contains many anecdotes about him, as a person Mò Dí remains largely a cipher. To a great extent, he functions as a neutral placeholder for the Mohist conception of the sage or moral saint. As depicted in the text, he is totally dedicated to morality and moral education and to pursuing the aims of the Mohist ethical, political, and economic reform program. He is clever, and not entirely humorless, but has next to no personality or interests outside his all-consuming commitment to morality. In this respect, he personifies Mohist ethics, which as we will see has a very thin conception of the individual good life. The Mohists' literary treatment of their founder contrasts with the fuller portrayal of Confucius in the *Analects*, which presents several sides of his personality.

Mohist texts give only a handful of clues about Mò Dí's life. One passage highlights his low social status, as it depicts a minister to King Xiàn Huì of Chǔ (488 B.C.E.–432 B.C.E.) questioning whether his ruler should accept the counsel of a lowly commoner (*Mz* 47/6–16). A late, probably embellished anecdote depicts Mòzǐ as a brilliant military engineer (50/1ff.). The *Huáinánzǐ*, a Hàn-dynasty text, reports that he was an apostate (Rú 儒), or Erudite, who rejected the teachings of Confucius because he found the rituals tiresome, the burial practices wasteful, and the prolonged mourning harmful to people's livelihood (*Hnz* 1459). This account seems merely a conjecture by the *Huáinánzǐ* writers, however. Nothing in the *Mòzǐ* or any other pre-Hàn text supports the claim that he originally studied as a Rú. The *Mòzǐ* depicts him as familiar with Ruist practices and a handful of Ruist sayings, but no more so than any resident of the Central States might have been.

A more persuasive conjecture about Mò Dí's background is that he was originally an artisan, perhaps a carpenter or wheelwright.⁹ This proposal explains why the *Mòzǐ* regularly depicts him giving examples and analogies based on the work of carpenters and wheelwrights. The many textual references to work, crafts, trade, farming and husbandry, warfare, and the welfare of the common people strongly suggest that Mohism was a product of the emerging middle class of artisans, merchants, small landholders, and soldiers that grew in size and political influence during the Warring States era.

This social background distinguishes the Mohists from most other early Chinese thinkers, who were typically from elite or privileged social groups, such as government officials or advisers, royal clients, or ritual priests. As Graham conjectures,¹⁰ the Mohists' low social origins may help explain why they make no use of the paradigmatic moral contrast of the Confucian *Analects*, that between the *jūnzǐ* 君子 (gentleman) and *xiǎo rén* 小人 (petty or vulgar person), terms that originally referred specifically to social rank (princeling versus commoner). It may also help explain the Mohists' frequent criticisms of the misguided judgments of the *jūnzǐ*, many of whom they regarded as ethically shortsighted upper-class conformists. For the Mohists, as for the Rú, idealized role models play a part in moral education and practical reasoning. But their models, such as the benevolent person (*rén rén* 仁人 or *rén zhě* 仁者), do not allude directly to elite as opposed to plebeian social status.¹¹

A corollary of these conjectures about their origins is that Mò Dí and many of his early followers—including the writers of much of the *Mòzǐ*—may have had limited formal education, leaving them relatively unversed in the Classical Chinese written language. Parts of the *Mòzǐ* appear to have been composed in colloquial, regional speech rather than in the more terse, graceful written language. The *Mòzǐ* does depict Mò Dí quoting ancient texts, and one anecdote emphasizes his love of book learning, describing him as traveling with a cartload of scrolls (Mz 47/32–36). However, such passages may be later embellishments added to portray him as more educated than he really was. The earliest parts of the *Mòzǐ*—such as the first books in the "Identifying Upward," "Inclusive Care," and "Heaven's Intent" triads—do not depict him quoting the classics. Given that these have the ring of oral compositions rather than written texts, Mòzǐ himself may have been a powerful orator but only marginally literate. Oral composition also helps to explain the repetitive, formulaic style of the earliest sections of the *Mòzǐ*, which are well suited to memorization and spoken delivery but distinctively ponderous and monotonous as written texts. An anecdote in the *Hánfēizǐ* suggests that the plain, repetitive Mohist style was deliberate, because the Mohists feared that even in rhetoric, ornamentation interferes with utility.[12] This story rings true given the Mohists' general indifference to aesthetic value. However, their characteristic prose style was probably also due partly to an emphasis on precision and clarity. Mohist writings are the oldest argumentative texts and perhaps the first examples of expository writing in the Chinese tradition.[13]

The Mohists' social origins probably also helped to motivate certain features of their thought, such as their focus on the material welfare of the common people and on applying objective standards of conduct. For the elite Rú, the aristocratic ceremonial etiquette of the waning Zhōu dynasty provided grounds for consensus in ethical judgments. Coming from lower social strata, the Mohists identified less with the Zhōu high culture and so looked for other, more universal guidelines. They felt little attachment to aristocratic customs such as elaborate burials and ceremonial musical performances, which to them seemed wasteful and pointless. As practical, down-to-earth artisans, merchants, soldiers, and farmers, they would have valued utility and believed there are objectively right and wrong—or at least reliable and unreliable—ways to do things. Their subelite origins dovetail too with their commitment to the interests of the poor and downtrodden, those most likely to starve or die because of the economic mismanagement or reckless military ambitions of autocratic rulers. A theme to which Mohist writings return repeatedly is the problem of meeting the common people's basic subsistence needs. Their conception of Heaven as a personal deity and their conviction that Heaven, ghosts, and spirits reliably punish the wicked and reward the good may also reflect popular religious beliefs that were less influential for Confucian and Daoist thinkers from higher social echelons.[14]

As Graham points out, however, there is no evidence that Mohism represents the ideology of a self-conscious lower or middle class seeking to restructure or overturn established political institutions or the prevailing social order.[15] Rather, the Mohists are ambitious, capable commoners for whom the passing of the old feudal system and the development of centralized, meritocratic bureaucracies have made promotion to the officer (*shì*) class a real possibility. Like most other early Chinese thinkers—with the notable exception of the Daoists—the Mohists advocate a powerful, centralized government bureaucracy directed by virtuous leaders, and they aspire to positions of responsibility within such a system. Hence their doctrine of "promoting the worthy" advocates promotion of anyone with ability, including farmers and artisans.

As their movement flourished in the fifth through third centuries B.C.E., the Mohists branched into a number of factions, each led by a *jùzǐ* 鉅子, or "grand master." Two early sources, the *Hánfēizǐ* (book 50, ca. 233 B.C.E.) and the *Zhuāngzǐ* (book 33, perhaps second century B.C.E.), mention a total of six such groups of Mohists. Another early text, *The Annals of Lü Buwei* (ca. 239 B.C.E.), mentions at least three other Mohist *jùzǐ*.[16] Evidence from the *Mòzǐ* and the *Annals* indicates that these Mohist groups were disciplined organizations devoted to moral and practical education, political advocacy, government service, and in some cases military service. Members undertook a period of study and training, after which the organization would find them positions in government or the military, perhaps in a Mohist regiment. They were expected to contribute funds to the organization and could be expelled for failing to fulfill their duties. The Mohists were renowned for their ethical principles, fervent commitment to their movement, austere lifestyle, and courage. The *Huáinánzǐ* says that Mòzǐ's followers "could all be commanded to rush into fire or tread on blades. In the face of death they would not turn their heels" (*Hnz* 1406). The *Zhuāngzǐ* "All Under Heaven" essay—a Hàn-dynasty history of thought—claims that many Mohists of its time believed they had a duty to emulate the altruistic labors of the legendary sage-king Yǔ:

> Many of the Mohists of later ages wear furs and rough clothing, clogs and grass slippers, never resting day or night, taking self-sacrifice as the highest. They say, "One who cannot do this is not following the way of Yǔ and doesn't deserve to be called a Mohist." ... They press each other forward in self-sacrifice until there's no flesh left on their calves or hair on their shins. (*Zz* 33/27–32)

Such external testimony—albeit from an unsympathetic source—presents a puzzle in interpreting Mohist thought, because the texts preserved in the *Mòzǐ* do not advocate selfless altruism. Some zealous Mohists may have taken their idealism beyond what orthodox Mohist ethics required. The same *Zhuāngzǐ* passage reports that different groups of Mohists quarreled over doctrinal details, calling one another "heretical Mohists." Self-sacrifice may have been one of the issues over which they disagreed.

Though they condemned military aggression, Mòzǐ and his followers were not pacifists. Remarks throughout the middle and later strata of the *Mòzǐ* indicate that they considered a strong defense force crucial to state welfare and themselves possessed considerable military expertise.[17] Some Mohists apparently concluded that since gratuitous warfare was wrong and social order was a paramount value, they had a duty to go beyond mere persuasion in assisting victims of aggression. They formed militias specializing in defensive warfare that would come to the aid of cities under threat of attack. These military experts produced a series of manuals on defense tactics and siege fortifications, which are preserved in the last twenty-one chapters of the *Mòzǐ*.[18] The militias were probably crucial in winning influence for the Mohists, since rulers of small city-states and fiefs would have been keen to befriend them and enlist their support.

Still another band of Mohists may have been responsible for the Mohist "Dialectics" (Mò biàn 墨辯), six books of the *Mòzǐ* that are among the most important texts in the history of Chinese ethics, philosophy of language, epistemology, ontology, and logic. The "Dialectics" writers were among China's earliest scientists, undertaking investigations in geometry, mechanics, optics, and economics. The thought of the "Dialectics" is tightly related to and probably developed out of that of the core chapters, but it is distinctive enough that its writers could have represented a separate branch of the movement.

THE *MÒZǏ*

Our primary source for the thought of Mòzǐ and his followers is a corpus of anonymously authored texts collected into an anthology called the *Mòzǐ*. Other, less-direct sources include anecdotes and comments about the Mohists preserved in early texts such as *The Annals of Lü Buwei*, *Hánfēizǐ*, *Zhuāngzǐ*, and *Huáinánzǐ* and criticisms of them by two of their major opponents, the Ruists Mencius (ca. 372 B.C.E.–289 B.C.E.) and Xúnzǐ (fl. 289 B.C.E.–238 B.C.E.). The *Mòzǐ* is a diverse compilation of polemical essays, short dialogues, anecdotes about Mòzǐ, and compact philosophical discussions. The different parts of the anthology probably range in date from the fifth to the third century B.C.E. Even single "chapters" or "books" (originally scrolls made by stitching bamboo strips together like a snow fence) tend to contain materials of diverse origin, some of which may have been assembled in stages.[19] No part of the anthology purports to be from the hand of Mò Dí himself.

According to a table of contents compiled during or before the Hàn dynasty, the *Mòzǐ* originally consisted of seventy-one *piān* 篇, or "books," of which eighteen are now lost. The books fall into six loose groups, likely of different origin and perhaps the work of different Mohist factions. The first comprises seven books containing mainly short summaries of Mohist doctrines from perhaps the middle to late third century B.C.E. or later.[20] The second is the core of the anthology, comprising the "Triads," ten sets of three books expounding the ten main doctrines of the school. The books in each triad share the same title—probably added by a later editor—followed by the Chinese equivalent of the Roman numerals I, II, or III. Of these thirty texts, seven are lost, leaving four of the triads incomplete. This block of texts probably contains the earliest parts of the corpus, some of the books, or sections of them, going back perhaps to Mò Dí's lifetime in the middle to late decades of the fifth century B.C.E. The texts appear to be of varied date and origin, however, and linguistic, organizational, and thematic features suggest they belong to several distinct strata. A plausible explanation of these features is that the books represent different stages in the development of Mohist thought. Some may be of considerably later date than others—perhaps as late as a century or more after Mò Dí's death.[21] The separate books in each triad might also represent the views of different factions, perhaps associated with different geographical regions.

The third group comprises two books devoted to denouncing the Rú, only one of which survives. Unlike the books in the "Triads," this book—"Condemning the Rú II" (Fēi Rú xià 非儒下)—presents no constructive Mohist doctrines, so it belongs in a separate category. Its first half resembles a debate handbook giving stock rebuttals of Ruist views. The second half is a series of slanderous anecdotes about Confucius.

The fourth group—books 40–45—are known as the "Later Mohist" texts or the Mohist "Dialectics" (Mò biàn). These include two books of short "canons" (jīng 經), two of longer "explanations" (shuō 說) of the canons, a brief but rich text on argumentation and logic, and a collection of fragments from two or more lost essays on ethics and on language. These books treat a variety of topics, including language, epistemology, analogical reasoning, ethics, geometry, mechanics, optics, and economics and are of the highest philosophical and historical interest. Unfortunately, the texts are also the most difficult and corrupt in all the classical Chinese literature. This section of the corpus is probably of a later date than most of the doctrinal books. A reasonable conjecture, based on their implied intellectual milieu, is that these texts were written between the late fourth and the middle of the third century B.C.E.

The fifth group comprises five books that I will call the Mohist "Dialogues," which present sayings attributed to Mòzǐ and brief conversations between him and various disciples, opponents, and rulers or officials. These books reflect a flourishing Mohist organization that trains students, recommends them for government posts, and dispatches them on military assignments. Given the organizational development they depict and their stylistic and doctrinal differences from the "Triads," a likely conjecture is that these texts date from the middle to late decades of the fourth century B.C.E. Many of the conversations they present are probably embellished or fictional, and it is difficult to judge how much of their content might go back to Mòzǐ himself. Doctrinally, these books—especially book 47, "Valuing Morality"—contain the most demanding formulations in Mohist ethics. They may be the work of a different branch of Mohists from those who produced the "Triads," or they may indicate a tendency toward more stringent ethical ideals in later generations of the movement. As I will suggest in chapter 5, they also seem directed at a different audience from the "Triads"—committed Mohist adherents rather than officers and officials from across society.

The final block of twenty-one books is devoted to military engineering and tactics for defending besieged cities. Ten of these books are lost. Many are organized as replies by Mòzǐ to questions from a leading disciple, Qín Gǔ Lí, who is referred to as Master Qín (Qínzǐ 禽子). This suggests the texts may have been written by Qín's followers. These writings are of great value to historians of ancient Chinese warfare, but since the focus of this book is Mohist philosophy, I will pass them over here.

All but three of the triad books begin with "Zǐ Mòzǐ yán yuē..." 子墨子言曰...," interpretable as "Our Master Mòzǐ states..." or "Our Master Mòzǐ pronounces...." Since much of the books' content is attributed to Mòzǐ in this way, readers have traditionally taken them to be records of his speech and treated him as their author. However, most writing in pre-Hàn China was anonymous, and it was common for writers to place their own words in the mouth of a venerated teacher or worthy predecessor, partly from respect and partly to give their ideas more authority. The "Triads" probably present and develop ideas and doctrines first set forth by Mòzǐ, and the oldest parts perhaps record his actual words. However, the books in each triad exhibit significant linguistic differences and sometimes present different, even incompatible, views. In some, such as books 14 and 16, in the "Inclusive Care" triad, or book 19, in the "Condemning Aggression" triad, much of the argument is presented in a narrator's voice rather than attributed to Mòzǐ. So it is likely that many of the statements, doctrines, and formulations in the texts are not Mòzǐ's own but represent developments, revisions, or new ideas introduced by his followers. Accordingly, instead of referring to the thought of Mòzǐ, it is becoming conventional to refer to Mohist doctrines, understood as a set of interrelated but evolving—and sometimes conflicting—views recorded by different members of the school over many years, perhaps even several generations. This is the approach I will adopt here. I will frequently point out differences and developments in the texts, rather than taking them to present a unitary, finished philosophical system. I will generally remain agnostic as to the authorship of particular views, leaving it unspecified whether they go back to Mòzǐ himself or are the work of his later adherents. At the same time, I will draw on the results of recent research yielding a tentative chronological stratification of the "Triads."[22] No decisive interpretive points hang on this stratification, but it helps to explain the differences between various books, and it provides a credible framework within which to sketch the development of Mohist ideas.

MOHIST THOUGHT: AN OVERVIEW

To introduce the discussion in succeeding chapters, this section gives a rough, bird's-eye view of central themes in Mohist thought. Later chapters will provide a detailed account to support this summary.

The Mohist movement originated in Mòzǐ's and his early followers' dismay at the war, feuding, crime, exploitation, economic mismanagement, and other wrongdoing they saw as endemic to their era. The Mohists urgently sought to restore society to the good order they believed China's ancient sage-kings had achieved in the distant past. They saw people as naturally social, concerned about their family and community, and generally committed to doing what they take to be right. If people disagree about what is right, however, or if they fail to distinguish right from wrong properly, conflicts may arise, leading to social disorder. The Mohists offered two main diagnoses of the causes of disorder. The first, and more fundamental, was moral disagreement. In the absence of proper political leadership, people will follow diverse conceptions of what is morally right, many of them presumably in ignorance of the correct moral norms. If they are strongly committed to their conception of what is right yet endorse different, incompatible norms, they are likely to come into conflict and may ultimately resort to violence. The Mohists' second diagnosis—partly a consequence of the first—was that, ignorant of proper moral norms, some people act without regard for others, willingly injuring them to benefit themselves.

As moral activists, the Mohists aimed to rectify moral disagreement and ignorance and thus achieve social order. This they proposed to do by unifying society around a single moral code, one that would incorporate concern for others' welfare as well as one's own. Ideally, this project would be carried out through a government administered by wise, virtuous leaders, who at each level of the state hierarchy—from the village up to the entire empire—would lead everyone to draw value distinctions according to unified norms. The major method of education would be model emulation. Leaders selected for their wisdom and moral merit would set an example of morally correct statements and conduct for all to emulate. To reinforce this training, correct conduct would be praised and rewarded, incorrect conduct criticized and punished.

This political and educational system would provide a means to train everyone to follow unified moral norms. But to achieve proper order, the content of the shared norms must be correct. The Mohists thus mounted a search for objective moral criteria, or as they saw it, reliable, easily applicable "models" or "standards" (fǎ 法) by which to guide judgment and action. These would guide everyone to distinguish right from wrong correctly, just as a straight-edged tool guides a carpenter in sawing a straight line. The models would provide the content of the unified moral norms.

In choosing such models, of course, we must be cautious. Human role models and traditional customs are all potentially faulty or unreliable. So instead of modeling ourselves on them, the Mohists proposed as an ultimate model the intentions of the noblest and wisest agent in the cosmos, Heaven (tiān 天, also "nature" or "the sky"), whom they revered as a quasi-personal deity. For the Mohists, Heaven is an ideal, infallible moral agent whom we can take as an exemplar by which to identify objectively correct moral norms, since it unfailingly sets an example of what is right. Heaven has not handed down any scriptures we can take as a guide. But by observing its conduct, we can determine its intentions, which can serve as our guidelines. From Heaven's conduct, the Mohists contend, we can know that it cares about and benefits all humanity. It gives all people life and the resources needed for survival. According to traditional lore, it rewarded the ancient sage-kings who advanced the welfare of all and punished the vicious tyrants who mistreated their subjects. Examples such as these show that Heaven desires that people "all-inclusively care about each other and in interaction benefit each other" and that moral right and wrong can be distinguished by the criterion of "promoting the benefit of all the world and eliminating harm to all the world." Morally right norms, practices, policies, and acts are just those that tend to advance the benefit of or eliminate harm to all.

The Mohist notion of the "benefit of all" is a conception of the public good comprising material welfare, an abundant population, and sociopolitical "order" (zhì 治). In providing for people's material welfare, the Mohists emphasize meeting the basic needs of the poor by providing food for the hungry, clothing for the cold, and rest for the weary. Core features of order are the absence of war, strife, crime, and hostility and the universal virtuous performance of the core social roles of ruler, subject, father, son, and brother. More broadly, order may include such goods as neighborly sharing of knowledge, surplus labor, and surplus resources and fair administration of the penal system. As this list of goods indicates, Mohist ethics is communitarian, not individualist. The goods that serve as criteria of morality are mainly collective or public—by contrast, for instance, with individual happiness, the basic good in classical Western utilitarianism. Despite this collective focus, however, Mohist ethics is not, as has been suggested, a form of "state consequentialism."[23] Right and wrong are determined by what benefits all the people of the world—or in some *Mòzǐ* passages, by what benefits Heaven, the ghosts, and people—not by what benefits the state.

Drawing on this framework of ethical, political, epistemological, and religious theories, the Mohists offered systematic arguments for norms they considered beneficial and against conduct and practices they considered detrimental to general welfare, such as military aggression, extravagant burials, and excessive public spending on nonessentials. Their consequentialism led them to develop a platform of ten ethical and political doctrines that they aimed to persuade rulers and officials of the day to adopt and promulgate.

THE TEN DOCTRINES

As their movement developed, the Mohists eventually came to summarize their teachings as a set of ten doctrines, organized into five pairs. A summary of the ten—which correspond roughly to the titles of the ten triads—provides a quick synopsis of the Mohist moral and political reform program.

According to the doctrine of "identifying upward" (*shàng tóng* 尚同), the aim of government is to achieve a stable social, economic, and political order by promulgating a unified conception of moral righteousness.[24] This project of moral education is to be carried out by encouraging everyone to "identify upward" with the good example set by exemplary social and political leaders. Those who do are rewarded; those who do not are punished. Government is to be structured as a centralized, bureaucratic state led by a virtuous monarch and managed by a hierarchy of appointed officials. According to "promoting the worthy" (*shàng xián* 尚賢), appointments should be made on the basis of competence and moral merit, without regard for candidates' social status or origin.

"Inclusive care" (*jiān ài* 尚愛) was the Mohists' signature doctrine. To promote the welfare of all, people should inclusively care about one another, being concerned for others and their families and communities as they are for themselves and their own, such that when interacting with others they seek benefit for both sides. Almost equally famous was the doctrine of "condemning aggression" (*fēi gōng* 非攻). Military aggression is morally wrong for the same reasons that theft, robbery, and murder are: it harms others in pursuit of self-interest and so fails to promote the benefit of all.

According to "moderation in use" (*jié yòng* 節用), wasteful luxury and useless expenditures should be eliminated to better ensure basic material welfare for all. "Moderation in burial" (*jié zàng* 節葬) calls for an end to the custom of rich, elaborate funerals and protracted mourning rituals—traditions staunchly defended by the Rú—in order to better promote prosperity and social order.

The doctrine of "Heaven's intent" (*tiān zhì* 天志) holds that since Heaven is the noblest, wisest moral agent in the cosmos, its intent should be followed as a reliable, objective standard of morality. Heaven rewards those who obey its intent and punishes those who defy it, so people should strive to be benevolent and do what is righteous. "Understanding ghosts" (*míng guǐ* 明鬼) contends that social and moral order can be advanced by encouraging belief in ghosts and spirits who reward the good and punish the vicious.

"Condemning music" (*fēi yuè* 非樂) denounces the extravagant, state-sponsored entertainment and luxuries enjoyed by the ruling elite, since these waste resources that could otherwise be used to feed and clothe the poor. "Condemning fatalism" (*fēi mìng* 非命) contends that fatalism must be rejected, since it does not conform to the example of the ancient sage-kings, correspond to what people observe, or promote the welfare of all. In fact, teaching that good or bad fortune is predestined and human effort is useless is harmful to society and thus morally wrong.

In presenting their ideas to rulers and officials, the Mohists would emphasize different parts of this platform, depending on the circumstances:

> If the state is in disorder, expound "promoting the worthy" and "identifying upward"; if the state is impoverished, expound "moderation in use" and "moderation in burial"; if the state overindulges in musical entertainment, expound "condemning music" and "condemning fate"; if the state is profligate and indecorous, expound "honoring Heaven" and "serving ghosts"; if the state is devoted to aggression and conquest, expound "inclusive care" and "condemning aggression." (Mz 49/61–64)

As this passage implies, the Mohists saw themselves mainly as a moral, political, and religious reform movement devoted to pursuing their vision of a morally right society and way of life, one that promoted the welfare of all. They were especially concerned to ensure the basic welfare of the worst off, whose needs they perceived as often going unmet. Because of this practical orientation, their ten-doctrine program alludes only indirectly to the underlying ethical and epistemological theories that support their proposals. The next several chapters will focus on these theoretical underpinnings, along the way tying them to several of the Mohists' key reform proposals. I will then discuss the remainder of the reform program in chapter 8.

THE SIGNIFICANCE OF MOHIST PHILOSOPHY

Why study the Mohists, an ancient school that faded away more than two thousand years ago and afterward had little direct influence on the Chinese philosophical tradition? Two sorts of considerations make the Mohists significant and interesting, some pertaining to intellectual history, others to the philosophical value of their ideas.

Mòzǐ and his followers had an immense influence on the intellectual discourse of classical China. A strong argument can be made that it is Mòzǐ, not Confucius, who deserves the title of China's first philosopher. Before the rise of the Mohist school, Ruist thought seems to have consisted mostly of wise aphorisms aimed at coaching pupils toward becoming virtuous performers of traditional social roles and rituals. Mòzǐ and his followers initiated philosophical reflection and argumentation in China. They were the first to engage—like Socrates in ancient Greece—in reflective criticism of traditional mores and the first to give explicit, tightly structured arguments for their views. They formulated China's first systematic ethical, political, epistemological, and logical theories. Their ethics was the world's earliest version of consequentialism, an important kind of ethical theory according to which whether something is morally right or good is determined by whether it produces better consequences than alternatives.[25] The classic example of consequentialism in the West is the utilitarianism of Jeremy Bentham (1748–1832) and John Stuart Mill (1806–1873), whose ethical views the Mohists predated by more than two thousand years. Moreover, structurally the Mohist theory is a sophisticated, indirect version of consequentialism, in some respects more advanced than classical utilitarianism.[26] The Mohists may also have been the first thinkers in the world to build a systematic ethics around an explicit conception of impartiality, expressed through their notions of *jiān* 兼, or "all-inclusiveness," and *tiān xià zhī lì* 天下之利, or "the benefit of all the world."[27]

The Mohists' ethics alone thus earns them an important place in the history of philosophy. Beyond their ethics, they also played a crucial role in articulating and shaping many of the central concepts, background theories, and issues of classical Chinese philosophical discourse. Through concepts such as *shì-fēi* 是非 (this/right versus not-this/wrong), *biàn* 辯 (distinction drawing, disputation, dialectics), *zhì* 治 (order), and *fǎ* 法 (models), they influenced all later thinkers of the classical period, in particular Xúnzǐ, the *Zhuāngzǐ* writers, and the Legalists, or the school of *fǎ* (models, laws). Their conception of a *dào* (way) as a set of skilled practices for guiding action by means of *shì-fēi* distinctions became a core element of the shared conceptual framework of early Chinese thought, developed in different ways by Ruist and Legalist thinkers and provoking insightful metaethical reflection in Daoist texts.[28] Their political theory initiated China's tradition of government through a centralized civil service with a merit-based appointment system. Their logic articulates a view of reasoning and justification common to all classical Chinese thinkers, which carries over to a shared conception of practical reasoning and thus shared assumptions in moral psychology. Their philosophy of language and epistemology are adopted more or less wholesale by Xúnzǐ, who extends them in interesting ways, and their theories in these fields incite a profound skeptical response from the *Dàodéjīng* and *Zhuāngzǐ*. As intellectual opponents, the Mohists motivate developments in the thought of Mencius, Xúnzǐ, and their followers, and they and the Rú jointly stand for a way of life against which the Daoists direct a radical critique. The Mohists' politics, ethics, and psychology also articulate communitarian, utilitarian, nonmentalistic assumptions that have been tremendously influential in Chinese civilization right down through the Communist era.[29]

Because Mohism died out in the Hàn dynasty, it is sometimes depicted as an isolated, anomalous school of thought not genuinely part of the early Chinese philosophical mainstream. Nothing could be further from the truth, however. Many features of Mohist doctrines directly reflect concepts, assumptions, and problems that became elements of mainstream Warring States intellectual discourse. Understanding the Mohists is an essential step toward fully understanding Confucianism, Daoism, and other early Chinese schools of thought.

Beyond the Mohists' historical influence, many of their ideas are inherently interesting philosophically and potentially instructive in working out our own views. Mohist ethics highlights fundamental questions such as how to articulate impartiality, what relation should hold between impartial justification and the moral agent's motives for action, and what values should ground moral judgment. The Mohists recognize that morality requires impartial consideration of everyone's interests and that moral reasons have a form of universality, in that what is right for one person would be equally right for anyone else in an analogous position. They see that the interests even of strangers can constitute reasons for us to act. Yet they struggle to articulate these insights in a viable form, partly because they tend to conflate the notion of impartial standards for action with that of the attitudes of an ideally impartial, beneficent agent—which in the end is not really an agent in the normal sense at all.

The Mohists hold, plausibly, that there is a fundamental link between morality and human interests or welfare. They develop this idea into an interesting communitarian version of consequentialism that raises in acute form some of the questions faced by any consequentialist theory, even a more nuanced and advanced one.[30] Are consequences really all that matters in determining moral right and wrong? How can we determine which consequences should count? Further questions arise from their conviction that the overarching model (fǎ) of "the benefit of all" provides a systematic, conclusive guide to morality. Can any single, determinate criterion or set of criteria be expected to resolve all ethical issues? The directive to follow practices that yield the greatest benefit may be of little help in cases when two or more conflicting practices seem to have equally beneficial consequences, when disagreement arises concerning what counts as "benefit," or when it is unclear what consequences a practice may have.

The Mohist dào tends to place moral righteousness (yì 義) at the very center of life, raising profound questions about the role of morality in our lives. (Yì can refer to morality, what is righteous or proper, a moral code, norms of conduct, or duty.) We might be tempted to characterize Mohist ethics as focusing exclusively on the right, or duty, rather than on the good, or what would count as an admirable or flourishing life for the individual.[31] Such a characterization would not be fully accurate, however. The Mohists do consider the question of the good life, but their answer seems to be that the best life is one dedicated to practicing and promoting righteousness (yì). In this focus on moral righteousness, Mohist thought comes closer to Kantian ethics than does any other view in the Chinese tradition. By way of justification, however, it lacks anything resembling Kant's idea that agents are inherently bound by the moral law because of their rational nature. Instead, we are to dedicate ourselves to righteousness because it is the most valuable thing in the world, since people are willing to sacrifice their lives for it (Mz 47/1), its practice benefits everyone (46/29), and it is desired by Heaven, the wisest and noblest moral exemplar (26/12). Like most early Chinese thinkers, the Mohists endorse the ideal of personal sagehood (47/19), which they equate with total dedication to righteousness.

Important as morality may be, we might wonder whether it should dominate life as it does for the Mohists. A good life is likely to involve commitments to other values as well, such as the development of one's talents, the pursuit of meaningful projects, intellectual inquiry, recreation with family members or friends, and the creation or appreciation of art. In some respects, the Mohist *dào* threatens to leave us unable to pursue such values. Indeed, it may direct us away from any sort of personal project, insofar as such projects interfere with promoting the benefit of all.

Other areas of Mohist thought are also philosophically interesting. The Mohists present a perfectionist political theory in which the paramount aim is to achieve social order by promulgating a unified system of values. The chief role of the state lies in moral education. Evaluating this theory is a worthwhile exercise in examining the justification and aims of the state, the legitimate scope of its power, and the importance of the individual's interests versus the community's. The theory also provides insights into the limits of an authoritarian system focused on social order. The Mohists themselves seem to have concluded that even if massive resources were devoted to social indoctrination, the genuine support of the people, earned through leaders' demonstrated commitment to the public good, would be crucial to making their political system work.

Epistemology is both one of the more undeveloped areas of Mohist thought and one of the most intriguing. The Mohists treat knowledge as a skill or an ability, namely the ability to correctly distinguish various kinds of things. Their view of knowledge is externalist, in that a subject can know something without being able to cite a justification for it. (An internalist view of knowledge is one on which a necessary condition for knowledge is that the subject have an explicit justification available.) The Mohist approach suggests that knowledge and justification could be less tightly paired than Western epistemology has typically taken them to be. Indeed, the two may have divergent roles, knowledge being more a sort of competence in interacting with the world, justification just one among other processes of belief formation, rather than a component or condition of knowledge. Mohist epistemology suggests that justification might be primarily a way of attaining or checking whether one has knowledge, rather than a constituent of knowledge.

On the Mohist view, the interface between mind and world lies not in representational relations between mental content and external things but in patterns of reliable, skilled activity. Knowledge is not just a matter of correctly distinguishing things in isolated instances, but a reliable ability to distinguish them properly in a variety of cases. Mohist epistemology thus shifts the focus of potential skeptical doubt from whether any one belief is true, or represents the world accurately, to whether certain patterns of drawing distinctions are the correct or most effective way to interact with the world. Whether we as knowers are firmly in contact with the world and can find *some* path through it is not in doubt. This fascinating approach to knowledge and the mind-world relation—which is representative of early Chinese philosophy more generally—deserves study and development.

Finally, Mohist moral psychology raises intriguing issues concerning practical reasoning, moral education and motivation, and the role of moral standards or principles in guiding action. Like their conception of knowledge, the Mohists' view of psychological processes such as reasoning or deliberation is based on the model of skills. They share with other early Chinese thinkers the assumption that the mind—or more specifically, the heart—is primarily a faculty for guiding action—and not, as in the Cartesian-empiricist tradition, an inner, private sphere in which the individual subject contemplates and manipulates representations of the external world. Action is guided through the heart's capacity to distinguish and respond to things, and the patterns of distinctions and responses we follow are learned largely through training in social practices. Deliberation and judgment are seen as processes of drawing distinctions. These need not involve inner ratiocination or running through the steps of an argument in one's head. At high levels of skill, they can be a matter of simply seeing a similarity or dissimilarity between cases and responding accordingly.

The Mohists thus understand practical reasoning and the structure of action differently from how they have often been conceptualized in recent Western philosophy. They apply a discrimination-and-response model of action, rather than the familiar belief-desire model rooted in Aristotle's practical syllogism and Hume's conception of motivation. Desires and affective states play a less prominent role as motives for action in their psychology than they do in approaches informed by the belief-desire model. For the Mohists, desire versus aversion is just one sort of action-guiding distinction among others. It is not the central or dominant motivational state, nor the focus of moral education or cultivation. What drives action is mainly ability or know-how (*zhī* 知), which is largely the result of skill training. Moral education and cultivation thus are processes similar in important respects to skill development. They aim mainly not at changing agents' motivations, understood as desires or other affective states, but at training them to discriminate and respond to situations in certain ways. A consequence of their psychology and logic is that the Mohists conceive of an ethical theory as guiding action through a network of skills learned by emulating models, rather than by reasoning from general principles.[32] No doubt people sometimes guide action through explicit moral reasoning along the lines of a practical syllogism, in which the agent reasons from a general principle to a particular conclusion about what to do. But it is also highly likely that we often act in the manner the Mohists suppose, through discrimination-and-response skills acquired by emulating role models or by learning how to respond to paradigmatic situations.

The Mohist approach raises intriguing questions about what role desires, emotions, and reasoning do or should have in directing action and about how people can initiate and sustain the process of moral improvement. One frequently discussed approach to moral development, associated with Mencius, emphasizes the activation and cultivation of morally relevant emotions, which are thought to reliably prompt appropriate action. Another approach, associated with Kant, emphasizes reasoning or rational persuasion, which, other things being equal, is expected to reliably motivate rational agents to do what is right. The Mohist view differs from both, offering a distinctive, intriguing perspective that tends to be overlooked in recent discussions of moral motivation.

To some, the Mohist theoretical picture might look suspiciously like a variety of psychological behaviorism. However, Mohist writings do not imply that action is guided merely by conditioned responses or that inner mental processes are explanatorily redundant. They simply suggest a distinctive view of the structure of mental processes, one partly shared by other early Chinese thinkers and interestingly different from prominent Western views, such as those of Aristotle, Hume, or Kant. A related concern is whether the Mohists can account for moral autonomy—for agents' ability to act on their own independent judgment, grounded in what they take to be objectively justified moral norms. If action is guided by dispositions and skills acquired through social training, one might worry that agents' conduct is reduced to robotic, programmed responses rather than autonomously chosen actions. Again, however, the Mohist picture does not threaten autonomy but simply presents an unfamiliar conception of judgment. Consider skills, which are often initially acquired through rote emulation of others. Once we have mastered a skill, its performance is neither robotic nor preprogrammed. Skilled performances require independent judgment in evaluating and responding to particular contexts, albeit judgment that is often instantaneous or involves no self-conscious thought. In taking skill as a model for judgment and action, Mohist thought may offer a distinctive, intriguing approach to thinking about agency and autonomy.

OUTLINE OF THE BOOK

The first two chapters explore some of the underlying concerns and background assumptions of Mohist thought. Chapter 1 describes the Mohists' concern with order, objectivity, and impartiality and their conception of the cosmos as supporting human efficacy. Chapter 2 gives an overview of their epistemology and logic. These shape the structure of the Mohist ethical theory and their conception of mind, which is in turn reflected in their political theory, ethics, and moral psychology. The next three chapters examine their moral and political philosophy. Chapter 3 treats their political thought, exploring how it balances individuals' values and motivations with the need for a stable political society. Chapter 4 discusses the Mohist conception of Heaven and explores its role in their ethics, in particular how it grounds their conception of objectivity and impartiality. Chapters 5 and 6 present and critique the Mohist ethical theory, including their basic consequentialist theory, their doctrine of inclusive care, and their replies to opponents' objections. Contrary to many previous interpretations, these chapters argue that the Mohists endorse the commonsense tendency to put the welfare of our circle of kin and associates before that of strangers. The discussion identifies an unresolved tension between the Mohists' ideas and their practices, however, and criticizes Mohist ethics for its narrow conception of value.

Chapters 5 and 8 also consider the Mohists' relation to early Ruism, or "Confucianism." Mohism is often depicted as motivated largely by opposition to Ruist ethics. I argue that such depictions are inaccurate. Though the Mohists vehemently criticize certain Ruist practices, opposition to Ruism was just one among many factors motivating their thought. In fact, they share important, core values with the Rú. Their criticisms primarily concern early Ruist doctrines and practices that are strongly downplayed by modern interpreters—such as the Ruists' fatalism and ritualism—and the Mohists' rejection of these points is largely convincing.

Chapter 7 surveys the Mohists' views on moral psychology, perhaps the most widely misunderstood aspect of their thought. The Mohists have been criticized for lacking a viable theory of moral development. Some writers claim they hold the implausible view that human motivations and dispositions are almost wholly plastic. Others suggest they cannot explain how morality is continuous with people's natural dispositions. I argue that these criticisms are misplaced. The Mòzǐ presents a rich, largely plausible view of human psychology, according to which most people have strong, untutored dispositions to do what they consider right. The Mohists acknowledge individuals' capacity for moral autonomy while also emphasizing the social nature of human life. Their moral psychology is in places too optimistic. However, its main flaw lies not in its account of moral motivation or development but in its assumptions about the kind of life people find beneficial and justifiable.

Chapter 8 explores the Mohist antiwar and economic-reform doctrines. Of great importance to the Mohists themselves, these doctrines are of less interest to contemporary readers, as the historical circumstances that motivated them no longer obtain. However, they do provide interesting examples of the application of Mohist ethical and political views, and the antiwar texts present one of the world's earliest just war theories. The brief concluding chapter offers several conjectures to explain the decline of the Mohist movement during the Qín and Hàn dynasties.

I
ORDER, OBJECTIVITY, AND EFFICACY

THIS CHAPTER LAYS the groundwork for succeeding chapters by sketching three central, pervasive themes in Mohist thought: the Mohists' concern for sociopolitical order, their search for objective moral standards by which to bring about that order, and their belief in the efficacy of human action, grounded in their theology.

ORDER

As we saw in the introduction, the fundamental motivation for Mohist thought is practical, not theoretical. The Mohists' basic project was social and political reform, not inquiry for inquiry's sake. Mòzǐ and his followers did not set out to examine philosophical issues in ethics, politics, or epistemology and develop theories about them. They were interested primarily in social and political problems. Their theories emerged from a reasoned attempt to solve those problems and to persuade others to adopt their solutions. Philosophical inquiry is a significant part of their project but not the main end.

What is that end? Ultimately, it is to achieve a world in which everyone reliably conforms to moral righteousness (yì 義). More immediately, it is to stop the intolerable military aggression, feuding, crime, and injury to others that the Mohists believe mar their society. They call such immoral conduct "disorder" (luàn 亂), a word that refers to disruption, disturbance, or chaos. In ancient Chinese thought, "disorder" is not a value-neutral description. To call a situation "disorderly" is to express a normative judgment: something is wrong with it. The contrasting, good state of affairs is called "order" (*zhì* 治), a word that refers to things being orderly, well governed, or under control. For the Mohists, order overlaps with righteousness in that what is in order is usually thereby morally righteous, and when things are righteous, they are also in order.

Several passages from the *Mòzǐ* help to elucidate the Mohists' conception of disorder—and, conversely, order—and indicate what they see as its two major, interrelated causes, which are addressed by two major tenets of Mohist thought. According to the first of the three "Inclusive Care" books—likely among the earliest Mohist writings—disorder refers to a range of disruptive behaviors, including subjects and sons failing to show proper filial devotion (*xiào* 孝) to their rulers and fathers; rulers and fathers failing in turn to show paternal kindness (*cí* 慈) to their subjects and sons; brothers failing to treat one another considerately; crimes such a robbery and theft; feuding between clans; and military aggression. In each case, the Mohist diagnosis is that disorder is caused by the offenders' selfish disregard for others. They care only for their own interests or those of their circle—their family, clan, or state—and so feel free to injure others in order to benefit themselves:

> Subjects' and sons' not being filially devoted [*xiào*] to their rulers and fathers is what's called "disorder" [*luàn*]. Sons care about themselves and don't care about their father, so they injure their father to benefit themselves; younger brothers care about themselves and don't care about their elder brothers, so they injure their elder brothers to benefit themselves; subjects care about themselves and don't care about their ruler, so they injure their ruler to benefit themselves—this is what's called "disorder."
>
> Even fathers being unkind to sons, elder brothers being unkind to younger brothers, rulers being unkind to subjects—this too is what the world calls "disorder." Fathers care about themselves and don't care about their sons, so they injure their sons to benefit themselves; elder brothers care about themselves and don't care about their younger brothers, so they injure their younger brothers to benefit themselves; rulers care about themselves and don't care about their subjects, so they injure their subjects to benefit themselves. Why is this? It all arises from not caring about each other.
>
> Even in the case of those in the world who are robbers and thieves, they too are so. Robbers care about their house and don't care about other houses, so they steal from other houses to benefit their house. Thieves care about themselves and don't care about others, so they injure others to benefit themselves. Why is this? It all arises from not caring about each other.

> Even in the case of high officials who disorder each other's clans and the various lords who attack each others' states, they too are so. The high officials each care about their clan and don't care about other clans, so they disorder other clans to benefit their own. The various lords each care about their state and don't care about other states, so they attack other states to benefit their own.
>
> The disorderly things in the world are all just these and nothing more. If we examine from what they arise, they all arise from not caring about each other. (Mz 14/4–12)

This is a diagnosis of the causes of disorder, not a general indictment of humanity or a depiction of untutored human nature. The text does not imply that people are inherently selfish or that everyone is disposed to sacrifice others' welfare for their own. The claim is simply that disorder arises from people's selfish failure to "care about each other." This problem is addressed by the doctrine of inclusive care, one of the Mohists' central ethical tenets (discussed in chapter 6).

Interestingly, in the course of describing people's disregard for others, the passage also shows that the Mohists share the characteristic early Chinese assumption that human beings are inherently social in nature. People are seen as naturally caught up in a web of hierarchical political and kinship relations, the central ones being between father and son, ruler and subject, and elder brother and younger brother.[1] They interact with others mainly as performers of these social roles. Ideally, their conduct is guided by the behavior and attitudes appropriate for each role—mainly subordinates (sons, younger brothers, subjects) showing filial devotion and loyalty to superiors (fathers, elder brothers, rulers), who in turn show them kindness. (This framework of paradigmatic kinship and political relations is sometimes misleadingly labeled "Confucian," but as this passage shows, it is fundamental to Mohist ethics as well.) People are seen as normally caring about and identifying not only with themselves but also with various social units—their immediate family, their clan, and their state. Some may be selfish, but in general people are not regarded as atomistic or self-centered individuals.

As depicted in the foregoing passage, disorder comprises mainly two sorts of behavior: failing to exercise filial devotion and paternal kindness toward those within one's circle of kinship and political relations and injuring those outside one's circle through crime or violence. Mohist political theory expands on this initial depiction in several ways. Outside the family, disorder includes failure to follow the norms of conduct for rulers and subjects, superiors and subordinates, and elders and youth, while within the family it is failure to observe the ceremonial proprieties governing fathers, sons, and brothers (*Mz* 12/5). In the most extreme circumstances of disorder, people live in a state of nature, "like animals" (11/5). Family members resent one another and split up, unable to live in harmony; people physically injure one another "with water, fire, and poison"; and community members refuse to share good teachings, surplus labor, and surplus resources (11/3–4).

Since order is the opposite of disorder, the Mohists' characterization of disorder also indicates how they understand order. At minimum, order requires that people care about others' welfare enough to refrain from harming them and that they perform their social roles virtuously, being devoted to superiors and kind to subordinates, within the family and without. Order may also require that family members live in harmony and community members share knowledge, surplus labor, and surplus resources. Since the absence of these circumstances characterizes *extreme* disorder, however, we cannot be sure the Mohists see them as part of the minimal conditions for order. Beyond these features, texts from the middle to late strata of the "Triads" tell us that order requires that the noble and wise govern over the foolish and lowly, rather than the other way around (*Mz* 9/2), and that rewards and punishments be distributed properly, the good being rewarded and the vicious punished (13/6). Moreover, since a central claim of their political thought is that order is achieved by leading everyone to follow unified moral norms, the Mohists may hold that order fully obtains only when such norms are generally observed. The achievement of order in this fullest sense would thus coincide with the universal practice of righteousness.

Besides linking disorder to disregard for others, the Mohists make a second, broader claim about its causes. In their political theory (described more fully in chapter 3), they trace the roots of disorder to general disagreement about moral norms, or standards of righteousness. In a state of nature, they suppose, before government is established, people all act on different views of what is righteous. Members of society are all stubbornly convinced that their view is correct and others' are wrong. This disagreement leads to rancor, violence, and thus disorder. So the root cause of disorder is disagreement about what counts as righteous.

The Mohists assume everyone will agree that disorder is disastrous for all. Moreover, they imply, people generally assume there should be a single, unified set of moral norms. In the state of nature, disorder arises precisely because people incessantly condemn one another for following what they each take to be the wrong norms—namely, norms different from their own. Accordingly, in the Mohists' view, people value order enough that they will set aside whatever else they disagree on to support a policy that eliminates disorder. The aim of the Mohist political program is to remove the second basic cause of disorder—disagreement about moral norms—by unifying everyone's norms of righteousness. People will then agree in their value judgments, eliminating potential reasons for conflict. The plan is to use the political system to promulgate unified, objectively justified moral norms. If everyone can be persuaded or trained to follow these norms, society can be brought to order. At the same time, the first cause of disorder—acting with selfish disregard for others—can be resolved, since the Mohists hold that the norms adopted will not permit acting without regard for others. In their view, self-interest alone cannot provide practicable standards of righteousness (for more on this, see chapter 5).

The emphasis on social order reflects the social or communitarian orientation of the Mohist project. For the Mohists, ethical issues are framed primarily at the level of society as a whole, not the individual agent. On this point, Chad Hansen rightly contrasts the Mohists with Socrates, the first Greek thinker to reflect critically on conventional mores in the way that Mòzǐ did in China.[2] Where Socrates's question is individualistic—how should one live?—the Mohists' is social: what system should we follow? Accordingly, the Mohist "Triads" are not directed mainly at individuals pondering how to live their lives or seeking to improve themselves. They are political tracts, addressed to "kings, dukes, ministers, officers, and gentlemen of the world"—that is, rulers, high-ranking officials, lower-level bureaucrats, and others of elite social status, who, if persuaded, had the power to change how society operated and bring order to "all the world." In this respect, Mohist texts also contrast with Ruist and Daoist texts. Though deeply concerned with political issues, Ruist anthologies such as the *Analects* and *Mencius*, along with portions of the *Xúnzǐ*, devote more space to addressing individual practitioners of the Ruist *dào* 道, one of their chief aims being to coach them along the path. The *Zhuāngzǐ* too takes up the question of the good life for the individual. By comparison, with the exception of some parts of the "Dialogues," the *Mòzǐ* approaches even personal moral improvement through the lens of society as a whole, asking not how I as an individual can become a better person but how all of us together can come to practice the *dào*. The implication is not that the Mohists see individual moral development as unimportant; their doctrinal books do address individual agents, particularly officials of various ranks. But their theoretical and practical focus is social and collective. They see the *dào* as inherently social and human life as inherently communal. The project of implementing the *dào* and thus bringing order to the world is a collective, political undertaking, which can succeed only with staunch, judicious political guidance and broad community engagement.

OBJECTIVITY AND IMPARTIALITY

The Mohists are clear that the moral standards by which we unify society and achieve order cannot be chosen arbitrarily, for if people see that the standards do not genuinely promote social and moral order, they will defy them (see chapter 3). So a crucial question is, how do we determine the content of the unified norms of righteousness?

One possible answer is to appeal to ritual or ceremonial propriety (lǐ 禮), a traditional code of etiquette specifying behavior appropriate for various social roles and situations. The Rú and perhaps other "gentlemen of the world" criticized by the Mohists maintain that we take the norms of ceremonial propriety, guided by the situational discretion of the virtuous gentleman, as a standard of conduct. The *Analects* famously depicts Confucius as saying that benevolence (rén 仁) lies in "overcoming the self and returning to ceremonial propriety." Asked to elaborate, he says, "If not in accordance with ceremonial propriety, do not look. If not in accordance with ceremonial propriety, do not listen. If not in accordance with ceremonial propriety, do not speak. If not in accordance with ceremonial propriety, do not move" (*LY* 12.1).[3] This suggests that the norms and practices of ceremonial propriety provide a comprehensive guide to conduct for someone aspiring to be a morally good person. Numerous passages describe the gentleman as someone who assiduously regulates his conduct by ceremonial propriety.[4] One passage describes ceremonial propriety as the concrete means by which one practices righteousness: "The gentleman takes righteousness as his substance, puts it into practice through ceremonial propriety, expresses it with modesty, and completes it with trustworthiness" (15.18). The practice of ceremonial propriety is among the keys to effective government: "If one can govern a state by ceremonial propriety and deference, what difficulties can there be?" (4.13). For "if superiors are devoted to ceremonial propriety, the people are easy to command" (14.41).[5] For some early Rú, social disorder might have amounted largely to a failure to conform to ceremonial propriety, which for them was a fundamental guide to proper behavior.[6]

Ceremonial propriety has a place in Mohist thought, but only a peripheral one. In a passage cited previously, for instance, disorder is associated with failure to conform to the ceremonial proprieties governing social relations (*Mz* 12/5).[7] This passage thus takes the proper performance of at least some aspects of ceremonial propriety to be a constituent of social order. Since (as we will see in chapter 5) the Mohists take order to be a basic good that partly determines moral value, they may treat some aspects of ceremonial propriety as elements of the morally right social *dào*.[8]

Overall, though, the Mohists found the sort of conservative, traditionalist stance embodied in ceremonial propriety an unconvincing moral guide. Customary ceremonial etiquette can function as a standard of conduct only if a rough consensus holds that the norms of ceremonial propriety are right or permissible. Early Ruist thought seems to take such a consensus for granted. Accordingly, the *Analects* and *Mencius* devote little attention to formulating an explicit normative theory to articulate and justify moral norms.[9] They focus instead on ethical development, on how to lead ourselves and others to follow the *dào* reliably. The content of the *dào* is not thematized as requiring articulation and justification. By contrast, in the Mohists' view, disagreement exists as to whether certain ceremonial practices are right or wrong. To them, elite ceremonial customs such as elaborate funerals, rich burials, prolonged mourning, and extravagant state rituals accompanied by music and dancing were wasteful and detrimental to the general welfare. In the face of wide-reaching social changes and political turmoil, it seemed futile to recommend ceremonial propriety as a basis for returning society to good order. The Zhōu social and political system was unraveling. Guidance by ceremonial propriety was in effect a *dào* that had been tried and found wanting. Its failure had contributed to the present chaos.

Even more important, the Mohists rejected ceremonial propriety as a fundamental moral guideline because, in a momentous philosophical step, they noticed the crucially important distinction between custom and morality.[10] Conceptually, ceremonial propriety simply cannot do the work of a moral code, because the fact that something conforms to the prevailing view of etiquette, ceremony, or propriety simply does not show it is morally righteous. Accepted social customs—in particular, customs such as elite ceremonial rituals, many of which were practiced by only a small, privileged segment of society—can be morally wrong. The Mohists make this point by calling attention—at roughly the same time Herodotus was making a similar point in Greece—to the wide variation in customs across cultures, not all of which can plausibly be taken to be morally right.

> Now those who uphold rich burials and prolonged mourning state, "If rich burials and prolonged mourning turn out not to be the Way of the sage-kings, then how do we explain why the gentlemen of the Central States perform them without ceasing and maintain them without choosing something else?!"

> Our Master Mòzǐ said, "This is what's called deeming their habits convenient and their customs righteous. In the past, east of Yuè there was the country of Gài Shù. When their eldest son was born, they chopped him up and ate him, calling this 'advantageous to the younger brothers.' When their grandfather died, they carried off their grandmother and abandoned her, saying, 'One cannot live with the wife of a ghost.' These practices superiors took as government policy and subordinates took as custom, performing them without ceasing and maintaining them without choosing something else. Yet how could these really be the *dào* of benevolence and righteousness?" (Mz 25/74–77)

Other cultures may practice customs we find morally abhorrent. There is thus an important distinction between moral concepts such as benevolence or righteousness and mere custom, be it ours or another culture's. That a practice is traditional or customary, as ceremonial etiquette is, does not show it is morally right, since in other cultures morally deplorable practices such as eating one's firstborn son or abandoning one's grandmother—or foot-binding, slavery, or female genital mutilation—may be just as traditional and customary as our most cherished conceptions of ceremonial propriety. Since other cultures' customs may be morally wrong, our own might too. Ceremonial propriety thus cannot serve as an authoritative guide to morality. Nor, for that matter, does the consensus of a majority make something morally right. As the Lord of Lǔ observes, in response to Mòzǐ's criticism of gratuitous military aggression, "If I look at it on the basis of what you say, what all the world calls acceptable is not necessarily so" (49/24). We need to find other, objectively justified standards.

This search for objective standards to guide action and reform society lies at the heart of the Mohist philosophical and political project.[11] A cardinal conviction driving Mohist thought is that in ethics and politics, as in any other practical field, we must find and apply such standards, which the Mohists call "models" (*fǎ* 法, also "paradigms" or "standards"). "Models and Standards," a relatively late summary of Mohist doctrines, explains the role of models as follows:

> Our Master Mòzǐ said, "Those in the world who perform tasks cannot do without models and standards. There is no one who can accomplish their task without models and standards. Even officers serving as generals or ministers—they all have models; even the hundred artisans performing their tasks—they too all have models. The hundred artisans make squares with the set square, circles with the compass, straight lines with the string, vertical lines with the plumb line, and flat surfaces with the level. Whether skilled artisans or unskilled artisans, all

take these five as models. The skilled are able to conform to them; the unskilled, though unable to conform to them, by following them in performing their tasks still surpass what they can do by themselves. Thus the hundred artisans in performing their tasks all have models to measure by.

"Now for the greatest to order the world and those the next level down to order great states without models to measure by—this is to be less discriminating than the hundred artisans." (Mz 4/1–5)

The Mohists see models as similar to tools used to guide and check the performance of skilled tasks, such as sawing a square corner or drawing a circle. They provide a clear standard against which we can compare things to judge whether they are correct or on the mark, just as we can use a set square or compass to confirm whether something is truly square or round. They are objective, reliable, and easy to use, such that with minimal training anyone can employ them to perform a task or check the results. Models are understood primarily as exemplars, not abstract principles or rules, although these too can be models. They may be role models, prototypes, examples, or analogies, or they may be tools or measuring devices. Any criterion or paradigm that helps us make correct judgments or act correctly can be a model. Models alone do not ensure success, nor do they erase the distinction between the skilled and unskilled—or between the virtuous and those still acquiring virtue—but for most of us they at least ensure that we will do better than we would without them.

A primary task in governing or ordering society, then, is to find reliable, objective models to guide our actions, practices, and policies. As with ceremonial propriety, however, the Mohists point out that any model or standard specific to our particular family, education, or community could turn out to be unreliable. "Models and Standards" continues,

That being so, then what is acceptable to take as a model [*fǎ*] for order [*zhì*]? If all model themselves on their parents, what would that be like? Those in the world who are parents are many, but the benevolent are few. If all model themselves on their parents, this is modeling on the unbenevolent. Modeling on the unbenevolent—it's unacceptable to take that as a model. (Mz 4/5–6)

Having rejected parents as a fundamental moral model, the passage next rejects "learning" (or "teachers") and rulers on the same grounds. We cannot be sure that the particular teachers we follow or our particular political leaders are indeed benevolent. The text concludes that "of these three, parents, teachers, and rulers, none is acceptable as a model for order." A reliable, objective standard is needed, one that is not fallible in the way that any particular role model or tradition of learning might be. The Mohists propose that we can find such a standard by considering the attitudes of an ideally impartial, beneficent, and reliable moral agent: Heaven, or nature itself.

> That being so, then what is acceptable to take as a model for order? So I say, nothing is like modeling on Heaven. Heaven's conduct is broad and impartial; its favors are rich and incur no debt; its brightness endures without fading. So the sage-kings modeled themselves on it. (Mz 4/9–10)

Obviously, we cannot emulate Heaven directly or completely, since we are not deities and lack its superhuman powers. The Mohists' idea is that we can take Heaven as a model in the sense of conforming to its desires or intent. Since Heaven is an exemplary moral agent, its desires or intent will invariably reflect the correct moral norms. In Mohist theology, Heaven generally does not inform people directly of its desires or intentions, typically doing so only during crises. However, the Mohists believe we can discover what it desires by inference from its behavior.

> Having taken Heaven as a model, our actions and undertakings must be measured against Heaven. What Heaven desires, do it; what Heaven doesn't desire, stop.
> That being so, what does Heaven desire and what does it detest? Heaven surely desires people to care about each other and benefit each other and doesn't desire people to detest each other and injure each other.
> How do we know Heaven desires people to care about each other and benefit each other and doesn't desire them to detest each other and injure each other? By its inclusively caring about them and inclusively benefiting them.
> How do we know Heaven inclusively cares about them and inclusively benefits them? By its inclusively possessing them and inclusively accepting offerings from them.
> Now in the world there are no great or small states—all are Heaven's towns. Among people there are no younger or elder, noble or common—all are Heaven's subjects. Hence none fail to fatten oxen and sheep, feed dogs and pigs, and prepare pure offerings of wine and grain to reverently serve Heaven. Is this not inclusively possessing them and inclusively accepting offerings from them? If Heaven inclusively possesses them and accepts offerings from them, how could it not desire people to care about each other and benefit each other? (Mz 4/10–16)

As presented here, the Mohist argument is mainly just a crude articulation of their religious beliefs, hardly amounting to a cogent justification of their position. Still, to an audience who shared their belief in a divine Heaven—as much of their actual audience would have, in one form or another—the underlying theological point is potentially powerful, and it can easily be reformulated in a more sophisticated way. Suppose there is a Heaven who created the world and governs over it, as the Mohists believe. Then indeed all people are equally Heaven's subjects, and it is plausible that, other things being equal, their interests carry equal weight with Heaven. We can assume that Heaven cares about its subjects, since it created the world that sustains them all. So presumably it desires that they all flourish, and indeed it seems to act accordingly to benefit them all by providing natural resources that sustain everyone. As the Mohists contend, then, Heaven probably also desires that people all "care about and benefit others," since everyone is more likely to flourish if we do. Moreover, the Mohists think they have concrete evidence that this is Heaven's attitude, since they believe it punishes those who despise and injure others and rewards those who care about and benefit them (Mz 4/16). For instance, according to history as they understand it, Heaven rewarded Yǔ, Tāng, Wǔ, and Wén, four great sage-kings who cared for and benefited people, and punished Jié, Zhòu, Yōu, and Lì, four cruel tyrants who despised and abused people (4/18–22).[12]

The main philosophical interest of this passage lies in how it reflects the Mohists' discovery of the role of impartiality in ethics. From the standpoint of Heaven, an unbiased and consistent moral exemplar, all people and all communities have equal status. Youths and commoners are on a par with elders and aristocrats; small, weak states are on a par with the great and powerful. All people are equally Heaven's subjects; it cares about and benefits all impartially.[13] Thus, as the Mohists see things, whatever the right norms are for ordering society, they must in some way be modeled on Heaven's impartial care for and benefit to all humanity. The Mohists' search for objectivity thus leads them to develop an ethical and political theory grounded in impartial care and benefit for all. This is an intriguing yet potentially problematic foundation. It incorporates the notion of impartiality, which seems likely to play a central role in any compelling ethical or political theory. The Mohists' conception of Heaven as an ideal agent provides strong grounds for arguing that morally everyone's interests deserve impartial consideration. However, the passage also ties impartiality to caring about and benefiting people. Many of us find it implausible that the correct ethical theory could require us to care about or benefit everyone impartially. So it is interesting to see how the Mohists unpack the idea of modeling ourselves on Heaven.

Modeling oneself on Heaven could mean emulating Heaven's attitudes and acting accordingly. We would seek to care about and benefit everyone equally, just as Heaven cares about and benefits all its subjects equally. For human beings, however, emulating the intent or actions of Heaven is an implausible, even incoherent, ethical ideal. Limitations on our time and resources make it practically impossible for us to act equally on others' behalf as well as our own. (I could not possibly make breakfast for everyone each morning—only for myself, my family, and at most a few neighbors.) Modeling ourselves directly on Heaven would probably also prevent us from realizing certain goods we normally think of as contributing to a flourishing life, such as fulfilling friendships and family relationships, a meaningful career, or creative projects. All of these seem to require devoting more care and benefit to ourselves and our circle of kin and close associates than to outsiders. Directly emulating the attitudes and actions of Heaven would probably demand so much attention to the welfare of others as to leave us with insufficient resources to live our own lives well. Indeed, the instruction to act equally on everyone's behalf might leave us unable to act at all, for any choice about what to do first would seem already to give priority to some people's interests over others' and thus to violate the instruction.

Fortunately, "Models and Standards" does not advocate anything approaching this level of altruism. All the text claims is that Heaven desires that people care about and benefit one another, to some unspecified degree. Heaven itself may care about and benefit everyone equally, but nothing in the text suggests that everyone else must do so as well.

Another way of developing the idea of modeling ourselves on Heaven would be to structure our practices and institutions so that society as a whole conforms to the general norms that Heaven follows. Heaven is committed to caring about and benefiting everyone equally. Instead of attempting the impossible task of caring about and benefiting everyone equally ourselves, as individuals, we could establish a framework of social practices and institutions to ensure that everyone receives equal care and benefits. This framework might entail different attitudes and conduct for agents in different circumstances. For instance, the ruler of a state might be required to care about and benefit all his subjects equally because of his special position of responsibility for them all. However, his subjects might not be required to care about and benefit one another equally. Everyone might be better off overall if people cared about and benefited primarily themselves, their kin, and their friends and associates, while directing only a basic, minimal degree of care and benefit toward strangers. The attitudes and conduct of both ruler and subjects might nevertheless be objectively, impartially justified if the system as a whole conformed to Heaven's intent by securing the welfare of all. Depending on how it is developed, an ethical theory of this general type—a form of indirect consequentialism—might be plausible. As we will see, the Mohists do develop their ethics in this direction, though without fully resolving the potential problems raised by the idea of taking Heaven as a model.

The proposal that we model ourselves on Heaven thus leaves the Mohists with the challenge of articulating the notion of impartiality in a persuasive way. At the same time, it puts them at risk of confusing impartial standards or justification with impartial motivation and action. Impartial, objective standards are the explicit aim of their search for reliable moral models. In their theoretical framework, such models function mainly as epistemic guidelines, to direct us in judging what sorts of conduct or practices to undertake. For discussion's sake, however, we can think of them as also providing an impartial justification for judgment and action. Impartial justification is probably a core element of any plausible ethical theory. A moral justification for actions and practices can be cogent only if it is impartial or unbiased, in the sense of giving due consideration to all morally relevant factors, including the interests of all affected. Justifications that are impartial in this sense possess a sort of universality. By the very nature of reasoning, what is a good reason for me to do something under certain conditions will also be a good reason for anyone else to do the same kind of thing under relevantly similar conditions.[14] A compelling justification is thus also impartial in a second sense, in that it can serve as a justification not just for you or me but for anyone in similar circumstances.

However, recognizing that justification must be impartial in these ways is very different from claiming that our motivation or attitudes must be impartial, like those of a divine agent such as Heaven. To say that others' interests as well as our own are morally relevant, and thus must be impartially taken into consideration, is not to say that we must care impartially about everyone's interests. Nor is it even to say that we must give equal weight to others' interests along with our own, as Heaven presumably does. The fact that others' interests are theirs, not ours, is also a morally relevant factor in determining what we should do.[15] We may have impartial grounds for caring more about some people, including ourselves, than about others. To give a simple example, from an impartial perspective friendship is a good: human lives are better if enriched by friendship. But friendship by its nature requires caring more about friends than about strangers, so we have an impartial justification for sometimes caring more about our friends.

Mohist ethics thus raises fundamental questions concerning the moral claim on us of others' interests, the role of impartiality in morality, and the elements of a good life—questions that remain vital in moral philosophy today. I take up these issues and the Mohists' response to them in chapters 5 and 6.

FATE AND EFFICACY

The Mohists' project of pursuing social order by promulgating norms of righteousness based on the reliable, impartial model of Heaven implicitly rests on a set of metaphysical views that play a crucial foundational role in their thought. These are their theories about Heaven, ghosts, and fate—three topics we can think of as constituting their theology. I will save detailed presentation and evaluation of these theories for chapter 4. Here my aim is mainly to sketch their architectonic role in the Mohist system.

The Mohists hold that Heaven itself conforms to the moral norms articulated in their ethical theory. Moreover, as the ruler at the apex of the cosmic sociopolitical hierarchy, Heaven rewards those who conform to these norms and punishes those who do not. Natural disasters, for instance, are Heaven's punishment for people's failure to conform to unified standards of righteousness (Mz 11/23). Ghosts and spirits also mete out rewards and punishments, in effect working as Heaven's allies or agents. The Mohists thus firmly believe in divine reward and punishment. Good conduct is supported, encouraged, and rewarded by Heaven and the ghosts; wrongdoing is punished.

If Heaven is indeed an impartial, beneficent, and consistent moral agent who follows and enforces objective moral norms, it is unlikely to punish people for outcomes they cannot control. Such punishment would be capricious and unfair—and thus not the conduct of an impartial, beneficent, and consistent nature deity. A belief in divine reward and punishment intuitively tends to go hand in hand with the conviction that, by and large, human beings control their actions and at least the immediate consequences of what they do. Hence, as we might expect, the Mohists adamantly reject predestination or fatalism. There is no such thing, they insist, as destiny or blind fate (*mìng* 命)—some mysterious power that determines whether we will enjoy wealth or poverty, a large or small population, order or disorder, and longevity or premature death, such that our own efforts are to no advantage (Mz 35/3–4).[16] No inscrutable force determines what happens to us, independently of the actions we choose. Prosperity and success are always open possibilities, potentially attainable through diligence and perseverance. Since Heaven—and thus the natural order itself—supposedly conforms to and enforces the moral norm of promoting the benefit of all, the Mohists see the cosmos as arranged such that achieving benefits such as prosperity and social order must be within our control, at least collectively and in the long term.[17]

The central, fundamental role in Mohist ethics of Heaven—and by extension, ghosts and spirits, the moral policemen of the cosmos—is obvious and unmistakable. By contrast, the importance of the Mohist rejection of fatalism is easy to underestimate. A naturalistic, scientific worldview shapes modern readers' attitudes so deeply that we tend to see the Mohist position as unremarkable common sense. Moreover, the triad on fatalism does not particularly call attention to the structural role of the rejection of fatalism in the Mohist system. The explicit content of these three books is notable mainly for presenting the Mohists' epistemological principles (discussed in chapter 2), which they apply to argue against the existence of fate.

In fact, however, the rejection of fatalism stands with the theory of Heaven at the base of the whole Mohist enterprise. Together, these views depict a world in which what happens to us is in principle within human control. Provided people band together under wise leadership, we can achieve social order and solve society's problems. If we diligently follow the correct moral norms, Heaven—that is, nature itself—will approve and support our efforts, without interference from obscure influences such as fate. Conversely, failure is our own fault, due to negligence in pursuing the opportunities open to us. The Mohists' theology thus underwrites confidence in the efficacy of human agency, which in turn is an implicit yet crucial premise of their entire ethical and political project.[18] If our actions were of little or no effect in determining what happens to us, a consequentialist ethics such as the Mohists' would collapse into incoherence. As we will see in chapter 5, the Mohists hold that the benevolent person seeks to promote the welfare of all and that righteousness lies in following practices that tend to promote the goods of material wealth, a large population, and social order. In their view, fatalism eliminates any reliable causal connection between our intentions or actions and promoting these goods. It thus generates two acute tensions, one motivational, the other conceptual. Motivationally, why try to do what is morally right when you have no control over whether you will succeed? Were fatalism true, in the Mohist view, the very idea of aiming to do what is right according to a consequentialist ethics would lose purchase. Despite good intentions, careful planning, and thorough execution, our actions might turn out to have bad consequences after all and thus be morally wrong. Conceptually, by putting the results of what we do beyond our control, fatalism makes it difficult or impossible to distinguish which sorts of conduct reliably produce good consequences. For the Mohists, it threatens to undermine the very distinction between morally right and wrong actions.[19]

The efficacy of human agency is thus a crucial precondition for the Mohists' brand of consequentialism. A natural corollary, in their view, is that confidence in the efficacy of our actions is a psychological prerequisite for commitment to the *dào*. Indeed, they diagnose the failure of some ancient governments to achieve wealth, a large population, and social order as the result of the prevalence of fatalists among the population (Mz 35/1–3). To the Mohists, the chief problem with fatalism as a metaphysical doctrine is not that it is factually mistaken. The problem is its pernicious practical consequences. In their view, fatalism breeds passivity and indolence. It robs people of initiative and leads them to see effort and virtue as pointless, since beneficial or harmful outcomes will occur regardless of what they do.[20] Those who subscribe to it will neglect their work, leading to disorder and poverty:

> If government officials trust in it, they will be neglectful in their apportioned duties. If the common people trust in it, they will be neglectful in undertaking work. If officials don't order affairs, there will be disorder. If farmwork is remiss, there will be poverty. Poverty and disorder are contrary to the root of government. (Mz 39/11–12)

For the Mohist social and moral reform program to succeed, it was imperative that neither rulers nor the general populace accept fatalism. People must be confident that their efforts to secure political stability and economic prosperity will pay off.

> Now why is it that kings, dukes, and great men go to court early and retire late, hearing legal cases and ordering government affairs, the whole day apportioning things fairly, not daring to be negligent? I say, they take it that if they work hard, there will surely be order, if they don't work hard, there will surely be disorder; if they work hard, there will surely be safety, if they don't work hard, there will surely be danger; and so they dare not be negligent.... Now why is it that farmers go out in the morning and come in at dusk, working hard at plowing and sowing, planting and cultivating, harvesting many crops, not daring to be negligent? I say, they take it that if they work hard, they will surely be wealthy, if they don't work hard, they will surely be poor; if they work hard, they will surely be full, if they don't work hard, they will surely be hungry; and so they dare not be negligent. (Mz 37/30–36)

Political order and material wealth are part of the "benefit of the world," the Mohist criterion of righteousness. If the doctrine of fatalism obstructs people's pursuit of these goods, then for the Mohists it is not merely an incorrect account of how things are but a teaching whose promulgation is morally wrong.

Unfortunately, according to the Mohists, fatalism was widespread in their day. They claim that the Rú, for instance, actively promulgated fatalistic doctrines, and indeed fatalism epitomizes the Mohist take on the difference between the two movements. The Mohists' central complaint against the Rú is that the doctrines and practices of Ruism as they know it—before the time of Mencius and Xúnzǐ, perhaps even before it came to be dominated by the figure of Confucius—interfere with promoting the benefit of all, either by wasting material resources, impeding their production, or passing over opportunities to benefit people. It is worth exploring the two schools' different views of fatalism, as these clarify the orientation of Mohist thought and exemplify the contrast between the Ruist tendency toward an inward focus on character and the Mohist tendency toward an outward focus on consequences.

The Mohists report the Ruist position as follows:

> Longevity or early death, poverty or wealth, security or danger are inherently fated by Heaven and cannot be decreased or increased. Failure or success, reward or punishment, good fortune or bad have fixed limits. People's knowledge and effort cannot do anything about them. (*Mz* 39/10–11)

Why would the Rú hold such a pessimistic view?[21] Intriguingly, the answer seems to grow out of a shared early Chinese belief in the moral authority of Heaven.

"Fated by Heaven" here corresponds to the Chinese phrase *tiān mìng* 天命. *Mìng* is typically interpreted as "fate" or "destiny." The word has a wide semantic range, however, and is sometimes appropriately interpreted as "to command" or "to designate." To say that some event is *mìng* is to say that it was mandated by forces beyond our control. "Heaven's *mìng*" is what has purportedly been mandated by Heaven. Traditionally, appeals to Heaven's *mìng* (the mandate of Heaven) were used to justify the political legitimacy of the Zhōu and later dynasties. Supposedly, a good ruler held the mandate of Heaven and so was authorized to exert sovereignty over his people. The overthrow of a dynasty was explained by the loss of Heaven's mandate. An incompetent or wicked ruler would displease Heaven, which would withdraw its mandate, allowing a challenger to depose him. The founders of the Zhōu, Kings Wén and Wǔ, were regarded as justified in overthrowing King Zhòu, the wicked last ruler of the Shāng dynasty, because Heaven had purportedly shifted its mandate to them.

The *Mòzǐ* mentions and endorses this doctrine in several places (for instance, at *Mz* 19/38). Mohist theology thus incorporates a pre-Mohist view of Heaven as a quasi-personal deity that rewards the good and punishes the vicious. Roughly this view also occurs in early Ruist thought, as recorded in the *Analects*. For example, in reply to a pupil who questions his meeting with a notorious woman, Confucius says, "If I have done wrong, may Heaven reject it! May Heaven reject it!" (*LY* 6.28). Another passage remarks that those who offend against Heaven have nowhere to turn in their prayers (3.13). Other passages depict Heaven as having chosen Confucius to preserve the Zhōu tradition and awaken the world to the *dào*. Heaven intends to use him as a bell clapper to rouse the world (3.24), and it will protect him from enemies, since it engendered the virtue in him (7.23) and chose him as its vehicle to transmit Zhōu culture (9.5).

These passages depict Heaven as acting for ethical reasons, a view that imbues the cosmos with moral authority. Sometimes, however, events occur for nonethical reasons, as when catastrophes happen to good people. If Heaven—and thus nature itself—is a force for good, why do bad things happen to undeserving victims? The Ruist answer seems to have been that such events are due to fate. When a worthy disciple falls terminally ill, for instance, Confucius is depicted as saying that the disease is due to fate (*LY* 6.10). Similarly, the premature death of Yán Huí, Confucius's most talented student, is attributed to his unhappily short fate (6.3). It seems, then, that Heaven is a force for good, which determines events at least partly by moral desert, while fate designates events beyond our control, which may occur arbitrarily.[22] As a well-known passage in the *Mencius* explains, fate refers to cases in which "seeking is of no benefit to obtaining, for the things sought are outside us" (*Me* 13.3).

Such remarks in early Ruism imply that material outcomes such as wealth, honor, and life span are ultimately beyond our control, so it is pointless to worry over them. This thought serves three functions. First, it partly answers the Ruist problem of evil, the question of why worthy people who devote themselves to the Ruist *dào* may nevertheless encounter misfortune. Misfortune occurs because, aside from the influence of Heaven, events may also be determined by fate without regard for agents' moral worth. Second, it offers solace in the face of adversity. Certain events are simply beyond our control, determined by fate, so we should accept them without fretting over or blaming ourselves for them. Third, and most important in the context of Ruist ethics, it redirects our concern as moral agents from uncontrollable material outcomes to what we can control: our conduct and intrinsic moral worth. Attention shifts from what is "outside" us, according to Mencius, to what is "within."[23] Poverty and obscurity—things we cannot control—are thus of no consequence to a good Rú. The *dào* lies in developing and exercising virtue while accepting whatever outcomes fate might bring.

Such fatalism presents few practical problems for the early Ruist way of life. Insofar as the Rú held that being a good person lay mainly in the cultivation of virtues and the committed practice of ritualized patterns of conduct, the consequences of one's actions were of relatively little importance ethically. One could be a worthy Rú by sincerely observing ceremonial propriety and offering moral or policy advice when asked. Embracing fatalism may have had little effect on the careers and lives of most Rú. Many were would-be candidates for official posts who in the meantime found employment performing ritual ceremonies. The official appointment process was largely nepotistic and out of their hands, so one could do little but wait and hope for a position. Seasonal rituals, state ceremonies, funerals, and other rites would have provided employment whether one exerted effort or not. Ruist attitudes might understandably have differed from those we saw the Mohists attributing to diligent officials and farmers, for whom fatalistic beliefs could have ruinous consequences.

In some early Ruist writings, however, the scope of fate is broader than merely the vicissitudes of one's career, health, and personal life. In one passage, Confucius dismisses concern over a potential threat to Zǐ Lù by saying that "whether the *dào* is practiced is fate; whether the *dào* is abandoned is fate" (LY 14.36). This seems to imply that whether the *dào* prevails in the world—whether society is in order or disorder—is beyond human control. Conceivably, this remark is consistent with the functions of fate identified earlier. Since ultimately we as individuals cannot control what will happen, we should accept events as they come and concern ourselves primarily with what we can control, namely our moral character and conduct. But it can easily be taken to imply that there is no point in actively seeking to promulgate the *dào*, since whether it is practiced is a matter of fate. This view the Mohists would have found dangerous and morally abhorrent.

This strong doctrine of predestination may not have been the view of Rú such as Confucius and Mencius. Franklin Perkins suggests that what these Rú had in mind may have been only the weaker position that our efforts are often not the decisive factor in what happens, and thus we can only do our best while consoling ourselves by attributing failed outcomes to fate.[24] Fate thus becomes a label for causal factors beyond our control. The problem is that, as Perkins explains, this view clashes with the function of fate in Ruist thought. For appeals to fate to offer consolation for failure or to justify redirecting our concern from material outcomes to personal moral qualities, we must take events to be not partly but wholly beyond our control. Otherwise, there is no discharging our responsibility for them. We should simply try harder to deal with more of the relevant causal factors.

This latter attitude is precisely the Mohist view. Adversity is never due to a mysterious, inevitable force called fate. Events may be caused by multiple, complex factors, which may be difficult to understand and control. In principle, however, these factors are at least potentially identifiable and manageable. In a conversation in the "Dialogues" (Mz 48/76–79), an ailing Mòzǐ is asked whether his illness shows that the ghosts and spirits do not reward the good after all. For why would they allow a sage such as himself to fall ill? He replies that illness can have many causes, the actions of the ghosts being just one. A person might please the spirits yet overlook other factors.[25]

Moreover, by contrast with the Rú, the Mohists doubt whether people can sustain their ethical commitments if the virtues are causally divorced from what happens to us. This doubt is implied by their claims about how fatalism affects people's response to rewards and punishments. The "Condemning Fatalism" books explain that the sage-kings brought order to society by setting forth laws and decrees to give people moral instruction and by instituting rewards and punishments to encourage proper conduct. According to the fatalists, however, "Those whom superiors reward, fate fixes that they will be rewarded; it's not that they are worthy and so are rewarded. Those whom superiors punish, fate fixes that they will be punished; it's not that they are vicious and so are punished" (Mz 35/30–35). The Mohists respond that if people act on the basis of this doctrine, they will fail to observe basic social manners or fulfill the relational virtues associated with core social roles—the ruler will not be righteous, his subjects not loyal, fathers not kind, sons not filial, and brothers not fraternal. In other words, if people suppose there is no causal connection between their conduct and whether superiors reward or punish them, they will fail to be virtuous. This view contrasts diametrically with the Ruist appeal to fate as a means of reorienting the agent's attention from desired outcomes to the cultivation and exercise of virtues. Why do the Mohists see fatalism as having such different implications for moral practice?

A quick, simplistic answer might be that they believe people are motivated to be virtuous only by the expectation of reward or punishment. This interpretation reflects at most only part of the story, however. It is one version of the uncharitable view that for the Mohists self-interest is people's dominant motivation, virtue never being its own reward.[26] As chapters 3 and 7 will show, the Mohists attribute to people a range of motives besides self-interest, and they see people as generally motivated to do what they take to be right, whether or not doing so directly furthers their own interests. Moreover, in criticizing fatalism about rewards and punishments, the Mohists do not suggest that only such material consequences can motivate people to be virtuous. Their point is rather that removing the causal connection between conduct and rewards or punishments robs people of the motivation to observe social norms and fulfill the relational virtues.

The Mohist claim, then, is that if no regular, predictable correlation obtains between what people do and whether they are punished, rewarded, or ignored, they will have no particular reason to perform their social roles in ways generally considered virtuous.[27] This claim is a special case of the Mohists' general view—reflected in their contention that fatalism breeds indolence—that some causal correlation must hold between what we do and what happens to us, or many of our reasons for acting one way or another lose their force. Without such a correlation, considerations we normally take to be reasons for action cease to function as such, and indeed the very notion of agency as acting for reasons is threatened. One role of rewards and punishments for the Mohists is to provide incentives and disincentives to educate and motivate people to behave well. Clearly, if people suppose there is no correlation between their conduct and any reward or punishment they might receive, this role collapses. As the quick answer of the preceding paragraph implies, the Mohists do think fair, public enforcement is needed to help motivate people to follow moral or social norms. But the deeper point is that if rewards and punishments are causally unrelated to actual conduct, the norms themselves begin to disintegrate.

Rewards and punishments normally indicate approval and disapproval. Mohist texts associate them with praise and reproach. The Mohists are contending that if the approval and disapproval of social superiors do not correlate with anything we do, we lose our reasons for exercising the relational virtues and observing basic manners. To be a righteous ruler, loyal subject, kind father, filial son, or loving brother is to be concerned about one's subjects, sovereign, children, father, and brothers and to interact with them in a way conducive to their welfare and to harmonious, fulfilling social relations. Such interaction presupposes a consensus concerning what sorts of behavior merit approval or disapproval, grounded in the norms governing the conduct of these roles and relationships. The absence of a regular correlation between agents' actions and others' approval or disapproval would undermine these norms as a guide to action and with them the basis for orderly social relations.[28] It would interfere with agents' motivation for treating others virtuously and their very ability to determine which actions count as virtuous. Why be loyal if doing so might only bring punishment? How can I be loyal if I cannot tell which actions the sovereign will approve and which he will punish? How can I be a devoted son if I cannot tell which actions will please my father and which will infuriate him? The absence of such correlations threatens the intelligibility of the norms, the associated virtues, and the status of these virtues as admirable character traits. For it becomes unclear on what grounds any particular pattern of conduct could be identified as virtuous and admirable or vicious and reproachable. Indeed, rewards and punishments lose their status as rewards and punishments. Instead of a means of endorsing and encouraging good conduct or condemning and discouraging bad conduct, they become purely fortuitous events—accidents that may happen regardless of what we do. Unlike the Rú, then, for whom the concept of fate grounds a focus on virtue, the Mohists see fatalism as threatening the motivation for and even the intelligibility of virtue, as it undermines our reasons for valuing purportedly virtuous character traits.

To sum up, in a cultural milieu in which religious belief in Heaven was widespread and one prominent view attributed adversity to fate, the Mohists' stance on Heaven and fatalism provided crucial grounds for their confidence in human efficacy, which in turn undergirded their ethical and political activism. Their belief in Heaven's agency and their rejection of fatalism jointly constitute a theological cornerstone for their ethics and politics. In their view, rejecting fatalism is a prerequisite for their consequentialist ethics and the success of their ethical and political reform program.

As an extended introduction to the more focused discussions in the chapters that follow, this chapter has sketched three broad, fundamental themes in Mohist thought: their concern with social order, their search for objective moral standards, and their belief in human efficacy. In the next chapter, I survey the epistemology and logic by which the Mohists support and apply their other doctrines. This background will help elucidate the grounds on which they reject fatalism, the justification for and structure of their ethical and political doctrines, and the details of their moral psychology.

2

EPISTEMOLOGY AND LOGIC

Drawing Distinctions

KNOWLEDGE CAN BE manifested in a variety of forms. Recent Anglo-American epistemology has tended to focus on propositional or factual knowledge, a form of knowledge sometimes called "knowing that," since it is the knowledge we have when we know that some statement is true. In daily life, however, we often apply other conceptions of knowledge. For instance, we speak of knowing people, places, or things, typically implying that we are acquainted with or recognize them. This kind of knowledge might be called acquaintance, recognition, or "knowing of." We also speak of "knowing how," the ability to perform some task or skill. Less idiomatically, we might speak of "knowing to," as in knowing to remove one's shoes on entering a Japanese home. This sort of knowledge amounts to a reliable disposition to conform to a norm or standard.[1]

Propositional or factual knowledge has been a prominent focus in Western epistemology since Descartes. To someone untutored in the modern Western tradition, however, propositional knowledge might not necessarily stand out as the most conspicuous type of knowledge. In reflecting on knowledge, an intelligent person uninfluenced by this tradition might reasonably focus on another form. If, as seems likely, Mòzǐ and many of his early followers were artisans or craftsmen, forms of knowledge such as knowing how to use a tool or knowing of various materials might have seemed more prominent to them. Such an alternative focus might even be more natural given that the syntax of their language, unlike ours, does not mark the distinction between knowing that and knowing how conspicuously or consistently.

As it turns out, the forms of knowledge that chiefly caught the attention of the Mohists and other early Chinese thinkers were what we might call knowing of, knowing how, and knowing to. The Mohists seem to have explained what we would call propositional knowledge by appeal to an implicit conception of knowing how. This feature of their epistemology is particularly interesting for students of the recent Western tradition, since their approach frames issues concerning knowledge, justification, and skepticism in a distinctive, relatively unfamiliar way. Mohist epistemology is also of special interest as part of an intriguing network of views on language, mind, and action that constitute a shared background for much classical Chinese thought. This epistemology had a major influence—both as a constructive resource and as a target of criticism—on other classical schools of thought, especially those represented in the *Xúnzǐ*, a collection of Ruist writings, and the *Zhuāngzǐ*, an anthology of Daoist texts.

This chapter presents an interpretation of early Mohist epistemology and logic and explains how their assumptions in these areas shape their ethics and psychology. For brevity, the chapter treats only the "Triads" and "Dialogues."[2] I argue that Mohist epistemology and logic are built around four core notions: *shì* 是 ("this" or "right") versus *fēi* 非 ("not" or "wrong"), *biàn* 辨 (drawing distinctions), and *fǎ* 法 (models). I first introduce these basic notions and then discuss how the Mohists apply them to treat knowledge and reasoning.

SHÌ-FĒI AND DISTINCTIONS

In Mohist philosophy—and pre-Hàn thought generally—perception, knowledge, judgment, reasoning, ethics, and action are all seen as grounded in the process of distinguishing what is *shì* from what is *fēi*. *Shì* refers to something being "this," the kind of thing under consideration. Technically, *shì* identifies something as part of the extension of a contextually specified "name" (*míng* 名)—a word or term used to denote that thing.[3] If we are discussing whether something is an ox, then to call it *shì* is to claim that it is indeed an ox—it is the kind of thing denoted by the term "ox." ("Ox" and "horse" are the Mohists' stock examples of terms for different kinds of things.) *Fēi* is the contradiction of *shì*. If the thing is not an ox, it is *fēi*. When early Chinese texts speak of *shì* and *fēi* in general, without specifying the term under discussion, *shì* usually refers to what is right and *fēi* to what is wrong. *Shì* and *fēi* can also be used as verbs meaning roughly "to approve," "to deem right," or "to deem this kind of thing" and "to condemn or reject," "to deem wrong," or "to deem not this kind of thing." To call something *shì* is to endorse doing it and, normally, to be motivated to do or encourage it. To call it *fēi* is to condemn or reject it and to be motivated to refrain from or discourage it. Early Chinese texts often mention *shì* and *fēi* as a pair, *shì-fēi*, interpretable as *shì* and *fēi* or *shì* versus *fēi*.

The act of distinguishing *shì* from *fēi* is called *biàn* 辨, roughly interpretable as "distinguish," "discriminate," or, when used as a noun, "distinction." *Biàn* 辨 (distinguish) is closely related to another word also pronounced *biàn* but usually written with a different graph. This second *biàn* 辯 is interpretable as "dispute," "debate," or "dialectics." In principle, the two words are distinct, but ancient texts often use the graphs for them interchangeably. Early Chinese thinkers did not distinguish the two concepts of *biàn* precisely, most likely because they regarded dialectics as an inquiry into how to draw distinctions and saw debate as a process of trying to convince others to draw distinctions in a particular way.⁴

Distinguishing *shì* from *fēi* is the core idea underlying early Chinese models of cognition and judgment, and so it plays a role in every area of philosophy in which cognition or judgment is relevant. Cognition is seen as a process of distinguishing *shì-fēi* with respect to various kinds (*lèi* 類) of relevantly similar things. To recognize something is to correctly distinguish it as the kind of thing it is, an attitude attested by our ability to apply the relevant name (*míng*) or term to it. Judgment is the attitude that something is *shì* or *fēi* with respect to some term—that is, the thing is or is not of the kind denoted by that term. The process of *biàn*, or drawing a distinction, is thus the early Chinese analogue of forming a judgment. To judge that some animal is an ox is to distinguish it as an ox, or, equivalently, to distinguish it as *shì* with respect to the name "ox." In the relevant context, uttering the term *niú* 牛 (ox) or the pronoun *shì* in the presence of some animal is functionally analogous to asserting the statement "This animal is an ox." Grammatically, however, the assertion might consist of only a single word, *niú* (ox).

The Mohists' term-based model of judgment contrasts with the sentence-based model we tend to take for granted today. In the sentential model, the cognitive attitude corresponding to judgment is belief. Beliefs are propositional attitudes, the attitude that the sentence or proposition that expresses the content of the belief is true. In contrast to this model, we might call early Chinese theorists' attitude of distinguishing something as *shì* or *fēi* a "predicate attitude," since it is the attitude of predicating a term of something.⁵ The term "fits" (*dàng* 當), and the associated attitude is correct, when the object on which the term is predicated is in fact the kind of thing the agent distinguishes it to be. What determines whether the object is that kind of thing are the norms for the use of the term. In Mohist thought, these norms rest on two grounds. One is the features of things that make them similar to one another in various ways and thus enable us to group them into kinds. The other is social practices based on perceptual evidence, precedents handed down from wise leaders, and the ethical norm of promoting the benefit of all. Fundamentally, in early Mohist thought, all *shì-fēi* distinctions are grounded at least partly in this fundamental ethical norm.

Distinguishing things as *shì* or *fēi* is thus itself a kind of norm-governed performance akin to a skill or ability. Correctly deeming something *shì* or *fēi* with respect to a term such as "ox" is a matter of following the norms governing the use of the term and the practice of distinguishing oxen from nonoxen. Correctly distinguishing *shì* from *fēi* in ethical contexts is a matter of reliably endorsing and performing ethically proper actions and condemning and avoiding improper ones.

Since *shì* and *fēi* refer both to what is "this" or "not" and what is right or wrong, *shì-fēi* distinctions pertain to both descriptive facts and normative values. They apply both to the descriptive, empirical question of whether or not something is a certain kind of thing and the normative question of whether some action or practice is morally right or wrong. In effect, *shì* and *fēi* refer to a very basic, general normative status that does not distinguish between the different flavors of correctness and error implicated in describing, commanding, recommending, permitting, or choosing. *Shì-fēi* distinctions may pertain to issues in areas as diverse as science, politics, ethics, prudence, and etiquette. Because of their normative use, they are seen as inherently evaluative terms with action-guiding force. In ethical contexts, this feature is obvious, as *shì-fēi* distinctions articulate values. Even in nonethical contexts, however, the attitude of deeming something *shì* or *fēi* is regarded as action guiding. In the context of distinguishing whether something is an ox, the attitude of deeming an object *shì* will normally prompt us to "select" (*qǔ* 取) it by applying the term "ox" to it. The attitude of deeming it *fēi* will normally prompt us to "reject" it with respect to the term "ox." The Mohists thus see cognition itself as inherently action guiding—minimally, by guiding our use of language.

The complex, dual character of *shì-fēi* attitudes—descriptive and normative, expressing a judgment and themselves the result of a norm-governed performance—reflects the shared assumption in early Chinese philosophy of language that a central purpose of language is to guide action, not simply to express facts or report how things stand.[6] To early Chinese theorists, an especially conspicuous type of speech act is uttering action-guiding instructions, teachings, or commands. Language is a vital tool of government, for directing and controlling subjects' conduct. Learning to use language is a process of learning to distinguish the things referred to by various words, while simultaneously learning to conduct oneself in the appropriate way toward those things. Distinguishing someone as "ruler" or "father" invokes a set of norms for interacting with that person; distinguishing something as "order" or "disorder" invokes norms for responding to that thing. As we will see in chapter 3, for the Mohists, moral education is carried out largely by having subordinates model how social superiors distinguish *shì-fēi*, learning by example what should be endorsed and practiced and what should be condemned and avoided. Among the countless action-guiding distinctions embedded in language, *shì-fēi* is the most general and fundamental.

MODELS

As explained in chapter 1, the Mohists refer to the objective moral standards they seek as "models" (*fǎ*). The concept of a model plays a central part in their ethics and their theories of language, knowledge, and reasoning. Models have a dual role, providing both evaluative standards or justificatory criteria and practical guidelines or decision procedures for judgment and action. In their justificatory role, they function as standards of correctness to which we can appeal in evaluating and justifying judgments, actions, practices, and institutions. In their action-guiding role, they serve as guidelines or decision criteria for practical reasoning and action. In this respect, they are an important part of the Mohists' explanation of how we learn language and ethical norms and of the cognitive processes by which we reason, form judgments, and act.

In the passages quoted in chapter 1, the candidates for models were not ethical rules or principles but virtuous agents, such as parents or rulers, whom we might take as role models. This observation yields a key to understanding both the concept of a model and, more broadly, the orientation of Mohist views about language, knowledge, cognition, reasoning, and action. The term "model" denotes any exemplar, standard, or tool used to guide or check the performance of a norm-governed activity. The Mohists conceive of models primarily as tools, paradigms, or benchmarks; their most commonly cited examples are the carpenter's set square and the wheelwright's compass. Models may also be measuring devices, such as a yardstick, a measuring cup, or a weight, or they may be role models, concrete examples, or even pictures. These sorts of models are all concrete, physical objects, but principles, guidelines, laws, or definitions can also be models. So can abstract concepts, such as "the benefit of all," which the Mohists treat as a model for identifying what is morally right. In short, any criterion or paradigm that reliably guides us in drawing distinctions and acting correctly can be a model.

The priority given to practical, concrete models or exemplars reflects two fundamental features of Mohist thought and arguably of classical Chinese philosophy generally. The first is that cognition, judgment, and inference are regarded as processes of pattern recognition—specifically, processes of distinguishing objects, events, or conduct as relevantly similar or not and thus deeming them *shì* or *fēi*.[7] Models are in effect reference prototypes to aid us in drawing such distinctions. The second is the practical orientation of Mohist thought. The focus is on correct performance, not theoretical knowledge or description. Structurally, the central concept in classical Chinese philosophy is *dào* (way), which refers to norms, patterns, techniques, or styles.[8] A *dào* is something to be practiced or performed, not merely grasped intellectually. The aim of *dào* practice is the reliable ability to follow norms or perform activities correctly. Models are aids to following *dào*, and so anything that helps to guide performance can serve as a model. A concrete exemplar to copy may often be more useful than an abstract principle or definition. Indeed, the Mohists understand the function of principles and definitions by analogy to that of paradigmatic concrete models such as the compass and set square, conceiving of them not as fundamental truths or descriptions of reality but as useful benchmarks for performing and checking practical tasks.

These features are illustrated by how the Mohists describe the use of models. For example, they explain the role of Heaven's intent as an ethical model by likening it to the compass, a benchmark against which a wheelwright compares objects to distinguish whether they are round:

> Thus our Master Mòzǐ's having Heaven's intent, to give an analogy, is no different from a wheelwright's having a compass or a carpenter's having a set square. Now the wheelwright grasps his compass and uses it to measure the round and not-round in the world, saying, "What conforms to my compass, call it 'round'; what doesn't conform to my compass, call it 'not-round.'" Hence round and not-round can both be known. What is the reason for this? It's that the model [*fǎ*] for round is clear. (Mz 27/63–65)

Applying Heaven's intent to distinguish moral right from wrong is analogous to judging what is or is not round by a perceptual comparison of similarity with a standard for measuring round objects. As a key passage in the "Dialectics" explains, "Models [*fǎ*] are what something is like and thereby is so" (*MB* A80). If something is "like," or relevantly similar to, the model, then it counts as being "so," or the kind of thing denoted by the term associated with that model. Distinguishing things as "alike" or not is a practical task that can be guided or checked by reference to a model. To know what is round or to check whether we have correctly deemed something "round," we can compare things with a relevant model.

The pivotal role of models in the Mohist conception of cognition, judgment, and reasoning makes them a key to understanding Mohist ethics, epistemology, and logic. Action, knowledge, and reasoning are all explained by appeal to drawing distinctions according to public norms. Models guide us in following such norms reliably. In ethics, models take the place of moral principles in guiding and justifying action. In epistemology, they are public criteria that justify or rebut knowledge claims. In argumentation, they provide the grounds for accepting or rejecting assertions.

Given this range of functions, it is instructive to compare and contrast models with the more familiar notions of a moral principle, a definition, and a reason or a justification. Models are similar to principles in some respects, but their structure and application are different. Both are a kind of general guideline for action. For instance, a moral principle might express a general moral norm in propositional form. A principle may be applied as the major premise in an argument, such as a practical syllogism, from which we derive a conclusion about whether something is right or wrong or should or should not be done. By contrast, models are conceived of as exemplars against which we compare things to distinguish whether or not they are similar. A principle or rule can be considered one type of model, but not every model is a principle or rule, since some are concrete objects, such as a set square.[9]

Models are like definitions insofar as they serve as guides for using words correctly and picking out the things a word refers to. What we call a definition could count as one kind of model. But models are neither semantic nor real definitions, since they do not purport to analyze concepts, capture meanings, or identify essences. Some models might function as nominal or ostensive definitions—definitions that indicate how to use a word without attempting to state its meaning or capture the essence of what it denotes. As the Mohists understand them, however, they are simply exemplars by which to distinguish the extensions of terms.

One role of models is to guide action, broadly construed to include distinction drawing and thus judgment.[10] But the passage likening the role of Heaven's intent to that of a compass also claims that by using a model, "round and not-round can both be known." As we will see, models enable us to know distinctions between *shì* and *fēi* and benefit and harm (Mz 35/6). They thus also have an epistemic role. As criteria for correct distinction drawing, they can guide us to knowledge and justify claims to know something. Matching a model establishes that something is *shì* or *fēi* and thus justifies the claim that it is. Comparison against a model can also explain how we know something. For instance, the Mohists claim we can know that people have strayed from righteousness by measuring their writings and utterances against the model of Heaven's intent (26/43). To persuade an audience that we have correctly distinguished something as *shì* or *fēi*, we can cite a generally accepted model and show that the thing conforms to it.

The role of models in justifying an assertion is distinct from that of a reason, however. The difference again arises from the fact that models are primarily exemplars or paradigms that serve as standards or examples of correct judgment or action, rather than principles or assertions that stand in a logical relationship to an assertion they support. With the exception of cases in which a model is formulated as an explicit rule or assertion, models themselves usually do not function as reasons, in the sense of serving as premises in an argument with some assertion as a conclusion. Rather, they function as standards or exemplars to which we can appeal in supporting an assertion. What conforms to the model is not the assertion but the thing it is about. To justify the assertion that the upper right-hand corner of this page forms a right angle, for example, we could hold a set square against the corner to see whether the two align. If they do, we would be justified in asserting that the corner is right-angled. Our justification would be based on an implicit analogical inference from the premises that the set square is right-angled and that the corner aligns with it to the conclusion that the corner is right-angled too. But the set square—the model—is not a premise in this reasoning, and it does not logically entail or support the conclusion. Were we to state our reasoning explicitly, the premises would be statements about the model, not the model itself. So models sometimes do their justificatory work indirectly, by providing the content of analogical judgments and inferences. Alternatively, we might say the justificatory power of a model lies in the similarity or dissimilarity between it and the thing under consideration, rather than in a logical relation between it and an assertion about that thing.

The Mohists tend to overestimate the power of models to lead people to conform to objective norms. They recognize that models alone cannot ensure correct performance. As we saw in chapter 1, their view is that "the skilled are able to conform to them," while "the unskilled, though unable to conform to them . . . still surpass what they can do by themselves" (Mz 4/3–4). Yet their discussions tend to emphasize the issue of identifying appropriate models without considering the details of how people are to apply them in practice. Models are not self-interpreting. We need to learn how to compare things with them and judge whether they conform, and very likely there will be room for error or disagreement when applying them in particular situations. On these points, the Ruist Xúnzǐ later corrects and fills out the theory of models. Xúnzǐ sees that the skill of applying models is usually learned from others, as an apprentice learns to use a compass or set square from a master. People thus need a teacher to guide them in learning to use models reliably. Xúnzǐ frequently refers to "teachers and models" in expounding his own view of moral education. Arguably, the teacher's role is implicit in the Mohist doctrine of identifying with superiors, but Xúnzǐ is the first to indicate explicitly that models alone are insufficient. He also recognizes that no model can directly cover all particular cases. Whatever the model, there will always be unforeseen situations in which they apply imperfectly or not at all. As Xúnzǐ sees, in such cases we need to rely on our trained judgment to extend the models to cover new cases.

KNOWLEDGE

Like other early Chinese thinkers, the Mohists conceive of knowledge in practical terms. Knowledge for them is not a matter of holding true, justified beliefs, of having mental representations that correspond to the world, or of understanding a theory about something. It is mainly a set of skills or abilities. To know something is to be able to do something correctly—most fundamentally, to be able to draw distinctions properly.

The Mohists apply several closely interrelated conceptions of knowing (*zhī* 知), of which probably the most common is a form of recognition, or "knowledge of." Knowledge of is manifested as the practical ability to correctly distinguish the referent of a term, or "name" (*míng*), that denotes the object of knowledge. To qualify as having knowledge of oxen, an agent must be able to reliably pick out the sorts of things denoted by the word "ox." The object of knowledge is typically a thing or event, denoted by a term, rather than a fact or proposition, expressed by a sentence. When the Mohists do discuss factual or propositional knowledge, they explain it in terms of the ability to distinguish things. To know that *a* is F is to know to distinguish *a* as the kind of thing denoted by the term F. Also, since to know a thing is to know how to distinguish it from other kinds of things, the object of knowledge is sometimes a distinction, as when the Mohists speak of "knowing the distinction between righteous and unrighteous" (Mz 17/13). What we regard as evaluating an assertion or determining the facts or truth about something for the Mohists is a process of drawing distinctions, such as discriminating *shì* from *fēi*, benefit (*lì*) from harm (*hài* 害), presence (*yǒu* 有) from absence (*wú* 無), or what is the same (*tóng* 同) from what is different (*yì* 異). In response to the fatalists' claim that wealth, longevity, and other matters are determined by fate, for instance, Mòzǐ contends that "we cannot fail to clearly distinguish [*biàn*]" the controversial doctrine (35/5)—that is, we must evaluate whether it is *shì* or *fēi* and leads to benefit or harm.

The Mohists' primary conception of knowledge is illustrated in the following passage, which indicates that knowledge lies not in making correct statements but in the ability to "select" the things denoted by a "name." The object of knowledge is not a proposition but concrete objects—white and black items.

> Our Master Mòzǐ said, "Now the blind say, 'What's bright is white, what's dark is black.' Even the clear-sighted have no basis for changing this. But collect white and black things together and make the blind select from among them, and they cannot know. So when I say the blind don't know white and black, it's not by their naming, it's by their selecting." (Mz 47/23–24)

The passage depicts the blind as possessing what we would call propositional knowledge about the colors white and black. Yet it claims that the blind do *not* qualify as knowing white and black, because they are unable to identify white and black things in practice. The criterion of knowledge here is not the ability to state facts or use words correctly—as when the blind "name the names 'white' and 'black' in the same way" as the sighted—but the ability to "distinguish the things" denoted by these words (19/5).

A natural response to Mòzǐ's claim here is that he himself implicitly acknowledges that knowing "names" constitutes a second type of knowledge distinct from knowing how to "select" things. The Mohists ought to distinguish between knowing how to use names—arguably a form of propositional knowledge—and knowing how to distinguish the referents of names. The later Mohist "Dialectics" categorizes knowledge more finely, recognizing that knowing how to use names—as the blind do—is itself a form of knowledge. Knowledge is still regarded as a type of ability, however, and knowledge of facts is treated only indirectly, as the ability to distinguish things properly. So for the Mohists early and late, knowledge is fundamentally a reliable ability to draw distinctions.

This view of knowledge thus illustrates the practical orientation of early Chinese thought. For the Mohists, knowing *x* does not require knowing the nature or essence of *x*, the definition of *x*, or a theory about *x*. It requires only the reliable ability to distinguish x from not-x. This practical view of knowledge contrasts with what we might call a semantic or realist orientation, as epitomized in the Greek tradition by Plato.[11] Indeed, it is interesting to compare the Mohists with Plato, since the two share similar concerns but seek to answer them in different ways. Like the Mohists, the Socrates of Plato's early dialogues is engaged in a search for objective standards to reliably guide judgment and action. In the *Euthyphro*, for instance, Socrates seeks criteria by which to judge which people or actions manifest the virtue of piety. He and the Mohists use similar metaphors. Both refer to what they seek as a "standard" or "model" (the Mohists' *fǎ*, Plato's *paradeigma*). Both compare these standards to measurement tools. Socrates seeks a criterion that can be applied in a way analogous to numbers, weights, and measures, which quickly settle disagreements about amount, heaviness, and size (*Euthyphro* 6e, 7b–d). The Mohists compare models to the artisan's compass and set square, which decisively show whether something is round or square.

But Plato's paradigms and the Mohists' models reflect fundamentally different theoretical orientations. The criterion Socrates seeks is a definition of each virtue that explains what is common to everything that manifests it and thus gives an "account" (*logos*) of that virtue. He wants to know, for instance, what all pious things share that makes them pious. He places several requirements on such a definition. It cannot merely report a general or majority opinion, because the lack of consensus about the virtues is precisely the reason we seek definitions. Also, it cannot just give examples of virtuous actions or list attributes associated with a virtue (*Euthyphro* 11a). It must state the "form" (*eidos* or *idea*) or essence (*ousia*) present in every instance of the virtue. Socrates assumes that all things of the same kind share an underlying, essential form or property that makes each individual the kind of thing it is (*Euthyphro* 6e). Without an account of this shared form, a person might more or less reliably distinguish instances of a virtue but would not have genuine knowledge (*episteme*) of it.

Unlike Socrates's *eidos*, the Mohists' models do not purport to capture the form or essence of things. They are just clear, easily applicable exemplars or tools to aid in distinguishing different kinds of things. The Mohists—and other pre-Hàn thinkers—do not explain the relationship between things of the same kind (*lèi*) by supposing that each kind has a shared essence or nature. Things count as the same kind simply by virtue of being similar to each other. For the Mohists, it is simply a brute fact that things have distinctive features, such as their shape or surface, by which they can usefully be distinguished into kinds. Nor is there a single, unique model for each kind; a variety of models might be useful in distinguishing them. (The "Dialectics" mentions three models for round things: a thought or an intention, a compass, and a concrete exemplar.) Unlike Socrates, the Mohists accept examples or lists of features as models—anything can be a useful model provided it reliably guides us in drawing distinctions properly.

Plato is also historically the source, in the *Theaetetus*, of the justified true belief, or "JTB," account of knowledge, which has dominated epistemology for most of the past century. On the JTB view, knowledge comprises three components or has three conditions: to know that the cat is on the mat, a subject must *believe* the cat is on the mat, this belief must be *true*, and the subject must have a good reason for the belief and thus be *justified* in holding it.[12] Unlike the JTB account, the Mohist conception of knowledge has no element corresponding to the justification condition. Instead, the Mohists treat knowledge simply as the ability to draw distinctions correctly. One reason they assign no role to justification is probably that their conception of correct distinction drawing implicitly incorporates reliability. The role of justification in the JTB account is mainly to disqualify accidentally true beliefs, such as lucky guesses, from counting as knowledge. The Mohists implicitly handle this issue by taking only correct distinction drawing that issues from a reliable ability to qualify as knowledge. Knowledge is not merely drawing a distinction correctly in one case or another but a consistent ability or disposition to draw distinctions correctly in a variety of cases:

> Now suppose there is a person here who, seeing a little black, says "black," but seeing much black says, "white." Then surely we'd take this person to not know the distinction between white and black. Tasting a little of something bitter, he says "bitter," but tasting much of something bitter, he says, "sweet." Then surely we'd take this person to not know the distinction between sweet and bitter. (Mz 17/11–12)

Here again, the Mohists' approach to knowledge reflects their overall focus on practical performance. Fundamentally, to them knowledge is not a matter of having mental states with certain features, such as being justified or corresponding to reality, but an ability to perform certain skills consistently. Accordingly, cognitive error—what we think of as false belief—is not explained as a failure of mental states to correspond to or represent the world accurately.[13] Instead, in early Chinese thought it is typically understood as "disorder" (*luàn* 亂) or "confusion" (*huò* 惑) in drawing distinctions, in effect a failure to perform a skill correctly. For instance, the Mohists criticize those who fail to condemn unprovoked military aggression for the "disorder" in how they distinguish what is righteous from what is unrighteous (17/14).

To guide us in distinguishing things properly, and by extension to evaluate or justify assertions, the Mohists again appeal to models. They develop a methodology for correctly distinguishing *shì-fēi* by reference to models (which I examine in the next section). So they typically answer the question of how we know something by citing models as criteria and then examining whether some statement or practice—or which of a pair of contrasting statements or practices—matches the model. Other common ways by which they explain how we know something are by giving examples to support a claim or by tracing out the causal consequences of some doctrine or situation to see whether they conform to a model. However, such models or examples are not components of knowledge, nor is referring to or citing them a condition of knowledge. Unlike the JTB account, an agent need not be able to cite a model or other grounds to count as knowing how to distinguish *shì-fēi*.

In today's terminology, the Mohists' position can be regarded as a brand of epistemic externalism. "Externalism" refers to views on which agents who hold a true belief can qualify as having knowledge despite lacking access to reasons that justify their belief. If the true belief was caused by a reliable process, for example, it may constitute knowledge even if the agent is unable to give a reason for it.[14] Externalism contrasts with epistemic internalism, according to which agents possess knowledge only if they can give a justification for their true beliefs. They must have good reasons, internal to their belief system, that justify the beliefs, even if they do not actually consider or apply these reasons in forming them. Insofar as the Mohists do not treat justification as a condition or component of knowledge, their conception of knowledge is probably externalist. Indeed, their approach suggests that knowledge and justification could be less closely linked than has generally been assumed in recent Western philosophy. Knowledge could refer mainly to a competence in interacting with the world, justification to a procedure for forming or checking beliefs, particularly in uncertain conditions. Rather than a component of knowledge, justification might serve as one among other processes of obtaining knowledge and as a procedure for checking whether one has knowledge. In both roles, it might pertain largely to intersubjective activities such as persuasion, explanation, education, and public evaluation of knowledge claims. As we will see in the next section, these are roughly the roles addressed by the Mohists' explicit account of justification.

THE THREE MODELS

So far, we have been reconstructing Mohist epistemology by interpreting the implicit conception of knowledge operative in various passages from the "Triads" and the "Dialogues." Unlike the "Dialectics," these writings do not treat the concept of knowledge explicitly, so this reconstructive work is inevitably partly conjectural. When we turn to the topic of evaluating and justifying statements, on the other hand, the *Mòzǐ* presents an explicit, though compact, theory based on the concept of models. Since, for the Mohists, to make a judgment is to draw a distinction between *shì* and *fēi*, evaluating whether a statement is correct is a matter of determining whether the underlying distinction has been drawn properly. To guide us in getting distinctions right, we can establish models as criteria. The act of comparing something against a model is a basis for evaluating and can serve to justify a statement. We can determine whether a statement is *shì* (right) or *fēi* (wrong) by examining whether it, or whatever it is about, conforms to a relevant model.

Setting forth a doctrine I call the Three Models, the Mohists propose three main criteria for evaluating what they term *yán* 言—statements, sayings, or pronouncements. Three slightly different versions of the doctrine are presented in the "Condemning Fatalism" books. In the first, and probably earliest, the criteria are called the three markers (*biǎo* 表). In the others, they are called models (*fǎ*), a change that probably reflects later terminological standardization. The first book begins by claiming that a reason some societies in the past failed to achieve material wealth, a large population, and orderly government was the many fatalists present among their people. It quotes the statement (*yán*) of the fatalists as follows:

> If fated to be wealthy, then wealthy; if fated to be poor, then poor. If fated to be many, then many; if fated to be few, then few. If fated to be in order, then in order; if fated to be in disorder, then in disorder. If fated to be long-lived, then a long life; if fated to be short-lived, then a short life. Given fate, even if one devotes great effort, of what advantage is it? (Mz 35/3–4)

Mòzǐ responds that "those who hold there is fate are unbenevolent. So as to the statements of those who hold there is fate, it's unacceptable not to clearly distinguish [*biàn*] them."

To grasp the significance of these remarks, we need to understand the role of "statements" or "sayings" in Mohist thought. A cornerstone of Mohist ethics is the conviction that the proper moral and political *dào* can be formulated and promulgated explicitly as statements, sayings, pronouncements, doctrines, or teachings. Such statements are regarded as dicta or instructions that guide action. The *Mòzǐ* frequently pairs statements (*yán*) conceptually with conduct (*xíng* 行). People's conduct is expected to correspond to their statements, and those who endorse contrasting statements can be expected to act in contrasting ways (Mz 16/24–29). In Mohist political theory (discussed in chapter 3), people are expected to follow their rulers' statements, and moral education involves emulating the statements and conduct—the words and deeds—of worthy leaders (11/13–22). Hence the Mohists are here proposing criteria by which to evaluate statements or teachings that guide conduct—in effect, explicit expressions of the *dào*.

The Mohists' discussion continues,

> That being so, then how do we clearly distinguish this doctrine? Our Master Mòzǐ stated, "We must establish standards. Making statements without standards is analogous to establishing sunrise and sunset on a potter's wheel. The distinctions between *shì* and *fēi* and between benefit and harm cannot be clearly known. So statements must have three markers." (Mz 35/6–10)

Biǎo, the word rendered here as "markers," refers to gnomons, wooden posts used in sets of three to fix the direction of sunrise and sunset on the horizon and thus to determine the cardinal directions.[15] The analogy is to having three marking posts or guideposts that align along an east-west axis and thus enable us to distinguish east and west from other directions. Making statements without proper standards is like trying to identify the directions by marking them on a spinning potter's wheel, rather than with three carefully fixed posts. Since the marks rotate with the wheel, one cannot distinguish east and west from any other direction.

The text specifies that the issue at stake—the purpose of the standards—is to distinguish *shì* from *fēi* and benefit from harm, using the term *biàn* ("distinguish" or "discriminate"), introduced in the first section of this chapter.[16] Evaluating a statement is regarded as a process of drawing distinctions. Formally, the outcome is not to establish whether an assertion or doctrine is true, but to distinguish whether it is *shì* or *fēi*, beneficial or harmful, and thus indicates the proper *dào* for social policy and personal conduct. These formal details are significant, for two reasons. First, as I have explained, *shì-fēi* distinctions may be either descriptive, normative, or some mixture of the two. The three standards thus apply to both empirical descriptions and normative prescriptions, without distinguishing between them. The Mohists do not see these as criteria specifically for evaluating empirical reports, moral teachings, or sociopolitical policies. Instead, they lump all three areas under the rubric of distinguishing *shì-fēi*. Second, as I discuss in the following, the criteria reflect an explicit concern not with truth, specifically, but with *dào*—the right way of individual and collective conduct and policy, including verbal pronouncements. Indeed, the text repeatedly refers to fatalism as "the *dào* of vicious people" (Mz 35/36) because of the harm it purportedly causes. The significance of this point is that in certain contexts issues concerning truth might diverge from those concerning the proper *dào*.

The "three markers" or "three models" are that statements must have a "root," a "source," and a "use":

> What are called the three markers? Our Master Mòzǐ stated: "There is rooting it; there is sourcing it; there is using it." In what is it rooted? Above, root it in the deeds of the ancient sage-kings. In what is it sourced? Below, source it by examining the reality that people's ears hear and eyes see. In what is it used? Implement it as a basis for the penal code and government and observe that it conforms to the benefit of the state and the people. This is what is referred to as statements having three markers. (Mz 35/6–10)

The "root" (*běn* 本) is the historical precedent provided by the deeds of the ancient sage-kings, moral paragons who reliably distinguished *shì-fēi* correctly. To give their doctrines such a "root," the Mohists typically cite the fabled achievements and practices of six exemplary ancient rulers of the Xià, Shāng, and Zhōu dynasties, the sage-kings Yáo, Shùn, Yǔ, Tāng, Wén, and Wǔ, on whose good example they claim their doctrines are based.[17] The "source" (*yuán* 原) is an empirical basis in what people see and hear. This requirement can be fulfilled by showing that some statement is consistent with common perceptual observation. The "use" (*yòng* 用), or application, is that if adopted as grounds for government policy and criminal punishment, a statement must benefit the state and the people. The first two criteria articulate views widely shared by classical Chinese thinkers. A common presupposition was that the ancient sage-kings were exemplars of wisdom and virtue whose practices could be taken as tried-and-true. Sense perception too was generally accepted as a reliable source of knowledge. The third criterion, benefit to society, presumably was considered justified by Heaven's intent. (I return to these justifications later in this chapter.) So if some statement or teaching conforms to the precedent of the sage-kings, is consistent with what people have seen and heard, and promotes the welfare of the state and people, it is thereby right.

With two exceptions, the differences between the three versions of the doctrine are probably philosophically insignificant. Some may be due to corruption or scribal error, rather than doctrinal differences or developments.[18] The exceptions occur in the second version, on grammatical evidence probably the latest of the three. In this version, the first model includes not only the deeds of the sage-kings but also "the intent of Heaven and the ghosts" (Mz 36/3). Arguably, this is just a more complete articulation of the Mohist system, not a change of doctrine, for the Mohists early and late seem to agree that the deeds of the sage-kings coincide with Heaven's intent. A more notable difference is that the second model, the "source," changes from the "reality" observed by "people's ears and eyes" to "verifying it in the documents of the former kings." This phrase refers to documents recording the laws, penal codes, and declarations of the sage-kings of the three dynasties, which according to the Mohists never endorse fatalism (35/17) and even explicitly reject it (36/24ff.). Unfortunately, textual dislocation and corruption make it difficult to assess the significance of this discrepancy. The extant book that presents the new version of the second model in fact cites what people have heard and seen, while the book that presents the first version cites only documentary evidence. The change could reflect the growing authority attached to documentary evidence as members of the Mohist movement became increasingly literate. It seems part of an overall trend throughout the middle and later strata of the "Triads" to cite purported documentary evidence in favor of Mohist positions. It could also represent a turn away from empirical evidence accessible to all toward traditionalism or authoritarianism,[19] but one of the political books from the same stratum of the Mòzǐ—book 13—actually seems less authoritarian than the others in its triad. The new version could also have been taken to apply mainly to cases in which perceptual evidence is irrelevant, such as when arguing for the doctrine of inclusive care. Considered along with the new version of the first model, the change could even be a halfhearted attempt to reflect actual Mohist practice, for in fact Mohist writings regularly cite not three but five models—the intent of Heaven, legends of the deeds of the sage-kings, ancient documents, perceptual evidence, and practical benefit. (A typical example is the argument in "Understanding Ghosts," which applies the latter four.)

The Mohists consistently apply the Three Models in arguing for their ten core doctrines. When the doctrine at stake concerns questions of existence, as when arguing for the presence of ghosts or the absence of fate, they employ all three models. In arguing against fatalism, for instance, they contend that, first, historical examples show that security and order depend on government policy, not fate: the ancient sage-kings achieved peace and security under the same social conditions in which the tyrants produced only turmoil and danger (Mz 35/11–12, 37/7–10). Second, no one has ever actually seen or heard fate (36/7). Third, fatalism has detrimental social consequences: if people listen to the fatalists, officials will be lax in governing the state and commoners lax in their work, resulting in disorder and poverty (35/42–43).[20] In arguing for the existence of ghosts and spirits who reward the good and punish the vicious, they point out that the sage-kings venerated the ghosts and spirits (31/45ff.); countless stories report cases in which ghosts have been seen and heard (31/14ff.); and the teaching that ghosts and spirits reward the worthy and punish the vicious has beneficial social consequences, since fear of punishment will deter people from wrongdoing (31/76–77).

In contexts where perceptual evidence that something exists is irrelevant, only the first and third models are applied. In condemning extravagant musical shows, for example, the Mohists contend that levying taxes to pay for expensive musical instruments contradicts the deeds of the sage-kings, who would tax the people only to pay for practical items such as boats and carts, which benefit all (Mz 32/8ff.). Grand concerts and feasts are pleasant, but on balance they do not benefit the populace, since they interfere with work and waste resources that could otherwise be devoted to goods such as food and clothing (32/12ff.). The doctrine of inclusive care is justified by citing its benefit to all (15/11–15, 16/13–15) and either the sage-kings' deeds (15/32ff.) or their documents (16/49ff.).

Doubts can be raised about the vagueness of the models and the potential for disagreement about their interpretation and application. The Mohists exalt several different sage-kings, each of whom performed many deeds. Some of these deeds might be inconsistent with one another. Which should serve as models? Disagreement might arise over which deeds are relevant and precisely how they bear on contemporary issues. Similarly, even if we accept the Mohists' conception of benefit as wealth, population, and order, there will be much room for argument about, for instance, whether one scheme of criminal punishments benefits society more than another. Moreover, the Mohists seem to overlook the possibility of conflicts between the models, such as the likelihood that certain practices of the sage-kings might not benefit society today. (In their defense, the first model stipulates only that we find some "root" in the deeds of the sages, not that we imitate them slavishly.)

How are the three models themselves justified? The texts that present the doctrine do not say explicitly. The first model the Mohists probably take to be beyond challenge, for a shared presupposition of their cultural milieu was that the ancient sage-kings were reliable moral and political exemplars. This view is less naive than it may seem, since it is effectively an appeal to experience and precedent—to norms and practices that were found ethically and practically satisfactory by wise, fair leaders in the past. Still, later Warring States texts such as the *Hánfēizǐ* and *Zhuāngzǐ* will rightly question whether policies developed under ancient social conditions remain applicable today and whether we can even know what those policies were. As to the second model—what people see and hear—the Mohists seem to assume that, at least as it bears on questions of existence, this criterion needs no defense. Sense perception is considered a reliable source of knowledge and attracts little discussion in early Mohist texts. The main criticism we might raise concerns the extent to which the Mohists themselves apply the model fairly and rigorously. Does recounting a series of legends about ghosts really count as showing that the common people have seen and heard them?

On the basis of the "Heaven's Intent" books, the Mohists would probably justify the third model, benefit to society, by appeal to Heaven's intent. That appeal they might justify in turn by Heaven's status as the wisest, noblest agent in the cosmos or by independent moral criteria such as impartiality, benevolence, and consistency, as suggested in chapter 1. Ultimately, the third model rests on the Mohist ethical theory; opponents who reject the theory are likely to reject this model as well. Clearly, a critic could argue that broad application of the third model to distinguish *shì* from *fēi* might be problematic, because good consequences may not always be a reliable guide to what is normatively or descriptively correct. Moreover, the critic might contend that the specific consequences the Mohists identify—wealth, population, and social order—are inappropriate grounds for distinguishing *shì-fēi*, especially in empirical matters such as the existence of fate or ghosts. Indeed, we might wonder how stringently the Mohists themselves would follow the third model if by chance the consequences went against their favored views. If, for instance, fatalism happened to have good consequences—say, by consoling the poor and downtrodden enough to keep them from giving up entirely—or belief in ghosts happened to have bad consequences—perhaps by leading people to spend an inordinate amount of time in worship or séances—would the Mohists reverse their position?[21]

In the Mohists' defense, however, the consequences of an empirical belief are sometimes relevant to our evaluation of it. Bad consequences can add to the reasons for rejecting a factually mistaken doctrine, by making it more objectionable—on moral or prudential grounds—than it otherwise would be.

Suppose a quack medical therapy not only is factually mistaken and ineffective but also prevents sufferers from seeking effective treatment. Promoting it is surely worse than propounding a view that happens to be false but has no real practical consequences. This line of thought suggests a way of viewing the doctrine of the Three Models that removes some of the oddness of applying a consequentialist evaluative criterion to empirical questions. The Mohists probably assume that evaluation by each of the models will generally yield the same result. For example, as they see it, fatalism fails the test of all three. It was not the practice of the sage-kings, nor is fate empirically observable, nor does fatalism have good consequences. They may see the empirical side of the issue as covered mainly or entirely by the first and second models—the sage-kings' experience and perceptual evidence—and the third model as providing supplementary moral or prudential considerations for accepting or rejecting a doctrine.

An obstacle to this line of interpretation, however, is that the Mohists do not explicitly address how to handle potential conflicts between the three models, and what little they do say suggests that the third model takes priority. A striking passage in book 31, "Understanding Ghosts," depicts Mòzǐ arguing that even if ghosts do not exist—and thus fail to coincide with the second model, since they cannot be seen or heard—we should still behave as if they do, because sacrifices to ancestral ghosts have good consequences: they provide an occasion for a social gathering and promote good relations among neighbors. (These benefits augment those the book has already argued for, mainly crime deterrence due to fear of ghostly retribution.)

> Now we prepare pure offerings of wine and grain to reverently and attentively sacrifice to them. Supposing in fact there are ghosts and spirits, this succeeds in providing food and drink for our parents and elder siblings. How is this not a rich benefit?! Supposing in fact there aren't ghosts and spirits, then this is just expending the resources used to make the offerings of wine and grain, that's all. Yet though we expend them, it's not that we just pour them in a sewage ditch and throw them away. Our relatives inside the clan and townspeople from outside the clan all get to drink and eat what's provided. Even supposing in fact there aren't ghosts and spirits, this can still make for an enjoyable gathering and build kinship among the townspeople. (Mz 31/99–102)

The priority of the third model here is remarkable, since it suggests that in some circumstances the Mohists may advocate using consequentialist criteria to resolve not only normative issues but also what we would consider empirical, descriptive ones, such as whether ghosts exist. Alternatively, the text could be interpreted as sidestepping the empirical question and contending that even if ghosts do not exist, acting as if they do is not a bad mistake, for it has good consequences.[22] Either way, the best underlying explanation of the Mohists' stance is probably that their fundamental concern is not the truth or falsity of the empirical claim that ghosts exist but the proper *dào* by which to guide social and personal life.[23] This focus on *dào* leads them to elide the abstract, descriptive question of whether ghosts exist and focus on the practical, normative issue of whether we should act on and promulgate the teaching that they do.[24] How they apply the Three Models thus reflects the practical inclination of their thought, in particular the background assumption, common among early Chinese thinkers, that a major function of language and judgment is to guide action appropriately.[25] The Three Models might also reflect a practical bent in another sense: they could have been chosen specifically because of their rhetorical force for audiences likely to acknowledge them as decisive criteria.[26] That is, the Mohists might see themselves not as offering an account of the ultimate theoretical basis for distinguishing *shì-fēi* so much as identifying what they take to be compelling, widely accepted criteria.

Interestingly, one could argue on the Mohists' own grounds that they should explicitly distinguish descriptive from normative issues, since doing so is probably more beneficial than not. Although counterexamples can be given, in the long run we probably benefit more from pursuing beliefs—or corresponding patterns of distinction drawing—that are true, rather than only instrumentally useful. In the Mohists' terms, we could say that ultimately we better satisfy the third model, practical benefit, if we guide our distinction drawing mainly by the second model, perceptual observation, rather than by the traditions of the sage-kings or by immediate benefit. If ghosts and spirits indeed do not exist—and thus are not routinely part of people's perceptual experience—then relying on fear of their wrath to deter crime will probably be less effective in the long run than developing reliable systems of moral education and law enforcement. Also, in practice, the alleged social benefits might not provide sufficient motivation for doubters to sincerely act as if ghosts exist or to follow a moral code based partly on commitment to the existence of entities they do not perceive. In effect, our criticism would be that, in their teachings on ghosts and spirits, the Mohists do not apply their own models judiciously enough.

LOGIC AND ARGUMENTATION

Besides its role in Mohist epistemology, the doctrine of the Three Models epitomizes the Mohist approach to logic and argumentation. The Mohists do not investigate formal logic or develop an explicit conception of logical consequence. Rather, since they see judgment as a matter of distinguishing whether something is one kind of thing or another, they tend to conceive of all reasoning on the model of informal, analogical inference. Particular pieces of reasoning in their texts may be deductive, inductive, analogical, or causal. But the Mohists themselves probably regard all these as special cases of the more general cognitive process of comparing things with models in order to draw distinctions between similar and dissimilar kinds of things.[27] That is, they tend to see all forms of reasoning as species of pattern recognition or analogical reasoning.[28]

For the Mohists, the process of supporting a statement by giving reasons and that of drawing out the consequences of one or more statements fall under the rubric of *biàn* 辯 (dialectics or distinction drawing). Although *biàn* may involve citing reasons, it is not understood as a matter of laying out premises and drawing a conclusion from them. Rather, it is a process of distinguishing something as "the same as" (*tóng* 同) another thing or kind of thing and predicating a term of it accordingly. The focus is on judging whether a thing falls within the extension of a term, rather than on grasping logical relations between statements of a certain form. So although such *biàn* involves inferences—in most instances analogical, but in some deductive or inductive—overall, it is concerned primarily with semantics, not logic. The distinction drawing or cognition on which it is based is typically learned, guided, and justified through the use of models. If a thing is similar to, or of a kind with, a model, then we distinguish and treat it similarly.

The Mohists' core conception of reasoning can be understood as having three parts. First, we cite one or more models by which to distinguish *shì* from *fēi* or to guide the use of some term, such as "benevolent" (*rén* 仁) or "righteous" (*yì* 義). Then we indicate how some object, event, or practice does or does not coincide with the model. Accordingly, the thing in question is distinguished as *shì* or *fēi*, benevolent and righteous or unbenevolent and unrighteous. What we think of as the major premise in a syllogistic piece of reasoning would be analogous, for the Mohists, to citing a model. What we call the minor premise, they would see as a claim that something coincides with the model. What we think of as drawing a conclusion, they would see as distinguishing whether or not something is of the same kind as the model. The "Dialectics" clearly indicates that this reasoning process is understood as a form of analogical inference, which one passage calls "extending kinds" (*tuī lèi* 推類)—that is, "extending" (*tuī*) our judgment of what counts as "the same kind" to include new cases. In practice, "extending kinds" amounts to taking the judgment that things are "of a kind" (*lèi*) in one or more respects as a basis for treating them as "of a kind" in some further respect.

The doctrine of the Three Models provides an example of this general type of argument by exemplar or analogy. The Three Models are not the only exemplars the Mohists employ, however. They regularly cite others, such as the conduct of the benevolent person or the filially devoted son. Mohist arguments typically proceed by establishing such a model or exemplar and then contending that Mohist doctrine conforms to it and thus is *shì*, or right. For instance, the main arguments for the doctrine of inclusive care begin by citing the model of the benevolent person, who "seeks to promote the welfare of all and eliminate harm to all" (Mz 16/1). The text goes on to argue that the doctrine of inclusive care promotes the welfare of all and so conforms to the model of the benevolent person. Inclusive care is thus benevolent and right. A second example is the chief argument against extravagant burials. It too begins by citing the benevolent person as an ethical paradigm, but here the opening move is to establish, by analogy, the attitude of the filial son toward his parents as a model for that of the benevolent person toward all the world: "The benevolent person's planning on behalf of the world, to give an analogy, is no different from a filially devoted son's planning on behalf of his parents" (25/1). Just as the filial son seeks to provide his parents with wealth, a large family, and good order, the benevolent person seeks these goods for society as a whole (25/7). The text argues that extravagant burials and prolonged mourning are antithetical to these goods, so these practices are mistaken (25/14).[29]

The inclusive care argument and the funerals argument also illustrate another common Mohist rhetorical strategy: exploring the causal consequences of a doctrine or policy, typically to show that Mohist doctrine yields results that tally with some model while an opposing doctrine does not. One passage describes this argument technique as jointly "developing" or "proceeding with" the two alternatives (Mz 16/23). In each argument, the Mohists identify two contrasting norms—inclusive versus exclusive care, in the one case, extravagant versus moderate burials, in the other—and explore their causal consequences. The norm that yields results conforming to the ethical model of "promoting benefit to all and eliminating harm to all" is *shì*, while the opposing norm is *fēi*.

Many other prominent Mohist arguments are also based on analogical reasoning. An example from among the earliest Mohist writings is the opening argument of the antiwar triad. The text describes a series of increasingly serious crimes, from petty theft to murder, claiming that each is more unrighteous (not *yì*) or unbenevolent (not *rén*) than the last because of the greater injury to the victim. All are similarly wrong, because they injure others for selfish benefit, and the relation between each pair of cases is similar, in that one of the pair concerns a more severe injury and so a more serious crime. The text criticizes "the gentlemen of the world" for failing to see that military aggression against another state is of a piece with but more serious still than the preceding examples:

> Now suppose a person enters someone's orchard and steals his peaches and plums. When the multitude hears about it, they deem him wrong [*fēi*]. If superiors who govern get hold of him, they punish him. Why is this? Because he injured another to benefit himself.
> In the case of seizing someone's dogs, hogs, chickens, and pigs, the unrighteousness is even greater than entering someone's orchard and stealing the peaches and plums. What is the reason for this? Because the more he injures another, the more he is unbenevolent and the heavier the crime.
> In the case of entering someone's stable and taking the person's horses and oxen, the unbenevolence and unrighteousness are even greater than seizing someone's dogs, hogs, chickens, and pigs. What is the reason for this? Because it injures another even more. If it injures another more, the more it is unbenevolent and the more serious the crime.
> In the case of killing an innocent person, stripping him of his clothing, and taking his spear and sword, the unrighteousness is even greater than entering someone's stable and taking the person's horses and oxen. What is the reason for this? Because it injures another even more. If it injures another more, the more it is unbenevolent and the more serious the crime.
> In these cases, the gentlemen of the world all know to deem these acts wrong and call them unrighteous. Now when it comes to the bigger case of attacking another state, they don't know to deem it wrong, and so they praise it, calling it righteous. Can this be called knowing the difference between righteous and unrighteous? (Mz 17/1–7)

The analogical inference to the conclusion is left implicit. Rather than explicitly stating that war is even more unrighteous than murder, the argument is framed as showing that "the gentlemen of the world" are "confused" in how they distinguish what is righteous from what is unrighteous (17/14). They know how to distinguish the two in the less serious cases of theft and murder but not in the most serious case of all, wars of conquest resulting in countless deaths. To us, the passage might be interpreted as giving examples of, or inductively supporting, a general principle, such as "the greater the intentional injury to others, the more serious is the crime." The Mohists instead see themselves as tracing out patterns of similarity on the basis of which to draw distinctions such as righteous versus unrighteous. The argument constructs analogies along two dimensions: all the examples are similarly unrighteous because of the injury to others, and each successive example is similarly *more* unrighteous than the last because of the *greater* injury to others. The gentlemen of the world fail to recognize that differences in the scale of injury do not nullify the similarity of these acts in being unrighteous; to the contrary, they render the larger-scale crime more deeply unrighteous. This sort of inconsistency the Mohists elsewhere label "understanding the little things without understanding the big things," or understanding small-scale, minor cases without grasping how large-scale, major ones are fundamentally the same.[30]

The opening of the first "Inclusive Care" book offers an example of an explicit analogical argument from the same early stratum of the text.

> The sage, who takes ordering [zhì] the world as his task, must know what disorder arises from; only then can he put it in order. If he doesn't know what disorder arises from, he can't put it in order. To give an analogy, it is like a doctor treating someone's disease. He must know what the disease arises from; only then can he treat it. If he doesn't know what the disease arises from, he can't treat it. How could putting disorder in order alone not be so? One must know what disorder arises from; only then can one put it in order. If one doesn't know what disorder arises from, one can't put it in order. (Mz 14/1–3)

Just as a doctor must know the cause of the disease he treats, a sagely ruler must know the cause of the disorder he seeks to rectify. The passage is also typical of the highly repetitive style of early Mohist writing, with its recurring parallel clauses.

The Mohists' conception of reasoning is effective in many contexts, particularly ethical, political, and legal argumentation, where arguments by analogy or appeals to precedent are a common form of reasoning. Their approach faces the same limitations as analogical reasoning in general, however. Arguments by analogy are not reliably cogent, because two items similar in many respects may be importantly different in others, and because the criteria by which we determine what counts as relevantly similar are always open to dispute. These two issues are central problems in the Mohist "Dialectics," as well as in other early Chinese texts that address argumentation, such as the *Xúnzǐ*, *The Annals of Lü Buwei*, and the *Zhuāngzǐ*.

CONSEQUENCES FOR ETHICS AND AGENCY

According to the interpretation presented in this chapter, the Mohists regard cognition, language, and reasoning as based on drawing distinctions between different kinds of things. Such distinctions are denoted most generally by the pronouns *shì* (this) and *fēi* (not). To guide ourselves in drawing distinctions correctly, we can compare things with models (*fǎ*), which are paradigms of different kinds of things. Distinguishing something as *shì* or *fēi*, belonging to a certain kind or not, is the functional equivalent of making a judgment. The resulting attitude is the analogue of holding a belief. Knowledge is the ability to draw distinctions properly. To learn whether something is *x* or to check a claim that it is, we can compare the thing with a model for *x*. Argumentation is most commonly a process of citing a model, claiming that something is or is not relevantly similar to it, and then distinguishing the thing as *shì* or *fēi* accordingly.

A philosopher's model of judgment and argumentation is likely to reflect, and may tend to shape, that thinker's conception of thought, knowledge, reasoning, and justification. By extension, it probably also reflects and shapes the thinker's conception of action and agency. The Mohists' epistemology and logic are thus interesting not merely in themselves: they have far-reaching consequences for other areas of their thought, such as their conception of moral reasoning, the structure of their ethical theory, and their view of agency.[31]

Western philosophers have commonly conceived of reasoning as having an argument-like structure. According to what we might call the argument model of thought, we reason by considering premises in sentential form and drawing conclusions from them. Interrelated with this conception of reasoning is a view of the structure of knowledge as an axiomatic or a deductive system, in which a core set of axioms, principles, or laws serve as the basis for theorems about or explanations of a variety of cases or phenomena. Similarly, an ethical theory is often thought of as comprising a few general principles that are applied to particular cases through deductive reasoning. One paradigm of moral reasoning—not the only one, of course—is to cite a general moral principle and a premise about a particular situation and then derive a conclusion about what to do or whether some action is right or wrong.

As we have seen, the Mohists conceive of reasoning as primarily distinction drawing. They regard moral reasoning or deliberation mainly as a process of considering models and discerning patterns of similarity and difference, not one of drawing conclusions from general principles. Moral reasoning for them is typically analogical: an action or practice is compared with a model and distinguished as *shì* or *fēi*.³² It is a process of extending our know-how in drawing distinctions to cover new cases. It is not the application of an innate reasoning ability possessed by each individual—as in Kant's ethics, for instance—but a practical skill that initially must be learned, usually in a social setting.

Ancient Chinese mathematicians had no notion of an axiomatic system. They saw mathematics as the study of algorithmic techniques for solving practical problems, which they organized taxonomically. The Mohists too have no notion of an axiomatic system, and their conception of knowledge as correct distinction drawing suggests that they too probably see knowledge as having a taxonomical rather than a deductive structure. Accordingly, they do not think of their ethical theory as structured like a deductive system, with axiom-like general principles from which lower-level principles and particular conclusions are derived. Instead, they see it as comprising models, at various levels of generality, which provide exemplars for agents to emulate in distinguishing *shì-fēi* and acting accordingly. The models are applied not through our capacity for reasoning, in the sense of drawing inferences, but through our capacity for pattern recognition—for mastering a way of noticing and responding to similarities and dissimilarities.

Familiar Western conceptions of agency tie it closely to reasoning and deliberation, understood along the lines of the argument model of thought. In thinking about action, many influential Western philosophers have focused on the process by which we decide what to do in particular cases.³³ The dominant model of practical reasoning—the process by which rational agents are understood to make such decisions—is the belief-desire model. This model represents and explains action by an argument-like structure in which premises representing the agent's motivational state and beliefs combine to entail a conclusion about what to do. Agency is seen as lying in the capacity to choose one's actions autonomously on the basis of such reasoning. Moral dignity is associated with the exercise of rational agency.

Since the Mohists and other early Chinese thinkers do not share the argument model of practical reasoning, they are unlikely to share this conception of agency. Rather, in thinking about action, as in thinking about knowledge and argumentation, they take their cue from the performance of skills. Skills depend mainly on a trained, reliable ability to discriminate and respond to things according to appropriate patterns. The focus of skill training is not on deciding what to do in particular situations but on developing the ability to perform consistently, producing a similar, appropriate pattern of action across a variety of cases. It would be awkward to conceptualize skills as having an argument-like structure like that embodied in the belief-desire model—such a structure hardly seems an informative way to explain what a pianist is doing while sight-reading a new piece of music, for instance. But it is quite natural to conceive of skills as having a discrimination-and-response structure of the type suggested by the Mohists' concept of distinction drawing as it bears on knowledge and reasoning.

I suggest that the Mohists—and most early Chinese thinkers—take for granted what I call a discrimination-and-response model of action.[34] Action is regarded as a skilled response to things or situations. It is triggered by the agent's distinguishing a thing or situation as being of a certain kind and thus invoking a relevant, normatively appropriate response. Instead of tying agency to our capacity for reasoning, this model bases it primarily on our capacity to acquire and exercise skills and virtues.[35] Autonomy lies in our control over how we discriminate and respond to things, which we do through training, sensitivity to particular situations, and sometimes reasoning. Reasoning plays only a subsidiary role in this conception of action. It is a skill invoked to guide action in complex cases where our other skills are insufficiently competent. Desires and other affective states represented in the belief-desire model also play only a minor role, as features of situations to which we might respond in various ways, such as by acting to satisfy them or by ignoring them. The predominant factors in guiding action are skills and virtues and the practical habituation and training by which we develop them. The consequences of these interpretive proposals are developed and explored in the ensuing chapters on Mohist political theory, ethics, and moral psychology.

3
POLITICAL THEORY

Order Through Shared Norms

AS WE SAW in chapter 1, a fundamental motivation for the Mohist movement was a concern with social order (zhì 治). The Mohists saw a well-functioning state as a necessary condition for social order, both as a means of achieving it and as one of its constituent features. A concern with politics is thus central to their thought. Moreover, because their ethics generally approaches normative and motivational issues from the perspective of society as a whole, rather than that of the individual agent, the Mohists see ethics and politics as inextricably intertwined. For these reasons, they devote much attention to political philosophy, articulating a range of views pertinent to the origin and justification of the state, the organization and aims of government, who should rule and by what methods, and the balance between state power and individual liberty. To a limited extent, they even take a position on the just distribution of wealth. They present insightful observations about human organizational behavior and the effects of appropriate or inappropriate administration of the state, or any organization, on people's motivation to cooperate with it.

This chapter discusses Mohist political theory as presented in the texts devoted to their two major political doctrines, "identifying upward" and "promoting the worthy." Along the way, I touch on how Mohist political thought relates to broader issues in political philosophy, including the justification and ends of the state, the question of who should rule, the distribution of wealth, and the scope of state power. The chapter closes with a few critical remarks about the Mohist political system.

ORIGIN OF POLITICAL AUTHORITY

Mohist texts present what is probably history's earliest account of the hypothetical origin of political society from a state of nature. Their myth about the intolerable circumstances in the state of nature and the transition to political society is interestingly different from the more familiar modern theories of Hobbes, Locke, or Rousseau. Unlike Hobbes, they do not depict social chaos as resulting from individuals' attempts to defend themselves while pursuing their self-interest in contention for limited resources. Unlike Locke or Rousseau, they do not tie chaos to conflicts arising from claims to private property. Unlike all three, they do not invoke a social contract to explain the origin of government. Nor do they ground political obligation in the voluntary consent of the people—though, as we will see, the choice and support of the people do play an important role for them.

The Mohist myth contends that in a state of nature violent disorder would arise from disagreement over values. People tend to do what they think is right. The problem is that everyone disagrees about what that is. As the Mohists put it, people in a hypothetical state of nature, before the origin of political authority, would probably each have their own yì 義—their own conception of what is righteous (Mz 11/1, 12/1). The Mohists usually use the word yì to refer to morality or what is morally righteous. In this context, however, it refers loosely to whatever norms of or guidelines for conduct people take to be proper, even if the sense of propriety in question does not coincide exactly with moral righteousness. For the purposes of this chapter, I will generally leave yì untranslated, with the understanding that it refers to norms or conceptions of righteous or appropriate conduct. According to the Mohists' hypothetical scenario, the root of disorder is that people have diverse yì—diverse norms—but also assume that yì is inherently social and shared, and so any conception different from their own is mistaken. The texts depict people as so committed to their own yì and so adamant in condemning others' that even family members are unable to live together harmoniously. People's criticism of one another's yì leads to resentment, belligerence, and wasted resources. Ultimately it drives society into violent disorder. The first of the Mohists' three versions of the myth describes the slide into chaos as follows:

> In antiquity when people first arose, before there were penal codes and government, probably the saying was, "People have different yì." Hence for one person, one yì; for two people, two yì; for ten people, ten yì—the more people, the more,

too, the things they called "yì." Hence people deemed their own yì right [shì 是] and by it deemed others' yì wrong [fēi 非], and so in interacting they deemed each other wrong. Thus, inside the family, fathers and sons, elder and younger brothers became resentful and scattered, unable to remain together with each other peacefully. The people of the world all injured each other with water, fire, and poison. It reached the point that, having surplus strength, they couldn't use it to labor for each other; letting surplus resources rot, they didn't share them with each other; and concealing good dào, they didn't teach them to each other. The disorder in the world was like that among the birds and beasts.[1] (Mz 11/1–5)

Disorder here lies in the breakup of families, injury to others, and refusal to share labor, resources, or knowledge. The need to rectify these evils provides the fundamental justification for political authority. Its primary purpose is to unify yì and thereby achieve social order, and so it is justified to the extent that it succeeds.

As the Mohists imagine them in the state of nature, people are autonomous agents who are strongly, even obstinately committed to their yì. The passage describes their attitude by saying that they "shì their yì and on that basis fēi others' yì, and thus fēi one another"—that is, they each deem their yì to be shì (right), on those grounds deem others' fēi (wrong), and thus fall into a cycle of reciprocal condemnation that eventually leads to social turmoil. This description has two important implications. First, people apparently assume that since their own yì is shì, any other yì is fēi and thus mistaken. Commitment to one's yì seems to entail the attitude that others are mistaken not to also affirm and practice that yì. Although people each have their own yì, then, they seem to assume that yì by its nature comprises public norms of conduct to which everyone should conform, not only themselves.[2] They thus share a belief that yì should be unified across society. Second, people's attitude of deeming their yì to be shì and others' fēi is apparently accompanied by a strong motivation to act on their convictions, which in the hypothetical scenario leads them to clash with one another. The best explanation of this point, I suggest, is that the Mohists take the attitude of deeming something shì or fēi to have inherent motivational force. In chapter 2, we saw that shì and fēi refer to a pair of basic cognitive and action-guiding attitudes, with roles analogous to those of a judgment or a reason for action. The description of the state of nature illustrates the role of shì-fēi attitudes and underscores their action-guiding character. Other things being equal, to deem something shì is also to be motivated to do, endorse, respect, or promote it, while to deem it fēi is to be motivated to avoid, condemn, prevent, or eliminate it.[3] Moreover, since people normally deem their yì to be *shì*, this motivation carries over to *yì* as well: people are normally motivated to do, endorse, or respect what they consider *yì*. The hypothesis that *shì-fēi* attitudes are inherently motivating helps to explain why the Mohist political program emphasizes having everyone emulate how their leaders discriminate *shì* from *fēi*. To distinguish *shì-fēi* in a certain way is not merely to see things one way rather than another but to have a disposition to act accordingly. Indeed, how one distinguishes *shì-fēi* is a core element of what it is to follow some *yì*.[4]

What are the various *yì* by which people in the state of nature act? One possible interpretation is that each person's *yì* is simply his or her self-interest. If the claim is that people in the state of nature are motivated only by self-interest, this interpretation is unsustainable. The text depicts people as motivated by their *shì* and *fēi* attitudes, not self-interest, and it is difficult to see how self-interest, rather than normative disapproval, would motivate them to clash with others simply on the grounds that they follow different *yì*. But probably this interpretation is better understood as claiming that the content of everyone's *yì* is self-interested. As Schwartz says, "The people's 'view of what was right' [*yì*] was simply that they should serve their own individual interests."[5] This would be one way to explain why the texts depict people as each having their own *yì*. Each person's *yì* could amount to "always act to benefit P," where P is that person.

Some of the diverse *yì* may indeed be self-interested. An anecdote in the "Dialogues" gives an example. Mòzǐ's opponent Wūmǎzǐ remarks that according to his *yì*, he would kill others to benefit himself, but not himself to benefit others (Mz 46/52–60). However, the thesis that all the people in the state of nature follow self-interested *yì* is implausible, for several reasons. First, if the Mohists do see all the various *yì* as self-interested, it is difficult to explain why they do not directly say so. Elsewhere, they explicitly attribute social disorder to people's pursuing their own interests at others' expense (14/5–8). If the state of nature scenario is meant to illustrate a similar idea, why not use equally direct language? Another problem is that there are not enough distinct versions of self-interested *yì* to account for the radical plurality of norms the Mohists envision. Schwartz's suggestion, that people's *yì* was for individuals to serve their own interests, is actually only a single *yì*, not a plurality. Other formulations of self-interested *yì* are available, of course, such as Wūmǎ's. But diversity on the order of "one person, one *yì*" would be more likely if the *yì* were not restricted to different norms for furthering one's own interests. A defender of the self-interest interpretation might suggest that each of the diverse, self-interested *yì* would be a distinct set of norms, since each would be directed at the interests of a different individual. However, it is unlikely the

Mohists would conceive of self-interested norms this way, because in contexts where they unequivocally do refer to self-interested conduct, they treat it as a single norm, such as "injuring others to benefit oneself."[6] A further point is that the Mohists simply do not regard people as predominantly self-interested. As we will see in chapters 6 and 7, they assume that people normally care about the interests of their family, city, and state. Even Wūmǎ's self-centered policy is not purely self-interested. His full statement of his yì indicates that in fact he does care about others, depending on the closeness of their relationship to him. He simply cares about them less than he cares about himself.

Finally, elsewhere the Mòzǐ gives examples of alternative yì that are not self-interested. In "Moderation in Burial," the Mohists point out that people sometimes erroneously "take custom to be yì"—that is, they mistakenly confuse contingent customs with what is genuinely righteous (Mz 25/75). Examples they give of such customs include rending and eating one's firstborn son, abandoning one's widowed grandmother, allowing the flesh of the dead to rot away before burial, cremation of the dead, and extravagant burials. Apparently these practices could in principle be taken to constitute different yì or aspects of different yì (erroneous ones, in the Mohist view). However, none of them are self-interested in content. One of the "Dialogues" depicts a man whose yì is to devote himself to farming and pottery (49/40). So it seems likely the Mohists would conceive of a radical plurality of distinct yì as including many different norms, some but not all of them self-interested in content. The most plausible interpretation of the statement that "people had different yì" is simply that people followed a diverse range of norms and policies. The point of the "one person, one yì" rhetoric is probably to underscore the radical disunity of these norms, not to assert literally that each individual had a unique conception of yì.

In the Mohists' hypothetical scenario, people apparently assume that yì by its nature should be a unified code of conduct to which everyone conforms, not only oneself. For they find the plurality of yì intolerable and criticize one another's yì specifically on the grounds that since their own is shì, any other is fēi. These features might suggest that the conception of yì held by people in the state of nature is already just that of morality. For morality is something about which many people believe there is a single, correct set of norms, such that any alternative, conflicting norms are mistaken.

The Mohists' own conception of yì very likely converges with our notion of morality or moral righteousness. As we saw in chapter 1, they distinguish their conception of yì from contingent social customs and tie it to the noble, wise, impartial, and beneficent standpoint of Heaven. These features of their view overlap enough with familiar conceptions of morality that we can justifiably take them to be getting at roughly the same thing. The various *yì* followed by people in the state of nature need not all share such features, however, and some of them likely fall short of what we would consider conceptions of morality or righteousness. Consider again the policy articulated by Wūmǎzǐ: he would sacrifice others' lives to benefit himself, but not his own to benefit others. In the anecdote, both Mòzǐ and Wūmǎ refer to this policy as his "*yì*," but there is no hint that Wūmǎ takes himself to be proposing a view of what we would call morality, nor expressing what he believes to be morally righteous. He is merely stating his personal code of conduct. Mòzǐ points out that if this *yì* were publicized, it would have self-defeating consequences, since people who endorsed it might kill Wūmǎ to benefit themselves, while those who rejected it might kill him for spreading a vile doctrine. The criticism suggests that, for the Mohists, a defensible conception of *yì* must meet a publicity condition and what I call a regular practice, or universalizability, condition, two further features that again indicate that their notion of *yì* corresponds roughly to our notion of morality.[7] At the same time, however, the anecdote indicates that a policy can count as an *yì* without purporting to satisfy these conditions and that a person can endorse an *yì* without considering it to satisfy them.

It seems likely, then, that not all the *yì* endorsed by people in the state of nature are conceptions of morality or righteousness as such. Many are probably only norms corresponding to what people consider right or proper in some broader or looser sense. Some might be conceptions of social appropriateness, others might be customs, still others norms that particular individuals take to be prudent. Again, this proposal helps to explain the radical diversity of conceptions of *yì* the Mohists envision. If all the *yì* were views of morality, it is difficult to see how there could be dozens, hundreds, or even thousands of them (as the third version of the myth states). If they include various customs, mores, and personal policies, however, there could easily be very many.

Still, even if not all these *yì* are conceptions of morality, the Mohists depict people as each holding that their *yì* is in some sense the right way to live and that others are wrong for not following it. People take it that *yì* should be unified and that the community should seek uniformity in norms. They recognize that the absence of a unified *yì* leads to disorder, which everyone finds intolerable. The origin of the state thus lies in their shared conviction that normative unity is needed and that it can be achieved only through the exercise of political authority. Presumably, since people each consider others' *yì* to be wrong, they assume that many or most of the divergent conceptions of *yì* are mistaken. Thus, though the texts do not explicitly say so, it seems that a leader is needed not just to unify *yì* but to guide people in following the correct *yì*.

Why is political authority needed? We might suppose that proponents of different yì could negotiate with one another and reach a consensus concerning a unified yì. However, the Mohists apparently assume that in a state of normative anarchy, discourse among peers cannot yield normative unity or even a partial, overlapping consensus about core values. This is not, I suggest, because they fail to imagine that the content of the various yì might overlap. More likely, it is because they imagine a scenario in which there are no shared standards on which people could base a consensus—the fact that all sides have different yì entails that they simply cannot reach agreement. An yì is a norm or set of norms governing people's evaluative attitudes and conduct. If two people follow different yì, then even if their attitudes do agree in places, they may lack shared grounds for privileging these points of agreement as a basis for interacting with each other. Ideas such as organizing public life around an overlapping consensus or respecting others and thus seeking compromise are themselves yì that, by hypothesis, people in the state of nature disagree about. So the very nature of the hypothetical scenario rules out people's finding any middle ground on which to develop a shared, compromise yì. In fact, most of them probably agree that violent disorder, for instance, is a disvalue. But agreement on this point is not enough of a basis to develop a shared yì. Society as a whole is trapped in a sort of bootstrapping problem. Everyone agrees that a unified yì is needed, but there is no means of arriving at one.

This is the problem that political authority is invented to resolve. For the Mohists, political authority is a necessary condition for the shift from normative anarchy to a unified normative order. The key is not simply the coercive power of the state, though coercion undoubtedly plays a role. It is the very nature of authority as such. In the state of nature, people lack any authoritative standard by which to arrive at a unified yì. Everyone's yì is on a par with everyone else's, and there are no privileged or unified grounds on which to build a consensus. Assigning authority to a leader solves this problem. Now there is one yì, the leader's, that has an authoritative status and can be taken as a basis for settling on a unified yì. Moreover, the Mohists apparently believe that people have an inherent respect for authority that predisposes them to identify with and follow leaders (Mz 16/72–81). Thus simply acknowledging the leader's status as leader will help motivate them to adopt the unified yì he promulgates. The implication is that, though people lack a tendency to respect the judgments of or find a consensus with peers, they do tend to respect and follow social authorities. A formal structure of political authority is needed because people cannot reach normative agreement without it.

Since the Mohists hold that Heaven provides a reliable model of *yì*, why do they not envision people in the state of nature solving the unification problem by appealing directly to Heaven as an exemplar? Probably the proposal to take Heaven as a model would still amount to just one of the many diverse *yì* and so would not be recognized as grounds for a unified *yì*. For the Mohists, the shift from anarchy to political society is simultaneously the origin of political authority and of the very idea of something possessing authoritative status. Heaven's status as an authoritative model is a product of this shift. The grounds of Heaven's moral authority are partly political, as we will see in chapter 4.

In the Mohists' myth, then, people recognize that the violent disorder they face—a disvalue by everyone's standards—arises from the absence of political authorities who could unify society's *yì*. So a morally and intellectually qualified leader is chosen to establish a government and unify *yì*.

> It was understood that the people lacked government leaders to unify the world's norms of righteousness, and so the world was in disorder. Thus the most worthy, sagely, and intelligent person in the world was chosen, established as the Son of Heaven, and commissioned to work to unify the world's *yì*. (Mz 12/5–6)

One person alone cannot handle the huge task of unifying the world's *yì*. To assist him, the Son of Heaven appoints three dukes, who help him divide the world into myriad states and appoint a lord to rule each. The lords in turn appoint other officials in their states, down to the level of the district, village, or clan head, until a comprehensive, hierarchical political system is established. The criteria for appointment to office are that a candidate be "worthy and capable" or "worthy, wise, and intelligent."

The first and second "Identifying Upward" books do not specify how the ruler is selected, nor how people manage to agree on a qualified candidate. In Classical Chinese, a predicate standing alone can be a complete sentence. In the original text, the sentences in the earlier passage that I have translated in the passive voice lack a grammatical subject, leaving it unclear precisely who understood that a lack of political leadership was the cause of disorder and who selected a worthy candidate to be the sovereign. The third of the three books fills in a subject, however, saying that "all under heaven"—that is, all human society—desired to unify the world's *yì* and so selected a worthy leader. This apparent reference to society selecting a sovereign has so surprised some commentators that they emend the text to say that "Heaven" (*tiān* 天), rather than "all under heaven" (*tiān xià* 天下), desired to unify the world's *yì*.[8] It is unlikely, however, that the Mohists' stance is that in the state of nature, the initial leader is selected directly by Heaven. First, the texts simply do not say this. The *Mòzǐ* presents three versions of the myth, and none gives Heaven a role in selecting the initial sovereign. All three do say, as we will see, that society must conform to Heaven's standards of *yì*, the first two indicating that Heaven will punish people for failing to do so. The texts are explicit about this role of Heaven, so if Heaven also selects the ruler, we would expect them to be equally explicit. Second, the first and second books indicate that a sovereign was selected because it was understood that disorder was due to a lack of political leadership. Since Heaven for the Mohists is a wise, omniscient deity, it probably would not need to wait until chaos ensued before discovering the need for political leadership. More likely, people reflected on the causes of disorder and concluded that leaders were needed to unify society's *yì*. Third, there are indeed a few references in the *Mòzǐ* to Heaven or the spirits rewarding worthy rulers by establishing them as the "Son of Heaven."[9] But these generally do not refer to the origins of the state or the initial selection of a sovereign.[10] They describe how Heaven rewarded the sage-kings—who were already in positions of power—for their virtuous leadership by helping them become rulers of all the world, or, conversely, punished the vicious tyrants by causing them to die ignominious deaths and scattering their descendants. Rather than selecting the original sovereign, then, Heaven's role seems to lie in facilitating the rise of leaders who have already shown themselves worthy or punishing those who have proven themselves vicious.

Most likely, the text is vague about the selection process because the writers envision no particular procedure for selecting the leader other than that enough people agree he is "worthy, wise, and intelligent" or "worthy and capable" (*Mz* 11/5) to bestow an authoritative status on him. The selection process need not involve a democratic vote or any other formal procedure. Nor do the texts say or imply anything about a contract or covenant between the people and the sovereign or state. It may be simply that a handful of people tacitly converge in treating someone as a leader and others fall in with this habit, or that one person asserts himself and others defer to him. The process might be similar to how a group of children regularly select or defer to an older, more talented, or more assertive child to determine who will be captain of a pickup ball team, or how people undertaking a project tend to follow the lead of whoever among them is the most experienced, successful, or assertive.[11] Once a leader is established among some portion of a population, others will likely acknowledge his authority as well, particularly if his leadership is perceived as effective.

However the sovereign emerges, the crucial point is that he is somehow chosen by society—even if only tacitly, as far as most of the population is concerned. The grounds for establishing political leadership are the shared realization that violent disorder is intolerable, that the solution lies in a unified *yì*, and that *yì* can be unified only through the functioning of political authority. Given these points, the Mohists suppose, people can agree to follow a leader even though they do not yet agree on the content of *yì*.

The grounds for selecting a particular candidate as sovereign are that he has the moral and intellectual qualities needed for the job. Political authority does not rest on people's explicit, voluntary consent, as expressed in a contract. But it is initially established by their implicit choice, or at least acceptance, of a system and a sovereign they expect will unify *yì* and achieve order. (As we will see, for the Mohists, this attitude of accepting, and thus identifying with, the state and its leadership is a prerequisite for successful government.) Once established, it is justified and maintained by success in achieving these ends. So the grounds for political authority as presented in "Identifying Upward" are consequentialist: at root, authority is justified by the sovereign's and the system's effectiveness in unifying *yì* and thus securing social order.

The Mohists' myth of the origin of the state is frequently compared and contrasted with Hobbes's, probably because both depict the invention of political society as a response to violent anarchy in the state of nature.[12] The exercise can be illuminating in revealing differences between the basic assumptions of an influential early modern Western thinker and an equally influential school of ancient Chinese thought. Hobbes sees violent disorder as arising from individuals' exercise of their natural right to seek self-preservation. In the state of nature, people are governed only by their own reason, which leads them to use any means they believe will best preserve their lives. People all seek their own felicity. Yet resources are limited, some people act without regard for others, and so conflicts arise. If people all act separately to protect themselves, as their reason directs, the result will be a war of all against all—the worst possible outcome in terms of each individual's rational aim to seek peace and security. So people realize that the most effective way to ensure their long-term self-preservation is to act not on their own decisions but by the uniform laws of a sovereign. Accordingly, they form a covenant by which they transfer their right of self-preservation to the state, agreeing to obey its laws in exchange for protection from violent death. This covenant is the source of the state's political authority. The primary duty of the state is thus to ensure people's physical safety. As long as their safety is assured, citizens have an absolute obligation to obey the state.

The Mohist theory does not share the individualist grounds of Hobbes's theory. For the Mohists, the basic good to be secured is social order, not individual survival. Disorder arises from clashes between people's different conceptions of *yì*, which they each take to be norms to be followed by all, rather than from individuals' rational pursuit of self-preservation. The immediate purpose of the state is to promulgate and enforce a unified *yì*, or system of norms, not to ensure its subjects' safety—although their safety is an obvious consequence of the unified *yì*. The state does not originate in a contract through which individuals entrust to it their right to self-preservation. The Mohist theory mentions neither a contract nor rights. Rather, the state originates in people's selecting a virtuous, wise leader to unify moral norms, and its authority is justified by his effectiveness in unifying norms and achieving order. Moreover, as we will see, the state does not unify norms and coordinate people's conduct through a system of laws, as in Hobbes's theory. Instead, it does so through what amounts to a community-wide education and training program.

IDENTIFYING UPWARD

The basic aim of government for the Mohists is to achieve a stable social order by promulgating and enforcing a unified conception of *yì*. The central task of the state thus lies in moral education—in training everyone to reliably conform to uniform norms in judgment and action. Collective identification with unified norms achieved through moral education provides the basis for achieving the various other ends of political society the Mohists mention, such as state defense, public security, economic management, and poverty relief. The state's responsibility for moral education is a distinctive theme of classical Chinese thought, prominent in both Mohism and Ruism and much criticized in Daoist texts.

Once the Son of Heaven and his government are in place, he initiates a scheme to unify the world's standards of *yì*. The main technique employed is model emulation. Leaders at each level guide their subordinates to "identify upward" with the good example set by their worthy superiors and not to "align together below." People are to emulate how their leaders discriminate *shì* from *fēi*, to learn from their good statements (*yán* 言) and conduct (*xíng* 行), and to report others' good and bad conduct. A second important technique is social and material incentives and disincentives. Successful emulation is encouraged with praise and rewards; failure is punished by criticism and penalties. By unifying people's view of *yì* at each level of political organization, from the village up to the empire, this scheme brings order to the world and thus justifies political authority.

> Once the government leaders were in place, the Son of Heaven issued a government policy to the people of the world, stating, "Hearing of good and bad, in all cases report it to your superiors. What superiors deem *shì*, all must deem *shì*; what superiors deem *fēi*, all must deem *fēi*. If superiors commit errors, admonish them; if subordinates do good, recommend them. Identify upward and don't align together below. This is what superiors will reward and subordinates will praise.
>
> "Or, if you hear of good and bad but don't report it to superiors; are unable to deem *shì* what superiors deem *shì*; are unable to deem *fēi* what superiors deem *fēi*; don't admonish superiors when they commit errors; don't recommend subordinates when they do good; align together below and don't identify upward, this is what superiors will punish and the people will denounce." (Mz 11/9–13)

Officials on each level of the hierarchy repeat similar instructions to their subordinates, urging them to model themselves on the good example set by the judgments, statements, and conduct of the leader the next level up. Since leaders must serve as role models for those they rule, moral wisdom and a virtuous character are crucial qualifications for political office.

> Thus the village head was the most benevolent man in the village. The village head issued a government policy to the people of the village, stating, "Hearing of good and bad, you must report it to the district head. What the district head deems *shì*, all must deem *shì*; what the district head deems *fēi*, all must deem *fēi*. Eliminate your bad statements and learn the good statements of the district head; eliminate your bad conduct and learn the good conduct of the district head." Then how could the district be in disorder?! Examine what put the district in order: it's just that the district head was able to unify the district's *yì*, and hence the district was in order. (Mz 11/13–16)

The process of identifying upward and unifying *yì* thus includes seven components. The Son of Heaven's initial edict mentions five: informing superiors of good or bad conduct; emulating the *shì-fēi* judgments of one's superiors; correcting superiors when they stray from the norms they have promulgated; recommending subordinates for their good conduct; and identifying upward rather than aligning below against the leadership. To this, the lower-level officials add that people must abandon their bad statements or pronouncements (*yán*) and instead emulate the good statements of their superiors. Likewise, they should abandon their bad conduct and emulate their superiors' good conduct. Incentives for compliance include praise from superiors and peers, material rewards, and, as we will see in the next section, "promoting the worthy," promotion in government service. Disincentives for noncompliance include criticism from superiors and peers, fines, the traditional five corporal punishments,[13] and demotion or dismissal from service.

Each village head leads his village to emulate the district head. As a result, the district head is able to unify the *yì* of the district and bring it to order. The district heads in turn lead their districts to emulate the lord of the state, aiding him in unifying the *yì* of the state and bringing it to order. The lords of states lead their people to emulate the Son of Heaven, thus unifying the *yì* of all the world and bringing it to order. The Son of Heaven is still fallible, however, and so cannot be the highest moral paragon. Above him is Heaven itself, to which the people must ultimately conform. In Mohist thought, politics is not fully distinct from ethics and religion, and unlike in Hobbes, the sovereign's power is not absolute, for he must answer to independent standards of *yì* enforced by Heaven.

> If the people of the world all identify upward with the Son of Heaven but don't identify upward with Heaven, then disasters still will not go away. Now if in the heavens whirlwinds and bitter rain come again and again, this is how Heaven punishes the people for not identifying upward with Heaven. (Mz 11/22–24)

A distinctive feature of the theory is that, as we might expect from the Mohists' conception of models, moral education is seen as similar to teaching a practical skill. It is mainly a process of emulating the judgments and conduct of moral exemplars, specifically how they distinguish *shì* from *fēi* and act accordingly. The basic source of moral guidance is thus practical training in social norms, which people are expected to master and extend to new cases. As in language learning, superiors teach chiefly not by dictating rules or instructions but by setting an example and then praising or correcting the learner's performance. Sometimes they may set forth models (*fǎ* 法) in the form of explicit rules or instructions, as when the Son of Heaven issues the original edict for everyone to identify upward and the lower-level officials make statements or pronouncements (*yán*) that people are to emulate. But moral education is not seen primarily as a matter of inculcating knowledge of rules. Nor does it lie in acquiring theoretical knowledge of the good, nor in the reflective habit of testing the maxims on which one acts against the Moral Law. It is seen mainly as a kind of training aimed at habituating people into the practice of distinguishing right from wrong correctly in speech and action. To perform this practice competently and reliably is to be a steadfast, virtuous performer of the *dào*.

In their theory as we have seen it so far, the Mohists present only a formal system for unifying *yì* and thus achieving order. Besides the good of "order" (*zhì*), the substantive content of the unified morality is largely left open. In fact, the theory of the state presented in the first two "Identifying Upward" books is incomplete, for neither text spells out the content of the unified norms of *yì*. Both state that the Son of Heaven must lead people to identify upward with Heaven, so the unified *yì* is neither indeterminate nor decided by the ruler but fixed by the model of Heaven. Still, the texts do not stipulate what exactly conformity to Heaven's example involves. Unlike the first two books, the third version of "Identifying Upward"—probably historically the latest of the three—fills in the content of the unified *yì*. Instead of having people emulate the *shì-fēi* distinctions and conduct of their leaders, this book advocates unifying *yì* by having leaders establish incentives for people to report those who "care for and benefit" or "detest and injure" their clan, state, or "all the world," so that goodness will be rewarded and viciousness punished (Mz 13/22–42). The clan heads, for instance, issue the following orders:

> If you see someone caring about and benefiting the clan, you must report it. If you see someone detesting and injuring the clan, you must also report it. If you see care for and benefit to the clan and report it, this too is being like someone who cares about and benefits the clan. When superiors get hold of them, they will reward them; when the multitude hears about it, they will praise them. If you see detesting and injuring the clan but don't report it, this too is being like someone who detests and injures the clan. When superiors get hold of them, they will punish them; when the multitude hears of it, they will deem them wrong. (Mz 13/23–25)

Here the central means of unifying *yì* has shifted from leading people to emulate the judgments and conduct of their leaders to leading them to encourage care and benefit to the community. The emphasis is no longer on model emulation but on reporting good and bad conduct, so that superiors are aware of the people's situation and can ensure that those who commit crimes are punished and those who do good are rewarded (13/1–4). Unifying *yì* is introduced as the only way to ensure that the leadership is fully aware of actual conditions throughout the community. For if people endorse the *yì* of the leadership, they will cooperate in reporting information the authorities need to maintain order, such as the whereabouts of criminals. If people practice an *yì* different from that of the leadership, they may align together against it, as they may disagree with its rule, in particular how it issues rewards and punishments. As the preceding passage illustrates, the Mohists hold that a unified *yì* requires publicity and transparency through all levels of society. Good or bad conduct is to be reported so that it can be praised or condemned by all. Subordinates can correct superiors, and superiors must be aware of actual conditions among their subordinates. A consequence of the system, claim the Mohists, is that people throughout society will aid the ruler in reporting events across the land, spreading his words to all, quickly developing plans, and promptly carrying out projects (12/65–68).

By specifying in the third book that the content of the unified *yì* should correspond to that of their ethical theory, the Mohists probably aim to ensure that the *yì* promulgated by the state is one people can genuinely endorse for themselves.[14] In recommending care and benefit for the community as a unifying standard, they seem to assume that people will generally tend to endorse broadly consequentialist norms as a basis for political life, or at least find it easy to cooperate with a political system grounded in such norms.[15] The Mohists repeatedly stress this crucial point: people must be convinced that the unified *yì* is correct and works in the public interest, or they may resist the leadership. Indeed, the third book states that only by "caring fervently" about the people and being "completely trustworthy" toward them can one succeed in leading them to identify with their rulers (*Mz* 13/56–58).

In its fully developed form, then, the Mohist political theory does not call for radical changes in people's motivation or values. To be sure, it demands that they give up their original *yì* and adopt that promulgated by political leaders. But the unified *yì* of the state is an *yì* grounded in values the Mohists think most people will share and find it easy to identify with—social order and the care and benefit of the community. So Mohist political theory does not assume that people's motivations and dispositions are "highly malleable," as some recent interpreters assert.[16]

Still, we can legitimately worry that, given its authoritarian structure and use of rewards and punishments, the Mohist system might be ripe for abuse. The success of the system depends heavily on the moral character of the sovereign and his officials. What if these leaders are misinformed or corrupt? What prevents them from abusing their power? In practice, abuse could surely become a problem in the Mohist system—as it might in any political system, for that matter. In principle, however, several constraints on the ruler's power are built into the Mohist model. First, in the fully developed theory, the unified *yì* is specified as norms of caring for and benefiting the community. The central aims of the state are social order, wealth, and population growth. So the unified *yì* is not arbitrary, to be decided at the sovereign's whim. A ruler who does not promulgate norms in line with the Mohist ethical theory will be publicly perceived as doing wrong and will be subject to criticism from those below him. Given the ruler's control over the coercive power of the state, we can doubt whether in practice people would dare to criticize him. But in principle, at least, the system incorporates objectively justified norms, grounded in Heaven's intent, and a mechanism for criticizing and correcting those in power when they deviate from the norms. Second, the Mohists believe that Heaven will punish a corrupt, vicious, or unscrupulous ruler by allowing a challenger to overthrow him. This belief reflects the traditional Chinese conviction that the sovereign rules by the mandate of Heaven. This constraint may be unpersuasive to us today, but it is nevertheless part of the Mohist system. Third, the Mohists hold that people have psychological tendencies that will lead the system to collapse in the hands of a corrupt ruler. If people judge that political leaders fail to govern fairly and in the interest of society as a whole, they will align below against them. According to the Mohists, even rewards and punishments lose their motivational effectiveness if people disagree with the standards by which they are administered. In such circumstances, the unified moral code disintegrates and disorder ensues. Since this outcome is antithetical to everyone's interests, including the ruler's, even a self-interested leader has a reason to govern in a morally correct way.

Indeed, taken together, the "Identifying Upward" books depict a delicate balance between people's respect for authority, their responsiveness to incentives, their commitment to a unified yì, and their original inclination to act on what they themselves autonomously deem yì.[17] For the Mohists, people are not passive subjects of indoctrination, following their rulers blindly, but active participants in the process of realizing social order through a unified yì. Besides praising or criticizing the conduct of their peers, they are expected to reproach their leaders for errors (Mz 11/10, 12/14). If the ruler appoints officials merely to surround himself with cronies and flatterers, rather than to govern effectively, people will band together in resistance and follow an yì distinct from his.

> Nowadays kings, dukes, and great men in administering the penal code and government are the opposite of [the sage-kings of old, who governed with the aim of benefiting the people]. They govern for the sake of flatterers, clansmen, fathers, brothers, acquaintances, and friends, placing them on their left and right, and installing them as government leaders. The people know that the superiors' installing of government leaders is not really to order the people. Hence they all ally together, concealing things, and none are willing to identify upward with their superiors. Thus superiors and subordinates have different yì. If superiors and subordinates have different yì, rewards and praise are not enough to encourage good, while punishments and penalties are not enough to discourage viciousness. (Mz 12/52–55)

In such circumstances, the unified *yì* fractures. The ruler's scheme of incentives and disincentives loses its power to motivate people, since they now reject his standards for reward and punishment (12/55–61, 13/17–22). The issue is not simply that one or two individuals protest, but that the community as a whole may come to condemn those the ruler praises and to praise and encourage those he punishes. Ultimately, the Mohists think, the moral approval or disapproval of the community is an even more powerful motivating force than any reward or punishment from a ruler whose judgment the community rejects.

> If superiors and subordinates have different *yì*, those the superior rewards are those the multitude condemns. It's said people dwell together in multitudes. If people are condemned among the multitude, then in this case even supposing they are rewarded by the superior, this is not enough to encourage them. . . . If people are praised among the multitude, then in this case even supposing they are punished by the superior, this is not enough to discourage them. (Mz 12/56–59)

If the community comes to reject the ruler's judgment in this way, the political system fails, and society falls back into normative anarchy like that in the original state of nature.

> If one is established to govern a state and to act as the people's government leader, yet one's rewards and praise are not enough to encourage good, while one's punishments and penalties are not enough to discourage viciousness, then isn't this the same as what I previously stated originally about when people first arose, before there were government leaders? (Mz 12/59–61)

Besides their role in establishing a leader in the state of nature, then, the people play an ongoing part in maintaining the leader's political authority. Without their approval, the unified *yì* that grounds political authority collapses.

These passages highlight the central role for the Mohists of rewards and punishments in government administration. In these texts, the Mohists see praise and censure, material rewards, corporal punishment, and other penalties as the primary tools of government. (In this respect, they anticipate so-called Legalist thinkers such as Hán Fēi, a political theorist who lived toward the end of the Warring States era.) Where we might speak of obeying laws and seeing that justice is served, they instead speak of rewards and punishments. Like many consequentialists, their justification for rewards and punishments is instrumental and forward-looking, rather than retributive and backward-looking.

Rewards and punishments are justified because they reinforce good and deter bad conduct (Mz 11/24–25, 12/42–49)—not because people deserve repayment for good or bad deeds.

Although Mohist communities enforced explicit penal codes and a version of rule by law—or, more precisely, rule by *fǎ* (models, laws)—the political system presented in their texts is fundamentally a form of rule of man.[18] Models or laws, the penal code, rewards, and punishments are decreed by the sovereign, who employs them to guide and control people's conduct. Still, the Mohists emphasize that the system of rewards and punishments—in effect, the legal system—is an embodiment of the unified *yì* that provides the basis for social order. To maintain order, the system must be administered fairly and consistently and must reflect values with which people can willingly identify. It must track the public good. If it does not, people will align together against it and the state will fail. This is probably why, in the third version of the theory, the Mohists stipulate that the way to unify *yì* is by encouraging care and benefit for the community. Mohist political thought is thus highly authoritarian while also assuming that broad endorsement among and the voluntary compliance of the people are needed for government to function properly.

Against this, one might argue that, provided the rewards are great and punishments severe, they can function effectively whether or not they reflect norms endorsed by the people. This is Hán Fēi's view. However, the Mohist position is more sophisticated than Hán Fēi's in two respects. First, a political system is likely to function more effectively with the willing endorsement of its people. Second, although the process may be slow, the Mohists are probably correct that if the people disagree with the sovereign's *yì*, they will tend to align together in resistance, ultimately causing the system to fail.

A further worry is that the Mohist system might abrogate people's autonomy or dignity by implementing a command morality, in which subordinates are forced into mindless, childlike conformity with superiors, who decide for them what is right and wrong. From the presentation of the Mohists' views in this section, however, it should be clear that this worry is unfounded. The system itself is established by the choice or acceptance of the people. The sovereign does not create the norms of right and wrong but only exemplifies, teaches, and enforces them. Moreover, as the sovereign's original edict makes clear, the system is not purely top-down, subordinates dumbly following their superiors. The subordinates are responsible for criticizing their superiors if they err. Clearly, those on lower tiers of the hierarchy are expected to have the capacity to exercise independent judgment. The overall aim of the system is education and cooperation, not passive obedience. The Mohist notion of a unified *yì* is two-sided. In one respect, subordinates conform to their superiors, who lead and educate them, but in another, those above conform to those below, for the system works only if the people genuinely approve of their leaders' decisions and conduct.

Outside the "Identifying Upward" texts, two features of Mohist political views complicate their account of political authority. First, according to Mohist theology, human political authority is subordinate to the moral and cosmic authority of Heaven. The human sovereign must lead the people in identifying upward with Heaven, which rules over him in a way analogous to how he rules over subordinates (Mz 26/17). Heaven can reward or punish a sovereign, and his legitimacy rests partly on its mandate. So in some sense the sovereign's authority derives from Heaven. As I argued previously, however, Heaven's role may be to grant legitimacy to the rule of a particular individual sovereign, not to ground political authority as such.[19] The existence of political authority may still ultimately be justified by its effectiveness in unifying *yì* and securing good order. Heaven in effect audits the performance of the human sovereign in this and other tasks and sanctions or censures him accordingly. (Chapter 4 discusses Heaven's role further.)

Second, as we will see in "promoting the worthy" and again in the Orderly Government argument in chapter 4, Mohist writings sometimes suggest that a constitutive feature of—and so a necessary condition for—social order is that "the noble and knowledgeable govern over the ignorant and common" (Mz 9/2–3). This idea is explicit in the books on Heaven's intent, which identify righteousness with "good government" on the grounds that whenever righteousness obtains, so does social order, and vice versa. (This latter point follows from the role of order as a basic good in Mohist ethics. The argument plausibly assumes that good government is characterized by social order.) The texts then contend that good government requires that the "noble and knowledgeable" or "those above" rule over the "ignorant and common" or "those below."[20] This reasoning suggests that the Mohists see a hierarchical political system led by worthy officials as inherently morally right. Since social order partly constitutes righteousness and obtains only through the functioning of a hierarchical system of rule, righteousness entails a hierarchical structure of political authority. A plausible implication is that some Mohist writers may have considered political authority intrinsically justified as part of righteousness, rather than justified by its good consequences.

How does this stance relate to the consequentialist account in "Identifying Upward"? The two make different assumptions and probably pertain to different rhetorical contexts. The conception of social order that drives the argument in "Identifying Upward" is weak and relatively uncontroversial, referring to harmonious social relations, neighborly cooperation, and the absence of violence. This conception could probably be accepted by many people in the hypothetical state of nature who hold diverse *yì*. The conception of social order operative in the argument of "Heaven's Intent" is stronger and potentially more controversial. Here the Mohist writers tie social order to a specific structure of authority and to their particular view of morality or righteousness. This conception of order and its relation to righteousness might well be rejected by others. "Identifying Upward" thus gives a consequentialist justification of political authority that is neutral across at least some different conceptions of *yì*, while "Heaven's Intent" assumes the Mohists' view of *yì* and explains how it requires a structure of authority in which the worthy rule. One way to relate the two is that "Identifying Upward" presents a political doctrine that is at least partly independent of Mohist ethics, while "Heaven's Intent" incorporates and articulates substantive details of Mohist ethics.

PROMOTING THE WORTHY

The doctrine of "identifying upward" argues for a centralized state with a hierarchical, tightly organized bureaucracy. The other central Mohist political doctrine, "promoting the worthy," concerns how this bureaucracy will be managed and staffed. According to "promoting the worthy," the "root of government"—the path to ensuring the state's success in securing wealth, a large population, and social order—is for rulers to employ worthy, capable personnel, making appointments to official posts on the basis of moral worth and expert ability. "Promoting the worthy" is probably partly a response to new administrative challenges arising from population growth, economic expansion, and military rivalry, which could be met only by moving beyond the traditional feudal system and developing a class of professional government officials. It is also a reaction against nepotism and incompetence and an appeal for equality of opportunity for outsiders and commoners, such as the Mohists themselves. Indeed, in this pair of doctrines, the Mohists initiate China's long tradition of government administration through a centrally directed, nominally meritocratic civil service open in principle to all qualified applicants.

The earliest book on "promoting the worthy" is concerned primarily with recruiting talented, capable personnel for government service. To do so, it advocates bestowing wealth, rank, respect, and praise on the worthy and allowing only those who are righteous to enjoy wealth, rank, and favored or close relations with the ruler. Those who already have privileged status must demonstrate merit to retain it. The poor, lowly, or physically distant from court, who in the past had no hope of official employment, are now to be considered. The book emphasizes equality of opportunity: even farmers and artisans may be recruited, if they are capable (Mz 8/17). According to the Mohists, a result of this policy will be that people throughout society "all compete to be righteous" (8/14), thus expanding the pool of qualified candidates for office and enhancing the community's overall moral quality. In this way, by enforcing consistent, merit-based criteria for social and economic status, the ruler motivates people to strive for moral and professional excellence. The Mohists thus recognize a tie between equality of opportunity and motivation. By opening up chances for advancement to all, even the nonelite, they expect that people throughout society will strive to improve themselves. At the same time, however, "promoting the worthy" reflects the Mohists' communitarian orientation. They do not advocate equality of opportunity on the individualist grounds that, other things being equal, people deserve to be treated similarly. Their argument is that the state is best served by employing the most capable candidates, regardless of their background.

The later two versions of the doctrine were probably composed at a time when recruiting an adequate supply of capable candidates was less of a problem. They shift emphasis from increasing the pool of candidates to the need to avoid favoritism and nepotism by basing appointments primarily on merit. The sage-kings promoted the worthy to high official posts, with corresponding rank and remuneration, without regard for kin, social rank, wealth, or physical appearance.[21] The unworthy they dismissed or gave only low rank, assigning them menial tasks. In this they were emulating Heaven itself, which does not discriminate on the basis of wealth, social status, place of residence, or kinship.

Recruiting worthy and capable officials is only the first part of the Mohist policy. Worthy officials must be employed properly, according to the "Three Roots": "If their rank is not high, the people will not revere them. If their salary is not rich, the people will not trust them. If their decrees are not authoritative, the people will not fear them" (Mz 8/18, 9/15–16). Appointees must be given high rank, a generous salary, important responsibilities, and the power to enforce their orders. The point of these benefits, according to the Mohists, is not to reward them but to ensure they are able to accomplish their tasks (8/19, 9/17). This claim has several dimensions. To enable capable personnel to bring their abilities into play and thus strengthen the state, one must entrust important tasks to them and delegate to them the power to get the job done. Also, if talented people are not given meaningful work and paid well, they will feel unappreciated, lack confidence in the ruler's sincerity, lose interest in service, and look elsewhere for employment (9/22–25). Moreover, the Mohists apparently see respect and obedience as crucial elements of political power, without which it cannot function properly. To win people's respect and obedience, officials must be granted not only considerable decision-making authority but also high social and economic status. Presumably, the Mohists regard these outward trappings of official status as concrete expressions of its value and power, which help incite respect and awe in those governed. At the same time, however, for people to respect the state and its officials, this high status must be perceived as something earned and maintained through merit.

> Ranks were assigned on the basis of virtue, tasks allotted on the basis of the office held, and rewards given on the basis of the labor expended; achievements were measured and salaries apportioned accordingly. So no official was permanently ennobled, while none of the people were forever common. The capable were elevated; the incapable were demoted. (Mz 8/19–20)

A key to maintaining people's respect and obedience is that officials must not enjoy the perquisites of their rank simply because they had the good fortune to be born or appointed to it. Their power is not irrevocable. Nor are commoners condemned forever to suffer at the hands of capricious or incompetent officials. Officials must earn and keep their positions on the basis of performance.

Recruiting talented personnel is obviously important to the success of any organization. But why stress it as "the root of good government"? The Mohists give three reasons. One invokes a constitutive feature of social order, mentioned earlier: order obtains only if "the noble and knowledgeable govern over the ignorant and common" (Mz 9/2–3). "The ignorant and common governing over the noble and knowledgeable" is a disorderly state of affairs. So a necessary condition for order is that honorable, wise, intelligent people be installed in positions of authority. A second reason is that for the Mohists, the criteria of good government include practical ends such as producing wealth, promoting population growth, and maintaining order. These ends are more likely to be achieved if competent people are in charge. Like Plato in *The Republic*, the Mohists appeal to a craft analogy to justify rule by an expert elite. Any ruler knows, they contend, that to make a suit of clothes, butcher an ox, heal a horse, or fix a bow, you hire a professional tailor, butcher, veterinarian, or bowyer. In such minor business, everyone values expertise. So it is simple ignorance not to apply the same norm to the major business of governing a state (9/32–34, 10/11–20). The third reason is that the doctrine of "promoting the worthy" must be applied consistently to maintain the integrity of the Mohist political system, specifically its grounding in unified norms of righteousness and its role in moral education. Promotion to office is one form of reward for meritorious conduct. Demotion is a punishment for improper or incompetent performance. If the wrong people are promoted or the incompetent are not dismissed, people will lose respect for and cease to identify with the system. In that case, as we saw in discussing "identifying upward," rewards and punishments will lose their motivational force and the unified *yì* may collapse.

The Mohists underscore this last point in discussing the consequences of failure to promote the worthy (Mz 9/25-29). If worthy officials are not employed, they argue, unworthy people will hold positions of power and respect. A ruler who places such people in office will be one who generally fails to praise and reward the worthy or reproach and punish the vicious. Such failure to allot rewards and punishments judiciously will cause the state's system of rewards and punishments to fail in a way similar to how fatalism causes it to fail, as discussed in chapter 1. The system of rewards and punishments will no longer encourage the worthy or discourage the vicious. People will cease to practice the relational virtues, be good neighbors, or even observe basic manners and social restraint. In the most extreme case (10/40-42), whether a person is as virtuous as the sage-kings or as incompetent and vicious as the tyrants will make no difference to whether the ruler respects or vilifies, rewards or punishes him. People may be rewarded without reason or punished despite their innocence. In such circumstances, "the people are all anxious and shattered, discouraged from doing good" (10/42). Just as in the state of nature—the text uses the same descriptions—they lose their motivation to contribute to society by sharing labor, resources, or knowledge (10/42-43). People go hungry and civil society breaks down.

As in their treatment of fatalism, the Mohists' point may be partly that fair, reliable enforcement of norms is needed to help motivate people to follow them. But the main point is probably deeper. The Mohists are addressing the social conditions necessary for people to identify with and contribute to society and develop flourishing relationships with others. Their position is again that a precondition for such identification and relationships is that society and its leadership observe consistent norms of conduct that the people themselves endorse—in this case by promoting officials who are demonstrably ethical and competent and dismissing those who are corrupt and ineffectual. Under such conditions, people can be expected to support the system even if they personally do not anticipate reward or promotion, since they can see that the system as a whole is fair and rewards and promotions go to the deserving. If people perceive the system as capricious and unfair—as when the undeserving are rewarded and the innocent punished—they will lose the motivation to participate in it.

"Promoting the worthy" is thus a crucial part of the project of unifying society's *yì*—its moral norms or standards of righteousness. A ruler who surrounds himself with corrupt or incompetent officials will alienate people from the state and society and cause the unified *yì* to disintegrate. If people generally believe that officials held up for praise are actually unworthy of emulation, the system of moral education founders, and its incentives and disincentives cease to motivate. Political leadership can succeed only with the cooperation and support of the people, earned through the leader's exercise of "virtue and righteousness" (Mz 9/71). Indeed, the Mohists warn that no one has ever succeeded in ruling the world by might and power alone, dominating people by threatening them with death (9/72–73). The effective way to rule is by promoting the worthy (9/73–74) and thus establishing a system of government with which people will identify and cooperate.

A further consequence of "promoting the worthy" is that the Mohists advocate equality of opportunity while simultaneously maintaining that merit-based inequality of status and wealth is crucial to effective political administration and thus to "the benefit of all." An orderly society is one with clearly distinguished ranks, such that the wise, worthy, and deservedly well-off govern over those less competent, virtuous, or wealthy. At the same time, however, the Mohist conception of "the benefit of all" gives priority to the subsistence needs of the poor over nonessential spending for the well-off. As we will see in chapter 5, a special concern is aid for orphans and the childless elderly, who lack any other means of support. Moreover, the Mohists hold that "the *dào* of being worthy"—and thus of qualifying for official appointments—is to share one's labor, wealth, and knowledge with those who are hungry, cold, and in disorder (Mz 10/33–34). So their system would allow significant inequality of wealth while providing a charitable safety net to meet the needs of the destitute.

CRITICAL REFLECTIONS

Mohist political thought offers many plausible insights. The Mohists are probably correct that social order is tied to the norms we follow—our *yì*—and that some degree of uniformity in norms is needed for society to function normally. If we all follow different norms—you drive on the left and I on the right—disorder might indeed ensue. Also plausible is their view that a structure of authority is needed to achieve and enforce the required level of unity. A special insight of their theory is that an effective political system will be one that people identify with and perceive as upholding publicly declared norms that benefit all. As they suggest, judicious or incompetent government policies probably affect the balance between "identifying upward" and "aligning below."

Still, the Mohists' conception of a unified *yì* and of social order are disturbingly totalitarian. They seem to assume that social stability and harmony require consensus not just on a minimal moral code—one that rules out murder and theft, for instance—but also on all value judgments whatsoever—all distinctions between *shì* and *fēi*. Even moderate diversity in how we draw such distinctions seems to count as disorder. We should question whether comprehensive agreement in *yì* is really needed to secure the level of order required for a political society to function and whether the Mohists' proposed political system and methods of rule are indeed the best way to achieve the required level of agreement.

The Mohists plausibly assume that if people have a unified *yì* they will live together harmoniously. Therefore, they conclude, unifying people's norms is the way to form a peaceful, stable society. The conclusion does not necessarily follow, however. Uniformity in *yì* might be a sufficient but not a necessary condition for social order. Perhaps, as in liberal societies today, agreement on only a core set of norms would be enough to yield good order. We could all agree on issues such as respecting one another's lives, liberty, and property, setting up a social welfare safety net for the poor, or driving on the same side of the road while also allowing pluralism about religious beliefs, career choices, aesthetic values, and leisure activities. Partial pluralism about values need not be a threat to social stability, especially if, as the Mohists seem to assume, people ultimately share a commitment to order. Indeed, given that, by the Mohists' own hypothesis, people start off tending to disagree extensively about norms, it is difficult to see how fully comprehensive agreement would be feasible. People who begin from divergent *yì* are likely to actively support uniformity in only whatever minimal set of norms is needed to ensure cooperation and social stability. By the Mohists' own lights, if people do not see that political policies and decisions work to the benefit of all, they are likely to withdraw support and "align below." So an overreaching demand for uniformity beyond the minimum level necessary might motivate resistance.

Similarly, authoritarian enforcement of uniformity in values might be a sufficient but not necessary condition for social order. Perhaps encouraging respect and tolerance for others would be equally or more effective. People in the Mohist state of nature clash because they obstinately criticize one another's diverse *yì*. Instead of promulgating a unified *yì*, perhaps leaders could resolve disorder by encouraging respect or toleration toward others' *yì* while jointly pursuing values we already share. Such an alternative approach might be more consistent with the Mohists' ideal of inclusive care and reciprocal benefit than their own authoritarian system is. Indeed, as their own remarks about peer relations hint, perhaps the key to social order is not to identify *upward* but to identify more with *one another*.

Of course, these criticisms assume that the scope of *yì* is comprehensive. Perhaps a charitable interpretation of Mohist political thought might propose that *yì* covers only certain pivotal *shì-fēi* distinctions, not all. We know from the exchange between Mòzǐ and Wūmǎzǐ that a maxim or two can be considered a distinct *yì*. Yet it seems likely that the Mohists' conception of their own *yì* encompassed the entirety of the Mohist *dào*. In *The Annals of Lü Buwei*, for instance, the Mohist grand master Mèng Shèng seems to refer generally to the Mohists' values and way of life as "the Mohist *yì*" (*LSCQ* 19/3). So probably *yì* was regarded as quite broad in scope.

The Mohists' assumption that enforced, comprehensive agreement in *yì* is the only way to achieve order is motivated primarily by two factors. First, they assume that in fact there is a single, uniform *dào* that everyone should follow, exemplified by Heaven or nature itself. (For details, see chapter 4.) Ultimately, in the Mohist view, the plurality of norms in the state of nature are almost all mistaken and so should be abandoned in favor of the correct norms discovered by following Heaven's model. Worthy rulers will seek to educate everyone in society to identify upward with these norms. Pivotal features of Mohist political theory thus probably reflect their metaethics and theology. Second, given their communitarian orientation, the Mohists are concerned with the interests of society as a whole, specifically wealth, population, and order. What is right for the individual is determined by whatever *dào* is right for society. The salient level of moral choice is that of the community's commitment to *dào*, not individuals' pursuit of their personal values. Individuals committed to *yì* are expected to take for granted that it entails conforming to the *dào* that is best for society. Mohist communitarianism acknowledges no distinction between public and private morality—between values everyone must share to maintain social flourishing and those about which individuals can disagree without disrupting social order. Individuals are seen as constituted largely by the hierarchical, relational social roles they occupy—ruler or subject, father or son, elder or younger brother, male or female, elder or youth, clan member or villager. We belong to political society by virtue of our place in a hierarchical structure—subjects of a regional lord or subordinate members of a clan, for example—not by virtue of being members of a community of peers. It is primarily as occupants of such social roles that we have norms to follow and interests to pursue. For the Mohists, a system in which members of society share a joint commitment to social order while pursuing their own diverse yì is simply not on the radar.

The Mohists' brand of authoritarianism did not want for critics in their own day, however. Their authoritarian conception of social order—along with those of Xúnzǐ and Hán Fēi, whom they probably influenced—epitomizes attitudes that Daoist writings vehemently attack. The Dàodéjīng and Zhuāngzǐ suggest that assertive, authoritarian policies such as "identifying upward" only disrupt people's spontaneous ability to achieve the minimal degree of order actually needed for society to function. Parts of the Zhuāngzǐ advocate letting people follow whatever path seems spontaneously appropriate for them, allowing a significant degree of liberty (Zz 7/11, 7/15).

4
HEAVEN

The Highest Ethical Model

HEAVEN PLAYS A central part in the early Mohist worldview, as an object of religious worship, an explanation for natural and historical events, and a fundamental model of what is morally righteous (yì 義). Mohist writings clearly indicate that Heaven is the Mohists' supreme moral authority. But what exactly is its role? One possibility is that, as a kind of ideal moral agent, it reflects and expresses the proper moral norms, specifically the consequentialist norm of pursuing "the benefit of all." Another is that its attitudes might be conceptually more fundamental than moral norms, such that they fix the content of morality. In that case, Mohist ethics might not be a brand of consequentialism after all but a divine will or divine command theory, the view that what is morally right and wrong is determined by the will or command of a divinity. Still another possibility is that Mohist ethics might be fundamentally deontological. Perhaps its basic guideline is not "benefit all the world" but "obey Heaven" or another guideline that makes Heaven a criterion of morality. The role of Heaven even raises the unlikely possibility that Mohist ethics could be a species of virtue ethics in which Heaven, an ideal moral agent, exemplifies admirable character traits and norms of conduct that we are to admire and emulate.

This chapter explores the various roles of Heaven in Mohist thought. Since Heaven is above all an object of worship for the Mohists, the first section surveys their religious beliefs, including their belief in sentient ghosts and spirits that share the cosmic sociopolitical hierarchy with Heaven and people. The next section examines the problem of evil that arises in Mohist theology. The third section explores the place of Heaven in Mohist ethics, particularly how it reflects their understanding of objectivity and impartiality and the grounds for their consequentialism. The penultimate section then considers a hypothetical, secularized version of the Mohist appeal to Heaven, in which a conception of Heaven as nature itself, rather than a deity, provides a basis for objective, impartial justification of moral norms. This discussion leads into a critique of the role of Heaven in shaping the structure of Mohist ethics.

HEAVEN AND MOHIST RELIGION

The Mohists' religious beliefs play a central part in their thought, providing a foundation for their view that an objective moral code obtains in the cosmos. Though brief, their descriptions of their beliefs and practices provide a rare direct glimpse into the religion of a portion of the subelite populace of ancient China.

Like much of traditional Chinese religion, Mohist beliefs are in effect an extension of the social and political hierarchy to include what believers see as the other sentient, intelligent entities with whom humans coexist in the cosmos: Heaven, the high god Dì 帝 (the "Lord on High"),[1] and a variety of ghosts and spirits, including those of deceased ancestors and those of mountains and rivers. These various entities constitute a personified natural setting that enforces morality by rewarding the worthy and punishing the vicious. Humans worship them as objects of devotion, gratitude, and fear, sacrificing animals and offering wine and grain to show respect and seek their blessings.

At the pinnacle of the cosmic sociopolitical hierarchy stands Heaven (tiān 天, also "sky" or "nature"). The word tiān refers most fundamentally to the sky. It also refers to nature itself and, for the Mohists, a benevolent, quasi-personal deity. Heaven created human beings and the world in which we dwell and provides us with the resources by which we live. It created kings, lords, and officers and made them watch over the people to administer rewards and punishments. It possesses the world just as the lord of a state possesses the state. All people are its subjects and beneficiaries and so owe it veneration for its nobility and wisdom and gratitude for its gifts (Mz 27/35–41). Heaven reigns virtuously over the human sovereign—the "Son of Heaven"—as an all-seeing, all-powerful parent-ruler who enforces the normative order of the cosmos. As the highest, noblest, and wisest moral agent, it embodies correct moral norms and serves as a model by which to judge the morality of practices and actions. It thus amounts to a personified, moralized conception of nature as an entity that follows and enforces ethical norms.

The Mohist concept of Heaven is dissimilar from the Judeo-Christian concept of God or Heaven in several ways. Heaven for the Mohists does not exist outside time, space, or nature. Rather than the creator of nature, it just is nature personified. Indeed, "Nature" with a capital N is a defensible alternative interpretation of *tiān*. Heaven has a personality but seems less anthropomorphic than the Judeo-Christian God. It has desires, intents, and affective attitudes—it desires that morality prevail, intends for people to care about one another, and cares for people. It can see and speak, though usually only as if thinking to itself, not directly to people. It typically does not communicate with people through revelation, although in crises it may dispatch spirit envoys to make proclamations. (Mohist religion has no scriptural tradition, although the declarations of the sage-kings and purportedly historical records of interactions between Heaven and humanity play a partly similar role.) It may intervene in human affairs to reward or punish people, such as by causing worthy proxies to prevail in battle or by manipulating the weather. People are expected to show their respect for Heaven by regularly performing ritual sacrifices, but they do not pray to it or address it directly. Generally, we discern its intent by observing and interpreting its conduct, which for the Mohists amounts to a conception of regular, reliable patterns of nature. For instance, we know that Heaven cares for all people because it supposedly provides life and sustenance to them, rewards those who benefit them, and punishes those who harm them. The Mohists see Heaven, and thus nature, as fundamentally intelligible, consistent, and predictable. If we act in line with its intent, it will reliably support and reward us; if we do not, it will discipline us. Consistent with the idea of Heaven as nature itself, the Mohists see Heaven's interactions with people as largely reactive, like the operation of regular natural patterns, albeit natural patterns that include moral and political norms. Throw a stone in the air, and it falls. Do good, and Heaven will support you; commit crimes, and it will punish you.

Heaven is a natural force that ensures that good or bad attitudes and conduct meet with appropriate consequences. This conception does not, however, imply that the Mohists regard the relation between humanity and Heaven as purely transactional, not devotional.[2] To the contrary, they hold that people should reverently serve and honor Heaven and the spirits by offering sacrifices and conforming to Heaven's intent, out of appreciation for its wisdom and nobility and gratitude for its benevolence. Failing to do so is like a son's failing to serve his father (a lack of filial devotion) or a subject's failing to serve his lord (a lack of loyalty) (*Mz* 27/32). The *Mòzǐ* approvingly describes in detail the meticulous rituals by which the sage-kings demonstrated their devotion to the spirits (31/46–55). Respect for Heaven is not founded simply on the desire to earn favors but on appreciation for its place in the cosmos. Heaven's status as the noble, wise ruler at the top of the cosmic hierarchy means that morality itself requires respect for and service to Heaven and its spirit attendants, as a properly devotional attitude toward them is part of good order (*zhì* 治).

The Mohists have no concept of religious salvation or of another realm to which we go after death. Their soteriological aim is simply to carry out the *dào* 道 by respecting and conforming to Heaven, improving the material conditions of human life, and achieving good social order. Moral virtue and religious piety are mainly ends in themselves; the only reward they bring is prosperity and social order. When people die, they become ghosts, who exist within the natural world as part of human beings' extended family and society. Unlike in the Abrahamic religions, people are not rewarded or punished in the next world for their deeds in this one. Rather, the Mohists hold that Heaven and the ghosts and spirits reward and punish people while they are alive (Mz 48/33, 70–71).[3] As one might expect, this belief raised questions about why some who followed the Mohist *dào* suffered adversity, while others who defied it prospered. We will consider this problem in the next section.

Another feature of the Mohists' enchanted conception of nature is belief in the sentience and efficacy of ghosts and spirits. Mohist texts frequently refer to Heaven and ghosts jointly: we are to "honor Heaven and serve the ghosts" (Mz 26/25–26). They recognize three types of ghosts and spirits: "sky ghosts" or "ghosts of Heaven," "ghosts and spirits of the mountains and rivers," and the ghosts of deceased humans (28/21, 31/97). These entities serve as Heaven's agents, handling most of the day-to-day enforcement of moral norms. Their agency is in effect an extension of Heaven's. An important social and moral duty for people is to regularly pay obeisance to the ghosts by sacrificing pure wine and grain at their altars, typically in an ancestral temple. Since many of the ghosts are worshippers' own ancestors, former rulers, or departed family members, such sacrifices are also a means of caring for deceased kin and associates. Ancestral sacrifices were also occasions for pleasant community gatherings (31/99–106). As in contemporary Chinese culture, once the honored ghosts had enjoyed their fill of the offerings, the living participants would consume the leftovers.

THE PROBLEM OF EVIL

Heaven, ghosts, and spirits jointly constitute a personified, moralized conception of nature that reliably conforms to and enforces a normative order. As we saw in chapter 1, for the Mohists, this normative order is unopposed by any countervailing force such as fate. Their theology thus depicts a world that operates according to consistent, predictable patterns, including both causal relations and moral norms and constraints. These patterns ground confidence in human efficacy, since their regularity and reliability allow us to choose our actions so as to control the outcomes we encounter. At the same time, however, this theological setting generates an acute version of the problem of evil. If the cosmos has an inherent moral order enforced by divine agents, we would expect people of moral worth to be reliably rewarded with security and prosperity and wrongdoers reliably punished. Yet sometimes the worthy fail to prosper, while the unworthy flourish. Why does Heaven allow such perverse outcomes? Moreover, if Heaven itself consistently follows the *dào* and Heaven created humanity, why didn't it make people such that all of us reliably follow the *dào* too?

In Judeo-Christian theodicy, the problem of evil concerns why an omniscient, omnipotent, morally perfect God would allow the existence of suffering due to moral or natural evil—suffering due to the harmful actions of moral agents or to harmful natural events, such as storms or diseases. Familiar attempts to answer the problem cite goods that supposedly outweigh the existence of evil but cannot exist unless evil does as well. For instance, perhaps God's preventing all evil is inconsistent with allowing people to exercise free will or with providing an orderly, predictable environment that follows natural laws. A fallback explanation is that in any case God will compensate worthy people in the afterlife for evils suffered on earth.

The Mohists lack such a backup explanation. Nor do they appeal to other goods that might outweigh the existence of evil. Yet they do hold that Heaven is reliably benevolent, omniscient about people's conduct, and extremely powerful. So why does evil exist? The Mohist answer, I suggest, draws on two aspects of their view of the cosmos. The first is causal pluralism. In the "Dialogues," Mòzǐ explains that even a worthy person may encounter adverse outcomes, such as illness, because events issue from multiple causal factors, some of which may be difficult to identify and control.

> Our Master Mòzǐ had an illness. Dié Bí entered and asked, "Sir, you take the ghosts and spirits to be sentient and able to bring misfortune or blessings. Those who do good, they reward; those who do bad, they punish. Now you, Sir, are a sage. Why do you have an illness? Could it be that some of your statements are mistaken? Or that the ghosts and spirits are insentient and unknowing?"
>
> Our Master Mòzǐ said, "Even supposing I have an illness, how is it that they are insentient? People can catch an illness in many ways. Some get ill from the

cold or heat, some from exhaustion. If there are a hundred doors and you close one of them, how is it that a robber has no way in?" (Mz 48/76–79; cf. 49/64–71)

According to the passage, the existence of natural evil does not disprove the doctrine of sentient ghosts and spirits who enforce moral norms. Natural evils such as disease may occur without the spirits' punishment and despite their rewards, since their intervention is only one of potentially many causally relevant factors. These factors are in principle intelligible, although perhaps not always practically manageable. Misfortune remains in principle avoidable and not determined by occult forces of fate. The key to good outcomes lies in human effort, in working harder to identify and protect against risks.

Still, why don't Heaven and the spirits protect the worthy person from these other potential causes of misfortune? The Mohists' answer probably lies in a second feature of their worldview, the quasi-naturalistic character of Heaven's agency. Heaven generally does not intervene proactively in human activity to prevent adverse outcomes. Its agency is mainly reactive, along the lines of natural causal regularities. Other things being equal, if we follow Heaven's intent—corresponding to the normative *dào* of nature—it responds by facilitating our endeavors. If we diverge from its intent, it does not prevent us but merely ensures that harmful consequences ensue. For example, in the Mohist worldview, Heaven beneficently provides materials by which we can build sturdy buildings. Despite its benevolence, if we foolishly decide to jump off a roof, it will not intervene, and when we do jump, it will cause us to fall. If we fail to avoid potential causes of misfortune, then, Heaven will not intervene on our behalf.

The reactive character of Heaven's agency also yields a Mohist response to the problem of moral evil. People are agents, who act on their understanding of *shì-fēi* 是非 (right versus wrong) distinctions. They sometimes behave immorally because they distinguish *shì-fēi* incorrectly or because they fail to act on the correct distinctions (for details, see chapter 7). Heaven does not intervene to prevent such incompetence or error but only responds with adverse consequences. In the Mohist interpretation of history, for example, Heaven does not prevent tyrants from misgoverning their states and harming their people. If they do so, however, it responds by punishing them, causing their eventual overthrow and premature death, the scattering of their descendants, and eternal condemnation by later generations.

The Mohist worldview thus balances precariously between the religious, enchanted conception of nature presented in their theology and a protoscientific attitude about causation that emerges from their stance on fate and their explanation of natural and moral evil. Recognizing that events can be caused by a plurality of factors, some difficult to control, is a step toward a scientific worldview. Yet the Mohists employ this idea for the most unscientific of ends, to render their doctrine of divine justice unfalsifiable, since any misfortune that befalls the worthy can be attributed to factors other than Heaven's failure to act. Ultimately, this response to the problem of evil undermines Mohist theology. By downgrading Heaven to the status of just one causal factor among many, it weakens or even relinquishes the picture of the cosmos as a strictly policed normative order that reliably rewards the good and punishes the bad. On the other hand, it is hard to see an alternative doctrine that would better serve the Mohists' purposes. A fully coherent approach to the problem of natural evil would probably entail giving up central tenets of their theology, by allowing that Heaven enforces the moral order only intermittently or by adopting a fully naturalistic, nontheistic view of Heaven, as Xúnzǐ will later do.

HEAVEN AS A MODEL OF MORALITY

The crux of the appeal to Heaven in Mohist ethics is that as the highest, wisest moral agent, Heaven conducts itself by a *dào* that unfailingly exemplifies correct moral norms. Its intent is reliably benevolent and righteous. To obtain an objective criterion of righteousness (*yì*), then, we need only observe its conduct and discover the norms it is committed to and desires us to follow—its "intention" (*yì* 意) or "intent" (*zhì* 志), two words that refer to the aim or object to which one's thoughts are directed. The Mohists believe that Heaven's norms are clear, intelligible, and easily discovered by anyone. So its intent can serve as a fundamental ethical model (*fǎ* 法) that anyone can apply, just as anyone can apply a craftsman's measuring tools.

> Thus our Master Mòzǐ's having Heaven's intent, to give an analogy, is no different from the wheelwright's having a compass or the carpenter's having a set square. . . . Above, he uses it to measure how the kings, dukes, and great men of the world administer the penal codes and government; below, he uses it to gauge how the myriad people of the world engage in writings and studies and present statements and discussions. Observe their conduct [*xíng* 行]: if it follows Heaven's intention, call it good intentions and conduct; if it opposes Heaven's intention, call it bad intentions and conduct. Observe their statements [*yán* 言] and discussions: if they follow Heaven's intention, call them good statements

and discussions; if they oppose Heaven's intention, call them bad statements and discussions. Observe their penal codes and government: if they follow Heaven's intention, call them good penal codes and government; if they oppose Heaven's intention, call them bad penal codes and government.

So he sets this up as a model [fǎ], establishes this as a standard, and uses it to measure the benevolence [rén 仁] or unbenevolence of kings, dukes, great men, secretaries, and ministers in the world, and, to give an analogy, it is like dividing black from white.

Thus our Master Mòzǐ said, "Now the kings, dukes, great men, officers, and gentlemen of the world, if, within, they really desire to follow the dào, benefit the people, and fundamentally examine the root of benevolence and righteousness [yì], then it's unacceptable not to follow Heaven's intention. Following Heaven's intention is the model of righteousness." (Mz 27/63–73)

Though the Mohists themselves do not explicitly draw the distinction, we can identify two interrelated roles that Heaven's intent plays. On the one hand, it serves as a criterion of what is morally righteous and thus a basis for ethical justification. In the preceding passage, for example, it is used to evaluate whether laws, policies, statements, and conduct are good (shàn 善) or not. On the other, it also serves as a practical moral guideline. In practice, when considering what to do, we can compare courses of conduct against it to determine how to proceed.

Having taken Heaven as a model, our actions and undertakings must be measured against Heaven. What Heaven desires, do it; what Heaven doesn't desire, stop. (Mz 4/10–11)

Heaven thus provides a fundamental guide to conduct: "It's unacceptable not to follow Heaven's intention" (Mz 27/73).

The Mohists have several reasons to appeal to Heaven in grounding their ethics. Doing so is an expression of respect for Heaven as the ultimately wise, virtuous role model and ruler of the world. It lends the Mohist dào special metaethical and epistemic authority, giving it an objective foundation in the purported norms of the natural order itself. The injunction to follow Heaven's intent, along with the threat of divine punishment, would have been rhetorically compelling to much of their audience. Also, as I discuss in the following, the conception of Heaven as a benevolent ruler concerned for the welfare of all metaphorically articulates the Mohist understanding of morality and its grounding in an objective, impartial standpoint. A further reason, touched on in chapter 1, is that Heaven's intent supposedly provides a clear, public standard of morality that is as simple to apply as a compass or set square, which makes distinguishing moral right from wrong as easy as telling black from white. The Mohists' enthusiasm for a straightforward criterion that simplifies moral judgment is understandable. As we will see, however, it tends to foster a narrow conception of value that may be among the main weaknesses of their ethics.

WHAT HEAVEN INTENDS

If Heaven's intent is indeed a reliable criterion of morality, what does Heaven intend? On the Mohists' interpretation, Heaven's actions show that it wants people to care about and benefit one another, rather than detesting and harming one another (Mz 4/11–12, 27/45). Following Heaven's intent means "inclusively caring about each other and in interaction benefiting each other" (26/22). Heaven desires that righteousness prevail, and so it desires life, wealth, and social order for people (26/9, 13). Its intent is that "government by righteousness" obtain rather than "government by force" (26/36, 28/35). The second "Heaven's Intent" book spells out the details of a society that conforms to Heaven's intent:

> Heaven's intention doesn't desire great states to attack small states, great clans to subvert small clans, the strong to tyrannize the few, the cunning to scheme against the ignorant, and the noble to be contemptuous of the common. This is what Heaven doesn't desire. It doesn't stop at this only. It desires people who have strength to work for each other, those who have *dào* to teach each other, and those who have resources to share them with each other. Also, it desires superiors to work hard in attending to government and subordinates to work hard in performing their tasks.
>
> If superiors work hard in attending to government, the state will be in order. If subordinates work hard in performing their tasks, resources will be sufficient. If the state is in order and resources sufficient, then within, there will be means to prepare pure offerings of wine and grain to sacrifice to Heaven and the ghosts, while abroad there will be means to prepare bracelets and disks of pearl and jade to send envoys to befriend neighboring states. The rancor of the various lords being calmed and fighting on the borders ceasing, within the state there will be means to feed the hungry, rest the weary, and support the myriad people. Then rulers and subjects, superiors and subordinates will be generous and loyal,

fathers and sons, elder and younger brothers kind and filial. (Mz 27/14–20; see also 26/36ff., 28/35ff.)

Heaven desires that people follow Mohist moral norms, such as inclusive care, and desires the goods posited by Mohist ethical theory, including peace, security, social cooperation, economic sufficiency, care and protection of the poor and weak, reverence for Heaven and the ghosts, and fulfillment of the relational virtues. In short, Heaven endorses the Mohist account of morality. The Mohists thus claim that their ethics reflects Heaven's intent. Their ethical theory is correct because it captures the norms of conduct affirmed by Heaven.

The Mohists have two basic arguments for their claims about Heaven's attitudes, both grounded in an inference from what they take to be Heaven's conduct to the content of its desires (yù 欲) or intentions (yì 意). The arguments stop short of justifying all the details in the passage just quoted. Instead, they attempt to justify mainly the claim that Heaven desires that people care about and benefit one another and thus that they jointly pursue the goods of wealth, population, and order. The passage amounts to an extended interpretation of the concepts of benefit and more specifically order.

The first argument is that Heaven's actions show that it cares for and benefits everyone. As we have seen, it created the world in which we live and furnishes the natural resources that sustain us. From such actions, we can infer that its intention is to care for and benefit all. So, the inference runs, it desires that people too should conform to this intention by caring for and benefiting one another. The most concise and explicit version of the argument was quoted in chapter 1. Heaven supposedly desires that "people care about and benefit each other" because it itself "all-inclusively cares about them and all-inclusively benefits them," which we know because it "all-inclusively possesses them and all-inclusively accepts offerings from them" (Mz 4/12–16).[4] The first "Heaven's Intent" book presents a variant of this argument. Heaven desires righteousness, and thus officers and gentlemen should lead people to do what is righteous. How do we know that Heaven desires righteousness? Because only when righteousness prevails is there life, wealth, and order, and Heaven desires life, wealth, and order (26/12–14). The text does not spell out how we know Heaven desires these goods, but the explanation is probably that since Heaven itself gives people life, resources, and a well-ordered natural world in which to dwell, it obviously desires these goods for us. Substituting "life" for "population," the goods in question are just those the Mohists take to constitute benefit, their criterion of righteousness.

The second argument is that Heaven surely cares deeply for people, because it enforces morality by avenging crimes against the innocent. It rewarded the six ancient sage-kings, who cared for and benefited the people, and punished the four tyrants, who despised and harmed them.[5] From Heaven's rewards and punishments, then, we can see that its intention is for people to care about and benefit one another, for it rewards those who do so and punishes those who do not.

We need not dwell on the flimsiness of these arguments. The first rests on a religious conception of nature in which natural objects and events are selectively treated as evidence of Heaven's agency. To us, nature has been thoroughly disenchanted: interpreting natural phenomena as if they were divine actions is a category mistake. The second amounts to a suspiciously circular interpretation of mythical ancient events. As I suggest later, however, the first argument may nevertheless serve as a fruitful metaphor by which to elucidate a plausible conception of morality.

WHY OBEY HEAVEN'S INTENT?

The Mohists offer at least six reasons why we should obey Heaven's intent. The first is a crude appeal to self-interest. If we do what Heaven desires, it will reward us by doing what we desire (Mz 26/10). More broadly, Heaven will reward us for doing right and punish us for doing wrong (26/21–23). Since this line of reasoning is based purely on our own interests, it provides only prudential, not moral, grounds for obeying Heaven. Nor does it give any reason to think Heaven's intent is morally good. Heaven could dish out rewards and punishments for capricious or wicked reasons.

A related but morally pertinent reason is that obeying Heaven has good consequences. Since Heaven rewards conformity to its desires and punishes disobedience, following its desires tends to bring about order, peace, and wealth (Mz 27/20–21). Since for the Mohists these goods constitute what is righteous, it is right to conform to Heaven's intent. A third, also morally relevant reason is gratitude or reciprocity. Heaven has given us many gifts, such as natural resources. Failing to obey its intent would be like a grown son failing to care for a loving father who provided for him as a child. Such conduct would be unbenevolent and impious (27/39–41). Out of benevolence (rén 仁) or gratitude, then, we should do as Heaven desires. These latter two reasons furnish moral grounds for obeying Heaven but fall short of establishing that Heaven is a guide to morality.

A fourth, philosophically more intriguing reason is that we should follow Heaven's intent because as the noblest, wisest authority figure in the cosmos,

Heaven provides a reliable, objective model of righteousness.[6] A further moral reason is that, given the Mohists' understanding of political order (*zhì*), for a morally righteous state of affairs to obtain, Heaven must govern and thus we must obey its intent (Mz 26/14–22). The second "Heaven's Intent" book extends this point into a sixth reason: because Heaven is the wisest, noblest agent in the cosmos, "righteousness turns out to issue from Heaven" (27/6) and thus "it's unacceptable not to heed Heaven's intention" (27/22). These last three reasons all support the claim that Heaven's intent is a model or paradigm of righteousness or moral right.

Mohist texts offer two main lines of argument for this claim. The first I call the Moral Exemplar argument. Heaven is a model of righteousness because it is a reliable, exemplary moral agent. Unlike human agents, Heaven is consistently benevolent, because "its conduct is broad and impartial; its favors are rich and incur no debt; and its brightness endures without fading" (Mz 4/9–10). That is, its activity is inclusive and impartial, it distributes goods generously, and it shines consistently. Although these grounds are articulated explicitly only in "Models and Standards"—a relatively late essay—impartiality, generosity, and constancy are implicitly attributed to Heaven in the "Triads." As we have seen, the Mohists claim that Heaven does not discriminate between the poor and wealthy, noble or low, near or distant, kin or strangers; it cares for and bestows gifts on all; it possesses and cares about all the world; and it created the regular, constant cycles of the heavens, seasons, and weather.[7] The import of these claims is that Heaven embodies various features of morality and so is a fitting guide to what is righteous. This characterization also helps to contextualize the Mohist view of Heaven as the noblest, wisest agent, which stands above the human sovereign. Heaven possesses this superior, noble status partly by its identity as the supreme, all-seeing deity (26/7). But its nobility and wisdom lie also in its moral qualities—its reliable, impartial generosity. The claim that Heaven is a guide to what is righteous thus rests on the moral claim that impartial, generous, and consistent conduct qualifies an agent to be a moral exemplar, combined with the religious belief that Heaven demonstrates this conduct.

If we grant the Mohists' religious beliefs about Heaven and its attributes, and if we grant their claims that features such as impartiality and benevolence are criteria of morality, the argument supports their contention that Heaven can serve as a model of righteousness. Obviously, these are big ifs. We may well reject their beliefs about Heaven or disagree that, for instance, generosity is a key criterion of morality. An even more important problem, however, is that the Moral Exemplar argument tends to undermine the appeal to Heaven to justify Mohist ethics. The argument draws so heavily on the very ethical views that Heaven is supposed to vindicate that Heaven's intent can hardly be considered an independent model of righteousness. Arguably, Heaven actually functions more as a metaphor for or an illustration of Mohist ethical ideals than as a source of justification.

The second line of argument we can call the Orderly Government argument, versions of which appear in each of the three "Heaven's Intent" books.[8] The argument is that we must follow Heaven's intent because "righteousness is [good] government" (Mz 26/14). In good government, "there is no such thing as subordinates governing superiors; it must be that superiors govern subordinates" (26/14), for "the ignorant and common don't get to govern over the noble and knowledgeable; people must be noble and knowledgeable and only then do they get to govern over the ignorant and common" (27/4–5). The common people do not govern themselves but are governed by officers, who in turn are governed by ministers, and so on up the hierarchy to the sovereign—the Son of Heaven. Similarly, the Son of Heaven does not govern himself but is governed by Heaven. Supposedly, we know this because the sage-kings led people to sacrifice to Dì on high, ghosts, and spirits and to seek blessings from Heaven (26/20) and because Heaven has the power to reward and punish the Son of Heaven (28/14–15). Thus righteousness requires that we follow Heaven's intent. The Mohists themselves do not use the terminology of necessary conditions, but in effect they take following Heaven's intent to be a necessary condition for a morally righteous state of affairs to obtain in society.

Of special interest is the second version of this argument (Mz 27/1–6). This version contends that if we examine "what righteousness issues from," we find that "righteousness turns out to issue from Heaven." For the Mohists, social order (zhì) is a criterion and a component of righteousness. If righteousness obtains, order does as well; if righteousness does not obtain, neither does order. Order obtains only if society is governed well. Thus "righteousness is good government," insofar as "good government" too can be considered a component of righteousness, and when righteousness obtains, so does good government. The Mohists assume that society can be well governed only if the noble and wise or knowledgeable rule. As we saw in chapter 3, they hold that "if the noble and knowledgeable govern the ignorant and common, there is order; if the ignorant and common govern the noble and knowledgeable, there is disorder" (9/1–2). So righteousness "issues from" the noble and knowledgeable specifically in the sense that social order, a good that determines whether righteousness obtains, exists only if the noble and knowledgeable govern. Since Heaven is the noblest, most knowledgeable agent, righteousness ultimately issues from

Heaven. Righteousness is brought about when people comply with Heaven's rule, by following its intention, because only then does social order obtain, and righteousness obtains only if order does.

Like the Moral Exemplar argument, the Orderly Government argument establishes Heaven as an authority to follow only by taking for granted major features of the Mohist ethical theory—in this case, the conceptual links between righteousness, social order, and leadership by the "noble and knowledgeable." Rather than supporting Mohist ethics, the argument rests on it. It retains interest, however, as an expression of the Mohist conception of righteousness as embodied in a hierarchical social structure in which everyone conforms to norms promulgated by a ruler who cares impartially about and is concerned to benefit all.[9]

A DIVINE WILL THEORY?

Heaven's role as the highest model of righteousness has prompted a long-running debate as to whether Mohist ethics might fundamentally be a divine will theory rather than a type of consequentialism.[10] According to a divine will theory, the feature that determines whether something is morally right or wrong is whether it conforms to the will or command of a deity. What is morally right has that status because the deity wills or dictates that it does.

To understand and categorize an ethical theory, it is crucial to distinguish its answers to two distinct questions: what factors identify acts, rules, practices, or traits as morally right or good, and why are those factors morally significant? The first question concerns the theory's account of the normative factors that determine whether something is right or wrong. The second concerns its account of the foundations of morality—its explanation of why those factors are the relevant ones.[11] A theory's answer to the first question may be different from its answer to the second, but it is the second answer that determines the fundamental nature of the theory. For example, a rule consequentialist theory might give a deontological answer to the first question, asserting that the factor that determines whether some action is right or permissible is whether it conforms to the correct moral rules. Nevertheless, the theory might remain foundationally consequentialist, since its explanation of why moral right lies in conformity to such rules could be that right and wrong are ultimately determined by what has the best consequences, and the best consequences follow from guiding conduct by a particular set of moral rules.

The Mohists' writings suggest that their stance on the factoral question is primarily consequentialist but also to some extent pluralist. The chief normative factor the Mohists attend to that makes an action, policy, or practice right or permissible is that it promotes "the benefit of all" (Mz 32/1–2). Sometimes the operative normative factor may be conformity to certain practices, models, or laws, such as the *dào* of the sage-kings (25/86–87) or models established by Mòzǐ (25/83). In a few contexts, they assign Heaven's intent a factoral role: "What Heaven desires, do; what Heaven does not desire, stop" (4/10–11). These observations leave the foundational question open, however. The Mohists' foundational account could be consequentialist. They could hold that, foundationally, a tendency to promote the benefit of all is the basic feature that explains why actions, models, policies, or practices are right or permissible. Or they could hold a divine will theory. Perhaps the benefit of all is a factor that determines right and wrong because Heaven intends that we promote the benefit of all. If Heaven's intent is the basis for their foundational stance, their ethics would be best interpreted as a divine will theory.

A number of *Mòzǐ* passages might at first glance seem to suggest a divine will theory. The first and second "Identifying Upward" books state that society's unified norms of righteousness must conform to Heaven or it will punish us. "Models and Standards" contends that Heaven is the only acceptable model of order and thus we should do what it desires (Mz 4/9–11). The first "Heaven's Intent" book emphasizes that just as officials at each level of the political hierarchy govern those below, Heaven governs the human sovereign (26/15–17).[12] For righteousness to obtain, we must follow Heaven's intent. As we have seen, the second "Heaven's Intent" book even claims that righteousness "issues from" Heaven (27/6). On closer inspection, however, none of these passages straightforwardly implies that Heaven's intent provides a foundational explanation of why the benefit of all is the factor that makes righteous actions, policies, or practices morally right. All of them could stem from a consequentialist foundational stance in which Heaven's role is that of a moral guide and enforcer.

The Mohists probably do not address the foundational issue clearly and coherently enough for us to identify their implicit view with complete confidence. The practical, nonessentialist orientation of their thought steers them away from the topic. As we saw in chapter 2, their theoretical attention is not directed toward the kind of definitional question to which a divine will theory provides an answer. Their concern is with drawing distinctions according to the *dào*, not with giving a realist or an essentialist explanation of why the distinctions are the way they are. Arguably, however, the very fact that they do not thematize such questions makes it unlikely that they would implicitly hold a divine will theory. What we can say with assurance is that, as we have seen, within their own theoretical framework they directly and explicitly assign two major roles to Heaven, corresponding to the Moral Exemplar and Orderly Government arguments. Close interpretation of these arguments provides no reason to think the Mohists regard Heaven's intent as a foundational explanation of why factors such as promoting the benefit of all are the relevant factors by which to distinguish moral right from wrong. A simpler, more direct explanation of their stance is that it is consequentialist at the foundational level as well as predominantly consequentialist at the factoral level.

The first and most prominent role of Heaven—the concluding message of each of the "Heaven's Intent" books—is that its intent is a model of righteousness, or what is morally right.[13] As chapter 2 explained, claims about models are generally not definitional or foundational. They are epistemic and practical: a model is a reliable tool or gauge by which to guide or check something, as a set square is a model for producing and checking square corners. Congruity with the set square is not a foundational explanation of what a square corner is.[14] When "Models and Standards" proposes and rejects parents as a model for social order (Mz 4/5), the writers are not considering whether our parents' conduct might provide a foundational explanation of the factors that identify order. Of course, the epistemic appeal to Heaven as a model does not logically preclude the Mohists from holding a foundational divine will theory. But Mohist writers typically express their ideas clearly and repetitively. If a foundational divine will theory were central or fundamental to their worldview, we would expect it to be a prominent, explicit theme somewhere in their writings. Instead, Heaven's role as a model is the centerpiece of each of their four extended discussions of Heaven.

The second major role of Heaven is that it occupies the supreme place in the cosmic authority structure, ruling over the human sovereign as he rules over those below him. Since righteousness requires order and order requires obeying superiors, humanity must conform to Heaven's intent. Righteousness "issues from" Heaven in the sense that for order, and thus righteousness, to obtain, Heaven must rule.[15] There may be a foundational stance behind these claims, but if so, it is not that Heaven's intent fixes the factors that determine moral right and wrong. It is that righteousness lies partly in a specific conception of social order, namely a hierarchical system in which the noble and wise rule. The three versions of the Orderly Government argument all tie righteousness to this conception of order and argue from it to the conclusion that we should obey Heaven's intent. The ties between righteousness, order, and the hierarchical structure are treated as conceptually prior to and holding independently of Heaven's role. It is unlikely, then, that the Mohists' foundational view could be a divine will theory. If they held a divine will theory, their explanation of why social order is morally righteous would be that Heaven intends it so. The view they present is almost the reverse of this. Their explanation of why we should obey Heaven's intent is that doing so is required for social order, which is righteous. The simplest, most direct explanation of this stance is that the Orderly Government argument is grounded in their conception of the morally righteous structure of social order, a conception they treat as independent of Heaven's intent.[16] As I suggested in chapter 3, Heaven's moral authority is grounded partly in the Mohists' conception of political authority. Nothing in the argument implies that Heaven's intent is the foundation of moral norms.

Another passage in the first "Heaven's Intent" book similarly suggests that the Mohists see morality as foundationally independent of Heaven. The passage contends that we know Heaven desires righteousness because when righteousness obtains, so do life, wealth, and social order, while when it is absent, so are these other goods (Mz 26/12). Heaven desires these goods, so it desires righteousness. (Presumably, we know it desires these three goods because it previously gave people life, resources, and an orderly natural world to live in.)[17] Like the appeal to Heaven as a moral model, this passage does not logically exclude a divine will theory. But if the Mohists thought Heaven's intent was the foundation of moral right and wrong, it is hard to see why they would need to argue that Heaven desires righteousness and why in this context they would not present an account of how Heaven's attitudes determine what is righteous. A more straightforward explanation is that they see the convergence between Heaven's desires and righteousness as requiring explanation because their view that righteousness is what produces life, wealth, and order is foundationally independent of Heaven's intent.

A final consideration is that one of the Mohists' reasons for obeying Heaven is itself explicitly consequentialist. In the second "Heaven's Intent" book, the Orderly Government argument is followed by the paragraph quoted earlier cataloguing the types of conduct that Heaven desires and the positive consequences that ensue from them. The writers then conclude,

> So if people understand about following Heaven's intention and promote and practice it throughout the world, then penal codes and government will be in order, the myriad people will be harmonious, states will be wealthy, resources will be sufficient, the people will all get warm clothing and filling food and be calm and free of worries. (Mz 27/20–21)

The implication is that the moral factors routinely applied in Mohist ethics—good consequences such as social order and economic prosperity—justify following Heaven's intent. If the writers held that Heaven's intent was the foundational explanation of why these factors are morally significant, it would be odd to then appeal to the same factors to justify following Heaven's intent.

IS MOHIST ETHICS FOUNDATIONALLY CONSEQUENTIALIST?

Since Mohist texts do not directly address foundational issues, it is difficult to say decisively what their foundational view, if any, is. Moreover, to the Mohists themselves, the distinctions between the factoral and foundational levels and between consequentialist and deontological theories were neither clear nor pertinent. Still, perhaps they say enough about related issues that we can offer a plausible conjecture about their foundational stance. They explicitly assert that Heaven's intent is the highest moral model and that social order requires conformity to Heaven. I suggest the reasons they give for assigning Heaven these roles probably reflect their implicit foundational view—their view of why the normative factors that Heaven identifies as distinguishing actions or practices as righteous are morally relevant.

These reasons are just those offered in the Moral Exemplar and Orderly Government arguments. Heaven is inclusive, impartial, generous, and constant—that is, it consistently benefits everyone. Social order requires that we conform to its guidance. A plausible inference is that Heaven is a reliable moral guide because it picks out moral factors that impartially promote the welfare of all and bring about social order.[18] The factors are morally relevant because they promote these good consequences. If these reasons are indeed indicative of the Mohists' foundational stance, then their ethics is consequentialist at both the factoral and foundational levels. The foundational explanation of why the factors that pick out what is morally righteous are the correct factors is that they contribute to social order and general welfare.

Besides consequentialism and a divine will theory, two other possibilities for foundational views are virtue theoretical and deontological views. Since the appeal to Heaven as an ideal moral agent is central to Mohist ethics, might their implicit foundational view conceivably be a virtue theory? On this proposal, the foundational explanation of the relevant moral factors would be that they are right because they align with the virtuous character traits exemplified by Heaven. This interpretation is probably implausible, however, because the Mohists' grounds for taking Heaven as a model are framed in terms of its conduct and its role in securing social order, not its character traits. Still another possibility is to read the Orderly Government argument as expressing a deontological view, namely that a hierarchical political structure in which authority is invested in "the noble and knowledgeable" is intrinsically right. However, the most fully developed version of the argument claims that this structure is needed to achieve social order, which is treated as extensionally equivalent to righteousness (Mz 27/3–6). Since it is clear from other contexts that the Mohists take social order to be among the goods that determine righteousness, the simplest explanation of the appeal to rule by a noble, wise elite is that it contributes to the goods taken as foundational in Mohist consequentialism.

These considerations are by no means conclusive, as we are conjecturing about a dimension of their ethics that the Mohists themselves do not address directly or explicitly. Still, the major lines of reasoning they give for taking Heaven as a guide to morality both suggest that the reason it is right to obey Heaven, and the corresponding explanation for the moral relevance of the normative factors Heaven indicates, is that doing so has good consequences. Probably, then, the Mohists hold a consequentialist position on both the question of what factors make acts or practices morally right and the foundational question of why those factors are morally pertinent. In the occasional instances when they cite rules or Heaven's desires at the factoral level, their foundational explanation would be that following the rules or Heaven's desires leads us to promote the benefit of all.

HEAVEN'S INTENT AND THE NATURE OF MORALITY

The role of Heaven in Mohist thought is motivated by religious beliefs that few readers today can share. I suggest, however, that even if we jettison these beliefs, the Mohists' appeal to Heaven remains relevant to our understanding of moral theory. A conception of Heaven as nature itself or as a hypothetical ruler of nature provides a powerful metaphor—albeit a potentially misleading one—through which to think about morality. The factors that make it misleading can help us identify flaws in Mohist ethics and better understand how a more defensible moral theory might be structured.

According to the Mohists, moral norms—as I will here construe yì 義—must be unified, or endorsed and followed by all. They must be impartial and objective, not merely the personal policy of a particular individual, the parochial customs of a particular clan or community, or the idiosyncratic teaching of a particular school. They must be public, social, and "constant" or "regular" (cháng 常), in that they can be promulgated through explicit models (fǎ 法) and statements (yán 言) and consistently followed by everyone without generating conflicts or self-defeating consequences (for more details, see chapter 5).

We can interpret the Mohist appeal to Heaven as a proposal for identifying norms that meet these criteria. Think about morality by considering what would be a "natural" set of moral norms, in the sense of one grounded in the standpoint of Heaven, understood as nature as a whole.[19] Since these would be norms of nature as a whole, including humanity, all of us could endorse and follow them. They would be objective and impartial, since they would transcend the limitations and biases of particular individuals or communities and take all individuals and communities into consideration. They could be publicized—elucidated and promulgated to everyone through models and statements. Moreover, they would be authoritative, as they would be the norms of the natural world itself. To the Mohists, then, such a "morality of nature" would seem an ideal candidate for the correct account of morality. Insofar as these criteria do offer—to some extent, at least—a plausible characterization of moral norms, the Mohist appeal to Heaven is an intriguing way of articulating the nature of morality.

The Mohists conceive of morality or righteousness as a *dào* of drawing and acting on *shì-fēi* distinctions. What general action-guiding distinction might be grounded in nature itself, in the sense that, as natural creatures, we instinctively tend to act on it? A prominent candidate with a Mohist flavor is benefit (*lì* 利) versus harm (*hài* 害). We all instinctively seek benefit and avoid harm for ourselves and our immediate circle—our family and close associates. Minimally, the benefits we seek include preserving life, obtaining adequate material resources, and ensuring peace and safety—roughly just the basic goods of Mohist ethics. The Mohists probably see benefit versus harm, the core action-guiding distinction of their ethics, as a "natural" value shared by all.

Benefit or harm for ourselves and our circle is a *shì-fēi* distinction we naturally tend to act on, but it is not the morality of nature as a whole. Actions motivated by this distinction would not be objectively or impartially justified if our benefit were obtained by harming others. Applied from each agent's individual standpoint, the benefit versus harm distinction does not generate norms that are objective, impartial, and can be followed universally without self-defeating consequences. However, this distinction might yield such norms if applied from the standpoint of nature as a whole. One way to do so might be to broaden how we apply the distinction so that instead of acting for our own and our circle's benefit, we act for the benefit of all. The result would be a morality that few could practice, however, since most of us lack the capacity or opportunity to act in a way that directly increases the benefit of all. Alternatively, we could take the morality of nature as a whole to be a system of norms for drawing *shì-fēi* distinctions whose shared practice by everyone has the aggregate result of promoting the benefit of all. This system would be objective and impartial, taking everyone into consideration, and could be followed by all, since doing so would work to everyone's benefit.[20]

This train of thought amounts to a secularized route to the same position the Mohists reach by reflecting on Heaven as a cosmic ruler motivated by the benefit-harm distinction at the level of the entire world. Their appeal to Heaven amounts to the proposal that we can identify objectively correct moral norms by considering what norms such a ruler would promulgate for its subjects to follow. The cosmic ruler could not reasonably ask everyone to emulate the ruler itself in directly pursuing benefit for all, since only it would have the status and power to do so. But it could intend that everyone follow norms whose general observance would benefit all. Such norms would be objectively, impartially justified, because their overall consequences would align with the norms an agent occupying the objective, impartial standpoint would follow. But they would not need to require that individual agents exercise impartial benevolence, directly seeking to benefit everyone.

As this discussion illustrates, Heaven's function in grounding the Mohists' ethics is in principle detachable from their religious beliefs. Their appeal to Heaven can be reconstructed as an approach to articulating the structure and content of objective, impartially justified moral norms. We can even reconstruct, in secular form, their claim of special authority for norms grounded in the standpoint of Heaven. Such norms would supposedly be authoritative by virtue of being universal norms of nature as a whole, rather than the local, contingent standards of any particular individual, community, or tradition. They purport to be norms of nature as a whole insofar as they take a basic action-guiding distinction instinctively applied by all natural creatures—benefit versus harm—and apply it from an impartial standpoint, taking into consideration "all under heaven."[21] In an implicit, inchoate form, this simple but profound idea may be the root inspiration for Mohist ethics. It epitomizes their tacit conviction that the very idea of objectively justified norms of conduct leads to a consequentialist ethics focused on basic material needs and harmonious social relations.

I suggest, however, that this way of recasting key features of Mohist thought highlights two interrelated weaknesses of their approach. The first is that their appeal to Heaven inherently leads to a narrow consequentialism that neglects potentially important sources of value and reasons for action. Heaven represents a hypothetical neutral standpoint from which all sources of fallibility or bias have been removed. In the process of eliminating bias, however, the Mohists also subtract from the normative basis for their ethics many of the particular concerns and circumstances that normally provide reasons for action, filtering out all values except for bare survival needs. Heaven has no personal interests, hobbies, or projects. It has no friends, associates, or community, other than the community of "all under heaven." It has no preferences besides furthering "the benefit of all." From its standpoint, the only values that matter are the bare minimum that nature prompts us all to seek—life, material prosperity, peace, and social harmony. To be sure, these are important values. However, many other goods that have nothing to do with benefit in the Mohists' sense may also have objectively justifiable value, such as the arts, pleasure, friendships, and personal projects. As we will see again in chapter 5, Mohist ethics seems to leave little room for such goods. For related reasons, we can doubt whether benefit versus harm as the Mohists understand it is indeed a "constant" or "regular" action-guiding distinction in the sense they suppose. Surely the components of benefit—prosperity, adequate population, and social order—are among the goods by which we sometimes guide action. However, other goods have a role too. Benefit does not always take priority, nor is it always applicable. Other action-guiding distinctions that are arguably equally natural include just versus unjust, beautiful versus ugly, and enjoyable versus unenjoyable, to give only a few examples.

Thomas Nagel has suggested that the search for objective values tends to lead to an account of the reasons for action that would engage us if we were to take up "a maximally detached standpoint"—one divorced from any details of our particular identity and situation, as the standpoint of Heaven is.[22] He sees a connection between this conception of objectivity and consequentialism through the idea that the only real or objective values are neutral or impersonal ones, and thus "the only reason for anyone to do anything is that it would be better in itself, considering the world as a whole, if he did it."[23] In its emphasis on an objective, impersonal point of view, a direct consequentialism of this sort fails to recognize that not all values are impersonal and that each of us is a particular person acting from a particular perspective.[24]

As a form of indirect consequentialism, Mohism avoids the letter of this critique but remains vulnerable to its spirit. In their appeal to Heaven, the Mohists do not commit themselves to the idea that the only good reasons—that is, the only appropriate action-guiding *shì-fēi* distinctions—are those that directly promote the good of the world as a whole. They hold that the proper *shì-fēi* distinctions are part of a system of norms and practices that if generally followed promotes the benefit of all. As their emphasis on the relational virtues shows, their ethics recognizes that individuals stand in special relationships to other particular individuals, toward whom they have distinctive responsibilities. Yet they do tie objectivity to a detached standpoint that discounts or excludes reasons other than those pertaining to a narrow, minimal set of goods shared by everyone.[25]

The second weakness highlighted by these reflections on the significance of Heaven is that the very idea of articulating objectivity and impartiality by appeal to a neutral, all-inclusive standpoint may be misguided. It is more helpful, I suggest, to think of objectivity or impartiality as lying in justification across particular standpoints, rather than in a purportedly neutral, overarching standpoint such as Heaven's. This point can be illustrated by the grounds Mohist writers themselves sometimes give in condemning unethical actions. Murdering a person to steal his clothing, sword, and spear is wrong, they explain, because it injures another to benefit oneself (Mz 17/4–5). Taxing the poor to fund a musical gala for the aristocracy is wrong because it amounts to "robbing the people's resources for clothing and food" (32/3). In these contexts, the Mohists justify their moral judgments by calling attention to how vicious, selfish actions harm the victims. Whether these actions are detrimental to the benefit of all or rejected from the overarching standpoint of Heaven is beside the point, we might contend. The crux is that they fail to give due consideration to others. One promising way to develop this idea is by requiring that actions be justifiable, or at least not unjustifiable, from others' standpoints as well as our own. Murdering someone for his clothing and weapons, for example, could never be justified from the victim's perspective. The proposal is then that objectivity and impartiality lie not in ascending to a higher-level, transcendent standpoint like that of Heaven but in being able to justify or defend actions or practices to the various parties affected.[26] Such an approach to impartial justification would probably lead away from consequentialism, however. From the perspectives of different agents, factors other than good consequences may often be relevant—factors such as fairness or justice, for instance. Indeed, this way of thinking of objective or impartial justification probably leads to a conception of morality quite different from the Mohists', one in which moral rightness refers mainly to an intersubjective justificatory status rather than a relation to certain goods.

This line of thought prompts us to notice that, compared with the standpoints of particular individuals, the standpoint of Heaven is not genuinely neutral after all, but merely different. It is the standpoint of a hypothetical sovereign, concerned with the community as a whole, rather than that of individual members of a community, who are concerned also with themselves and their relations to one another. The appeal to Heaven is thus another manifestation of the Mohists' communitarian orientation and their tendency to merge the spheres of the ethical and the political. They approach morality or righteousness primarily as a social and political policy—the path an ideal ruler would lead the community to follow—rather than as a guide for individual agents. The benefit of all is their central criterion of morality partly because their theoretical stance is implicitly political and collective.

CONCLUDING REMARKS

The religious aspects of their belief system aside, the Mohists' appeal to Heaven is an intriguing way of expressing a conception of objectivity and impartiality, one whose basic structure is at least initially appealing. It leads the Mohists to conceive—plausibly—of morality as requiring that we take everyone into consideration and that we interact with others in a way that is in some sense impartially justified. They themselves think of such impartial justification specifically in terms of benefit: justified conduct or practices are those that work to the benefit of all. The flaw in this view is that it is incomplete, not false. Having good consequences for all affected is surely among the reasons that can sometimes justify conduct or practices. The problem is that it is not the only such reason, nor is it always decisive.

In their discussions of Heaven's intent, the Mohists are careful not to conflate the norms followed by Heaven, an ideally impartial and benevolent agent who occupies an abstract, decontextualized stance, with those Heaven desires that people follow. Heaven impartially benefits all, but its desire for human agents is only that we care about everyone such that we interact with others in mutually beneficial ways. The "Heaven's Intent" books do not ask that we emulate Heaven in caring equally for all or seeking to benefit everyone impartially. As we will see in chapter 5, however, elsewhere the Mohists proclaim that the benevolent person "seeks to promote the benefit of all the world and eliminate harm to all the world" and that righteousness involves, in our intentions, taking "all the world" as our "portion," on whose behalf we act.[27] Such remarks seem to advocate adopting the impartial standpoint of Heaven ourselves—doing so is morally good and perhaps was even regarded as obligatory among some later Mohists. If so, Mohist writers may at times have run together the idea of objective, impartial justification with that of adopting an objective, impartial point of view, such as Heaven's.

In one respect, the doctrine of Heaven's intent is a development of the traditional doctrine of the mandate of Heaven. In another, it originates the widely shared tendency in the Chinese tradition of seeking special authority for one's *dào* by attempting to ground it in nature itself. As the *Zhuāngzǐ* will later point out, however, such an appeal to Heaven ultimately raises more problems than it solves. Arguably, anything that is actual is thereby also natural. So a follower of any actual *dào* whatsoever can attempt to defend it as natural or originating from Heaven. The Mohists imply that seeking material wealth and social order is natural. But perhaps the Rú could argue that immersing oneself in elaborate traditional ceremonies is natural, since carrying on cultural traditions comes as naturally to us as seeking material prosperity and social order. In the end, appeals to Heaven or nature provide little or no concrete guidance, since nature apparently engenders a plurality of *dào*, all of which may seem obvious and useful to their followers. An isolated fragment in the later Mohist "Dialectics" seems to acknowledge that Heaven's intent is of no help in identifying moral norms, as it can be twisted to justify almost anything. A criminal might claim it is right for him to be selfish, because Heaven gave him a criminal disposition.[28] This snippet lacks context and is potentially corrupt, so we should avoid consigning much interpretive weight to it. Still, it is interesting that the ethical portions of the "Dialectics" make no appeal to Heaven to ground their normative stance.

5
ETHICS

The Benefit of All

IN THIS CHAPTER and the next, I examine the Mohists' concrete proposals concerning the content of the unified moral norms purportedly modeled on Heaven's intent and promulgated through the political system. Doing so entails reconstructing and interpreting the Mohist ethical theory from the arguments in the "Triads" and other texts. These writings do not present the Mohist ethical theory in a rigorous, systematic form, so my work is necessarily partly tentative. Still, to support their doctrines, the texts regularly employ a coherent set of consequentialist arguments, which provide grounds for reconstructing the Mohists' implicit ethical theory with reasonable confidence.

These chapters focus mainly on the ethics of the "Triads," using material from the "Dialogues" and "Dialectics" only to fill out the discussion of the concept of righteousness (yì 義), the status of special relationships, and the stringency of Mohist ethics. To keep the length of the chapter manageable, I have had to forgo sections focusing specifically on the ethics of the "Dialogues" and the "Dialectics." Interested readers are invited to consult the detailed treatments of both I have published elsewhere.[1]

The first section here sets the stage for the discussion that follows by reviewing pertinent features of the Mohists' historical context. The next section discusses the central notions of benevolence (rén 仁) and righteousness, which jointly shape the structure of Mohist ethics. I then present the ethical theory of the "Triads," elucidate the goods to which it appeals, and offer a hypothesis about its structure. Given the Mohists' emphasis on impartial consideration of the benefit of all, a controversial issue in interpreting their ethics is whether it conflicts with people's natural—and probably justifiable—tendency to attach special value to close personal relationships. The third major section of the chapter argues that, far from rejecting traditional views about values such as filial devotion (*xiào* 孝), the Mohists treat these as a cornerstone of their ethics. Another prominent worry about Mohist ethics is whether it might ask too much of people—so much that few people could live up to its demands. The fourth section contends that Mohist writings address at least two distinct audiences. Those directed at influential members of society present norms that are moderately but not unrealistically demanding. Teachings on self-cultivation intended for committed Mohist adherents, on the other hand, present a more stringent *dào* 道 aimed at attaining Mohist sagehood. The chapter concludes with a critical assessment of Mohist ethics, focusing on what I suggest are its two main flaws: the Mohists' approach to impartiality and their conception of value.

THE ORIENTATION OF MOHIST ETHICS

In interpreting Mohist ethics, it is vital to keep in mind the orientation of Mohist thought, particularly the Mohists' motivation and intended audience.[2] Doing so helps both to avoid misunderstanding of what the Mohists say and to explain some of the shortcomings of their views.

Outside the "Dialectics," the Mohists are not concerned with philosophical inquiry for inquiry's sake. Nor are they especially concerned with the nature of the good life for the individual, the details of character development, or evaluating alternative ethical theories. Their primary concern is social and political problems arising from selfish conduct harmful to others, such as war, feuding, banditry, burglary, poverty, and economic exploitation. Their earliest moral and political doctrines are presented as a platform for resolving these problems, not a contribution to philosophical discourse or a response to proponents of other ethical doctrines. Indeed, at the time of the earliest Mohist writings—the first essays on "Inclusive Care," "Condemning Aggression," and "Moderation in Use," for instance—it is unclear whether there were any prominent rival doctrines to respond to. These texts are the earliest known argumentative essays in the Chinese tradition, suggesting that the Mohists initiated public debate about the *dào* and were among the founders of the discourse to which later thinkers and texts contributed. The middle and later strata of the "Triads" record the growth of this discourse, in the sections devoted to addressing objections to Mohist proposals and the essays criticizing those who advocate fatalism or deny the existence of ghosts.

The primary audience for the Mohists' proposals thus was not rival thinkers or activists. Who was it? The "Triads" explicitly address two overlapping audiences. Most of the books begin or conclude with an appeal to "kings, dukes, great men, officers, and gentlemen," a phrase that refers to government officials at all levels, from rulers of states down to low-level bureaucrats, such as tax collectors (Mz 32/34–36). Many books also address objections from "the gentlemen of the world." For the Mohists, the term "gentlemen" (jūnzǐ 君子) seems to refer specifically to a social rank that contrasts with the masses or the common people.[3] This rank includes middle- and low-level government officials and perhaps also aspiring candidates for office, landlords, military officers, wealthy merchants, and others of comparable status. "The gentlemen of the world" probably included some Rú 儒, or "Confucians." As the Mohists use the phrase, however, it refers not to the Rú in particular but to a broad class of influential, socially prominent men who constituted the core of society, or "the establishment." These are the people who have the power and influence to put Mohist teachings into practice, if they can be persuaded.

These historical points help to deflect several potential misconceptions about Mohist ethics. Accounts of early Chinese thought routinely portray the Mohists as motivated primarily by opposition to Ruist ethics or, specifically, the ethics of Confucius.[4] They are depicted as engaged in a broad critique of "tradition," specifically Ruist traditions.[5] They are said to reject a purportedly "Confucian" (that is, Ruist) family-centered ethical and political system.[6] They are generally construed as advocating a narrow conception of the good focusing purely on material welfare.[7] Although there is some truth to these characterizations, by and large they are misleading.

Mohist ethics is not motivated primarily by disagreement with prevailing ethical ideals or doctrines, Ruist or otherwise. It is motivated by dismay at people's failure to conform to minimal, commonsense moral standards, such as fulfilling familial and political responsibilities and refraining from violence, theft, and exploitation. The Mohists plausibly assume that most well-meaning people will agree with their concerns, if not their solutions. Accounts that depict Mohism as driven primarily by opposition to Ruism anachronistically assign the Rú far more influence and sophistication than they had during the formative period of the Mohist movement, at least as seen through the lens of the Mòzǐ. The "Triads" do not frame Mohist doctrines in opposition to Ruist ethical ideals, let alone a purported Ruist orthodoxy. Mohist criticisms of the Rú play no role in the essays presenting core ethical teachings such as inclusive care, condemning aggression, or moderation in expenditure. In particular, the Mohists do not condemn a supposed Ruist doctrine of "graded care" or "love with distinctions," according to which our degree of concern for others should vary proportionally to the closeness of our relationship to them, such that we favor family over outsiders.[8] (As we will see, the Mohists agree that we should devote special concern to those closest to us.) The Rú are treated prominently in two places, one of the "Dialogues" (*Mz* 48) and "Condemning the Rú" (39), both most likely written long after the earliest "Triad" essays. Even in these texts, however, the Mohists do not really engage substantively with Ruist ethical doctrines. To be sure, they denounce the Rú for violating several of the core Mohist teachings, accusing them of impiety toward Heaven and the ghosts, recklessly extravagant burial and mourning rituals, wasteful dancing and music, and fatalism (48/49–58). But they never consider whether the Rú might have any meaningful grounds for their practices. Indeed, as depicted in the *Mòzǐ*, the Rú hardly have any ethical doctrines of significance. The teachings attributed to them are mostly inane, such as "the gentleman must be ancient in his speech and attire, only then can he be benevolent" (48/22, 39/17). To the Mohists, the Rú seem simply one feature of the social landscape, a band of pretentious devotees of ancient ceremonies, costumes, music, dance, and poetry, not proponents of an ethical stance deserving serious examination.

Nor is Mohist ethics driven by opposition to traditional mores. The Mohists endorse the established social and political structures of their time, such as the family or clan and a hierarchical, autocratic government. They advocate traditional values such as filial devotion and political loyalty. They devoutly perform traditional sacrificial rituals expressing reverence for Heaven, ancestral ghosts, and nature spirits. They self-consciously position their *dào* as following the model of the ancient sage-kings. They do apply the distinction between custom and righteousness to argue that some popular customs, specifically extravagant burial and mourning practices, are misguided, as they have become harmfully excessive and have diverged from the moderate practices of the sage-kings. However, recognizing this distinction does not prompt them to launch a wholesale attack on tradition.

Finally, Mohist texts indeed apply a narrow conception of the good, focused on material welfare and social order. They devote relatively little discussion to details of the individual moral life, such as improving one's character or achieving various psychological goods. However, the earliest Mohists do not advocate a narrow view of the good in explicit opposition to some richer, more well-rounded alternative. Nor do they focus on social goods in deliberate contrast to an alternative *dào* centered on personal moral development. For them, issues such as meeting the community's subsistence needs and preventing war, crime, and exploitation were so pressing that other values simply did not attract their attention. Their ethics arises from a historical context in which, as they see it, fulfilling basic material needs presents so urgent a challenge that a collective, social *dào* focused on securing material welfare and social order is the obvious and only path.

THE WAY OF BENEVOLENCE AND RIGHTEOUSNESS

In their seminal argument against conflating morality with parochial customs (discussed in chapter 1), the Mohists ask how alien cultural practices such as rending and eating one's firstborn son or abandoning one's widowed grandmother could really be "the *dào* of benevolence and righteousness" (Mz 25/77). Mohist essays frequently open or conclude with an appeal to "the gentlemen of the world" who "desire to be benevolent and righteous" (25/86, 27/1). As these examples suggest, benevolence and righteousness are the Mohists' central terms of moral evaluation. How do they understand these notions?

RIGHTEOUSNESS

Let us take righteousness first, since we have already treated it in chapters 3 and 4. For the Mohists, righteousness refers to moral norms or standards by which we evaluate statements, intentions, conduct, practices, legal codes, government, and circumstances to determine whether or not they are good and thereby deserving of approval, praise, or reward.[9] As we have seen, the Mohists place several constraints on a defensible conception of righteousness. Politically, to achieve social order, norms of righteousness must be unified, such that everyone in the community endorses and follows the same standards of right (*shì* 是) and wrong (*fēi* 非). The unified norms must conform to Heaven's intent and thus be objectively correct, not merely the personal policy of a particular leader, the parochial customs of a particular clan or community, or the idiosyncratic teaching of a particular school. They should be explicitly expressed and promulgated in the form of statements or pronouncements (*yán* 言),[10] which serve as models (*fǎ* 法) for proper conduct. Such statements must conform to the Three Models: they must be rooted in the deeds of the sage-kings, based on empirical observation (where relevant), and yield beneficial consequences when applied in legal codes and government policy.

The third of the Three Models generates a pair of further constraints, which reflect the Mohist focus on morality as a public, social code to be followed by all. The point of the third model is that any plausible moral norm must yield beneficial results when promulgated and enforced by the state. As the Mohists apply this requirement, it implicitly entails a publicity condition and what I call a regular practice condition—a loose version of a universalizability condition. Candidate norms must prove beneficial when widely publicized and regularly practiced by all. Minimally, they must not generate conflicts between agents or lead to self-defeating consequences. These latter conditions are illustrated by a passage in the "Dialogues"—mentioned briefly in chapter 3—in which Mòzǐ rejects a statement by his opponent Wūmǎzǐ as "empty jabbering" on the grounds that it is of "no benefit" (Mz 46/52–60). The statement is Wūmǎ's declaration, by way of explaining why he cannot practice inclusive care, that for him "there is killing others to benefit myself, but not killing myself to benefit others." Mòzǐ and Wūmǎ both refer to this pronouncement as Wūmǎ's yì—his norm or policy concerning what is righteous. The implication is that statements such as Wūmǎ's express conceptions of moral norms. Mòzǐ rebuts Wūmǎ's statement as follows:

> Our Master Mòzǐ said, "Your yì, will you conceal it? Or will you tell it to others?"
> Wūmǎzǐ said, "Why would I conceal my yì? I will tell it to others."
> Our Master Mòzǐ said, "That being so, then if one person is pleased with you, one person desires to kill you to benefit himself; if ten people are pleased with you, ten people desire to kill you to benefit themselves; if all the world is pleased with you, all the world desires to kill you to benefit themselves. If one person is displeased with you, one person desires to kill you, taking you to be spreading an inauspicious statement. If ten people are displeased with you, ten people desire to kill you, taking you to be spreading an inauspicious statement. If all the world is displeased with you, all the world desires to kill you, taking you to be spreading an inauspicious statement. This is what's called 'What passes from your own mouth is what takes your life.'" (Mz 46/52–60)

Wūmǎ's policy cannot be publicized without self-defeating consequences. Its aim is to promote his own benefit. Yet anyone who hears of and acts on it will be inclined to harm him, while anyone who hears of and rejects it might also be inclined to harm him.[11] To qualify as beneficial, and thus correct, a norm of righteousness or an action-guiding statement must not yield self-defeating or harmful results when proclaimed throughout society and regularly practiced by all. These conditions dovetail with the Mohist view that an effective action-guiding statement should be made "constant" or "regular" (cháng 常)—that is, widely and regularly proclaimed.[12] Regularly uttering statements that are useless in guiding conduct is "empty jabbering," just as Wūmǎ's statement is.

Statements adequate to repeatedly guide conduct, make them regular. Those not adequate to guide conduct, do not make them regular. To make regular those not adequate to guide conduct is empty jabbering. (Mz 46/37–38, 47/18–19)

Part of Mòzǐ's criticism is that Wūmǎ's statement, and thus his policy, cannot consistently and effectively be made regular. For the Mohists, the *dào* is a guide to conduct that can be explicitly expressed and consistently advocated and practiced by all.[13] An implicit part of their case for the Mohist *dào* is that Mohist norms supposedly fulfill these conditions while alternatives such as Wūmǎ's policy do not.

BENEVOLENCE

Whereas "righteous" refers to a status of conduct, practices, and circumstances, "benevolence" refers primarily to a character trait, a virtue. To the Mohists, benevolence is a species of ethical goodness akin to kindness, humaneness, or goodwill. It is used primarily for people and, by extension, for the dispositions, attitudes, conduct, and practices of those who possess it, which reflect concern for the benefit of all. Mohist writings do not use the concepts of benevolence and righteousness in a strictly precise, consistent way, just as we sometimes do not distinguish exactly between the good and the right.[14] Generally, however, "righteous" refers to conduct, policies, or states of affairs being morally right, "benevolent" to persons or their actions being morally good.

The crux of the Mohists' construal of benevolence is expressed by their repeated statement that "the task of benevolent people is surely to diligently seek to promote the benefit of the world and eliminate harm to the world."[15] Benevolence motivates a person to promote the benefit of all. In a pivotal statement of their ethical values, the Mohists explain the benevolent person's attitudes by analogy to the model of a filially devoted (*xiào* 孝) son's attitudes toward his parents.

> Our Master Mòzǐ stated, "The benevolent person's planning on behalf of the world, to give an analogy, is no different from a filially devoted son's planning on behalf of his parents."
> Now a filial son's planning on behalf of his parents, what will it be like?
> He said, "If his parents are poor, he undertakes to enrich them; if their people are few, he undertakes to increase their number; if their multitude is in disorder, he undertakes to put them in order. When he is in these situations, there are indeed cases when his strength is insufficient, his resources exhausted, or his

knowledge lacking, and then he gives up. In no case would he dare spare any effort, conceal any scheme, or withhold any benefit without pursuing them on behalf of his parents. These three duties—a filial son's planning on behalf of his parents is indeed like this."

Even the benevolent person planning on behalf of the world is also like this. He said, "If the world is poor, he undertakes to enrich it; if the people are few, he undertakes to increase their number; if the multitude is in disorder, he undertakes to put them in order. When he is in these situations, there are indeed cases when his strength is insufficient, his resources exhausted, or his knowledge lacking, and then he gives up. In no case would he dare spare any effort, conceal any scheme, or withhold any benefit without pursuing them on behalf of the world. These three duties—the benevolent person's planning on behalf of the world is indeed like this." (Mz 25/1–7)

The benevolent person is mindful of society's needs just as a devoted son is mindful of his parents' needs. Both diligently pursue the "three benefits": material wealth, adequate population, and good order. Few of us are positioned to take society's needs into consideration just as we do the needs of our family or clan. But recall that the Mohists' primary audience is men of influence, many of them government officials, and their primary concern is social policy. So a key segment of their audience may indeed be gentlemen in a position to make considerations on behalf of "all the world," or at least a significant portion of it.

The passage reflects the two foci of concern in Mohist ethics: our kin, or in-group, and the community of humanity, or all the world. Rather than contrast consideration for kin with benevolence toward others, it affirms the value of filial devotion and adopts it as a paradigm for our attitudes toward the larger community. Benevolence is an analogical broadening of filial devotion to incorporate "all the world." This idea overlaps that of the Ruist thinker Yǒuzǐ, recorded in the *Analects* (LY 1.2), that filial devotion and brotherliness are "the root of benevolence." In both Mohist and Ruist thought, then, we find the proposal that benevolence involves an extension to outsiders of attitudes and conduct normally found within the family.

The Mohists are sometimes said to treat virtues as if they were reducible to right conduct or to have a purely "outer-directed" ethics, concerned only with whether people's outward behavior conforms to moral norms, not with whether they have morally appropriate motives.[16] The preceding characterizations of benevolence and filial devotion suggest that such descriptions are unjustified. These virtues comprise not only dispositions to conduct oneself in certain ways but also one's pattern of thought and motivation, especially how one takes one's parents or all others into consideration in determining plans for action.

A prima facie tension obtains between the description of benevolence and the emphasis on filiality. The virtuous person will probably be both benevolent and filially devoted. Any one person's time and resources are limited, however, so benevolently devoting all one's effort to benefiting the world will tend to conflict with filially devoting all one's effort to benefiting one's parents. This is one of many instances in which Mohist rhetoric exaggerates, yielding mildly incoherent claims. For example, different passages variously identify the chief cause of social disorder as the absence of political leaders, gentlemen's ignorance of Heaven's intent, people's failure to care about one another, ignorance of retribution from the ghosts, and the spread of fatalism. The charitable reading is simply to discount slightly from the Mohists' formulations. The filial son and benevolent person devote *much* effort to benefiting their parents and society, not *all* their effort. Moreover, there is an important distinction between the two virtues. Unlike filial devotion, which is directed at particular family members, benevolence is a more abstract attitude directed at "all the world," not specific individuals. It could be manifested by supporting institutions and practices that contribute to the benefit of all, rather than by directly benefiting individual persons. A further point is that for the Mohists filial devotion counts among the beneficial attitudes and conduct that the benevolent person supports. One way for benevolent people to do their part in promoting the benefit of all is through devotion to their parents and other elderly kin. Filial devotion is part of benevolence, not a competing value.

Still, compared with the moral norms associated with Heaven's intent (discussed in chapter 4), this characterization of benevolence seems demanding. Benevolence involves working to benefit all the world with the same kind of devotion we direct toward our parents. As described here, the attitudes and conduct of the benevolent person seem more similar to those of Heaven itself than to what we earlier suggested Heaven asks of people. It seems, then, that for the Mohists benevolence is a more stringent ideal than righteousness. Righteousness refers to what is right, the minimal moral norms we all must live up to. Benevolence is an ideal of moral goodness that goes beyond the basic requirements of righteousness. The two are linked through the concept of benefit. Righteousness refers to norms whose general observance benefits all, whether or not each discrete righteous act actually benefits everyone. The benevolent person goes beyond such norms to directly pursue the benefit of all.

The similarity between benevolence and the attitudes of Heaven itself helps to explain the rhetorical role of benevolence in Mohist ethical argumentation.

The Mohists' arguments for their doctrines of inclusive care, moderate burials, and refraining from costly entertainment are grounded in the model of the benevolent person, whose attitudes are treated as a standard of right and wrong. In the process of evaluating a general practice, such as moderate burials, the attitudes of the benevolent person reflect the standpoint of Heaven and are thus a guide to identifying practices that are morally right.

MOHIST CONSEQUENTIALISM

What, then, is the *dào* of benevolence and righteousness, as indicated by the model of the benevolent person? For the Mohists, the chief feature of this *dào* is that it promotes benefit and eliminates harm to all. "The benefit of all the world" provides a general standard of moral permissibility.

> Our Master Mòzǐ stated, "The task of the benevolent is surely to diligently seek to promote the benefit of the world and eliminate harm to the world and to take this as a model throughout the world. Does it benefit people? Then do it. Does it not benefit people? Then stop." (Mz 32/1-2)

> Our Master Mòzǐ said, "In all statements and all actions, what is beneficial to Heaven, ghosts, and the people, do it. In all statements and all actions, what is harmful to Heaven, ghosts, and the people, reject it." (Mz 47/16–18)[17]

Some passages go beyond the simple distinction between what does and does not benefit people to recognize differences in degree. The extent to which something is right or wrong is determined by the degree to which it benefits or harms others. "The more someone injures another, the more he is unbenevolent and the more serious the crime" (17/2).

"Benefit" (*lì* 利) includes three sorts of goods, which are mainly social or collective: material prosperity, an adequate population or family size, and sociopolitical order, including social stability and personal and national security. These three goods are the concrete criteria against which the Mohists evaluate statements, conduct, practices, and institutions. Those that advance them are benevolent and righteous. Those that do not must be rejected. Elaborate funeral practices are an example:

> Might it be that, supposing we model ourselves on their statements, use their plans, and have rich burials with prolonged mourning, this can really enrich the

poor, increase the few, secure the endangered, and bring order to the disordered? Then this is benevolent, righteous, and the task of a filial son. In planning for others, it is unacceptable not to encourage it. The benevolent will promote it throughout the world, establish it and make the people praise it, and never abandon it.

On the other hand, suppose that, modeling ourselves on their statements, using their plans, and having rich burials and prolonged mourning, this really cannot enrich the poor, increase the few, secure the endangered, and bring order to the disordered. Then this is not benevolent, not righteous, and not the task of a filially devoted son. In planning for others, it is unacceptable not to discourage it. The benevolent will seek to eliminate it from the world, abandon it and make people deem it wrong, and never do it. (Mz 25/12–16)[18]

The justification for the first and third of these goods is obvious: material wealth, personal and national security, and social stability are all basic subsistence needs. (As the preceding passage illustrates, in referring to wealth, the Mohists have in mind eliminating poverty, not idle accumulation of assets.) The importance of the second good, a large population or family, may be less plain. In the Mohists' time, a substantial head count was crucial to the economic prospects of families and the economic and military strength of states. A bigger family increased the household labor supply and ensured the elderly would have relatives to support them; a larger population helped increase tax revenue and ensured a more formidable defense force. The Mohists' concern is not with population for its own sake but with increasing the population when insufficient.

Consequentialist arguments appealing to one or more of these three goods are offered to justify nine of the ten core Mohist doctrines. The tenth doctrine, Heaven's intent, elucidates and illustrates the justification for the consequentialist theory.

BENEFIT

Wealth, population, and social order provide only a general characterization of "the benefit of all the world." Fortunately, in the course of describing the problems they hope to solve and the expected consequences of their doctrines, the Mohists fill in further details of their conception of order and wealth. In preceding chapters, we saw that order (zhì 治) for them includes four sorts of conditions regarded as constitutive of flourishing social life. First, people refrain from harming or mistreating others, and so peace, social harmony, and public security prevail. War, feuding, robbery, theft, violence, oppression, deceit, and other forms of harassment, abuse, and injury cease.[19] Second, people fulfill the relational virtues—virtues associated with the primary, relational social roles of ruler or subject, father or son, and elder or younger brother. Rulers are generous, subjects loyal, fathers paternally kind, sons filially devoted, and brothers fraternal.[20] Third, society is governed by wise, virtuous leaders, who administer rewards and punishments fairly, and everyone follows a unified set of moral norms.[21] Finally, community members habitually share knowledge, surplus labor, and excess goods.[22] This mutual assistance amounts to neighborliness or community spirit, not altruistic self-sacrifice. The sharing comes out of surplus resources, not basic necessities, and people can expect reciprocal assistance from others when needed.

As to wealth, the Mohists seek to ensure there are sufficient resources to offer sacrificial food and drink of the required purity to Heaven and the ghosts, to give suitable tokens of friendship to other states, and "to feed the hungry, rest the weary, and support the myriad people" (*Mz* 27/19). Feeding and clothing the people are core concerns mentioned repeatedly.[23] The Mohists assume most families can provide for their own needs if the government maintains public security, avoids war, and refrains from predatory taxation and wasteful expenditure. Only two groups are expected to regularly need assistance, specifically on the grounds that they lack families to support them: orphans and elderly, childless widows or widowers (15/37–38, 16/18). Otherwise, people can be expected to need aid, mainly from state reserves, only in times of crisis, such as a plague or failed harvest (16/42–43). Besides food, clothing, and housing, references to wealth probably also include vehicles and boats, weaponry and armor, and city fortifications.[24]

To sum up, "the benefit of all the world" is a general conception of material and social welfare comprising economic prosperity; a thriving population or family; social harmony and public security; sharing of information, labor, and resources; charity toward those without families; flourishing social relationships, manifested through the relational virtues; and effective government by qualified officials. It is composite and complex, constituted by a variety of different types of goods.[25] Mohist texts seem to assume that these goods will generally not conflict with one another: pursuing some will not interfere with pursuing others. If, in a particular case, a conflict does arise, presumably the Mohist stance—according to a fragment in the "Dialectics," not the "Triads"—is to choose the greater of two available benefits or the lesser of two unavoidable harms (*MB* EC8).

A fascinating feature of the Mohist conception of benefit is its communitarian or collectivist orientation. No doubt the general practice of the Mohist *dào* in its original historical context would have enhanced the welfare of many individuals. Yet the goods that constitute the Mohists' criteria of morality are mainly collective or public. Again, this reflects their focus on a social system rather than individual conduct and their tendency to merge ethics and politics. It also explains why they do not consider whether "the benefit of all" refers to the total sum of welfare in society or to individuals' average level of welfare. The benefits they have in mind are primarily benefits of the community as a whole—security, stability, and harmonious relationships, along with sufficient food and clothing for all.

DÀO CONSEQUENTIALISM

The Mohists' structural focus on *dào* means that their ethical theory does not fit neatly into familiar categories such as act or rule consequentialism. In contemporary ethics, consequentialist theories are classified into types depending on what they take as a primary evaluative focal point—that is, the focus of the evaluations that are basic for that theory.[26] For instance, in rule consequentialism, rules are the primary evaluative focal point. Rules are evaluated as right or wrong by whether they produce better consequences than alternatives. The rules then provide the basis for evaluating other focal points, such as acts. An act is right if it conforms to the correct rules. In act consequentialism, individual acts are the primary evaluative focal point. Acts are evaluated as right or wrong directly by whether they produce better consequences than alternatives. Examples of other possible primary focal points include motives, character traits, practices, and institutions.

Mohist ethics sometimes employs rules or rulelike formulations to evaluate or guide action. Some models are presented as rulelike statements that stipulate proper conduct, such as the sage-kings' model for moderate burials, which specifies the details of how to inter the deceased (Mz 21/14–15). However, rules are not the Mohists' primary evaluative focal point. We do not see them referring all other evaluations back to rules or focusing on formulating rules as basic tenets. Moreover, formally they regard their ethics as comprising various models to be emulated, not a system of rules to be followed. So their theory probably cannot be adequately described as a brand of rule consequentialism.

The Mohists also sometimes directly evaluate acts as right or wrong, without appealing to rules. Although they would surely have rejected any general rule permitting false promises, a story in the "Dialogues" depicts Mòzǐ justifying a false promise by its good consequences (Mz 48/62–66). The "Dialectics" considers how to weigh benefits and harms in order to evaluate particular actions (MB EC8). When harm is unavoidable, the lesser of two harms can be the right act, even though causing harm would normally be wrong. Still, given the attention Mohist writings devote to models, norms or practices (such as inclusive care or moderate burials), and policies or institutions (such as promoting the worthy), it is unlikely their implicit theory is act consequentialist.

Some of the Mohists' models are not rules or norms but exemplary figures, such as the sage-kings, the benevolent person, or the filially devoted son. The character traits exemplified by these figures are another evaluative focus. People devoted to morality are expected to be benevolent and filially devoted, for example. But these character traits are also unlikely to be the Mohists' primary evaluative focal point. These models do not have explanatory or justificatory priority over others—the sage-kings are just one of the Three Models. Moreover, usually the models the Mohists cite are the sage-kings' or the benevolent person's deeds or intent, not their character traits. Also, as we saw in chapters 2 and 4, models generally are not normatively basic for the Mohists but are only useful guides to action.

Instead of rules, acts, or character, I suggest the Mohists' primary evaluative focal point is *dào*.[27] They frequently use the term *dào* to refer to proposals they defend or rival views they reject, as when they reject the Ruist *dào* on account of its harms (Mz 48/50). When contrasting custom and morality, they ask how abhorrent customs can be the *dào* of benevolence and righteousness (25/80). They repeatedly urge audiences to practice their doctrines on the grounds that they coincide with "the *dào* of the sage-kings" (16/83). They claim their teachings are "really the *dào* of ordering the state and clan and benefiting the myriad people" (31/77). They evaluate different views by asking whether, through "modeling on their statements, applying their plans, and practicing their *dào*," one benefits Heaven, the ghosts, and humanity (10/27). Accordingly, if we are positioning Mohist ethics with respect to familiar varieties of consequentialism such as rule or act consequentialism, it can plausibly be labeled "*dào* consequentialism."

Classifying Mohist ethics this way reflects the structure of their ethical theory as they themselves understand it and ties together the diverse evaluative focal points they employ. To them, the primary unit of human activity and the focus of ethical reflection are not discrete acts by individual agents but a social *dào*. A *dào* can include practices, mores, and institutions, along with models, guidelines, attitudes, and dispositions. To follow a *dào* is not simply to act in certain ways but to be a certain kind of person. Unsurprisingly, then, in some contexts, the Mohists evaluate actions, norms, practices, and institutions by comparison with models or statements, while in others they may evaluate them directly by their consequences or by whether they coincide with the activities of virtuous exemplars. In still other contexts, they evaluate people's character by whether it realizes virtues such as benevolence or filial devotion. Performing proper acts, observing appropriate norms, guiding action and judgment by relevant models, emulating virtuous figures and so cultivating virtuous attitudes and dispositions—all these activities are part of following a *dào*. All can be evaluated by whether they conform to the proper *dào*, the *dào* of promoting the benefit of all.

SPECIAL RELATIONSHIPS

There is a long tradition, stretching back to Mencius, of interpreting the Mohists' doctrine of inclusive care and their commitment to the benefit of all as incompatible with affirming the distinctive value of special personal relationships and the responsibilities arising from them.[28] "Special relationships" here refers to relationships with others that generate distinctive motives and norms beyond the default attitudes and norms that apply to strangers. Examples include relationships with family members and friends, whom we care about and attend to in ways distinct from how we feel about and act toward outsiders. If the Mohists advocate all-inclusive caring about the benefit of all, the interpretation runs, they cannot also value special emotions toward and preferential treatment for kin and other close associates. For inclusive care seems to entail having similar emotions toward everyone and treating everyone similarly, thus denying the special status and demands of family, friends, and other associates.

In fact, however, as we have seen, special relationships are a cornerstone of Mohist ethics. The relational virtues are among the elements of social order and thus count among the goods that determine what is righteous. In discussing order, the Mohists repeatedly mention six types of relationships: those between states or cities, families or clans, and people in general, and those between ruler and subject, father and son, and elder and younger brother. The first three of these are relations between entities or individuals who share no particular tie. These I will call relationships with outsiders. The latter three are relationships between people who share a particular bond of kinship or political association. Such relationships I will call relationships with one's circle. The three types of relationships with one's circle that the Mohists mention are in their view the primary social relationships, in that they constitute the basic social framework within which men of their time inevitably found themselves.[29] People were born, alongside their siblings, into a particular family or clan, within a particular political community under the rule of a sovereign. So an orderly society, as the Mohists see it, is one of healthy relationships between the ruler and his subjects, parents and children, and siblings (most likely including cousins).

Promoting the benefit of all involves balancing the interests of our circle with those of outsiders. Promoting the benefit of our circle in turn involves balancing the interests of our kin with those of our sovereign and state. People thus have three domains of duties toward others: relationships with kin, with the sovereign or state, and with outsiders. As the Mohists depict them, these domains invoke contrasting types of responsibilities or duties. Within our circle, we have a positive duty to promote the welfare of our family, clan, and state. In dealing with outsiders, we have mainly a negative duty to refrain from harming them, along with a secondary, positive duty to share surplus resources when needed (*Mz* 11/4). Since this sharing comes out of our surplus, the Mohists imply that normally the needs of our circle take priority. Duties toward both our circle and outsiders are understood to be reciprocal: others' duties toward us mirror ours toward them.

An intriguing aspect of the Mohist conception of social order is that orderly relations with our circle are characterized by what I have been calling the relational virtues—virtues associated with excellent performance of the relational roles of ruler, subject, father, son, and elder or younger brother. What the texts specify as elements of order are not flourishing relationships with our circle, specifically, but the virtues manifested by those bound together in such relationships—the generosity (*huì* 惠) of rulers toward their subjects, the loyalty (*zhōng* 忠) of subjects to rulers, paternal kindness (*cí* 慈) toward children, children's filial devotion (*xiào* 孝) toward their parents, and fraternal love (*tì* 悌), respect, or harmoniousness. Apparently the Mohists see these virtues as the distinguishing feature of healthy, orderly relationships. A flourishing ruler-subject, father-son, or elder-younger brother bond is just one in which both sides manifest the corresponding virtues. Accordingly, since these virtues are among the basic goods of their ethics, the Mohists think it righteous to be a loving or respectful sibling, devoted child, kind parent, loyal subject, and generous superior.

The implications of the role of the relational virtues in Mohist ethics have been widely overlooked. The Mohists are often taken to hold that "one should have equal concern for, and has equal ethical obligations toward, promoting the well-being of every person, regardless of any special relation a person might have with oneself."[30] Given the place of special relationships and the associated virtues in Mohist ethics, however, this cannot be their view.[31] Barring a radical reconstrual of these relationships and virtues, one cannot be a kind parent, devoted child, or fraternal brother without having distinctive emotions toward family members, devoting special attention to their needs, and giving them preferential treatment over outsiders. Nor can one be a loyal subject or generous ruler without special concern for and preferential treatment of political associates. Nothing in the Mòzǐ suggests the Mohists understand these virtues in some unusual, unconventional way. They thus agree with the commonsense view that our duties to our circle are greater than and take priority over those to outsiders and that special concern for our circle is justified. Indeed, the "Dialectics" codifies this stance into a doctrine it calls relation ranking (lún liè 倫列), according to which we are expected to benefit some people more and others less in proportion to their relation to us (MB EC9). The content of these various duties is determined by the norms of righteousness—by whatever set of practices best promotes the benefit of all.

This aspect of Mohist ethics has been widely neglected, no doubt mainly because the doctrine of inclusive care asks us to care about everyone, viewing others' states and families as we do our own or being committed to the welfare of others' states and families as we are to our own. As the next chapter explains, it is not obvious precisely how we should interpret these descriptions. Whatever interpretation turns out most justified, however, the Mohists clearly expect that our attitudes and conduct toward our circle will be different from those toward outsiders, as the relational virtues entail distinct attachment, attention, and treatment toward those in our circle. The Mohists insist that such attitudes and treatment are compatible with inclusive care, which actually contributes to fulfillment of the relational virtues (Mz 16/64–72).

The status of special relationships is often taken to be a major point of contrast between Mohist and Ruist ethics. The Rú are taken to advocate "graded care" or "care with distinctions," the view that our moral concern for and obligations toward others should be proportional to their relationship to us, such that we have greater concern for and duties to our circle than to outsiders. (Finding a direct statement of such a doctrine in early Ruist texts turns out to be surprisingly difficult, however.) Scholars often construe "graded care" and Mohist inclusive care as logically contrary. In fact, however, some Rú, such as Mencius, advocate extending our concern for our circle outward to include outsiders (Me 1.7, 13.15), while as we have seen, the Mohists endorse special attitudes and treatment toward our circle. Although the details of Mohist and

Ruist views may differ, then, the value they attach to special relationships and the duties they associate with them are fundamentally similar. Any differences between the two sides are likely to be quite narrow.

One possible difference might lie in the relation between special relationships and general moral norms or values. The *Analects* states that filial devotion and brotherliness are the root of benevolence (*LY* 1.2). The *Mencius* suggests that the paradigm of benevolence is children's loving attitude toward their parents, while that of righteousness is the parallel attitude of respect for elder brothers. Moral improvement lies in extending these attitudes to others (*Me* 13.15). These passages imply that in some vague sense general moral norms develop from the attitudes characteristic of special relationships, the latter being conceptually or psychologically basic. Perhaps the general norms are interpreted or justified by analogy to special concern for one's circle, or the ability to follow them is grounded in attitudes developed in family life. The proposed difference from Mohism would be that perhaps for the Mohists the general norms or values are more basic. Special relationships are valued as part of the benefit of all, which is more fundamental. Filial devotion would be valued as a specific expression of the general virtue of benevolence. In fact, however, the Mohists do not ground the relational virtues in the more general values of benevolence and righteousness. The relational virtues are not derived from a more basic conception of benefit; they constitute part of what benefit is.[32] Moreover, since the Mohists model benevolence on filial devotion, the latter seems conceptually more basic, or at least equally basic. As to moral development, the Mohists depict the moral attitude of inclusive care as a matter of expanding our commitment to our own and our circle's welfare so that it includes outsiders (discussed in chapter 6). This relation again implies that they see the moral attitudes as generalizations of attitudes toward our circle, rather than seeing the relational virtues as specifications of general moral attitudes.

Another proposal for distinguishing the role of special relationships in Mohism and Ruism might be that the Rú hold a pluralistic view of value, on which special relationships and the public good are distinct sources of value, while for the Mohists there is only a single source of value, the benefit of all, from which special relationships derive their value.[33] As a result, for the Rú, special relationships may sometimes create duties that conflict with our commitment to the public good. However, this second proposal is also difficult to sustain. The Mohist conception of benefit is complex, including the relational virtues, material wealth, public order, interstate peace, neighborliness, and so forth. These are distinct goods and thus sources of potentially conflicting duties. So for the Mohists too special relationships generate duties that may conflict with broader goods or with duties to outsiders.

A genuine contrast may be that the Mohists' overarching consequentialism gives them a more principled approach to resolving such conflicts. They are likely to advocate taking the course that most increases benefit or reduces harm for society as a whole. By contrast, the Rú sometimes seem to favor duties arising from special relationships. A famous passage in the *Analects* (LY 13.18) contrasts Confucius's *dào* with that of an upright man who reported his father for stealing. Confucius remarks that where he comes from, uprightness lies in family members covering up for one another. The implication is that special duties to family trump public justice. Potential conflicts between special relations and other demands of morality are treated prominently in a series of stories in the *Mencius* about the sage-king Shùn. In one, Mencius is asked what Shùn, a paragon of filiality, would have done had his father committed murder (*Me* 13.35). Mencius replies that as king, Shùn would not have interfered with the magistrate's authority to arrest his father. As a filial son, however, he would have abdicated the throne and helped his father escape. Unlike Confucius's remark, this reply acknowledges the conflicting values at stake—devotion to kin versus Shùn's duty to uphold the law—while nevertheless giving priority to filiality.[34] Mencius proposes, in effect, that Shùn would dissolve the conflict between filiality and his legal role as sovereign by finding a way to nullify one of these sources of duty. For Mencius, filiality takes priority, so Shùn nullifies his legal duties by abdicating and fleeing the state with his father. Self-exile allows him to abrogate his responsibilities as ruler while acknowledging he has violated his duty to the state.

The *Mòzǐ* addresses such conflicts between special relationships and other aspects of morality only obliquely. In a passage in the "Dialogues," Mòzǐ criticizes a prince of Chǔ for rejecting, at the cost of his life, an offer of the throne from the rebel who deposed his father and murdered his elder brothers (*Mz* 49/76–81).[35] To the prince, filial devotion and loyalty ruled out accepting the throne. Mòzǐ's view is that these values were outweighed by the likely benefits of accepting the offer, since once the prince had taken power, he could have restored good order. The implication is that the good consequences of taking power outweighed the prince's devotion to kin. However, the story is inconclusive as to whether the Mohists would generally give duties to kin lower priority than other goods. The prince's choice was between a purely symbolic sacrifice of his life out of respect for his murdered brothers, which offered no concrete benefit to anyone, and an action that might eventually have benefited many people, perhaps including his deposed father. Had he taken the throne, his abrogation of the relational virtues would have been limited, while the potential benefits might have been substantial.

Two stories in *The Annals of Lü Buwei* hint that when special relationships collide with other duties, the Mohists indeed tend to take the course of action likely to yield greater benefit. After the only son of Fù Tūn, an aged Mohist grand master, killed a man, the King of Qín offered to pardon him for Fù's sake. Fù explained that even if the king spared his son, he was obliged to carry out the Mohist *fǎ* (model, law) of punishing homicide by death and maiming by mutilation. "This is how killing and maiming others are prevented, and preventing killing and maiming of others is the most important *yì* (norm of righteousness) in the world." He had his son executed.[36] Like Shùn in Mencius's scenario, Fù holds a position of authority and must choose between protecting a family member and enforcing righteousness on behalf of the community. Unlike Shùn, he does not seek to nullify one of the conflicting duties. Where Mencius places familial duties above other duties, even when the latter are weighty, Fù holds that the overall demands of righteousness and his duties as grand master outweigh his responsibilities to kin, since abrogating the law would have far-reaching harmful consequences.

The other story complicates the picture, as it depicts another Mohist grand master, Mèng Shèng, giving a special relationship priority over his life and those of 180 followers. Mèng formed a covenant with his friend the Lord of Yángchéng to defend his fief in Chǔ (*LSCQ* 19/3). Yángchéng sided with the losing faction in a Chǔ power struggle and fled. Chǔ dispatched an army to confiscate his territory, presenting Mèng with a dilemma. Defending the fief against the vastly larger Chǔ force would be hopeless and pointless, since Yángchéng had already abandoned it. Yet the covenant remained in force and could be dissolved only with both parties' agreement. Mèng reasoned that because of his special relationship to Yángchéng as the latter's teacher, friend, and subject, his only admissible course of action was to uphold the covenant by sacrificing his life, even though doing so was of no immediate benefit to anyone. Sacrificing his own and his regiment's lives would preserve the Mohists' reputation as diligent teachers, worthy friends, and loyal subjects and so exemplify their *yì* and perpetuate the Mohist vocation. He dispatched two envoys to transmit the title of grand master to another Mohist leader and then led his followers to their deaths, most likely by mass suicide. Mèng's stance was that the long-term benefits of preserving the Mohist reputation for virtue in special relationships outweighed the death of an entire band of Mohists. To him, these relationships were so central to the Mohist *dào* that the covenant could not be set aside— even at no cost to the other party—without undermining Mohist values.

These stories imply a contextual approach that seeks the greatest long-term benefit rather than invariably favoring either duties arising from special relationships or more general duties. In the Chǔ prince's case, according to Mòzǐ, a minimal violation of duties to kin would yield substantial benefits for the community, so the latter take priority. In Fù Tūn's case, the harm to his son is extreme, but he plausibly contends that the harm of abrogating the law would be even worse. Mèng Shèng holds that his special duties to Yángchéng plus the consequences of preserving the Mohist reputation for upholding such duties outweigh a massive loss of life. Unless the Ruist position is that duties grounded in special relations *always* trump other morally relevant factors, there is probably no fundamental disagreement between Ruism and Mohism on the value of special relationships. Any differences concern details of how representatives of the two schools weigh different factors in particular contexts, the Rú perhaps favoring special duties, the Mohists greater overall benefit.

HOW DEMANDING IS MOHIST ETHICS?

Mohist ethics has a reputation for being extremely demanding.[37] Ideals such as seeking to promote the benefit of all or caring all-inclusively for others as for oneself may seem impracticably difficult. Ancient sources outside the *Mòzǐ* indicate that some Mohist factions were fervently dedicated to self-sacrificing activism. A well-known *Zhuāngzǐ* passage, quoted in the introduction, describes Mohist groups who sought to emulate the strenuous altruism of the mythical sage-king Yǔ (*Zz* 33/27ff.). Other early sources depict Mohist militias as fanatically devoted to their cause (*LSCQ* 19/3, *Hnz* 1406). We have just seen how Mèng Shèng and his followers chose suicide rather than risk damaging the Mohist reputation for loyalty.

Still, Mohist texts insist that their ethical doctrines are not especially difficult to practice (*Mz* 15/19, 16/81). How do we reconcile this disparity between the Mohists' reputation and their claims? The answer, I suggest, depends on what audience they are addressing and what aspect of their *dào* we are considering. The "Triads" are addressed to "the gentlemen of the world"—especially government officials—and present norms of righteousness these gentlemen are to lead all of society to follow. As we have seen in this and the previous chapter, these norms are not especially stringent. They amount to refraining from harming others, neighborly sharing of know-how, labor, and resources, donating some of our surplus to provide for others with no means of support, and conducting ourselves virtuously toward our circle. By today's standards, all this adds up roughly to being a considerate family member, a responsible member of society, and a decent, helpful neighbor willing to aid the destitute. The Mohist conception of righteousness is at most only slightly more demanding than norms widely accepted in contemporary liberal democratic societies. The formulations by which the Mohists express the attitudes associated with some of these norms can sound demanding. One formulation of inclusive care, for instance, calls on us to "regard others' persons as we regard our own person" (15/12). But the concrete conduct associated with these formulations is roughly just what many people today would consider basic moral decency. Indeed, one factor contributing to the Mohists' reputation for strenuous moral standards may have been that they were the first in their clan-centered, quasi-feudal society to strongly advocate general norms of decency applicable to those outside one's circle—people to whom one was not related in any way. Theirs was a traditional, largely agricultural society in which most people were related as kin or neighbors to nearly everyone they knew and norms of conduct were largely determined by one's relational social role. In this context, the idea that we should care about outsiders may have sounded radical.

As previously noted, the Mohist conception of benevolence is a more demanding ideal than righteousness. Righteousness requires only conforming to norms whose general observance promotes the benefit of all. Benevolence may require sometimes acting directly to promote the benefit of all. Yet it is righteousness, not benevolence, that constitutes the minimal moral standard the Mohists expect everyone to meet. To fall short of righteousness is to do something wrong and so be blameworthy. By contrast, to be benevolent is to achieve a degree of moral goodness that exceeds the basic requirements of righteousness. A person whose conduct conforms to righteousness yet falls short of benevolence has room for moral improvement yet may not be blameworthy. So even if the demands of benevolence are relatively stringent, Mohist ethics as a whole might be only moderately demanding, since not everyone is expected to consistently meet the standard of benevolence. Moreover, if we again consider the chief audience for the "Triads," the virtue of benevolence may be intended to appeal to officials and other powerful figures for whom, given their social status, taking direct action to promote the benefit of all may have been a reasonable demand—indeed, it may again have amounted to little more than basic decency. For people of less-influential status, perhaps even the demands of benevolence could be met simply by following and promoting the Mohist dào.

Unlike the "Triads," parts of the "Dialogues" advocate a considerably more stringent ideal of self-cultivation aimed at moral sagehood.[38] Here we do find hints of the self-sacrificing extremism that, according to the Zhuāngzǐ, many

Mohists adopted late in the movement's history. One passage suggests that righteousness lies largely in helping others (Mz 49/42). Another implies that if righteousness does not prevail in the world, one can only work even harder to achieve it (47/6). Still another advocates eliminating the influence of emotions and other potential sources of bias and dedicating oneself wholly to righteousness, so as to become a sage or moral saint:

> Our Master Mòzǐ said, "You must eliminate the six biases. When silent, ponder; when speaking, instruct; when acting, work. Make these three alternate and surely you will be a sage. You must eliminate happiness and eliminate anger, eliminate joy and eliminate sorrow, eliminate fondness and eliminate dislike, and use benevolence and righteousness. Your hands, feet, mouth, nose, and ears undertaking righteousness, surely you will be a sage." (Mz 47/19–20)

The "six biases" are affective attitudes or passions—happiness, anger, joy, sorrow, preferences, and aversions. We are to reject easily biased emotions and preferences as grounds for action in favor of guidance by the virtue of benevolence and the objective, impartial norms of righteousness. The passage calls for total dedication to morality. One is to devote every thought, utterance, and action to benevolence and righteousness, setting everything else aside. No room is left for any activity without positive moral value, derived from contributing to the benefit of all. Morality here is not merely a constraint on our conduct or a normative status but an all-encompassing end in itself. This sage ideal is thus considerably more demanding than the doctrines of the "Triads," which require only that everyone live by norms whose collective practice promotes the benefit of all.

However, these passages—and the "Dialogues" as a whole—are probably aimed at a different audience from the "Triads." The sage ideal is directed at devoted Mohist followers, who had dedicated their lives to the movement's ideals. Given the religious character of the Mohist movement, the injunction to purge the "six biases" and devote oneself wholly to morality is comparable to the strict self-discipline adopted by adherents of a devout religious order. Contemporary analogues would be members of an elite military unit, ascetic religious community, or other organization devoted to an austere code of conduct. Just as we do not expect everyone to join the Marines or the Jesuits, however, the Mohists give no indication that they expect the entire populace to pursue moral sagehood or enlist in a Mohist militia. If we consider its likely audience, the sagehood ideal is easy enough to understand. It is hardly surprising that, in a world of scarcity and turmoil, some people might dedicate their lives to pursuing a morally more satisfactory state of affairs. Indeed, the commitment to pursuing sagehood can be seen as a profound expression of spirituality or religiousness.[39] Nor was this level of dedication unusual among adherents of rival *dào*. The life of the Rú was arduous, requiring years of intense study of classical poetry, history, and music, along with mastery of rituals governing all aspects of life, including the minutiae of one's posture, gait, and countenance. Living up to Daoist ideals would have required formidable dedication. Many ethical-religious movements place stringent demands on devotees while allowing more moderate norms for laypeople.

In one respect, I suggest, the Mohists' *dào* may indeed have been too demanding of the layperson. This stringency arises mainly from their economic doctrines, however, and only indirectly from their ethical teachings. To help ensure adequate resources in times of hardship, the Mohists advocated an extremely frugal, plain lifestyle for everyone. As chapter 8 explains, this austerity grew partly from legitimate economic concerns, partly from their overly narrow conception of benefit. Although in times of deprivation the Mohist economic program might save lives, in a more prosperous society people would almost surely have found it excessively severe.

CRITICAL ASSESSMENT

Mohist ethics deserves praise for recognizing the importance to morality of impartiality and of benefit or welfare. Both these features of the Mohist ethical theory are probably crucial elements of a defensible moral theory. At the same time, however, the major flaws in Mohist ethics arise from its treatment of precisely these two points.

First, extending a point raised in chapter 4, I suggest that in the end there remains a tendency in Mohist ethics to conflate the impartiality required for morality—impartial justification—with an attitude of impartial commitment to promoting the interests of all. In chapter 4, we saw that the Mohists successfully avoided conflating the norms and attitudes of an impartial, divine Heaven with those that morality requires of us. Rather than advocate that we directly emulate Heaven, they advocate following norms that Heaven intends for us to follow. Still, the Mohist conception of benevolence suggests that the attitudes of a person who is morally excellent will indeed resemble those of Heaven itself. The task of such a person "is surely to diligently seek to promote the benefit of all the world" (Mz 16/1). So in the end perhaps the Mohists do not distinguish impartial justification from impartial motivation clearly enough. (This problem arises yet again in chapter 6 when I discuss inclusive care.) The Mohists' consequentialism perhaps inclines them toward the same confusion. Since their criterion of morality is what promotes the benefit of all, they may tend to think of a commitment to doing what is morally right as a standing commitment to promote the benefit of all.

The second major shortcoming of Mohist ethical thought is its excessively narrow conception of value. A flaw in itself, this narrowness also prevents the Mohists from noticing and addressing other potential problems. The "Triads" and "Dialogues" ground moral value in a conception of benefit that comprises only material wealth, sufficient population, and orderly, harmonious social relations. Granted that these are important goods, a natural thought is that other goods ought to count as benefits too—examples might include psychological happiness, physical pleasure, or personal fulfillment through meaningful projects. The "Triads" sidestep the problem of justifying their account of benefit by focusing on a narrow range of basic goods that the Mohists reasonably assume their audience will agree are indispensable. We can grant that if, through no fault of their own, members of our immediate community are starving, providing for their basic needs should take priority over funding entertainment that pleases the rest of us. Indeed, the Mohists may be right that any society in which some people's subsistence needs go unmet while others enjoy lives of excess has strayed from the *dào*.[40] However, suppose Mohist policies were actually put into practice, with brilliant results: society was well governed, people's material needs were provided for, state defense was robust, the economic outlook was stable, and the community's wealth was growing steadily. Society having achieved these goods, even the most austere Mohist would be forced to address the issue of just what—beyond wealth, population, and order—should count as benefit. A consensus might be difficult to come by, as critics could plausibly argue that enjoying luxury items and musical entertainment or allowing a plurality of overlapping but distinct conceptions of *yì* might contribute to the benefit of all, by providing more goods to more people.[41]

Beyond these problems, I suggest the Mohists' conception of morality is also too narrow insofar as benefit alone serves as a source of moral value. To be sure, the Mohist conception of benefit is complex, comprising different types of goods. Still, the concept of benefit alone probably cannot explain why all the various things we consider morally good or right are such. Indeed, some of what the Mohists themselves include within the scope of benefit, such as the relational virtues or preventing exploitation of the poor, ignorant, and weak, could probably be explained more directly and plausibly by acknowledging distinct kinds of moral value, such as the intrinsic value of personal relationships or of individuals' dignity.

Doubting that benefit is the only source of moral value naturally also prompts us to question whether consequentialism is the correct approach to ethical theory. This book is not the proper place for a detailed critique of consequentialism, but in the context of evaluating Mohist thought, it is worth sketching the problem, even if the exposition is too brisk. Let's grant that good or bad consequences—benefits or harms—are often relevant to determining what course of action is morally justified. The difficulty for the Mohists and other consequentialists lies in establishing that consequences are the *only* such relevant factor. Consider an example the Mohists themselves touch on: slavery.[42] They argue that, along with other aspects of military conquest, enslaving the people of a defeated state is immoral. Their official explanation is that this and other consequences of war benefit neither Heaven, the ghosts, nor people.[43] But is slavery wrong merely because it harms its victims? Suppose the enslaved prisoners were from an impoverished, crime-ridden state, and after their capture they lived comfortably as servants in a wealthy, orderly state. By the Mohists' criteria, one might argue that enslavement had benefited them. Still, most of us—probably including the Mohists—would deny that this benefit justifies their enslavement. The challenge for the Mohists is to explain why not. Non-Mohists can suggest that slavery is wrong not just because it is usually harmful but because it contravenes other crucial values, such as people's autonomy, dignity, or exercise of their characteristic capabilities. A Mohist might rejoin that trampling on such values amounts to harming people, and so Mohist ethics can indeed explain why benevolent slavery is wrong. However, subsuming such values under the concepts of benefit and harm seems redundant and gratuitous, a Procrustean attempt to assimilate into consequentialism reasons that are fundamentally not consequentialist.[44] Indeed, this redundancy sometimes emerges even in the Mohists' own explanations of immoral conduct. One passage explains that theft is wrong because the stolen items are the product of others' labor and thus not the thief's property (Mz 28/57). According to their ethical theory, the Mohists' official explanation of why theft is wrong must be that the practice of appropriating what is not one's own is harmful to all. To a critic of consequentialism, however, this explanation will seem redundant. Other things being equal, that thieves take what is not theirs is already a sufficient explanation of the wrong. Indeed, it is not obvious that theft actually is harmful to all, nor that, were it beneficial, it would thereby be right. Without purporting to offer a knockdown critique of Mohist-style consequentialism, then, I suggest that a more persuasive ethical theory would acknowledge different types of moral value rather than subsuming all moral value under the single label of benefits to be promoted.

A third respect in which the Mohist conception of value seems too narrow is that the Mohists tend to assume that moral value is the only kind there is, or at least the only kind that matters. As I have remarked, they disregard aesthetic value and devote little attention to personal happiness or fulfillment or to a conception of well-rounded human excellence. For them, the best sort of life—for a committed Mohist—is that of the benevolent person or the sage, a life of total devotion to morality and to promoting the benefit of all, construed as material welfare, sufficient population, and social order. Their texts hint at recognition of other values, as when they point out that ancestral sacrifices offer an occasion for an enjoyable gathering (Mz 31/102) or enthusiastically describe dialectics as a path to knowledge of the myriad things (45/1). However, their texts, especially the "Dialogues," give the impression that morality is all that really counts. The problem with this stance is that morality may not be all that matters, and a life of total devotion to it may not be the best sort of life. Many goods that enrich our lives are morally neutral; examples might include beauty, knowledge, humor, and excellence in various activities. A flourishing, well-rounded life may be one that makes a significant place for the pursuit or appreciation of such nonmoral goods.[45]

Mohist ethics thus contrasts with the dominant orientation of classical Greek ethics and that of classical Chinese texts as diverse as the Ruist *Xúnzǐ* and the Daoist *Zhuāngzǐ*. Much ancient ethical thought, in both Greece and China, is concerned with the good or flourishing life of the individual. A widely shared assumption is that leading a morally good life is in the individual's own interest, since such a life is the most excellent or happiest for us as individuals. The morally good and prudentially good life converge: what is morally best turns out to be what is also prudentially best for us as persons.[46] For the Mohists, by contrast, we seek to be benevolent and righteous simply for the sake of being benevolent and righteous, not because this is prudentially the best life for the individual qua individual. Much as Mòzǐ himself tends to disappear as a person into his teachings, Mohist ethics tends to make individuals vanish as particular persons into their devotion to the collective welfare. A formula repeated throughout the middle and later strata of the "Triads" hints at the Mohist ideal of the good individual life. People who, "within, really desire to be benevolent and righteous and seek to be superior officers; above, desire to conform to the *dào* of the sage-kings; and below, desire to conform to the benefit of the state and the people" will not fail to examine and practice Mohist doctrines.[47] The aim of an excellent life—that of a superior person—is simply to be benevolent and righteous, living according to the *dào* of the sage-kings and so promoting the benefit of all. Such a life is justified because it emulates the highest ethical models, the sage-kings and Heaven. There is no implication that it is good or fulfilling for the individual as an individual, nor any hint that a fulfilling individual life might be something of value in itself.

Of course, the goods that underwrite the Mohist conception of righteousness are just basic prudential goods such as material wealth, a flourishing family life, stable, harmonious social relations, and public security. Those who commit to the Mohist *dào* can expect to enjoy such goods, along with praise and recognition from peers and superiors and perhaps even honored status as officers (*shì* 士) in their community. So the Mohist *dào* will not clash with individual adherents' material interests and may even promote them. The issue is that the operative conception of prudential interests is very thin.

To reiterate a point with which I began the chapter, however, the Mohists' historical context makes it easy to understand and excuse their constricted conception of value. They do not endorse this conception by way of rejecting some more well-rounded view.[48] Rather, they simply assume it as obvious. Their texts imply economic and political circumstances in which adversity is never far off and meeting the subsistence needs of the poor is an urgent task to which any conscientious person should attend. Moreover, the "Triads" are addressed chiefly to socially and politically influential gentlemen the Mohists see as responsible for ensuring society's needs are met. For this audience, in circumstances as difficult as those depicted, a life devoted to benevolence and righteousness, in the Mohists' narrow sense, might indeed be justified. Adversity is not a universal or perpetual feature of human life, however. An adequate *dào* must address more prosperous circumstances as well. Though excusable, the narrowness of the Mohist conception of value is nevertheless a flaw in a general account of "the *dào* of benevolence and righteousness," which the Mohists do seem to be offering.

CONCLUDING REMARKS

The basic structure of Mohist ethics is simple yet profound. At its base stands the notion of impartial concern for the benefit of all, as epitomized by the standpoint of Heaven, an ideally benevolent, impartial agent who cares equally about everyone's welfare. From this foundation, the Mohists develop a consequentialist theory of benevolence and righteousness in terms of a set of goods that constitute benefit or welfare. Practices, policies, and actions are justified by their effectiveness in promoting the benefit of all. The theory strikes a balance between the importance of special relationships and universal duties to all. It recognizes that individuals live within a web of social relations, which partly define their identities and duties, and that flourishing social relationships are a crucial part of human welfare. It assigns virtues a role in guiding action and in constituting good social relations. The theory is loosely formulated, inelegantly expressed, and supported by rudimentary, at times simplistic, arguments. Yet the general consequentialist approach it sets forth remains one of the major alternatives in ethical theory today and can easily be modified and extended in sophisticated ways.

The problems with Mohist ethics arise mainly from its ambitiousness and one-sidedness, both of which are instructive in helping us better understand the nature of morality. The Mohists' approach is unrealistically ambitious insofar as it attempts to resolve all ethical issues by referring back to a single model, the benefit of all. It is one-sided in holding that benefit alone, and indeed a highly restrictive conception of benefit, is the only value that need be considered in guiding conduct. This one-sidedness is the basis for the one sound criticism that Mencius directs at Mohism. Mencius accuses Mòzǐ of "injuring the *dào*" by "grasping one thing"—the benefit of all—to the neglect of a hundred others (*Me* 13.26). To be fair, the Mohist conception of benefit is complex and incorporates multiple sources of value. Still, Mohist ethics does advocate guiding conduct by a single, master action-guiding distinction, benefit versus harm. The implication of the Mencian criticism is that the *dào* cannot be this simple. The range of values we recognize and constraints we actually encounter are too varied and complex to be subsumed under any single good, let alone one as narrow as the Mohist conception of benefit.

6

INCLUSIVE CARE

For Others as for Oneself

THE ETHICAL MODEL (*fǎ* 法) for which the Mohists are most well known is inclusive care (*jiān ài* 兼愛), the attitude of caring about others as we care about ourselves. This chapter presents an interpretation of inclusive care, explains the Mohists' arguments for it, and considers to what extent it is justified.

Discussions of Mohist thought occasionally characterize inclusive care as the central principle of Mohist ethics.[1] In fact, the Mohists' arguments clearly indicate that inclusive care is based on the more fundamental norm of promoting the benefit of all. Still, the conceptual link between inclusive care and benefiting all is tighter than these arguments might suggest at first glance, for the mark of those who care inclusively about everyone is just that they are inclined to benefit others as well as themselves. Inclusive care is thus one manifestation of commitment to the benefit of all. The Mohists depict it as the psychological attitude that underlies and motivates the practice of interacting with others in a mutually beneficial way. As we will see, the link they presuppose between care and benefit explains why, in their ethics, care must be all-inclusive and even equal for all.

The doctrine of inclusive care is sometimes mistakenly taken to imply that we should feel equal or impartial love for all or that we have equal obligations to everyone, even distant strangers.[2] These misunderstandings prompt the criticism that Mohist ethics is impractically demanding or conflicts with the deep-seated human tendency to feel greater affection for one's circle and to place their interests before others'. As this chapter will explain, inclusive care does not in fact entail that we should feel the same emotions toward or that we have equal obligations toward all. It is only moderately, not excessively demanding, and it is compatible with having distinctive emotions and obligations toward those we hold near and dear. Inclusive care is in effect the Mohist analogue to equal regard for all or equal consideration of everyone's interests, attitudes some philosophers today view as fundamental to morality.[3] Indeed, it overlaps roughly with what on some views of morality we might call the moral attitude.

The first major section of the chapter examines how the Mohists use the words "inclusive" (*jiān* 兼) and "care" (*ài* 愛) and thus what the phrase "inclusive care" (*jiān ài*) implies for them. The next section interprets the doctrine of inclusive care on the basis of the major arguments for it. Rather than a single doctrine of inclusive care, the texts actually present a range of positions. For brevity, I focus on spelling out and critiquing the strongest version. The third major section examines the Mohists' responses to four objections to inclusive care. The chapter concludes with a critical evaluation of the doctrine.

PRELIMINARY REFLECTIONS

The phrase *jiān ài* is sometimes translated as "universal love" but is more aptly interpreted as a kind of all-inclusive care about or all-embracing consideration for everyone. *Jiān* is typically used as an adverb interpretable as "together" or "jointly" or as a noun referring to an aggregate or a whole. In the phrase *jiān ài*, it has the connotation of including everyone together, such that our attitude of *ài* is directed at the whole of humanity. *Ài* (care, love, concern) has a wide semantic scope, ranging from strong affection to dispassionate concern. It may refer to a parent's love for a child, a woman's affection for a good-looking man, or fondness for someone's physical appearance. But it can also refer to begrudging wasted expenses, concern about the health of one's livestock, or concern for the welfare of one's political subjects.[4] Although *ài* may be accompanied by emotions, it need not involve a feeling of affection or any other occurrent emotional state. As we will see, on the weakest construal consistent with what the Mohists say about it, *ài* may refer simply to a commitment to others' welfare such that one is disposed to treat them well, if they are members of one's circle—those with whom we have kinship or political relations—and to refrain from harming them, if they are not. "Care" seems the English word with the most similar semantic range, along with a similar degree of vagueness and ambiguity. Like *ài*, "care" allows for potential confusion between affection and a much weaker attitude, roughly just a preference. So I will render *ài* as "care" and *jiān ài* as "inclusive care."

To understand the Mohist conception of care, we need to understand its relations to several other notions with which it is regularly paired or contrasted. Mohist writings draw a tight connection between care and benefit (lì 利). In its full form, as presented in the middle to later strata of the "Triads," the doctrine of inclusive care is that people are to follow the model of "inclusively caring for each other and in interaction benefiting each other" (Mz 15/10, 16/48). The texts regularly pair care with benefit, referring to the two jointly as "care and benefit" or speaking of "caring about and benefiting the people," "caring about and benefiting others," and "caring about and benefiting each other."⁵ Apparently, the Mohists see the attitude of care and the beneficial conduct associated with it as both causally and conceptually related. The relation is underscored by the attitudes and conduct they contrast with care. The antithesis of care is detesting or showing contempt (wù 惡) for others. The absence of care is associated with disorderly conduct injurious to others, such as military aggression, clan feuding, theft or robbery, oppression, exploitation, and failure to fulfill the relational virtues. Care for the Mohists thus does not contrast with a neutral attitude of having no preferences or dispositions toward others, whether positive or negative. It contrasts with disregard for them and a willingness to injure them to benefit oneself. The sharp dichotomy built into this conception of care explains why the Mohists advocate all-inclusive and even equal care for everyone. Given their understanding of care, to have any regard for others at all we must care about them. To give people equal moral consideration, we must care equally about them all. As we will see, this distinctive conception of care explains key features of Mohist ethics but also generates deep problems.

Two passages contrast the attitude of care with that of using someone or something as a means. In one, well-qualified but underpaid officials complain that their ruler does not really care about them but has appointed them to high-ranking yet low-paying posts merely as a pretence for using them (Mz 9/23). The result, according to the Mohists, is that people will not trust the officials—since they will need to find ways to augment their income—and the officials in turn will not feel kinship with their ruler. The other passage, from the "Dialectics," explains that "caring about oneself is not in order to use oneself. Not like caring about a horse" (MB A7). We care about the welfare of a horse because we use it as a means of transportation. By contrast, the morally pertinent form of care is to care about others for their own sake.⁶

Building on the conceptual link between care and benefit, we can characterize the Mohists' core moral notion of care as the attitude of being committed to or positively disposed toward a person's welfare, for that person's own sake and not as a means, such that we are attentive to the person's well-being, and, other things being equal, distinguishing something as beneficial to the person tends to move us to pursue it on the person's behalf, while distinguishing something as harmful to the person tends to move us to prevent or eliminate it. Inclusive care would then entail being committed to everyone's welfare in this way.[7] In calling this a "core" moral notion of care, I mean that care might also frequently, or even typically, be associated with emotions, desires, or other states. However, for the Mohists, the sort of attentiveness and responsiveness I am describing are probably sufficient to ascribe care to someone. In addition to explaining the links between care and benefit sketched so far, this characterization of inclusive care coheres well with a fragment in the "Greater Selection" implying that care for a particular person arises from consideration of the person's benefit. That is, according to the fragment, the habit of taking a person's welfare into consideration in some sense produces the attitude of care.[8] On the interpretation I propose, the attitude of inclusive care springs from regularly considering the benefit of all, rather than only oneself or one's circle.

The "other things being equal" disclaimer in this characterization is crucial, since much of the time other things will *not* be equal. Various factors may override the disposition to pursue benefit on behalf of those we care about, such as another, more important good, the benefit of others who take priority, or distance from the objects of care. For instance, according to Mohist ethical theory, filial devotion (*xiào* 孝) and other relational virtues are elements of the benefit of all. As a general social practice, inclusive care cannot require that we forgo these goods to contribute to the welfare of strangers, lest it reduce, rather than promote, the benefit of all. Moreover, care for others might not be manifested by directly pursuing benefit for each of them as individuals. It could be manifested by following norms that, practiced jointly by everyone, promote the benefit of all.

On the proposed interpretation, then, the Mohist conception of care amounts roughly to a reliable disposition to take the welfare of those we care about as a reason for action. Consistent with the implications of Mohist epistemology and logic, sketched in chapter 2, however, the Mohists do not frame their position in terms of the reasons we recognize and act on. Indeed, an interesting question about their ethics is why they express their normative stance in terms of inclusive care, rather than simply what we are morally justified in doing. The answer, I suggest, is that they conceive of action as generally springing from dispositions, habits, and skills to discriminate and respond to things in certain ways, not from explicitly recognized reasons or deliberate reasoning processes. Roughly, inclusive care is simply a reliable disposition to benefit others in the ways Mohist normative theory endorses. The Mohists' theoretical focus is on justifying this disposition and developing it in their audience, rather than on advocating that people's conduct should follow from certain processes of reasoning or certain sorts of reasons.

This characterization of care also helps to clarify an important difference between the roles of care and benefit in Mohist ethics, signaled by the modifiers in the two parts of the slogan "Inclusively care about each other and in interaction benefit each other" (*jiān xiāng ài, jiāo xiāng lì* 兼相愛, 交相利). The Mohists advocate that our caring attitude be all-inclusive, encompassing everyone. But beneficial conduct will generally be directed only toward people with whom we actually interact.[9] Since care refers primarily to an attitude—a commitment to people's welfare—rather than to actual conduct, we can care about others without actually benefiting them.[10] Hence the Mohists hold that we can care about people all-inclusively without benefiting everyone or treating everyone equally.

THE ARGUMENT FROM CONSEQUENCES

The *Mòzǐ* presents three main arguments to justify inclusive care. The chief argument, which I will call the Argument from Consequences, is the centerpiece of each of the three "Inclusive Care" books. The argument contends that the practice of inclusive care is right because it has beneficial consequences. It thus corresponds to the third of the Mohists' Three Models, as introduced in chapter 2. The second argument is that inclusive care conforms to two further criteria proposed in the doctrine of the Three Models: the deeds of the sage-kings and the documents of the former kings. Since the Mohists present this argument in replying to the "Objection from Impossibility," I will touch on it briefly in the later section devoted to that objection. The third argument is that caring for others is Heaven's intent. This argument was discussed in chapter 4, so I will not address it further here. The Argument from Consequences will be the focus of this section.

In outline, the argument is that harm to all is caused by people's excluding other persons, families, cities, and states from the scope of their care. This exclusion leads to injury, crime, violence, and failure to fulfill the relational virtues. Were people to practice inclusive care, they would eliminate these harms and promote the welfare of all. The three "Inclusive Care" books present different versions of the argument, which articulate three somewhat different conceptions of inclusive care.[11] The differences are twofold, pertaining to how the attitude of inclusive care is characterized and the examples that illustrate its practice. Comparing the three versions, we find that the Mohists' stance appears to have grown moderately more demanding over time.

VERSION 1: CARING ABOUT OTHERS

The first "Inclusive Care" book likely predates the full development of the Mohist ethical theory as presented in the middle to late strata of the "Triads." It makes no mention of promoting the benefit of all, the fundamental norm in most Mohist writings. Its basic good is order (zhì 治), not benefit. It does not use the technical term "model," and unlike most of the "Triads," its argument is based on the abstract model of an ideal sage, rather than the benevolent person or the historical sage-kings. Instead of the full list of relational virtues, it mentions only two, subordinates' filial devotion toward superiors and superiors' paternal kindness toward subordinates. Mohist texts usually associate these virtues only with familial relations, but here they cover both familial and political relations. Where objections and replies make up the bulk of the other two essays, this brief text concludes immediately after the main argument. Intriguingly, the text does not attribute the argument to Mòzǐ, presenting it instead as an elucidation of a single dictum ascribed to him: "It's unacceptable not to encourage caring about others" (Mz 14/19).

The text argues that to bring order to the world, the sage must know the causes of disorder, just as a doctor must know the cause of a disease before treating it. The cause of disorder, it claims, is failure to care for one another, which leads people to injure others in pursuit of their own benefit. A passage I translated in chapter 1 (Mz 14/4ff.) contends that all the disorderly conduct in the world—people's failure to treat their circle virtuously, robbery and theft, feuding between clans, and wars between states—arises from the failure to care about one another, which leads people to injure others in order to benefit themselves.[12] Were inclusive care to be practiced, disorder would vanish:

> Suppose all the world inclusively cared about each other, caring about others as they care about themselves. Would there still be those who are not filially devoted? Viewing their father, elder brother, and ruler as themselves, how could they behave without filial devotion? Would there still be those who are not paternally kind? Viewing their younger brother, son, and subject as themselves, how could they behave without kindness? So there would be no unfiliality or unkindness. Would there still be robbers and thieves? Viewing others' houses as their house, who would steal? Viewing others as themselves, who would injure them? So there would be no robbers or thieves. Would there still be high officials

disordering each other's clans and various lords attacking each other's states? Viewing others' clan as their clan, who would disorder them? Viewing others' states as their state, who would attack them? So there would be no high officials disordering each other's clans or various lords attacking each other's states. (Mz 14/12–16)

Thus "if all the world inclusively cares about each other, there is order; if in interaction they detest each other, there is disorder" (14/18–19). The text concludes that "as to our Master Mòzǐ saying 'It's unacceptable not to encourage caring for others,' this is the reason for it" (14/19).

The first point to note is that the argument is not explicitly a moral one at all. The concepts of benevolence and righteousness are not mentioned. Order is assumed as a basic value, but for all the text says this value could be prudential, not moral. (Again, these features suggest an early date of composition.)

"Inclusively caring about each other" is characterized in two different ways, as "caring about others as one cares about oneself" and also as viewing others' persons, houses (or families), clans, and states "as one's own." Interpretation of both is complicated by the hypothetical formulation of the argument. The text does not directly advocate caring about others as we care about ourselves, but only suggests, counterfactually, "suppose all the world inclusively cared about each other, caring about others as they care about themselves." It explicitly advocates only the weaker doctrine of encouraging "caring about others" (ài rén 愛人). "Care" here probably refers primarily to consideration for others, not an emotion. When the text says that people injure others because they do not care about them, the implication is probably not that they lack affection for others but that they fail to take anyone but themselves into consideration.

For this text, the practical demands of inclusive care are not at all demanding. Were everyone to care about one another, people would refrain from harming others and would treat their circle virtuously: "State and state would not attack each other, clan and clan would not disorder each other; there would be no robbers and thieves; rulers and subjects, fathers and sons could all be filially devoted and paternally kind" (Mz 14/17). In terms of conduct, inclusive care requires only that we refrain from injuring others and fulfill the relational virtues. The ideal of benefiting "all the world" has not yet been introduced.

VERSION 2: MUTUAL CARE AND BENEFIT

The argument of the second book begins by characterizing the conduct of the benevolent person, a moral exemplar. The benevolent person takes as his purpose "promoting the benefit of the world and eliminating harm to the world" (Mz 15/1). Harm is identified as "states attacking each other, clans subverting each other, people injuring each other, rulers and subjects not being generous and loyal, fathers and sons not being paternally kind and filially devoted, and elder and younger brothers not being peaceful and harmonious" (15/2–3). An excerpt from this argument translated in the introduction claims that these and other harms arise from a failure to care about one another (15/4ff.). People these days care only about their own state, clan, or person, and so do not hesitate to harm others. Thus the benevolent person condemns the failure to care about others and replaces it with the model of "inclusively caring about each other and in interaction benefiting each other." Whereas the first essay characterizes inclusive care as caring about others as we care about ourselves and viewing others "as oneself," this essay describes it as viewing others as one views oneself:

> That being so, then the model of inclusively caring about each other and in interaction benefiting each other, what will it be like? Our Master Mòzǐ stated, "View others' states as you view your own state; view others' clans as you view your own clan; view others' selves as you view yourself." (Mz 15/11–12)

If people adopt this model as a guide to conduct, all forms of harm to and abuse of others will cease:

> Thus if the various lords care about each other, they will not go to war; if the heads of clans care about each other, they will not subvert each other; if people care about each other, they will not injure each other. If rulers and subjects care about each other, they will be generous and loyal; if fathers and sons care about each other, they will be paternally kind and filially devoted; if elder and younger brothers care about each other, they will be peaceful and harmonious. The people of the world all caring about each other, the strong will not oppress the weak, the many will not intimidate the few, the wealthy will not humiliate the poor, the noble will not be contemptuous of the common, and the cunning will not deceive the ignorant. All the world's calamities, subversion, resentment, and hatred, what can prevent them from arising is produced by caring about each other. Hence the benevolent praise it. (Mz 15/12–15)

The benevolent person—a model of what is benevolent and righteous—seeks to promote benefit and eliminate harm to all. "Caring about each other" is beneficial to all and failure to care harmful. So the benevolent person praises inclusive care and condemns failure to care. Unlike the argument in the first essay, this is explicitly a moral argument, based on the model of the benevolent person. Although the argument does not directly contend that inclusive care is morally right, the book concludes by claiming that we must practice inclusive care because it will increase people's wealth, reduce poverty, and is "the model of the sage-kings, the *dào* of order in the world" (15/41–42). Since this coda mentions several Mohist criteria of righteousness, the implication is that inclusive care is morally right.

The major development in this version is that the care ideal is now spelled out explicitly as "inclusively caring about each other and in interaction benefiting each other," a model that specifies both the attitude of care and the associated conduct, mutual benefit. People are each to care about everyone else, such that their interactions with others are to both sides' benefit. The sorts of mutually beneficial interactions implicated are again limited in scope and not especially demanding. As before, people are to fulfill the relational virtues toward those in their circle while refraining from mistreating outsiders. This version of the argument goes beyond the first in specifying that, besides aggression and crime, such mistreatment includes oppression and exploitation of the powerless, minorities, the poor, the common, and the ignorant.

The appeal to the model of the benevolent person raises the question of how benevolence relates to care. The benevolent person seeks to promote the benefit of all and thus presumably cares about everyone. Might inclusive care simply be another label for a benevolent attitude? Instead of presenting a case for inclusive care as a distinct moral norm, perhaps the Mohists are merely elucidating their conception of benevolence. I suggest, however, that benevolence and inclusive care are indeed distinct, in several ways. The benevolent seek to promote the benefit of all, regardless of whether anyone benefits them in turn. Benevolence might sometimes require altruistic self-sacrifice in pursuit of the greater good. By contrast, inclusive care is specifically a reciprocal ideal, not an altruistic one,[13] and as such is significantly less demanding. It does not ask people to directly pursue the benefit of all. It asks them to care about one another such that their interactions benefit both sides. In principle, it does not demand that people regularly act in others' interest at a cost to themselves. As we will see in the following, the Mohists eventually indicate that inclusive care calls for limited altruism toward certain groups who may be unable to reciprocate, such as the elderly poor. But the core idea is for people to treat one another in mutually beneficial ways. Another difference from benevolence is that inclusive care is specifically a social ideal. The virtue of benevolence can be realized by a single person independently of others. By contrast, because of its reciprocal nature, inclusive care can be fully realized only when a group of people practice it jointly.

VERSION 3: FOR OTHERS AS FOR ONESELF

In substance, the third version of the Argument from Consequences is similar to the second. The benevolent person seeks to promote the benefit of all. Inclusive care promotes the benefit of all and so is *shì* 是 (right); its opposite has harmful consequences and so is *fēi* 非 (wrong). The two arguments have interesting differences in formulation, however, the doctrines in the third essay being more fully developed and probably of a later date. "Inclusion" (*jiān*) is introduced as a technical term denoting "caring about others and benefiting them," while "exclusion" (*bié* 別) is introduced to denote its opposite, "detesting others and injuring them" (Mz 16/6). The more abstract concept of *wèi* 為, "for the sake of" or "on behalf of," replaces the earlier formulations "caring for others as one cares for oneself" and "viewing others as one views oneself." One might argue that the metaphor of viewing others as we view ourselves is confused, since logically and psychologically it is impossible to view others "as ourselves," given that we are distinct persons. The new formulation mitigates this problem, at least partly. The attitude of "caring about others and benefiting them" is now characterized as being "for others," or committed on their behalf, as we are "for" ourselves.[14] The crux of this version runs as follows:

> That being so, then what is the reason that inclusion can replace exclusion?
>
> He said, "Suppose people were for others' states as for their state. Then who alone would deploy his state to attack others' states? One would be for others as for oneself. Were people for others' cities as for their city, then who alone would deploy his city to assault others' cities? One would be for others as for oneself. Were people for others' clans as for their clan, then who alone would deploy his clan to disorder others' clans? One would be for others as for oneself. That being so, then states and cities not attacking and assaulting each other, people and clans not disordering and injuring each other, is this harm to the world? Or is it benefit to the world? Then we must say, it is benefit to the world.
>
> "If we try to fundamentally investigate what these many benefits are produced from, what are they produced from? Are they produced from detesting others and injuring others? Then we must say, it's not so. We must say, they are produced from caring about others and benefiting others. If we demarcate and

name caring about others and benefiting others in the world, is it 'exclusion'? Or is it 'inclusion'? Then we must say it is 'inclusion.' That being so, then doesn't this interacting by inclusion turn out to produce great benefit to the world?"

Thus our Master Mòzǐ said, "Inclusion is right [shì]." (Mz 16/9–15)

As in the second version, the text implies that, besides eliminating aggression and crime, inclusion will prevent mistreatment of the powerless, minorities, the common, and the ignorant and will help people fulfill the relational virtues (Mz 16/2–4). The conclusion again indicates that inclusion will promote public security and ensure economic sufficiency for all (16/83–85). Beyond these good consequences, the text now also claims that if inclusion is practiced, "acute ears and keen eyes will see and hear for each other," "strong limbs will work for each other," and "those who have dào will diligently instruct each other," while "the elderly without wives or children will have sustenance to live out their lives" and "the young, weak, and orphaned" will have the resources they need to reach maturity (16/18–20). In other words, people will share information, labor, and know-how, and the community—perhaps mainly through the efforts of political leaders—will provide for the those who lack families and cannot fend for themselves. The argument explicitly points out that inclusion yields great benefit. The implication is that it is thereby morally right.

This third version of the Argument from Consequences thus presents two main developments. First, inclusion is now characterized as a commitment to others as ends similar to our commitment to ourselves as ends. By switching from the phrasing of caring for or viewing others as ourselves to that of being committed to their welfare as we are to our own, the text makes it clear that inclusive care refers primarily to a commitment to people's welfare, not an emotional attachment to them. The contrast between inclusion and exclusion also clearly indicates that exclusion does not refer to so-called graded care, the view that our moral concern for others should vary proportionally with the closeness of our relationship to them. The text explicitly specifies that "exclusion" refers to excluding others' interests from consideration altogether, such that we ignore their needs (Mz 16/24) and do not hesitate to "detest and injure" them (16/6). Second, the standards of conduct associated with inclusive care have become moderately more demanding. Now, beyond fulfilling the relational virtues and refraining from mistreatment of outsiders, we are to share information, labor, and know-how and to help support those among the very young and very old who lack families to care for them. Arguably, reciprocal sharing of information, labor, and know-how is simply a way of filling out what the second book denoted by "benefiting each other." But the requirement to help support destitute orphans and seniors is new and is not explicitly reciprocal (though of course orphans might reciprocate when grown).

The practical consequences of inclusive care described in the three essays display an interesting pattern.[15] All three claim that inclusive care will prevent war, clan feuding, and crime while promoting the relational virtues.[16] The second adds that inclusive care will end mistreatment of the weak, minorities, the poor, the lowly, and the ignorant. The third contends further that it will bring security to rulers and material sufficiency to the people (Mz 16/84). It will lead people to help one another and, most important, will ensure the welfare of the weakest, worst-off members of society, destitute orphans and elders. The concrete consequences of inclusive care thus become broader in scope and more ambitious as we move from the first to the second and then to the third essay. While maintaining their commitment to the general good, the Mohists express increasing concern for the poor and helpless. It seems, then, that their conception of the requirements of inclusive care may have grown gradually more stringent over time. At first, they saw it as demanding only that we refrain from harming others, in the sense of committing violence or crimes against them, and that we treat our own circle virtuously. Later, they expanded their conception of harm to include oppression, intimidation, humiliation, and deception. Eventually they came to see inclusive care as requiring that we assist and cooperate with those outside our circle and, in particular, that we help support those with no other means of sustenance.

JUST WHAT IS INCLUSIVE CARE?

From the three "Inclusive Care" books, then, we can extract a half dozen or more distinct formulations or explanations of Mohist teachings on care, some simple and undemanding, others more complex and stringent. The different texts do not even use a consistent label for the view they advocate. Sometimes they call it "caring about others" (ài rén 愛人), sometimes "inclusively caring about each other" (jiān xiāng ài 兼相愛), sometimes "inclusion" (jiān 兼). Use of the phrase "inclusive care" (jiān ài) seems to have been a gradual, relatively late development.[17] The variety of ways in which the Mohists present their ideas, along with the likely shifts in their position over time, means there is no single, exact doctrine of inclusive care to evaluate. There is only a set of overlapping claims, some easier to justify than others.

For brevity, let's focus on the strongest version of the doctrine that emerges from the three presentations of the Argument from Consequences. This version seems the latest of the variants in the "Inclusive Care" books and so may be representative of the Mohist stance during the movement's apogee. We can formulate what I will call strong inclusive care as follows.

> *Strong inclusive care.* We are to be "for" others as we are "for" ourselves—that is, committed to their welfare as we are to our own—such that
> - we do not injure, exploit, or mistreat others;
> - we share information, labor, and know-how with one another;
> - we aid those who have no means of provision, such as orphans and the childless elderly; and
> - we fulfill the relational virtues toward those in our circle.

Individuals within a community—a clan, city, or state—are expected to practice inclusive care toward one another, while communities and their leaders are to practice it toward other communities.

Inclusive care has two dimensions, the psychological attitude of being "for others as for oneself" and the conduct that ensues from this attitude. The norms of conduct associated with strong inclusive care are only moderately demanding. By today's standards, they amount roughly to refraining from taking advantage of others, treating our circle well, being a good neighbor, and contributing to charity for those who have no other means of support. Though we are to help strangers with urgent needs, radical altruism is not required. In a society in which strong inclusive care were widely practiced, we would normally care chiefly for our family and ourselves, share information and labor with our neighbors, and donate some of our surplus resources to others with urgent needs.[18] The burden of supporting the destitute would be distributed across the community and so would probably not be onerous. The only people expected to work directly to promote the benefit of all would be government leaders, who because of their position are responsible for benefiting all their subjects. Inclusive care would be more demanding than a minimal conception of morality on which we have only negative obligations to avoid harming others or infringing on their rights. But it seems at most only moderately more demanding than what many people today would consider simple moral decency.[19]

The psychological attitude associated with strong inclusive care is more challenging to interpret precisely. The words the texts use for the relation between our attitudes toward ourselves and toward others—*ruò* 若 and *yóu* 猶—can connote either equality or similarity. So the phrase "for others as for oneself" could refer to having exactly the same commitment to others' welfare as to one's own or a commitment similar in kind but different in degree. Evidence from outside the "Triads" favors the first, stronger interpretation. Fragments in the "Dialectics" imply that care is to be equal for all, even though our treatment of others varies with our relationship to them. In characterizing inclusive care, these passages repeatedly use the phrase *xiāng ruò* 相若, which elsewhere refers specifically to being equal, as points on the circumference of a circle are an equal distance from the center (MB A54). One fragment states that "inclusive care is equal and care for each one is equal" (EC13). Another indicates that although we do more for ourselves than for outsiders, we are to "care neither more nor less" (EC10). These fragments are from some of the most textually corrupt sections of the "Dialectics," so any interpretation must be tentative. Still, they suggest that later Mohists construed inclusive care as equal care for all. Also pertinent is the conversation in which Mòzǐ's interlocutor Wūmǎzǐ contrasts inclusive care with caring proportionally more or less about people depending on the closeness of his relationship to them. Mòzǐ accepts the contrast without comment, suggesting that inclusive care indeed refers to caring equally for all (Mz 46/52–60). Hence "for others as for oneself" probably refers to our having an equally strong commitment to everyone's welfare. This construal also coheres well with the rhetoric of "viewing others as oneself" or "viewing others as one views oneself."

If this interpretation is correct, then for the Mohists "care" (*ài*) is effectively a technical term, with a sense that overlaps but diverges from everyday uses of the word. In everyday use, whether in Chinese or in English, we associate a greater degree of care with the greater affection, attentiveness, and devotion toward family members that accompany relational virtues such as paternal kindness and filial devotion. The Mohists, however, see the relational virtues as compatible with an equal commitment to the welfare of all, which they refer to as "care." For them, special attitudes and treatment toward those in our circle are either subsumed within the relational virtues or are regarded as greater "endearment" or "kinship" (*qīn* 親) rather than greater care.[20]

As the Mohists understand the relation between care and conduct, to avoid inconsiderate, harmful treatment of others, we must care about them. In their theoretical framework, equal care for all is the counterpart to more familiar normative attitudes such as recognizing people's equal moral worth, showing equal regard for all, or impartially considering everyone's interests.[21] "For others as for oneself" is their way of articulating the idea that from an impartial, moral standpoint, everyone's welfare counts equally. In ethical contexts, for the Mohists caring about people is not primarily feeling affection or attachment toward them (although nothing in the texts rules out its being accompanied by such emotions). It is taking the normative stance that their welfare matters in determining our conduct. Inclusive care is the attitude that everyone's welfare matters equally. From the Mohist perspective, to allow unequal levels of care—more for those near and dear, less for the more distant—would amount to allowing that, since some people count for more than others, we can justifiably injure those who matter less to benefit those who matter more. As we saw in chapter 5 when discussing Mòzǐ's dialogue with Wūmǎzǐ, such a stance could not be a public, social *dào* regularly followed by all, as it would likely lead to a vicious, self-defeating cycle of reciprocal harm. The only sustainable, constant *dào*, in the Mohist view, which prevents harm to all and promotes the general good, is for everyone to care about everyone equally. Acting on this attitude does not require that we treat everyone equally, but that we jointly follow a social *dào* that collectively promotes the welfare of all—the *dào* articulated by the norms of conduct the Mohists associate with inclusive care.

If we accept the Mohists' consequentialist premises and the conceptual relations that determine the content of inclusive care, then the Argument from Consequences provides plausible grounds for the norms of conduct they advocate. No doubt there could be alternative norms that might be similarly or more justified, such as a system similar to theirs in which we give more assistance to impoverished families or omit the emphasis on the relational virtues. However, such alternatives would likely fall within a fairly narrow range of positions roughly similar to theirs. Any serious weaknesses in their position probably lie in the implicit assumptions that drive the argument—that the correct *dào* is to promote the benefit of all and that the attitude of care is the only alternative to disregard for others. If the right *dào* is not consequentialist, the argument fails. If care is not the only alternative to disregard, the argument may rest on a false dilemma. Before pursuing these issues further, however, let's consider several objections to inclusive care that the Mohists themselves discuss.

OBJECTIONS AND REPLIES

Is inclusive care consistent with deeply held values such as the welfare of one's family? Is it something people can feasibly adopt and carry out? Is it even practically possible? Four objections along these lines are treated in the latter two of the "Inclusive Care" books. The gist of the Mohist responses is that inclusive care is consistent with people's existing values and motives—at least those that are morally justified—and so with a bit of encouragement we already have the motivation and ability to practice it. The main purpose of the replies is not to establish that inclusive care is morally justified. They presuppose that the Argument from Consequences has already done so. Nor do the replies attempt to show that inclusive care better fulfills people's existing values than does any alternative dào—such a heavy argumentative burden far exceeds their ambit. Their aim is simply to show that inclusive care is practically feasible because it coheres with values and tendencies that people already have. Along the way, the replies help to fill in details of just how the Mohists understand inclusive care.

THE OBJECTION FROM DIFFICULTY

The first and most prominent objection to inclusive care is the Objection from Difficulty: inclusive care is just too difficult to carry out (Mz 15/15–29, 16/72–83). The Mohist response is that it is not too difficult, because according to historical accounts, rulers have led people to perform far more demanding deeds in the past. The texts relate the stories of Duke Wén of Jìn, fond of rough clothing, whose courtiers dressed in coarse, uncomfortable clothes; King Líng of Chǔ, fond of slender waists, whose courtiers dieted until weak from hunger; and King Gōujiàn of Yuè, fond of courage, whose soldiers leapt into a burning boat to save the national treasures he told them were stored there. All these feats, the Mohists claim, were much more difficult than practicing inclusive care. Yet with their rulers' encouragement, people performed them. Were rulers to encourage inclusive care, then, they could easily lead everyone to practice it.

The response in "Inclusive Care II" further contends that inclusive care is not difficult because it is beneficial (Mz 15/16–17) and because people reliably reciprocate beneficial or detrimental attitudes and conduct (15/18–19). Those who care about and benefit others will be cared about and benefited in turn, either by the recipients of their kindness or by others. Those who detest and injure others will likewise themselves be loathed and harmed. Let's refer to this pattern of attitudes and behavior as reciprocity. The response claims that, given people's inclination toward reciprocity, all that is needed to put inclusive care into practice is for rulers to adopt it as policy and commoners to adopt it as a basis for conduct. The response in "Inclusive Care III" contends that, because inclusive care is "beneficial and easy" (16/81), rulers need only delight in it and promote its practice through suitable incentives, and people will take to it readily, "as fire tends upward and water tends downward" (16/83). The general principle behind this claim complements the theory of identifying upward: "within a generation, the people can be changed" to the practice of inclusive care because they seek to identify with their rulers (16/80–81).

Between them, then, the two responses offer four reasons that inclusive care is not difficult to practice. First, it is beneficial to everyone, and, other things being equal, getting people to follow norms that are beneficial is not too hard. (The point is not that self-interest motivates people to practice inclusive care but that convergence with self-interest makes doing so relatively easy.) Second, the concrete demands of inclusive care are not especially arduous—or at least they are much easier than many genuinely challenging things people have done. Third, people tend to conform to their leaders' wishes, especially if these are backed by praise and incentives. Last, people tend to practice reciprocity, which dovetails with the practice of inclusive care. All four of these reasons are plausible (chapter 7 discusses them further). The only claim that might invite challenge is that inclusive care is "easy." The norms of conduct associated with strong inclusive care are moderately demanding but would probably be easy enough to observe in a community where they were encouraged and widely practiced. Psychologically, developing an equal commitment to everyone's welfare sounds difficult, and I explore this potential weakness in the following. But the Mohists' responses imply that for the typical member of the community, inclusive care amounts merely to a commitment to reciprocally care about and benefit others—roughly what we think of as being a good neighbor. They compare it to physical achievements—dieting, wearing coarse clothing, leaping into a fire—implying that they understand it primarily as a practice, not a conscious attitude or feeling.

The claim that people are inclined toward reciprocity is probably the core of the Mohist explanation of why inclusive care is not difficult. It is the centerpiece of the first response to the Objection from Difficulty. It is unmentioned but probably assumed in the second response, because it is the key premise in the immediately preceding argument that inclusive care is consistent with filial devotion (Mz 16/64–72). It helps explain why inclusive care can be expected to benefit us and thus, other things being equal, why we are unlikely to find it difficult. Even more important, it points out that people have predispositions that align with inclusive care and facilitate their developing and sustaining the attitudes and habits that constitute its full-fledged practice.

Given this predisposition toward reciprocity, why isn't inclusive care the prevailing norm? "It's just that superiors don't adopt it as a basis for governing, while officers don't adopt it as a basis for conduct" (Mz 15/19–20). As a reciprocal, social practice, inclusive care is contingent on political enforcement and adoption across society.[22] People's inclination toward a virtuous cycle of reciprocal care and benefit can be engaged only if others respond in kind. Even more important, political leadership must ensure inclusive care is widely adopted, because its practice by less than a self-sustaining critical mass within the community might impair, not promote, the benefit of all. Suppose a minority attempting to practice inclusive care were exploited by a majority who had no intention of benefiting anyone in turn. Since the welfare of the minority might suffer badly, overall benefit might decrease, defeating the justification for inclusive care.

THE OBJECTION FROM IMPOSSIBILITY

The second objection is the Objection from Impossibility (Mz 15/29–41, 16/45–63), a variant of the Objection from Difficulty. Here the worry is that inclusive care is practically impossible, on the order of "picking up Mount Tài and leaping over the Jì River" (15/30). The Mohist reply is that it is indeed possible, because the sage-kings actually practiced it. The texts cite purportedly historical examples and documents to show that the sage-kings ruled fairly and impartially, benefiting all. Yǔ carried out flood-control projects that benefited people throughout the known world, including foreigners, and defeated the Miáo tribe to achieve peace and security for all. Wén protected the interests of the weak, minorities, and farmers and ensured that the elderly, solitary, and orphaned were provided for. Wǔ and Tāng offered themselves in sacrifice to atone for any wrongdoing by their subjects. Wén and Wǔ allocated goods equitably, rewarded the worthy, and punished the vicious without partiality toward kin. Thus "the model for what our Master Mòzǐ calls inclusion is taken from" these six sage-rulers. Again, the examples all involve actions the sage-kings took on behalf of all, not their affections or attitudes. They may have felt relevant emotions—sympathy for disadvantaged, for instance—but they exemplify inclusive care because of their impartially benevolent deeds, not a particular attitude or feeling.

The aim of the appeal to the sage-kings is only to demonstrate that inclusive care is practically possible. Against the background of the Three Models, however, the argument also has normative force, since the deeds and documents of the sage-kings are a guide to what is right.

A critic might reject the Mohist response on the grounds that the sage-kings are a special case. As rulers of "all under heaven," they count among their subjects all people, even foreigners, and so their circle of special relationships expands to include everyone. Naturally, then, they are committed to everyone's welfare. Moreover, they have all the resources of the empire at their disposal. That inclusive care is possible for them does not show it is possible for you and me. In this regard, the reply to this objection seems less compelling than that to the Objection from Difficulty. The worry holds only if we are thinking of inclusive care from the standpoint of the individual, however. One implication of the Mohists' citing the deeds of the sage-kings is that inclusive care is primarily a social and political *dào*, not an individual code of conduct. The sage-kings do not illustrate the practice of inclusive care by the typical person. They illustrate its adoption as a state policy.

THE OBJECTION FROM USE

The third challenge—like the fourth, found only in "Inclusive Care III"—is the Objection from Use. The Mohists' opponents doubt whether inclusive care can be "applied" or "used" (*yòng* 用). There are two versions of the objection, one dealing with social peers (*Mz* 16/21–34), the other with rulers (16/34–45). The first version grants that inclusive care is a good thing but exclaims, "How can it possibly be used?!" The Mohists typically use the word "use" or "apply" to refer to putting a doctrine, policy, or plan into practice. A prominent example is that use is the third of the Three Models for evaluating statements or doctrines: we observe whether they have beneficial consequences when promulgated as a basis for government administration and the penal code (35/9). So the question the Mohists aim to answer here is, granted that inclusive care is a good thing, can we really apply it as a social *dào* to be publicly promulgated and followed by all? They interpret this as a challenge to establish that we can practically choose inclusive care as a *dào* to be followed by others with whom we associate. (In their view, the question of whether we can follow it ourselves has already been handled in answering the Objection from Difficulty, and the question of whether it has good consequences has been handled in the Argument from Consequences.) Their response aims to show that we can indeed apply inclusive care as such a *dào*, because doing so converges with our commitment to our family's welfare.

To establish that inclusive care can be "used," the Mohists present the "Caretaker" argument,[23] a hypothetical choice argument purporting to show that, in at least some circumstances, even those who verbally reject inclusive care would select it as a *dào* to be followed by their associates. The argument posits a scenario in which a soldier or envoy departing on a distant, hazardous mission has a choice of entrusting the care of his wife, children, and parents to either a fellow officer who practices inclusion or one who practices exclusion. The inclusive officer is committed to his associates' and their families' welfare just as he is to his own and his family's, so he reliably aids friends in need. "If his friend is hungry, he feeds him; if cold, he clothes him; if ill, he tends to him;

if dead, he buries him" (Mz 16/27–28). The exclusionist officer scoffs at the idea of such concern for others and so offers no help to associates facing hardship. The Mohists contend that the obvious choice for the soldier or envoy is to entrust his family to the inclusive person:

> Suppose there is a wide plain or vast wilderness here, and a man is donning armor and helmet about to go to war, and the balance of life or death can't yet be known. Again, suppose a lord or minister has dispatched him on a distant mission to Bā, Yuè, Qí, or Jīng, and whether he can get there and return or not can't yet be known. That being so, then may I ask, I wonder to which one he would entrust his household, to look after his parents and support his wife and children? I wonder, to the one who deems inclusion right? Or to the one who deems exclusion right? I take it that when they are in this situation, there are no ignorant men or ignorant women in the world. Even those who deem inclusion wrong would surely entrust them to the one who deems inclusion right. This is deeming inclusion wrong when making statements, but selecting inclusion when making choices—so this is statements and conduct contradicting each other. (Mz 16/30–33)

In the face of uncertainty about their family's welfare, according to the Mohists, even critics of inclusive care would choose it as the *dào* to be followed by a person to whom they entrust their family. The implication is that on the basis of a robust, shared value—our family's welfare—anyone would prefer inclusion over exclusion as a *dào* to be practiced by others with whom we associate. So inclusive care can be used: in practice we are already disposed to choose it as a social *dào*. Indeed, critics are allegedly guilty of a practical contradiction in rejecting it, as their conduct (*xíng* 行) fails to conform to their statements (*yán* 言). Their view cannot be promulgated and practiced consistently. It is thus their view, not the Mohists', that cannot be "used."

The second version of the objection questions whether inclusive care might be applicable only to our choice of officers (*shì* 士)—middle-class peers who live alongside us—and not to our choice of a ruler. Might it be a *dào* for individuals to practice toward one another but not for the state to practice toward its subjects? The Mohists respond with a second hypothetical choice argument, this time concerning a choice between a ruler who espouses and practices inclusion and one who espouses and practices exclusion. The Ruler argument parallels the Caretaker argument, with two differences. First, the inclusive ruler puts his people's welfare before his own, rather than being equally committed to both (Mz 16/39). His norm thus may be more demanding than inclusive care. However, the conduct ascribed to him—feeding his people when they are hungry, clothing them when they are cold, tending to them when they are ill, burying them when they die—parallels that of the inclusive officer. Second, the argument specifies that the choice is made not in the face of uncertainty but in a catastrophic social and economic scenario, in which an epidemic rages, people face economic hardship, and multitudes lie dead by the roads (16/42–43). Again, the Mohists contend, in such a situation, "there are no fools in the world": everyone would choose to be a subject of the inclusive ruler.

To sum up, the arguments sketch easily imaginable circumstances in which anyone would prefer inclusive care as the *dào* to be followed by our associates and political leaders. That way, should we or our family face hardship, we can count on assistance. The upshot is that people can and would use inclusive care, because it converges with our own and our family's welfare.

A natural criticism is that the arguments pose a false dilemma. The hypothetical choice is limited to inclusion versus exclusion, when it seems there could be alternative *dào* in which our commitment to others varies in scope or degree between these extremes. Perhaps, for instance, instead of a caretaker who cares all-inclusively about and shares resources with everyone, our family would be better off with someone who cares mainly about his circle and devotes most of his resources to them, cares somewhat about and devotes some resources to us, and ignores everyone else.[24] The charge that inclusive care rests on a false dilemma is potentially cogent, and I will return to it later. In this specific context, however, the Mohists could reply that the criticism misconstrues their conception of care. As we have seen, care is the attitude of acknowledging others' normative significance to what we do. We either take them into consideration or not; there is no middle ground. Moreover, the arguments need to show only that inclusive care can be used, not that it is preferable to all other alternatives. In any case, endorsing inclusive care does not settle the question of how much attention or assistance people are to give others in a particular practical scenario. Just as inclusive care licenses us to meet our circle's needs before contributing to outsiders', the inclusive caretaker could justifiably favor our family, whom he has taken in as dependents, over outsiders he has not agreed to assist.

A more serious problem is the hypothetical framing of the arguments. That people prefer inclusion as their associate's or ruler's *dào* in a narrowly defined hypothetical scenario in which their family's welfare is at risk does not really justify the claim that it can be applied generally, in actual circumstances. Even if the arguments do show that inclusive care can be used in some situations, they fall short of showing it can be used as a constant or regular *dào*. So they make only a weak case for the contention that inclusive care can be applied as a universal social norm. Perhaps the most charitable view is that they work as vivid illustrations of the plausible claim that the social practice of inclusive care complements our commitment to our own and our family's interests. If the Mohists are confident that the Argument from Consequences has already given a moral justification for inclusive care, then all they really need to show here is that it is consistent with deeply held values such as one's family's welfare.

This evaluation of the Caretaker and Ruler arguments turns on my interpretation of their relatively limited aims. Several previous treatments construe the arguments as aimed at justifying inclusive care over alternative norms by appeal to a shared value, the welfare of one's family. The arguments have been interpreted as contending that the Ruist "partialistic" value of placing the welfare of one's kin ahead of the welfare of others is better served by adopting inclusive care than by the Ruists' own *dào*. However, nothing in the text implies that the arguments are directed against Ruism, nor that their aim is to refute a partialistic *dào*. If we attend to their stated theme, they do not set out to show that a partialistic *dào* is incoherent or implicitly commits its proponents to inclusive care. The writers do, as an afterthought, rebuke critics of inclusive care for the supposed practical contradiction between their statements and their hypothetical conduct. But the arguments themselves do not target a rival ethical doctrine, nor do they attempt to justify inclusive care beyond merely showing that it can be used.[25]

THE OBJECTION FROM FILIALITY

The fourth objection is that inclusive care might fail to coincide with one's parents' welfare and thus interfere with filial devotion (*xiào*) (Mz 16/64–72). Presumably, the worry is either that pursuing our parents' welfare might sometimes require us to seize resources from others, thus harming them, or, more likely, that helping others takes away from the resources we could otherwise devote to our parents. The Mohist response is that filially devoted children would want others to care about and benefit their parents, not detest and injure them. To achieve this end, we should care about and benefit others' parents, prompting others to respond in kind. (As in the reply to the Objection from Difficulty, the Mohists assume people have a tendency to reciprocate good or bad treatment.) The widespread practice of inclusive care would thus dovetail with filial devotion. The argument is persuasive, provided the conditions for inclusive care are fulfilled—it is a widely practiced social norm and does not require extensive self-sacrifice, since most people have sufficient resources to support their parents while also sparing some resources to benefit one another.[26]

The underlying point of this response parallels that of the Caretaker and Ruler arguments. All three seek to show that as a social practice inclusive care is consonant with bedrock values such as our own welfare, our family's welfare, and filial devotion. The Caretaker and Ruler arguments are imperfect but dramatic attempts to make this point by appealing to hypothetical scenarios in which help from others might be pivotal to fulfilling such values. The filiality argument is more powerful, however, precisely because it is not hypothetical. It claims, plausibly, that the practice of inclusive care in actual, everyday circumstances would support, not interfere with, the ends of filial devotion.

STRONG INCLUSIVE CARE: A CRITIQUE

Once we understand that "care" is in effect a technical term for the Mohists, with tight conceptual links to benefit and harm and through them to the Mohist ethical theory, it is easy to see why they take inclusive care to be justified. As they see it, the alternative would be to hold that it is permissible to disregard others such that we can injure them to benefit ourselves. If we accept the Mohists' conception of care, along with the consequentialist framework in which it is embedded, their case for inclusive care is strong. However, elucidating the inferential relations between care, benefit, harm, righteousness, and other components of their theory also helps us to see why, with due sympathy for their views, we might nevertheless disagree with them—not so much because we question one or another step in their arguments but because we reject the whole package of concepts and assumptions that undergirds their position.

Inclusive care is the Mohists' distinctive way of articulating the widely shared conviction that all people have equal moral status. It is their version of the basic moral attitude that we think of as equal, impartial regard or consideration for others. However, strong inclusive care—caring equally for all—may not be the most appropriate way to express this conviction, for at least two reasons. First, assuming we agree that everyone has equal moral status, this status need not be directly reflected in our having an equal or impartial action-guiding attitude toward each person. All that is needed is for our attitudes and conduct to conform to norms that are impartially justified, in the sense that they do not unfairly favor some people over others. In advocating that we be "for others as for oneself," the Mohists ask individual agents to be equally committed to promoting the benefit of all. Arguably, this position misguidedly locates the impartiality characteristic of moral justification in the action-guiding attitudes of the individual agent, instead of in the *dào* that justifies those attitudes. The Mohists could instead simply require that agents commit to the impartially justified *dào*, or to doing what's right.

The second, deeper point is that care may not be the most suitable attitude through which to express regard for others' moral significance. Care is significantly stronger than mere respect for others. It calls for us to be positively disposed to promote their welfare, not simply to respect them as deserving moral consideration. The springboard for the Argument from Consequences is the harm caused by disregard for others. For the Mohists, the stance that contrasts with disregarding and harming others is caring about and benefiting them. But the solution to harmful conduct need not be for everyone to care about and benefit one another. It could be simply to respect others' interests or ends and so refrain from harming them. Accordingly, an impartially justified *dào* that embodies regard for others need not entail a commitment to benefiting them. It might call on us only to acknowledge their interests by refraining from harming them and interacting in a way acceptable to both sides.

These reflections suggest that if we reconsider the relations between harm, benefit, and care, there are alternative psychological attitudes besides strong inclusive care that affirm the moral significance of others. So the Argument from Consequences may indeed pose a false dilemma after all. The Mohists could respond that the alleged false dilemma is irrelevant, because inclusive care is obviously more beneficial to society than is, for instance, neutral respect for others' interests. Here the Mohists and our hypothetical critic might seem to reach an argumentative impasse. To a consequentialist, that inclusive care yields greater benefit than alternative normative attitudes is a conclusive justification. To a critic who doubts that moral regard for others amounts to a disposition to benefit them, such a consequentialist argument may be unconvincing and even irrelevant.

The critic could press her case on the Mohists' own grounds by arguing that another approach to acknowledging people's equal moral status might have consequences as good as or better than those of strong inclusive care. In formulating strong inclusive care, I identified two dimensions, a psychological attitude and the norms of conduct the Mohists associate with this attitude. The critic could contend that an alternative attitude or set of attitudes—a combination of respect, civic-mindedness, and neighborliness, for instance—might support the patterns of conduct the Mohists envision as well as or better than the stronger attitude of being "for others as for oneself." Such an alternative would prevent harm to others, just as inclusive care would. It could motivate aid for the destitute or reciprocal assistance for special projects, as when neighbors assist one another with harvesting or barn raising. Most important, it would eliminate the conceptual tension in the Mohist theory between equal care for all and differential treatment for our circle, yielding a position that is simpler, more coherent, and probably easier to practice. For in the end, the attitude of caring equally about all does seem incongruous with the relational virtues—even if we accept a distinction between care and endearment, and even if we understand that inclusive care entails only commitment to a *dào* that benefits all, not equal treatment for everyone. It seems doubtful that we could wholeheartedly exercise virtues such as filial devotion or paternal kindness without also caring more about our parents or children, in the Mohists' own sense of being attentive to their welfare and disposed to benefit them.

The Mohists themselves tie care conceptually to benefit, so by their own lights arguably there is conceptual pressure to allow care to vary proportionally with the degree we are expected to benefit others. What blocks them from doing so is their brand of consequentialism—their conviction that the moral standpoint inherently requires an impartial commitment to the benefit of all and thus that we must be "for others as for ourselves." The briefest critique of this view is that we simply cannot be "for others" exactly as we are "for ourselves," because in the end we are distinct people, standing in different relations to one another. The Mohists urge all humanity to identify with one another such that we are equally committed to the welfare of all persons, families, and communities. But to care about others' persons, families, or communities just as I care about my own is to undermine the identity of my person, family, or community as a distinct person, family, or community. If I care about other families' welfare just as much as I care about my own family's welfare, then it seems I am not really regarding my family as my *family*.[27] The same holds for caring about myself, my friends, or my community. A more defensible stance concerning the psychological dimension of inclusive care—one that coheres better with the actual norms of conduct the Mohists endorse as following from that attitude—would be to advocate that we adopt a range of caring attitudes toward others depending on our relationship to them.

CONCLUDING REMARKS

Inclusive care is the Mohist counterpart to moral attitudes such as devoting equal consideration to all or acknowledging each person's equal moral status. In this regard, it is indeed, as Mei remarked long ago, an "epoch-making" doctrine.[28] It is among the world's earliest systematic developments of the fundamental, attractive idea that the appropriate moral attitude is one by which, in some sense, everyone counts equally. The Mohist proposal is that we recognize people's moral status appropriately when we commit to a *dào* that impartially promotes the welfare of all. In their view, by following such a *dào*, we count as caring equally for all—as being "for others as for oneself."

The Mohists are surely right that morality involves regarding others as on a par with us in some respect. Moreover, by articulating this regard as care, a disposition to benefit others, they present an important, provocative position. Someone who cares not at all about others' welfare—someone utterly unmoved to assist an injured accident victim or a helpless, starving orphan—certainly seems morally deficient. Still, as the preceding section argued, we have reasons to question the Mohist advocacy of caring "for others as for oneself." Acknowledging people's equal moral status need not entail our taking up an equal action-guiding attitude toward everyone. Moreover, giving due moral consideration to others might entail only a commitment to respect their interests, not to benefit them. "For others as for oneself" seems to overstate what morality requires and to hastily identify moral regard with benefit rather than only respect.

These criticisms are not necessarily fatal. A hypothetical modern-day Mohist might resolve worries about inclusive care being too strong by scaling back its formulation so that caring about others is only all-inclusive, not equal. After all, the concluding slogan of "Inclusive Care I" urges us only to "care about others," not to care about everyone equally. The Mohist could allow our degree of care to vary proportionally with our relation to others and the level of benefit we are expected to provide them. Distant strangers would receive a basic degree of care, corresponding to a commitment to respect their interests and help in emergencies. Those with closer relations would receive more. The doctrine of "relation ranking" (described in chapter 5) could be revised to allow different degrees of care on the same consequentialist grounds that justify different degrees of beneficial treatment: doing so would better promote the welfare of all. These changes in formulation would probably prompt only minor changes in the conduct associated with inclusive care. The norms of conduct sketched in the "Inclusive Care" books are already a fairly plausible candidate for "the *dào* of benevolence and righteousness."

The more challenging criticism is that care may not be the appropriate attitude by which to reflect others' moral status. Morality may be a matter primarily of respecting others rather than of being disposed to benefit them. This criticism reflects a fundamental disagreement about the nature of morality, however, and a critic cannot simply assert that the Mohists' consequentialist stance is mistaken without begging the question against them. Moreover, we should keep in mind the religious orientation of Mohist ethics. Both the Mohists' consequentialism and the ideal of being "for others as for oneself" might ultimately reflect their religious convictions rather than an attempt to give a secular account of morality or righteousness. To the Mohists themselves, inclusive care could be less an ethical ideal than a religious one, an expression of spirituality or holiness.[29] All-inclusive care is the attitude of Heaven itself. By striving to be "for others as for oneself," we more closely emulate Heaven. This exalted status, rather than an accurate characterization of morality, could be the Mohists' foremost goal.

7

MOTIVATION

Changing People in a Generation

MÒZĬ AND HIS followers saw themselves largely as social and political reformers, dedicated to eliminating war, eradicating poverty, and promoting prosperity and social order. The aim of Mohist ethical and political thought thus was not just to elucidate the *dào* 道 but also to lead society as a whole to follow it. Despite this practical orientation, however, the Mohists are widely regarded as having only a thin, crude view of human motivation—one so simplistic as to leave them without a plausible account of how to lead people to put their *dào* into practice.[1] This chapter elucidates aspects of the Mohist view of motivation and defends it against this criticism. The discussion draws on the interpretations presented in preceding chapters to show that in fact the *Mòzĭ* presents a rich, nuanced picture of a variety of sources of moral and prudential motivation that the Mohists could reasonably view as sufficient to guide people to practice the core tenets of their ethics. The Mohists had a feasible program for carrying out their social reforms and "changing people within a generation," as they put it (*Mz* 16/74).

The widespread opinion to the contrary is probably due mainly to two factors. One is a misunderstanding of just what Mohist ethics demands, which I address briefly in the following section. The other is a failure to understand the Mohist conception of action and motivation, which I address in the subsequent section. One reason for this failure may be a tendency in the literature to focus on ideas prominent in Mencian and Xunzian discussions of motivation, such as the role of spontaneous affective responses or that of desires arising from people's nature (*xìng* 性). Because the Mohist approach does not center on affects or desires, it is considered simplistic. As I will show, however, once the

Mohists' conception of action and motivation is elucidated, they can be seen to have a sophisticated, defensible approach to motivation.

Let me begin by clarifying the conceptual and methodological basis of the chapter. By "motivation," I refer broadly to psychological states and dispositions that play, or potentially play, a direct causal role in producing action. For my purposes here, I include beliefs and analogous cognitive states among an agent's motivating states, since, as this chapter will show, the Mohists themselves seem to do so. Besides such states and dispositions, a treatment of motivation will typically also touch on a range of other psychological traits and capacities less directly connected to action. I take it that to be justified, claims about motivation or about these other aspects of human psychology need not state exceptionless universal truths but only credible generalizations about how people tend to think, feel, and act. The features they describe need not be innate or spontaneous, nor aspects of people's inherent dispositions or nature, however understood. For my present purposes, it is enough that they obtain regularly and widely and thus count among the conditions that a moral theory or reform program such as the Mohists' can or must work with—what features such a theory or program can take for granted, for instance, and what obstacles or constraints it faces. Thus I take the Mohists' depiction of certain features as widely observed in people as grounds for including them in my interpretation of their view of motivation.

Unlike the three major classical Ruist anthologies—the *Analects*, *Mencius*, and *Xúnzǐ*—the *Mòzǐ* contains relatively few passages that focus specifically on motivation. A likely explanation is that the core books of the *Mòzǐ* are roughly the equivalent of political reform pamphlets, aimed mainly at convincing rulers and officials to adopt Mohist policies. They are neither theoretical treatises (as much of the *Xúnzǐ* is) nor records of an ethical mentor's day-to-day coaching or instruction (as much of the *Analects* and *Mencius* seems to be). Still, in presenting and defending their ethical and political doctrines, the Mohists frequently make claims about human traits, dispositions, or behavior that bear on the topic of motivation. Other claims they make seem best explained by attributing to them certain implicit assumptions about motivation. My approach here will be to draw some of these explicit claims and implicit assumptions together into a sketch of their view of how to motivate people to practice their *dào*.

The next section rehearses the nature and content of the Mohist ethical and political project, since we cannot evaluate their view of motivation fairly without keeping in mind just what they hoped to lead people to do. The following section reconstructs their conception of action and contrasts it with familiar conceptions based on the practical syllogism and the belief-desire model. The subsequent section explains how their understanding of action affects their approach to motivation. The next two sections survey the major motivational techniques the Mohists employ and the sources of motivation on which they rely. The chapter concludes with a brief critical evaluation.

THE MOHIST REFORM PROGRAM

The Mohists' approach to motivation is intertwined with their ethical and sociopolitical reform program. To understand and evaluate their approach to motivation, we need to review the nature of this program and the normative ideals that they hope people will pursue. In this section, I highlight three aspects of Mohist ethics that are crucial to understanding their practical aims.

First, the Mohists are concerned primarily with social reform and only secondarily with the individual moral life.[2] This is not to suggest that personal moral development is unimportant to them; the core books of the *Mòzǐ* do address individual moral agents, particularly officials of various ranks. But their theoretical and practical focus is social and collectivist. The central question for them is not, how can I be good? but, what is the *dào*, and how can we collectively lead everyone to follow it? In the core books, their approach to guiding people to practice the *dào* emphasizes political policy and social interaction, rather than individual reflection and self-improvement. (Personal moral development is a more prominent theme in the "Dialogues.") One reason for this orientation lies in the nature of moral discourse in their time. Their primary audience, as they saw it, was not individual members of society but government officials, from rulers of states down to low-level officers, who they hoped would lead society to follow the *dào*. Another reason is that the Mohists, like most early Chinese thinkers, tended to employ a communitarian, rather than individualist, conception of what it is to be human. They regarded people primarily as members of social groups—specifically, the family or clan and the political community—and not as atomic individuals. A further reason is that central Mohist normative ideals presuppose collective practice of the *dào*. The Mohist ideal of social order, for example, requires collective adherence throughout society to a unified set of moral norms. The norm of inclusive care is explicitly reciprocal: people are to "care inclusively about each other and in interaction benefit each other" (Mz 15/10–11). Hence a single agent alone cannot practice inclusive care; for the norm to be realized, it must be practiced by the majority of some community. A corollary is that some of the motivational resources the Mohists invoke to explain how people can practice inclusive care—such as people's tendency toward reciprocity—are contingent on others' practicing it as well. For all these reasons, the Mohist approach to motivation is oriented mainly at leading communities to follow the *dào*. This orientation helps to explain, among other features of their position, why they assign a central role to encouragement and enforcement by political authorities.

A second point is that, as we saw in chapters 5 and 6, the ethical norms by which the Mohists seek to reform society are not exceptionally onerous. One factor driving the impression that Mohist moral psychology is untenably simplistic is the assumption that Mohist ethical norms are heroically demanding—so much so that no one could live up to them without elaborate, extensive training.[3] Many writers assume, for instance, that Mohist ethics demands complete impartiality toward others, in the sense that we have an equal obligation to benefit all people, regardless of their relationship to us.[4] The Mohists themselves clearly do not regard their *dào* as especially demanding, however. Though they acknowledge that opponents perceive inclusive care as difficult, they insist this is a misconception: compared with genuinely difficult feats, inclusive care is actually quite easy to practice (Mz 15/19, 16/81). In fact, as chapters 5 and 6 explained, Mohist moral norms seem only moderately stringent, going at most only slightly beyond what many of us today would consider common decency. Although, as we saw, early non-Mohist sources report fervent altruism among later bands of Mohists, these groups comprised ardent Mohist devotees, whose role was analogous to that of a disciplined religious order or elite military squad. They do not represent the typical member of a Mohist-inspired society. The general standards of conduct the Mohists expect everyone to follow are the norms of morality or righteousness (yì 義), which include mainly refraining from harm to and oppression of others, neighborly sharing of knowledge, labor, and resources, fulfilling the relational virtues, and aiding orphans and the childless elderly. These hardly amount to burdensome demands.

The third point is that, again as we saw in chapters 5 and 6, people's natural tendency to feel special affection and responsibility for family and friends presents no obstacle to the practice of Mohist ethics, because the Mohists endorse distinctive attitudes toward and treatment of those closest to us. The Mohists are often taken to hold that we should be impartially concerned for everyone and so should devote no special attention or treatment to our circle. Granted that the doctrine of inclusive care entails some form of equal consideration for all, given what else the Mohists say about inclusive care, it is compatible with and even requires special attitudes and treatment toward those with whom we have close personal relationships. For the Mohists justify the doctrine partly on the grounds that it helps to fulfill the relational virtues—virtues they associate with the core social relationships of ruler and subject, father and son, and elder and younger brother. They hold that inclusive care is right partly because, for example, it furthers filial devotion and political loyalty (Mz 15/13, 16/85). Virtues such as filiality and loyalty are normally understood to entail distinctive emotions, duties, and treatment toward those with whom we stand in the relevant relationships, and nothing suggests the Mohists think otherwise.

In advocating that we be committed "for others as for oneself," then, the Mohists do not intend to displace traditional kinship and political relationships from the center of social and ethical life. What they probably mean is that we should have the same degree of consideration for others' welfare that we do for our own. "Inclusive care" amounts to a label for the attitudes and conduct of an agent who has such equal consideration for all and accordingly has internalized a *dào* that promotes the welfare of all. It contrasts not with special concern for the welfare of one's family and associates—people simply could not be filial or loyal without special concern for their parents and associates—but with the attitude that others can be disregarded and freely harmed in pursuit of our interests (Mz 15/12–15).

THE MOHIST CONCEPTION OF ACTION AND MOTIVATION

A key to understanding the Mohists' approach to motivation is to grasp their conception of practical reasoning and the psychological antecedents of action. This conception is the basis for their view of how to prepare people psychologically to act in a normatively correct way—that is, how to educate and motivate them to follow the *dào*.

As I suggested in chapter 2, familiar conceptions of action in Western thought have been deeply influenced by argument-like models of practical reasoning. Aristotle's practical syllogism is one such model; the belief-desire model is another.[5] Such models inspire the view that the psychological antecedents of action are states whose content corresponds to premises in pieces of practical reasoning. According to the belief-desire model, for instance, action springs from a combination of a cognitive state—a belief—represented by one premise in a practical argument and a conative state—a desire or other pro-attitude—represented by another.

The Mohists are similar to Aristotle, Hume, and other Western thinkers in tying their conception of the structure of action to their conception of the structure of practical reasoning. However, their conception of the structure of reasoning is significantly different from Aristotle's and from the sentential, deductive models that inspire the belief-desire model. As we saw in chapter 2, the Mohist conception of reasoning is not syllogistic, nor even deductive. It is analogical and concerns mainly terms, not sentences. The Mohists understand reasoning as a process of discrimination or distinction drawing, which they call *biàn* 辯. Discrimination typically proceeds on the basis of comparisons of similarity to a model (*fǎ* 法), resulting in an attitude of deeming something *shì* 是 (this, right) or *fēi* 非 (not, wrong) (Mz 35/6). These attitudes are typically indexed to a contextually specified kind (*lèi* 類) of thing, denoted by a general term, such as "ox" or "horse." They correspond functionally to the judgment that an object is or is not of that kind, and thus that the term for the kind can correctly be predicated of it. The kind may be an aggregate of similar concrete objects, such as oxen or horses, or an aggregate of events or situations that share some abstract status, such as being morally righteous. Examples of particular *shì* or *fēi* attitudes, then, include the attitude, directed at some animal, that it is or is not an ox and the attitude, directed at some course of conduct, that it is or is not morally right. Besides alluding to a contextually specified kind, *shì* and *fēi* can also be used to refer generally to anything that is correct, right, or prudent, on the one hand, or incorrect, wrong, or imprudent, on the other. Thus they can also be construed as general pro and con attitudes.

Consistent with this model of reasoning and judgment, the Mohists apply what I call a discrimination-and-response model of action.[6] The structure of action, as they understand it, is that the agent discriminates an object, a situation, or a course of conduct as *shì* or *fēi*, typically with respect to some kind, and then responds to it according to norms appropriate for interacting with things of that kind. For example, an agent might distinguish an animal as *shì* with respect to the kind "ox" and then respond to it by calling it "ox" or using it to pull a cart. Or the agent might distinguish some course of conduct as *fēi* with respect to the kind *yì* (morally righteous) and respond by condemning and refraining from it. What drives action is a combination of *shì-fēi* attitudes and the norm-governed positive or negative responses to various kinds of things that these attitudes prompt.[7] Some of these responses may be innate, such as an infant's response to food. Many are probably acquired in roughly the same way we learn manners or skills. At the highest, most abstract level, when no specific kind is invoked by the context, *shì* and *fēi* themselves can directly prompt action via their role as generic pro and con attitudes.[8] Aside from occasional instances of akratic thought or action, then, to deem something *shì* is to be motivated to do, endorse, or promote it, while to deem it *fēi* is to be motivated to avoid, condemn, or eliminate it.

Shì and *fēi* are not the only motivating attitudes the Mohists recognize. Another prominent pair of action-guiding attitudes they mention is desire (*yù* 欲) versus aversion or detestation (*wù* 惡). For instance, they claim that Heaven's conduct provides evidence of what it desires and detests—it rewards those who care about and benefit others and punishes those who detest and injure others. The conceptual pairing of care and benefit suggests that they also see the attitude of care (*ài* 愛) as prompting beneficial actions and the opposing attitude of despising (*zēng* 憎) or detesting (*wù* 惡) others as prompting harmful ones. Like *shì-fēi*, these other attitudes are conceptualized as binary, positive-negative pairs, which induce positive or negative responses. One way of interpreting them is that they may in effect be specifications or special cases of *shì-fēi* attitudes. Desire and detestation, for example, may be a specification of generic *shì-fēi* or pro-con attitudes relating to whether something is to be pursued or avoided. Another interpretation is that the Mohists may recognize multiple, mutually irreducible pairs of action-guiding pro-con attitudes—including others beyond those mentioned here—each of which can incite action through a pattern of discriminations and responses. With respect to motivating people to practice their ethical and political doctrines, however, the pivotal attitudes for the Mohists seem to be those of deeming things *shì* or *fēi*. This is probably at least partly because, unlike desiring versus detesting or caring versus despising, *shì-fēi* attitudes carry an explicit evaluative valence, expressing approval or endorsement versus disapproval or opposition. It may also be because the Mohists assume that for many or most of their audience, what people desire or care about generally aligns with what they deem *shì*, while what they detest aligns with what they deem *fēi*. Throughout the "Triads," for instance, the Mohists repeatedly urge that if "kings, dukes, great men, officers, and gentlemen of the world" indeed "desire to be benevolent (*rén* 仁) and righteous" and "desire to conform to the *dào* of the sage-kings," they should carefully examine Mohist teachings, which they will find correspond to these values.[9] The operative assumption seems to be that many of this elite audience already endorse benevolence, righteousness, and the *dào* of the sages and moreover desire or aim to pursue these ideals. Accordingly, all that is needed is to convince them that Mohist teachings indeed embody benevolence, righteousness, and the *dào*.

The conception of action I have been sketching is illustrated by the Mohists' hypothetical account of the state of nature, examined in chapter 3. According to the Mohists, people in the state of nature are strongly, even obstinately, committed to their personal conception of what is morally right. Since different people's conceptions of right disagree, this commitment leads to conflict. The

Mohists describe people's attitudes by saying that they "*shì* their *yì* and on that basis *fēi* others' *yì*, and thus *fēi* each other" (Mz 11/2). That is, they deem their conception or norm of *yì* to be *shì*, on those grounds deem others' *fēi*, and thus fall into a pattern of reciprocal disapproval. A key observation is that people's attitude of deeming their view of righteousness to be *shì* and others' *fēi* is accompanied by a strong motivation to act on their convictions, which ultimately leads to social turmoil. This correlation between *shì-fēi* attitudes and conduct is underscored by the tight link Mohist political theory draws between emulating the *shì-fēi* attitudes and statements (*yán* 言) of political superiors, who serve as moral role models, and emulating their conduct (*xíng* 行).

The Mohist position that *shì-fēi* attitudes are typically sufficient to move agents to act converges in some respects with the views of influential contemporary writers who argue that rational or moral agents normally tend to do what they believe there is most reason to do.[10] Other things being equal, moral agents do not need some further motivation to move them to act beyond their discrimination, based on what they hold are compelling grounds, that something is right, or *shì*.[11] That they sometimes fail to act as they deem best shows only that a breakdown has occurred between motivation and action, not that they lack sufficient motivation.

The theoretical role of *shì* and *fēi* attitudes corresponds partly to that of judgment or belief, and the Mohists apparently hold that these attitudes alone can be sufficient to motivate action. Hence their position can to some extent be characterized as anti-Humean.[12] However, they do not necessarily hold that purely cognitive attitudes alone are sufficient for motivation, without the influence of conative or affective attitudes. Without question, *shì-fēi* attitudes generally have a cognitive aspect or component. The Mohists see them as shaped by cogent reasoning, and indeed they play a central role in the Mohist conception of cognition. To recognize a square object as square or an ox as an ox is to distinguish it as *shì* with respect to the kind "square" or "ox." In some contexts, *shì-fēi* attitudes may verge on being purely cognitive. But in ethical contexts, they can express approval or disapproval (for instance, see Mz 17/1), and so they may also have a conative aspect, intertwined with their role as general pro and con attitudes. They may have an affective aspect as well. When the Mohists condemn as *fēi* such conduct as theft, murder, war, and exploitation of the poor, their words ring with moral indignation (for example, 32/22–23). Conversely, when they approve a practice as *shì*, their claims often carry a tone of moral satisfaction, even exultation (16/15). In their account of the state of nature, they envision people's *fēi* attitudes toward others as motivationally so potent that they lead to violence. Family members' *fēi* attitudes toward one another spark resentment intense enough to overwhelm familial love and respect, driving them to split up (11/3).[13] Given the passion apparently associated with shì-fēi attitudes in morally fraught contexts, they may either incorporate affective elements or be closely associated with affective states.[14] Most likely, they are neither purely cognitive, conative, nor affective but, depending on the context, may incorporate all three dimensions.[15] In focusing on the motivational role of shì-fēi attitudes, then, the Mohists are probably not overlooking conative and affective attitudes. Rather, they may subsume these within the scope of shì-fēi attitudes.[16]

The Mohists consider the ability to draw and act on shì-fēi distinctions properly a form of competence or know-how (zhī 知), akin in some respects to the ability to perform a skill. Hence their primary explanation for an agent's failure to act properly is that the agent lacks the relevant know-how. As they understand it, such failure is typically due not to insufficient motivation but to ignorance or incompetence in distinguishing shì from fēi and responding accordingly. Mohist texts depict three overlapping types of cases of such ignorance or incompetence. The first occurs when the agent simply does not know how to distinguish shì from fēi properly, as when people fail to distinguish wars of aggression as fēi and even deem them righteous (Mz 17/9–13, 28/50). The texts especially call attention to cases of partial incompetence, in which people distinguish shì from fēi properly in some but not all relevant instances—as when they rightly condemn theft and murder but wrongly support unprovoked warfare aimed at seizing the wealth and slaughtering the people of other states. Another is when they apply a norm such as "employing the capable" properly in some cases, as when hiring a professional bowyer to repair a bow or veterinarian to cure a horse, but not others, as when they appoint an inexperienced relative to an official post (10/10–20). Such cases represent a failure "to know the distinction between righteous and unrighteous" (17/13). Perhaps the agent knows the correct way to draw distinctions only with respect to "the little things" (minor instances) but not "the big things" (major ones) (49/25).

The second type of case is when an agent verbally draws distinctions correctly but then fails to act properly. The agent may mouth the right words about righteousness yet lack the practical know-how to reliably distinguish and choose what is right and reject what is wrong (Mz 19/4–6, 47/23–26). These are cases in which agents' conduct fails to conform to their statements. To count as having moral know-how, the agent must respond to shì-fēi distinctions not just by making the appropriate sort of statements but also by reliably performing appropriate actions.

A third type of incompetence is when an agent endorses the *dào* and undertakes to act on it yet fails to do so. The agent commits to the *dào*, and presumably has some grasp of the distinctions and responses it entails, but falters in carrying it out, perhaps because of doubt or confusion about what to do, a lack of self-confidence, or motivational inertia. In the Mohist theoretical scheme, this sort of failure to follow a *dào* one endorses is analogous to akrasia, or weakness of will, since it amounts to a failure to do what one intends or deems best. However, rather than framing the problem as a failure to act on one's best judgment or to carry out one's intention to perform some discrete act, the Mohists view it as a lack of ability or competence in carrying out a *dào* one has embarked on. One *Mòzǐ* passage addresses the issue as follows:

> If you undertake righteousness but are not able, you must not abandon the *dào*. To give an analogy, a carpenter who saws a straight edge but is not able doesn't abandon the marking line. (Mz 47/20–21)

The emphasis on ability (*néng* 能), paired with the carpentry analogy, suggests that—as in the second type of case, when people say the right things but then fail to act properly—the Mohists ascribe this sort of akratic failure to a form of incompetence, not insufficient motivation. This incompetence is analogous to a deficiency in performing a skill, such as sawing a straight edge. So they probably see the remedy for akratic failure as analogous to that for ineptitude in a skill: the agent should continue training himself to recognize and act on evaluative distinctions properly, with the *dào* as his guide, until he can do so reliably—just as the novice carpenter should keep practicing his sawing technique, with the marking line as his guide, until he masters his craft. For the carpenter, the eventual outcome is skill mastery; for the moral agent, it is virtue.[17]

The discrimination-and-response model should not be confused with psychological behaviorism, the view that action can be explained without appeal to mental states and controlled simply through conditioning. The model does not imply that the Mohists see agents as capable only of primitive, unreflective pro or con attitudes and conditioned responses. The point is that their conception of the psychological states and processes that produce action is different from conceptions associated with the practical syllogism or the belief-desire model. On their model, our most basic psychological operation is one of distinguishing different kinds of things and adopting *shì* or *fēi* attitudes toward them accordingly. The content and consequences of these attitudes vary depending on the context. Reasoning lies in adopting further *shì* or *fēi* attitudes on the basis of perceived analogical relations between things. This model of cognition and reasoning is at least initially plausible, given that discriminating between kinds is simply pattern recognition, a basic cognitive process that underlies many more complex processes.

Nor does the Mohist approach to action entail a concern only with outward conformity to the *dào*, rather than character development aimed at following the *dào* spontaneously, from virtuous motives.[18] The Mohists are clearly concerned not simply to modify what people say and do but to have them develop the underlying *shì-fēi* attitudes that motivate proper statements and conduct (Mz 11/9–22). To suggest they are concerned only with behavior and not motives or character would be to overlook the role of *shì-fēi* attitudes. Having the right *shì-fēi* attitudes simply is having the right motives, and developing reliable moral know-how simply is developing a virtuous character. The Mohists' aim is for people to internalize the relevant *shì-fēi* distinctions and normative responses so that they acquire a reliable disposition to respond, smoothly and directly, to morally pertinent situations according to the *dào*. Of course, pending development of the appropriate *shì-fēi* attitudes, the Mohists might provisionally settle for behavioral conformity, partly as a second-best outcome and partly as a means of habituating agents into the right attitudes.[19] Thus in some contexts, as we will see, they appeal to prudential, nonmoral considerations either to help motivate people or to show that those who do not yet endorse their *dào* on moral grounds nevertheless have other good reasons to follow it or at least not oppose it. But the fundamental aim is to win people's moral approval of the Mohist *dào* and to bring their evaluative and motivating attitudes fully into line with it. This stance is clearly reflected in *Mòzǐ* passages that tie moral worth to action-guiding attitudes such as intentions (*yì* 意) and commitments (*zhì* 志) and to robust, stable aspects of agents' character.[20]

FRAMING THE PRACTICAL PROJECT

The Mohists' model of action and motivation affects how they frame the practical project of leading people to follow the *dào*. Because they see *shì-fēi* attitudes as the key form of morally relevant motivation, they view this project as one of guiding people to distinguish *shì-fēi* correctly and to act accordingly.

The overall project can be divided into two parts. The primary task is to use education, including persuasion and training, to modify how people distinguish *shì-fēi*. In some respects, education can be regarded as a process of redirecting existing motivation, rather than developing new motivation. It aims to redirect people's existing general motivation to do what they deem *shì* by convincing them that courses of action they previously did not endorse are indeed *shì*. It also appeals to motivating attitudes the Mohists assume are shared by all—such as valuing social order—and seeks to redirect these toward practicing the Mohist *dào*. In other respects, education can be regarded as producing new motivating attitudes, as it may lead people to acquire entirely new habits of distinguishing *shì-fēi*, some of them perhaps in areas of conduct that they previously did not attend to. It may also reshape people's motivational structure in various ways. For instance, it may eliminate inappropriate motivation by helping people see that certain of their *shì-fēi* attitudes are mistaken, as when the Mohists seek to show war-mongering rulers and their supporters that wars of aggression are in fact *fēi*, not *yì* (righteous) (Mz 17/12–14). Or it may remove motivational obstacles by showing people that certain apparently conflicting attitudes actually converge with the *dào*, as when the Mohists seek to show that filial devotion is consistent with inclusive care (16/64–72).

Because *shì-fēi* attitudes are normally sufficient to produce action, successful persuasion and education will be sufficient to lead most people to conform to moral norms with some degree of reliability. People occasionally fail to act on their *shì-fēi* attitudes, however. So the second major part of the practical project is to improve the reliability with which people translate *shì-fēi* attitudes into action. This task can be conceived of abstractly as one of strengthening people's character. More concretely, the aim is to improve their moral competence or know-how so that they more smoothly and reliably perform the actions that follow normatively from their *shì-fēi* attitudes. This part of the project is carried out through concrete practice in acting properly, backed by moral coaching in the form of instructions and encouragement, presentation of role models, praise and material incentives for success, and criticism and disincentives for failure (Mz 11/9–22, 12/12–31). Such coaching may come from social superiors, peers, or oneself.[21] The Mohists recognize that the process of strengthening people's character and moral competence is gradual, not instantaneous. They claim only that leading people to practice inclusive care would be much easier than getting them to perform more difficult practices—such as dieting to the point of starvation or wearing uncomfortable clothing—that rulers in the past nevertheless led their subjects to adopt "within a generation" (16/80).[22]

Given this conception of their practical project, the central question to ask in evaluating the Mohist approach to motivation is whether they offer a plausible account of how people can acquire the discrimination-and-response dispositions—that is, the virtues—needed to practice their *dào* reliably. The next two sections aim to show that they do.

MOTIVATIONAL TECHNIQUES

The Mohists either employ or propose to employ at least five interrelated techniques for educating and training people to distinguish *shì-fēi* properly and act accordingly. All five, I suggest, are widely agreed to be effective methods of guiding and modifying people's conduct.

The most prominent of these techniques is normative persuasion and explanation. Since *shì* and *fēi* attitudes have motivational force, a convincing argument or explanation that some practice is *shì* or *fēi* will generally be sufficient to move agents to perform or avoid it, as appropriate. This point partly accounts for the emphasis on normative argument throughout Mohist ethical writings. It is also reflected in the concluding summaries of many Mohist essays, which urge people who desire to do what is benevolent and righteous, or who desire the goods that Mohist ethics takes to be criteria of morality, to carefully "examine" Mohist doctrines (Mz 10/46, 19/63, 25/86). The underlying assumption is probably that if people evaluate for themselves the grounds for Mohist teachings, seeking to understand them and distinguish whether and why they are *shì* or *yì*, they will generally be led to practice them.[23]

A second, interrelated technique is to establish explicit verbal statements or teachings (*yán*) and verbal or nonverbal models (*fǎ*) by which people can direct their conduct. By committing to a statement or model as a guide to conduct, people become motivated to act in line with it, and repeatedly doing so trains them to act on the values it articulates. The Mohists allude to this technique when they remark that statements that are effective in guiding conduct should be made "regular," or repeated frequently (Mz 46/37–38, 47/18–19). It is reflected in their concern with evaluating whether particular statements, such as those of fatalists (35/5) or of advocates of rich burials and prolonged mourning (25/12), are right or wrong, and thus whether they should be taken as a guide to conduct. It is also reflected in the emphasis throughout the *Mòzǐ* on guiding and evaluating conduct by comparison with clear, measurement-like models akin to the carpenter's set square or wheelwright's compass (26/41ff.).[24] Among the models the Mohists introduce are general goods, such as "the benefit of the state and the people" (35/9); general norms of conduct, such as "inclusively caring for each other and in interaction benefiting each other" (15/10); concrete guidelines, such as detailed specifications for burial practices (25/83); and exemplary figures or role models, such as the historical sage-kings (35/8) or the "superior officer" (16/26). Guiding and checking one's performance by such models amounts to a training process that habituates agents to follow the *dào*.

A third approach to motivating people to act according to the *dào*, intertwined with the preceding, is model emulation. The Mohists seek to harness people's tendency to emulate admired role models, including political leaders, exemplary historical figures such as the sage-kings, and ideal types such as the benevolent person or the filial son. They explicitly employ forms of model emulation to justify their doctrines (Mz 25/1–16), demonstrate their feasibility (16/47–63), and educate people to follow them (11/9–22). I suggest that in all three of these sorts of cases they also implicitly invoke the motivational power of model emulation. People are likely to become motivated to follow the Mohist *dào* because it is the *dào* of admired and respected leaders, heroic historical figures, and paradigmatic archetypes.

A fourth method of motivation is social encouragement and pressure, from both superiors and peers. Mohist political theory proposes a society-wide scheme for moral education and training in which virtuous political leaders serve as moral teachers, instructing people to conform to a unified set of moral norms and setting a good example for them to follow, while members of society provide positive and negative reinforcement by praising one another's good conduct and criticizing transgressions (Mz 11/9–13).

A fifth, final technique is material incentives and disincentives. To help ensure conformity to the *dào* even among those who are not motivated by normative considerations or social pressure, the political system also incorporates material rewards and penalties for proper or improper conduct. The Mohists expressly state that the aim of criminal punishment is not retribution but to bring into the fold those who will not identify with political leaders in following unified moral norms (Mz 11/24–25, 12/48–49).

SOURCES OF MOTIVATION

The Mohists identify at least six distinct sources of motivation that they seek to bring into play through the techniques just described. All six may contribute to a particular agent's overall motivation to practice the *dào*.[25]

Perhaps the most prominent source of motivation for the Mohists is people's normative attitudes. As we have seen, the Mohists take *shì-fēi* attitudes to be inherently motivating. Since whatever people deem righteous they will normally also deem *shì*, the motivational force of *shì-fēi* attitudes carries over to the distinction between righteousness and unrighteousness: people are normally motivated to do, endorse, or defend what they deem righteous and to avoid, condemn, or prevent what they deem unrighteous. The motivational role of the benevolent (*rén*) versus unbenevolent distinction is similar, though perhaps more complex. Conceivably, the attitude that something is benevolent may motivate people to endorse and defend it without feeling compelled to pursue it themselves. However, Mohist argument strategies make it clear that people are expected to find the benevolent person's deeming something *shì* or *fēi* convincing grounds for deeming it *shì* or *fēi* themselves and becoming motivated accordingly (Mz 15/1–15, 32/1–7).

Numerous passages in the *Mòzǐ* illustrate the assumption that distinguishing something as righteous or unrighteous normally motivates agents to act accordingly. Most prominent is the account of the hypothetical state of nature discussed in chapter 3. Other examples include a passage claiming that people will fight to the death over a statement because they value righteousness over everything else and another claiming that anyone would give a hand to a worker struggling with a heavy load because doing so is righteous (Mz 47/1–3, 43–44).[26] Particularly telling is the Mohists' explanation of why war-mongering rulers and their supporters wage immoral wars of conquest: they do not know that doing so is unbenevolent and unrighteous but instead take their actions to be righteous (17/9–14, 19/4–6, 28/50–55). The Mohists' rhetorical strategy here rests on the assumption that how people distinguish righteous from unrighteous determines their conduct. The aim is to show that, like robbery and murder, wars of aggression are unrighteous. Were rulers to correctly deem them unrighteous, they would desist from them.

Besides a formal commitment to doing what they deem moral or righteous, according to the Mohists, people also share substantive beliefs about righteousness or morality (*yì*) that can be expected to help motivate them to follow the *dào*. As we saw in chapter 3, Mohist political theory assumes, for instance, that people share the conviction that righteousness comprises public, objective norms of conduct to which everyone should conform, that such unified norms are a prerequisite for social order, and that unified norms can be achieved only by having everyone in society obey the leadership of morally worthy political authorities.

A second source of motivation to which the Mohists appeal is widely shared values that they contend are promoted by their *dào*. They assume that most people—particularly government leaders—value social order, economic prosperity, and sufficient population, the goods they identify as constituting "the benefit of all the world," their criterion of what is morally right. One component of social order, as they understand it, is the exercise of the relational virtues, goods that again they assume most people value. Hence they plausibly hold that people's preexisting motivation to promote these goods carries over into motivation to practice the Mohist *dào*.

A third important source of motivation is prudential self-interest, in the broad sense of an interest in both one's own welfare and that of one's immediate kin. That self-interest is a common, even universal motive is presupposed by the "Caretaker" and "Ruler" arguments defending the "usability" of inclusive care (Mz 16/22, 35), discussed in chapter 6. Self-interest also grounds the Mohists' belief in the power of social and material incentives and disincentives to modify people's attitudes and conduct—though only, they specify, if these are perceived as distributed fairly (12/52–55), with equal opportunity for all (8/9–14), and in a way that makes people feel cared for, rather than merely used as means (9/23–24). The Mohists expect self-interest to converge with, and perhaps contribute to, people's motivation to practice their ethics, since they hold that their *dào* is consistent with and even tends to promote self-interest. One's own interests count among "the benefit of all," the basic criterion of morality. So morally right practices are expected to promote one's own interests as much as everyone else's.

A further source of motivation engaged by Mohist ethical norms is people's general tendency to reciprocate beneficial or detrimental attitudes and conduct (Mz 15/18–19, 16/70–71). The abstract phrasing the Mohists use to describe this tendency—"those who care about others will surely be cared about"—suggests they expect not only those with whom we have previously interacted directly but also people in general to treat us as we treat others. This tendency is thus a potentially powerful source of motivation that converges with the norm of inclusive care. For as we have seen, inclusive care is a reciprocal ideal: it calls for us each to care about everyone else such that we interact in ways that benefit one another. A tendency toward reciprocity thus means that people are predisposed toward just the sort of attitudes and conduct that constitute the practice of inclusive care. Of course, this tendency is only a formal inclination to respond to others in kind, whether they have treated us well or badly. It is not a substantive inclination to care about and benefit one another. Still, it does predispose people to sustain the virtuous cycle of care and benefit that the Mohist *dào* calls for.[27]

A fifth important source of motivation is people's inclination to respect and follow leaders (Mz 16/72–81). According to the Mohists, an effective political leader can motivate people to carry out difficult, even life-threatening acts, let alone follow moral norms that are not particularly stringent and promote the benefit of all. As we saw in chapter 3, however, the Mohists see such motivation as conditional on people's confidence that the leader governs fairly and in the public interest. If people perceive that their ruler fails to meet these criteria, they will align together in resistance against him (12/53–55). The motivational force of a leader's influence is thus constrained and, when the political system functions properly, reinforced by a sixth and final source of motivation, people's tendency to seek peer approval. The Mohists emphasize that people live together in communities, and community approval or disapproval ultimately has a greater influence on their conduct than any reward or penalty from a ruler whose judgment the community rejects (12/56–59).

In the ideal Mohist political society, the ruler employs the techniques sketched in the preceding section to govern in such a way that all six of these sources of motivation converge to support practice of the *dào*. He explains, exemplifies, and enforces unified norms of conduct grounded in values people either already share or find it easy to endorse, thus winning their respect and support. He sets forth explicit statements and models as guides to the norms and brings into play people's tendency to conform to authority and seek peer approval. By fairly and reliably enforcing the norms, he gives miscreants and free riders an incentive to cooperate and prevents them from harming the interests of the morally conscientious. He thus helps to ensure that conformity to the *dào* converges with self-interest and that people's tendency toward reciprocity is engaged in a beneficial rather than harmful direction.[28]

CONCLUDING REMARKS

Is the Mohist approach to action and motivation plausible? I suggest the Mohists' understanding of the structure of action is at least initially plausible, and indeed it may provide rich material for comparative work in the philosophy of action. Their conception of *shì-fēi* attitudes as inherently motivating is compelling, as is the view I have tentatively ascribed to them, that such attitudes can comprise both cognitive and conative or affective aspects. The five motivational techniques identified from their texts I think are widely agreed to be effective. Of course, we might question whether some are as powerful as the Mohists claim. For educated adults, for instance, model emulation and encouragement from political leaders may be less potent than the Mohists think. But commonsense experience strongly suggests that all these methods do work, within certain limits (some of which the Mohists explicitly recognize).

The sources of motivation to which the Mohists appeal probably are indeed genuine features of the typical agent's motivational system. People do tend to be motivated to act on what they endorse as right. They do tend to share at least some of the values the Mohists appeal to, and they obviously tend to pursue self-interest at times. Respect for authority and peer pressure can indeed play a role in motivating action, and people probably do tend to reciprocate others' attitudes and treatment, though perhaps less consistently than the Mohists envision. Even if none of these sources of motivation by itself is perfectly reliable, jointly they could add up to a powerful, reliable inclination to follow the Mohist *dào*. I think we can conclude that the Mohist approach to motivation is rich, nuanced, and reasonably plausible, even if in some respects incomplete.

Difficulties in motivating people to practice the Mohist *dào*, I suggest, probably would not arise from defects in the Mohist approach to motivation, nor from any failure to provide for the character development agents need to become virtuous, reliable performers of the *dào*. Mohist texts sketch a thorough, sophisticated social program for character development. Motivational obstacles would more likely stem from substantive weaknesses in the Mohists' normative conception of the *dào*. Without question, many aspects of Mohist ethics are persuasive. There are good reasons to think that unprovoked wars of aggression are indeed wrong, that others' welfare should count in determining how we act, that society should help provide for the care of orphans, and that impoverished farmers should not be taxed to buy luxury goods for despots, to cite just a few Mohist ethical claims. But other aspects of the Mohists' *dào*—such as their extreme parsimony—are much less convincing. By the Mohists' own lights, the most serious motivational obstacle to practicing an ethical teaching is a cogent argument that it is unjustified. Many of us find the normative justification for certain Mohist doctrines less than wholly persuasive, and thus we may reasonably lack the motivation to practice them.

8

WAR AND ECONOMICS

IN THE INTRODUCTION, I summarized the ten Mohist doctrines that constitute the planks in their social, moral, and political reform program. Their two major political doctrines, "identifying upward" and "promoting the worthy," were treated in chapter 3. Their central ethical doctrines, "Heaven's intent" and "inclusive care," were addressed in chapters 4 through 6. Their rejection of fatalism and commitment to the existence of spirits were treated in chapters 1 and 4. I now want to take a closer look at the four remaining doctrines. These are the antiwar doctrine, "condemning aggression," and the three economic doctrines, "moderation in use," "moderation in burial," and "condemning music." In addition, because the Mohists' criticisms of the Ruist *dào* focus mainly on the economic consequences of Ruist practices, the chapter includes a brief section summarizing the Mohist critique of Ruism.

To contemporary readers, the doctrines discussed in this chapter may be less interesting philosophically than those treated in previous chapters. To the Mohists themselves, however, they were vitally important. These were among the chief practical components of the Mohist reform program—concrete proposals arrived at by applying their ethical ideals to social and political problems that many among the wealthy and powerful would have preferred to ignore. These doctrines thus constitute a crucial element of early Chinese intellectual history and are essential to a full portrait of Mohism, as they were among the Mohists' most distinctive and renowned positions. Opposition to war was one of their two most prominent doctrines—inclusive care being the other—and their attack on the lavish entertainment and extravagant funerary practices of the aristocracy and the wealthy scandalized elite conformists, including the Rú. These doctrines also help to explain the Mohists' decline in the Hàn dynasty. Some of the details of their economic doctrines are the most idiosyncratic and least appealing of their views, and both these and their anti-aggression stance were eventually rendered obsolete by economic and political developments in early imperial China.

CONDEMNING AGGRESSION

The Mohists were renowned for their strenuous opposition to military aggression. "All Under Heaven," a Hàn-dynasty retrospective of Warring States thought found in the *Zhuāngzǐ*, says that Mòzǐ "cared universally, benefited all-inclusively, and rejected fighting" (Zz 33/18). A story in book 50 of the *Mòzǐ* depicts Mò Dí walking ten days and nights to reach the powerful southern state of Chǔ in time to dissuade its king from attacking the small, central state of Sòng.

Mohist texts opposing wars of aggression contain one of world history's earliest versions of a just war theory. They distinguish three sorts of warfare: defensive wars (*shǒu* 守), punitive wars (*zhū* 誅), and aggressive wars (*gōng* 攻). Defensive wars they take to be justified when unavoidable. Punitive wars they consider justified only in rare circumstances, in which demanding criteria are fulfilled. Aggressive wars they consider unjustified without exception. Unlike many antiwar activists, however, the Mohists themselves were keen, expert participants in military affairs, who considered a robust defense force a cornerstone of a state's political and economic strength. Since a state may need to engage in defensive warfare and possibly also punitive warfare, the Mohists advocate maintaining a high level of military readiness and devoting due attention to city fortifications. Indeed, the Mohists' own reputation as defense experts appears to have provided diplomatic leverage to help them dissuade potential aggressors from launching unjust wars.

DEFENSIVE WAR

For the Mohists, a justified state policy must promote the benefit of all and eliminate harm to all. Presumably, then, they consider defensive war justified insofar as it promotes benefit or reduces harm, at least for the community under attack. Of course, defensive war may not always promote benefit or reduce harm, compared with letting one's state be peacefully absorbed by an aggressor. Any war is likely to waste lives and resources. A failed defensive war might provoke harmful reprisals that are worse than the consequences of immediate surrender. If the costs of defensive warfare are too high, compared with surrendering one's state without resistance, Mohist ethical theory should justify surrender.[1] However, the Mohists depict the consequences of invasion in their day as horrific: a conqueror might pillage or destroy all the defeated state's resources and execute or enslave its people (Mz 19/10–14, 28/47–50). For a state under attack, it seems likely that defensive warfare, even with the risk of defeat, might have promised better consequences than peaceful surrender.

Defensive war for the Mohists includes not only self-defense but also the defense of other states, specifically allies and "innocent" small states targeted by belligerent larger states (Mz 19/12). Good statesmanship requires cordial, mutually beneficial relations with other states, such that all are prepared to come to one another's defense (19/57, 5/1–2). Through orderly domestic government and mutually beneficial diplomatic relations, states establish themselves as innocent and thus deserving of defense assistance.

One conversation in the "Dialogues" suggests that diplomacy and even political submission to a powerful aggressor may sometimes be preferable to defensive war. Fearful of an attack by the powerful state of Qí, the Lord of Lǔ asks Mòzǐ what can be done to save his state (Mz 49/1–4). Mòzǐ cites the examples of four sage-kings, who by teaching loyalty and practicing righteousness rose from small fiefdoms to rule the world, and the four tyrants, who through enmity and violence lost their empires. Disaster can be avoided, he suggests, by "honoring Heaven and serving the ghosts above, caring about and benefiting the people below, and richly preparing furs and coin, making your remarks humble, urgently paying respects to the neighboring various lords, and leading the state to serve Qí." These remarks suggest two concurrent courses of diplomacy. Lǔ should develop friendly ties with neighboring states, so that they support its defense, while diplomatically subordinating itself to Qí if needed to avoid war. The passage hints that diplomacy is preferable to defensive war even when the cost might be vassalage to a larger state. The Mohists' reasoning was probably that whatever harm might come from diplomatic subjugation would be less than the harm of war, or at least a mismatched war with little likelihood of success. Although this interpretation is conjectural, the passage may be applying an implicit criterion of probable success to argue against war, or it might reflect the view that defensive war is justified only as a last resort, when no peaceful diplomatic alternative is available.

AGGRESSIVE WAR

Aggressive war for the Mohists is always unjustified. A war of aggression, as they understand it, is an offensive war against a state that is "innocent" (Mz 19/12). Mohist texts do not directly spell out criteria for "innocence," but several conditions can be inferred from their stories about justified punitive war. In at least some cases, they consider punitive war justified when a state or its leader has fallen into "great disorder" (19/33), insulted Heaven and the spirits (31/84), attacked other states (49/16), or inflicted atrocities on its people (31/89). For a state to qualify as innocent, then, minimally its leaders must be orderly, devout, peaceful toward other states, and benign to their subjects. If a state is innocent, in this sense, there can be no morally sound justification for aggression against it.

The Mohists offer both moral and prudential arguments against wars of aggression. The moral arguments aim to show that, for various reasons, wars of aggression are morally wrong. The prudential arguments seek to show that such wars are also against the interests of the aggressor, since the costs outweigh the benefits. In Mohist ethics, of course, since the distinction between benefit and harm determines right and wrong, demonstrating that the harms of some action outweigh the benefits is tantamount to showing it is morally wrong. So the prudential arguments also support the conclusion that aggressive war is immoral. One argument combines moral and prudential concerns, contending that even if a ruler wages war for morally admirable ends that converge with his personal interests, aggression is a poor means of pursuing these.

The moral arguments are presented in three books, the first and third "Condemning Aggression" essays and the third "Heaven's Intent" essay. The shared theme of the arguments is that aggressive war fails to meet the basic moral standard of promoting the benefit of all. The penultimate section of chapter 2 quoted much of the first version of the moral argument, from the earliest "Condemning Aggression" essay (*Mz* 17/1–7). The gist is that unprovoked military aggression is unrighteous for the same reason that theft and murder are: because "it injures another to benefit oneself." Indeed, war is worse than these crimes, for the same reason that murder is worse than theft: "It injures another more. If it injures another more, the more it is unbenevolent and the more serious the crime." In the third "Heaven's Intent" essay, a similar argument explicitly criticizes rulers of the day for their inconsistency. In governing their states, they prohibit killing people, yet they deem it right to kill as many people of a neighboring state as possible (28/66–67).

The third "Condemning Aggression" essay presents a more elaborate moral argument (*Mz* 19/15–19). Everyone knows that what is good or moral is what benefits all denizens of the cosmos: Heaven, the ghosts, and people (19/3–4). But wars of aggression do not benefit Heaven. Just the opposite: they employ some of Heaven's people to massacre others, while dispossessing spirits from their shrines, overthrowing the altars of soil and grain, and slaughtering the sacrificial animals. They fail too to benefit the ghosts and spirits, since they result in the death or scattering of their worshippers. Nor do they benefit people: obviously, those who die do not benefit, and much of the survivors' material resources are wasted. Since such wars are harmful at all three levels, they are morally wrong.

The prudential argument that wars of aggression are against the aggressor's own interests is the main theme of the second "Condemning Aggression" essay and reappears in the third. The argument amounts to a litany of the costs and harms of war for the aggressor. War interrupts planting or harvesting. It wastes innumerable quantities of weapons, military supplies, vehicles, and livestock. People die because of harsh weather, insufficient food, illness, and injury in battle. The spirits suffer because of the death of their worshippers. Warlike rulers might rejoin that these costs are offset by the fame and plunder that victory brings (Mz 18/10). The Mohist reply is that the spoils of war are never enough to make up for the costs (18/11). Warlike states do not lack territory, yet they waste what they need—human lives—in pursuit of what they already have in abundance—villages, cities, and land. Governing in this way is contrary to the proper ends of the state (18/15). To the objection that some states have indeed benefited from aggression, increasing their territory and population, the Mohists reply that a handful of successes among a myriad failures shows that aggression fails to conform to the right *dào*, just as a doctor who treats many patients but heals only a few fails to genuinely treat disease (18/18–20). (Recall that for the Mohists, the *dào* must be a way that everyone can follow regularly and consistently with beneficial results for all.) To the objection that with competent leadership, wars of aggression promise to be profitable, they cite historical examples of competent, even brilliant generals whose initially successful military adventures eventually brought reprisal, defeat, and ignominious death (18/27–39).

A further argument against aggression combines prudential and moral concerns. The third "Condemning Aggression" essay considers the view that aggression might be justified if the aggressor's motive is not material gain but "to establish a name throughout the world through righteousness and to attract the various lords through virtue" (Mz 19/55). For prudential, self-interested reasons, the aggressor aims to achieve an admirable moral status and considers wars of conquest a reliable way to do so. A reputation for righteousness and virtue is a laudable ambition, the Mohists agree, but aggressive war is a misguided means of pursuing it. To achieve this aim, a ruler should instead conduct diplomatic relations in good faith, distribute military and economic aid generously to other states, and govern morally and effectively in his own state—thus befriending other states while strengthening his own. In this way, he would bring innumerable benefits to all and have "no match in all the world" (19/55–61). Wars of aggression are unjustified even if driven by praiseworthy motives.

PUNITIVE WAR

The third "Condemning Aggression" essay, chronologically the latest of the three, raises an important objection to Mohist criticisms of aggressive war. According to historical accounts widely accepted in the Mohists' era, several of the sage-kings they admired as moral paragons carried out successful offensive military campaigns. Yǔ suppressed the Miáo tribes, Tāng overthrew the tyrant Jié of the Xià dynasty, and Wǔ toppled the tyrant Zhòu of the Shāng dynasty. If wars of aggression are harmful and unjust, as the Mohists contend, why did the sage-kings launch these offensive wars? The Mohist reply is that these campaigns were not wars of aggression (gōng 攻). They were punitive missions (zhū 誅) (Mz 19/32–33), a type of offensive warfare that overlaps partly with what we would call humanitarian intervention. The Mohists allow that in the case of punitive missions, offensive campaigns may sometimes be justified.

To vindicate these wars, the text presents a series of elaborate historical stories, replete with portents from Heaven and visits from spirit emissaries. Although the stories amount mainly to a concocted apology for the sage-kings' wars, they jointly illustrate a series of conditions under which the Mohist writers consider punitive war justified. Intriguingly, despite the fanciful, mythical trappings of the Mohist doctrine, their implied conditions for justified punitive war overlap significantly with mainstream views today of the conditions for just war.[2]

The first and most prominent condition justifying these punitive wars is that all were purportedly conducted with divine sanction.[3] According to legend, Heaven expressed its condemnation of the targets of these invasions through miraculous portents, including freak weather, crop failure, midnight sun, rains of blood and flesh, screeching ghosts and animals, and fantastic creatures, such as a giant bird with a human head. Even more important, it dispatched spirit envoys to publicly authorize the sage-kings' campaigns. Heaven's sanction does not correspond directly to any condition in just war theory today. However, in the Mohists' philosophical and religious context, the mandate of Heaven can be interpreted as fulfilling the condition of proper authority for punitive war. One Mòzǐ passage draws an explicit analogy between Heaven's punishment of those who launch aggressive wars and a sovereign's punishment of criminality within a state (*Mz* 49/12–16). A plausible implication is that the only authority that can legitimately initiate a punitive mission is Heaven itself.

The grounds the Mohists give for Heaven's sanctioning punitive missions correspond to several criteria of just war commonly cited today. First, Heaven does not sanction punitive wars capriciously or arbitrarily. It does so for good reasons, which correspond to the condition of just cause in contemporary just war theory. In each of the Mohists' examples, the punished state had purportedly fallen into disorder. The tyrants Jié and Zhòu blasphemed Heaven and the spirits and massacred their people (*Mz* 31/83–84, 89). Zhòu is accused of abandoning the elderly, murdering children, torturing the innocent, and slicing open the wombs of pregnant women (31/89). Justified punitive missions thus aim to eliminate chaos and atrocities and restore peace and order. Although Heaven's sanction is a major criterion for just punitive war, the fundamental grounds for Heaven's decision are the familiar goods of Mohist consequentialism: the punitive war will supposedly promote the benefit of all or eliminate harm to all. Second, a punitive war must be waged with good intention. Specifically, the Mohists explain, it should be waged not for self-interest but, as in Yǔ's campaign against the Miáo, "to promote benefit to the world and eliminate harm to the world" (16/54–55). Each of the purportedly just wars was launched with the aim of securing peace and stability, which corresponds to the condition of right intention in modern just war theory. Third, the sage-kings had good reason to believe their punitive wars would succeed, as the spirits who commanded the attacks expressly guaranteed success. Although today we would reject alleged proclamations by spirits as grounds for expecting victory, these features of the stories correspond to the condition of probable success in modern just war theory.

A natural worry is that the doctrine of just punitive war could be exploited to excuse illegitimate aggression on the pretext that it is punitive rather than aggressive war.[4] In practice, however, probably no supposedly punitive war could ever meet the Mohists' stringent justification conditions. Since they expect Heaven's mandate to be attested by numerous publicly observed miracles, the criterion of divine sanction in practice puts the justification for punitive war permanently beyond reach.[5] Absent miraculous omens signaling Heaven's approval, what could justify punitive war? This question arises in a dialogue in which Mòzǐ dismisses a proposed justification for a punitive mission.

Lord Wén of Lǔ Yáng said, "Sir, why stop me from attacking Zhèng? My attacking Zhèng follows Heaven's intent. For three generations, the people of Zhèng have murdered their ruler. Heaven has punished them, causing three years of scarcity. I will assist Heaven in punishing them."

Our Master Mòzǐ said, "For three generations, the people of Zhèng have murdered their ruler and Heaven has punished them, causing three years of scarcity. Heaven's punishment is sufficient. Yet now you deploy your army to attack Zhèng, saying, 'My attacking Zhèng follows Heaven's intent.' By analogy, suppose there is a man here whose son is hale and hearty but worthless, so his father whips him with a bamboo cane. The father of the neighboring family then beats him with a wooden staff, saying, 'My beating him is following his father's intent.' How is this not perverse?!" (Mz 49/16–20)

The grounds for a legitimate punitive war cannot be simply that the offending state is disorderly or has committed crimes. Stronger grounds are needed, such as an explicit divine mandate. Without such grounds, the very evidence that Heaven is displeased with a state—such as that the state suffers from scarcity—is at the same time evidence that Heaven itself has already punished it. Further punishment is redundant and would lack proper authority, just as the head of one family lacks the authority to punish another's child.

Mòzǐ's remarks in the passage hint at inchoate recognition of a further condition in just war theory, proportionality of the means of justified war to the ends. If the end is to punish Zhèng, then Lǔ Yáng's invasion violates proportionality, since Heaven has already dealt sufficient punishment. The passage can also be read as implying a condition of last resort, by which war cannot be justified as long as peaceful alternatives remain. For a consequence of Mòzǐ's response is that a punitive mission could be justified only if one first waited to see whether Heaven itself would punish the offender. Hasty intervention without Heaven's explicit sanction would never be justified. If the offending state were to suffer a series of misfortunes on its own, without military intervention, these would already constitute sufficient punishment for its actions.

Given Mòzǐ's response in this passage, then, I suggest that the Mohists probably hold that punitive war is effectively never justified. For the Mohists, the doctrine of punitive war has mainly a rhetorical function, as an apology for the wars of the sage-kings. In practice, without unequivocal public portents signaling Heaven's mandate, no supposedly punitive war can be considered right. Is no form of offensive warfare ever justified, then? In principle, Mohist ethics should allow that, even without Heaven's mandate, an offensive campaign might be justified if on balance it significantly promoted the benefit of all. Given the expected harm to the people of the targeted state, however, such a justification would be difficult to establish. An offensive mission could perhaps be justified if aimed at morally good ends, such as eliminating a proven threat to people's welfare or reversing the harms inflicted on a conquered territory. Indeed, two Mòzǐ passages hint at a conception of justified retributive offensive war to liberate conquered territories and eliminate future threats from a serial aggressor (Mz 49/5–8, 18/27–41). Such offensive campaigns could probably be considered one aspect of just defensive war, however, rather than war for offensive ends. Moreover, the criteria of justification would be stringent. An offensive campaign could be justified only if the targeted state had committed severe aggression or atrocities, war was the only plausible means of achieving the morally good ends intended, and without intervention the offending state was unlikely to suffer misfortune proportionate to the harms it had caused. These criteria are strict enough that they would only rarely be met.[6]

MODERATION IN USE

The Mohists advocated three doctrines based on moderation in the use of resources. These include a general doctrine of moderation in use, covering housing, clothing, diet, weaponry and armor, transportation, luxury goods, and sexual relations, and two special applications of this doctrine to elite customs the Mohists perceived as especially wasteful: extravagant burial and mourning practices and "music," or lavish entertainment.

By the close of the Warring States era, in their critics' eyes, the Mohist movement was distinguished largely by these doctrines on economic moderation. They are the grounds for attacks on them by Xúnzǐ and for most criticisms of them in Hàn texts, such as the Zhuāngzǐ "All Under Heaven" essay and the Shǐ jì (Records of the grand historian). A common element of the criticisms is that Mohist practices allegedly recognize no distinctions in rank, treating different grades of aristocrats, officials, and commoners alike—a consequence these conservative, elite writers find intolerable. The Mohists were perceived as attacking elite rank and privilege. To some extent, Mohist economic doctrines would indeed have restricted elite entitlement. As we saw in chapter 3, however, the Mohists themselves advocated government by a meritocratic elite and believed that the proper functioning of the state depended on there being significant inequality in status, salary, and power between superiors and subordinates. They were not opposed in principle to a social system in which a minority enjoyed special rank and privileges, provided these were based on merit. They simply did not see the customs they rejected as necessary for marking such status distinctions.

Mohist doctrines concerning economic moderation thus were not motivated by any fundamental opposition to the prevailing sociopolitical system of the preimperial Central States. Rather, they grew out of two concerns facing prudent, economically middle- and lower-class residents of these states, which the Mohists assume ought to be shared also by political leaders: ensuring general material welfare and maintaining the state's economic and military strength. A joint premise of these doctrines is that poverty is a constant, imminent threat, one that can easily provoke social unrest among the disadvantaged. Thus in rejecting wasteful upper-class practices, the Mohists are not attacking the very idea of elite privilege or tradition. They are simply insisting that priority be given to ensuring the livelihood of the common people, preserving social order, and protecting society against war and economic hardship. In light of the pressing need for these goods, the elite should refrain from luxury items and extravagant entertainment, which do not promote "the benefit of all." If economic circumstances were as harsh as the Mohists imply—and I suggest we accept their testimony that for many commoners, hardship was never far off—then their strictures against excessive state spending and other misuse of resources are surely compelling.

The Mohists' focus on the welfare of the people and the state is clear from the central themes of the three extant essays on the general theme of moderation. The earliest "Moderation in Use" book contends that a state can double its resources by eliminating useless expenses and refraining from war. When a sage-king governs, "in issuing decrees and undertaking affairs, employing the people and using resources, he does nothing that doesn't add usefulness. Thus he uses resources without wasting anything, the people are not weary, and he promotes much benefit" (Mz 20/2–3). The second "Moderation in Use" book explains that the practice of the sage-kings, grounded in their deep care for the people, was to avoid doing "anything that added expense without adding to the people's benefit" (21/4). The much later essay "Avoiding Excess" claims that in primitive times people had not yet discovered how to build houses, make textiles, cook food, or construct vehicles and boats. In each case, the sage-kings invented these items for their benefit. But "any expenditure of resources or exertion of labor that did not add benefit was not done" (6/3). The texts thus advocate not austerity or parsimony but eliminating useless or wasteful expenses.

By "useless" consumption, the Mohists are referring primarily to elite extravagances. Their examples of useless goods are generally items that only the aristocracy could have afforded—jewelry, ornaments, exotic animals—and they directly criticize aristocratic indulgences, such as specially decorated vehicles for high officials or large harems for rulers. "Avoiding Excess" presents the most detailed complaints about such extravagances:

> As to the rulers of today . . . they inevitably collect heavy taxes from the people, robbing the people of their resources for clothing and food, to build palaces and pavilions with zigzagging views and decorations of colorful paint and carvings. The ruler builds his palace like this, so those on his left and right all model themselves on him. Hence their resources are insufficient to prepare against scarcity or famine or to relieve the orphaned and widowed. So the state is impoverished and the people are difficult to put in order. . . . They collect heavy taxes from the people to prepare various gourmet meats, along with steamed and broiled fish and turtles. In a great state, the dishes total a hundred, in a small state ten. On a table with ten-foot sides, the eye cannot see all the dishes, the hand cannot reach them all, the mouth cannot taste them all. In winter, the uneaten food freezes; in summer it spoils. The ruler eats and drinks like this, so those on his left and right emulate him. Hence the wealthy and noble are wasteful, while the orphaned and widowed are cold and hungry. (Mz 6/6–25)

The text criticizes such excess with respect to elite housing, clothing, diet, vehicles, and harems. A similarly themed passage in the "Dialogues" ties wasteful elite consumption to military weakness. Mòzǐ is depicted urging a minister of Wèi to exchange his harem for a regiment of soldiers:

> Wèi is a small state, situated between Qí and Jìn. . . . Now inspecting your house, we find hundreds of decorated carriages, hundreds of grain-fed horses, and hundreds of women clothed in finery. If we took the cost of decorating the carriages and feeding the horses and the resources needed for the fine clothing and used them to maintain soldiers, surely there would be in excess of a thousand men. If there were a crisis, you could station several hundred in the front and several hundred in the rear. Compared with stationing several hundred women in the front and rear, which would be more secure? (Mz 47/36–40)

The Mohists' primary target is thus aristocratic excess, waste, and imprudence. Still, their strictures on consumption go beyond ruling-class extravagance. They are presented as entirely general, applying to all levels of society. The texts stipulate that the function of clothing, for instance, is to warm the body in winter and cool it in summer, and so plain bluish-gray clothing of light, simple fabric that fulfills these functions is enough. Food should be nutritious and filling but need not be especially tasty and should not include rare, imported ingredients. Swords should be sharp and durable, armor light and tough while preserving agility. Vehicles should be strong, safe, and easy to pull. Palaces and houses should protect from the elements, be clean enough to perform religious sacrifices, and have appropriate partitions to separate the sexes. Any feature that does not contribute to the basic functions of these items should be eliminated. Specifically, the texts interpret "benefit" (*lì* 利) or "utility" (*yòng* 用, "use") as excluding almost anything of primarily aesthetic value, including all decoration or ornamentation in housing, clothing, armor, weapons, boats, and vehicles. One passage even implies that an interest in attractively decorated clothing leads people to become licentious and unruly (Mz 6/19–20). On the whole, then, the economic texts advocate an austere, parsimonious way of life devoted almost entirely to pursuit of narrow material utility. People are to refrain from any sort of personal indulgence, aesthetic enjoyment, or other activity that does not provide for basic material needs. Individual self-expression is discouraged to the extent that, in the interest of state utility, one passage advocates regulating even the age at which people marry—twenty for males, fifteen for females—since young people's fertility is a resource not to be wasted (20/11–14).

The Mohists surely succeed in establishing their main point, that aristocrats are wrong to exploit the disadvantaged to pay for their own extravagances. Were they to argue for only this claim, their position would be hard to fault. But their arguments commit them to a narrow, simplistic view of the good that they neither explicitly acknowledge nor defend. The problem is that they apply a highly restrictive conception of human welfare, acknowledging no form of benefit beyond material livelihood and social order, while overlooking such goods as aesthetic value and appreciation, self-expression, emotional enjoyment, and sensual pleasure.[7] Perhaps because of this omission, they see no middle ground between excess and parsimony: any expenditure beyond the essential minimum counts as indefensible extravagance. Moreover, they envision no economic conditions other than scarcity, not even as a long-term outcome of their own constructive economic policies. They never consider whether circumstances might improve enough to justify moderate spending on nonessentials or whether discretionary spending might contribute to economic growth and thus ultimately provide more resources for all. Again, however, as mentioned in chapter 5, they do not explicitly reject a thicker view of the good, nor expressly advocate a thin view. They simply do not seriously consider any goods other than material livelihood, population growth, and social order. Their narrow conception of the good is a by-product of their overall sociopolitical program, with its emphasis on basic general welfare, not a considered position that they deliberately articulate and defend.[8]

Given their social and historical background, it is easy to understand why the Mohists take such a thin view of the good for granted. As members of non-elite socioeconomic groups living in an ancient, primarily agricultural society, Mòzǐ and his early followers may never have experienced an economic climate in which it would have been prudent to allow spending on nonessentials. They could have been so scarred by deprivation that—like many survivors of hard times—they habitually saved every spare penny. Poverty may have been common enough in their time that it seemed only natural to direct all surplus resources toward relieving and preventing it. The plausibility of their outlook, given their historical context, is underscored by the fact that no other Warring States text criticizes them for their narrow conception of the good or argues for the importance of the goods they overlook.[9]

The one early critic who directly responds to Mohist economic doctrines is Xúnzǐ, who accepts without question their focus on material welfare and social order and grounds his own counterarguments in these goods. Xúnzǐ presents two arguments against Mòzǐ, one purporting to show that moderation in expenditure is unnecessary, the other that it undermines social order. First, he contends, the Mohists are simply mistaken that economic scarcity is a widespread problem. Nature provides such abundance that with proper crop and herd management, food and clothing will always be in surplus (Xz 10/48–51). Moderating expenditures is thus unnecessary. Of course, economic conditions could have changed enough between the early Mohists' time and Xúnzǐ's that both sides might have been justified in their views. The Mohist doctrine of moderation originated among artisans, merchants, farmers, and soldiers of the fifth century B.C.E. who seem to have lived mainly in small, relatively weak states, such as Lǔ. Xúnzǐ was a high-ranking official who lived almost two centuries later in the large, powerful states of Qí and Chǔ. However, even supposing the economic outlook was more encouraging in Xúnzǐ's day, his exaggerated optimism about nature's bounty seems facile and uninformed, and he wholly misses the Mohist point about exploitation of the common people. Even if natural resources were in principle unlimited, people's labor is not. Moreover, their prosperity in any one year is subject to hazards such as failed harvests, flood, drought, and disease—all worries mentioned in the *Mòzǐ*. As a privileged urban official, Xúnzǐ may simply have not understood how precarious economic conditions could be among the rural poor.

Xúnzǐ's second argument is that the practice of moderation will lead to social disorder and thus poverty. If material rewards were dispensed only in moderation, he contends, they would lose their power to motivate people, thus eliminating the ruler's primary means of governing. He goes on to claim that for the ruler to govern effectively, he must be able to unify, control, and intimidate the people through ostentatious displays of authority and wealth. So elaborate music, regalia, and banquets, along with vast throngs of retainers, are necessary for effective government (Xz 10/53–67). Both parts of this argument are far-fetched. It is unlikely a policy of moderation would prevent rewards or punishments from motivating people; nor are rewards the only means the ruler has of encouraging cooperation.[10] Granted, effective government requires people's respect, which in turn rests partly on the public display of status and power. (Xúnzǐ seems unaware that the Mohists make the same point, as we saw in chapter 3.) But Xúnzǐ offers no reason to think maintaining such respect requires extravagant, rather than moderate, displays of wealth.[11] His argument here amounts to little more than a strained apology for ruling-class indulgence.

Xúnzǐ's objection to the doctrine of moderation thus was not that it assumed too narrow a conception of the good, nor that it condemned people to a life of austerity. It was that it might diminish the ruler's power and thus undermine social order.[12] This objection is also reflected in his repeated complaint that the Mohists blur the distinctions between social ranks.[13] When Xúnzǐ famously criticizes Mòzǐ for being so "blinkered by utility" that he "did not know wén [文, pattern, form, adornment, culture]" (Xz 21/21), perhaps his point is not that Mòzǐ was blind to aesthetic value, a common interpretation of this remark. Given Xúnzǐ's arguments, the point may instead be that the Mohists do not sufficiently acknowledge the role of outward cultural forms or protocols in producing utility—that is, the need for ceremonies, music, palaces, regalia, and other trappings of power in order to achieve utilitarian ends such as social order.

In summary, then, although the narrow conception of the good the Mohists employ in their economic arguments may strike us as a salient shortcoming, it was neither unusual nor especially controversial in their milieu. Indeed, it may simply reflect shared presuppositions of early Chinese political discourse.

The general doctrine of moderation in use was the basis for two further economic positions, the Mohists' opposition to protracted mourning and rich burials and their disapproval of what they unfortunately referred to as "music."

MODERATION IN BURIALS

During the Mohists' time, a custom developed among some of the aristocracy and the wealthy in the Central States of giving deceased relatives and officials extravagant burials—the higher one's social rank, the more lavish.[14] The deceased would lie in state for up to three months, after which the corpse would be dressed in several layers of fine clothing or shrouds, placed in a set of nested coffins—from two for an officer up to seven for a king—and buried in the main room of a large, multichambered tomb filled with rich burial goods, ranging from jewels, trinkets, and clothing to weapons and carriages. Sometimes concubines, slaves, attendants, or entertainers might be sacrificed to accompany their master or mistress in death. Above a royal tomb, a vast mound would be built and a large memorial palace erected, with towers, courtyards, halls, and chambers that, according to one contemporaneous account, resembled a city (LSCQ 10/3). One such complex designed for a Warring States king, his two queens, and two concubines occupied a walled plot of land over 410 meters wide and 176 meters long.[15] The deceased's surviving kin would undertake a complex, protracted series of mourning rituals lasting in some cases as long as three years. (In practice, "three years" meant "into the third year," and so the "three-year" mourning was in fact usually twenty-five to twenty-seven months.) Mourners were required to wear sackcloth mourning robes, reside in a thatched hut, sleep on the ground on a mat of twigs, walk with a cane, and eat only thin gruel.

These customs probably arose from aristocratic rivalry in conspicuous consumption and public demonstration of virtue, specifically filial devotion. They then spread downward throughout society, people striving through lavish burials and protracted mourning to demonstrate their households' wealth and their virtuous devotion to the deceased. With the exception of human sacrifice, such practices were encouraged and defended by the Rú, who as specialists in rituals and ceremonies stood to profit from them. A vitriolic passage in "Condemning the Rú" depicts them as living off the fruits of others' labor, "chasing after large funerals, their sons and grandsons all in tow." News of a death in a wealthy family fills them with glee, claims the text, since for them "this is the source of food and clothing" (Mz 39/15–17).

The Mohists rejected these exaggerated funerary practices as detrimental to the welfare of the state and its people. They offer three arguments against them, all grounded in the doctrine of the Three Models. The main argument rests on the third of the models, benefit to society. The Mohists observe that those who support and those who oppose rich burials and lengthy mourning both contend that their position reflects the *dào* of the sage-kings, the first model. Hence appealing to that model cannot settle the issue. Nor, in this case, can the issue be resolved by empirical observation, and so the second model—what people see and hear—must be set aside. So the matter comes down to the third model. In a passage I translated in chapter 5, the Mohists highlight the relevance of this model by suggesting that just as a filially devoted son spares no effort in pursuing for his parents the "three benefits"—wealth, a large family, and social order—the benevolent person spares no effort seeking prosperity, a large population, and social order for "all the world." Since rich burials were considered an expression of filial devotion, the analogy reassures audiences that the Mohists are committed to filiality while implying it is nevertheless not the only pertinent value.

The first argument asks whether the practice of extravagant burials and prolonged mourning enriches society, increases the population, and yields stability and order (Mz 25/12–16). The Mohists argue that for each of these goods, elaborate burial and mourning practices have detrimental consequences (25/17–55). They impoverish the state, since they cause much wealth to be buried in the ground and take people away from their work for extended periods. They do not increase the population, since the unhealthy living conditions imposed by the mourning rituals can cause illness or death and the prolonged separation of married couples interrupts sexual relations. They interfere with social order in numerous ways. They keep officials from their duties, leading to negligence in government administration and law enforcement. They interfere with the common people's work, causing economic scarcity. Scarcity in turn makes it difficult for parents, elder brothers, and rulers to provide for their children, siblings, and subordinates, who, if they lack the relational virtues, may come to resent them. Lacking adequate food and clothing, malicious people may turn to banditry and thievery. Moreover, by impairing economic prosperity, population growth, and social order, these customs reduce the resources available for state defense. The resultant poverty, depopulation, and disorder even interfere with the provision of timely, ritually clean sacrifices to the Lord on High, ghosts, and spirits, whose blessings thus cannot be sought and who may in response decide to punish the people.

The second argument addresses the objection that, whether or not rich burials and lengthy mourning contribute to wealth, population, or social order, they are nevertheless the *dào* of the sage-kings. Here the Mohists set aside their reservations about appealing to the first model—the deeds of the sage-kings—and assert that, according to traditional lore, the sages Yáo, Shùn, and Yǔ were all given very simple burials (Mz 25/58–64).

The third argument concludes the important passage, discussed in chapter 1, in which the Mohists distinguish between custom and morality, pointing out that a practice may be customary without thereby being right. The passage cites three examples of exotic funeral customs that people of the Central States would have found abhorrent: abandoning the wife of one's deceased grandfather, discarding the rotting flesh of the deceased and burying only the bones, and cremation on an open pyre. These foreign customs, the Mohists contend, are too meager, while those of the Central States are too extravagant. Some practices being inadequate and others excessive, moderation is called for. Just as moderation is needed in our use of clothing and food, which benefit the living, so too is it needed in funerary practices, which benefit the dead. The passage thus seems to imply a refinement of the third model, benefit to society. Since insufficiency and excess are both contrary to benevolence and righteousness, the text implies, the correct *dào* is one in which benefits are enjoyed in moderation. The text goes on to claim that Mohist funerary norms neglect the benefit neither of the dead nor the living (Mz 25/86), thus hinting as well at a further criticism of extravagant burials, that they are insufficiently impartial, favoring the welfare of the deceased over that of the survivors.

In place of lavish burials, "Moderation in Burial" proposes two overlapping versions of moderate norms, one attributed to the sage-kings (Mz 25/55–57), the other to Mòzǐ (25/83–85). Both are roughly similar to common practices today. The two versions agree that the coffin should be three inches thick, the corpse wrapped in three layers of shrouds, and the burial neither so deep as to reach water nor so shallow as to allow odor to escape. The sage-king version specifies a grave mound "about three crop rows wide," the Mòzǐ version one "large enough to mark the spot." The sage-king version stipulates that "once the deceased has been buried, the living must not cry for long but hurry to undertake work, people doing what they can to benefit each other in their interactions." The Mòzǐ version instructs that people are to wail on the way to and from the burial, but on returning should set to work producing food and clothing. Afterward, they are to regularly perform sacrificial rituals to express filial devotion toward the deceased. Neither formulation specifies exactly how long the funeral and mourning rituals are to last, nor just how quickly mourners are to return to work. A passage in the "Dialogues" indicates that a three-day funeral and mourning period was standard (48/42–43).

The Mohists were not alone in opposing extravagant funerary practices. Two essays—possibly Mohist inspired—in *The Annals of Lü Buwei* argue that, far from expressing appropriate respect and concern for the dead, lavish burials actually harm them, since they attract grave robbers (LSCQ 10/2–10/3). Xúnzǐ responds to this argument by optimistically claiming that under the ideal government of a sage-king, grave robbery will not occur, since there is material sufficiency for all and people are ashamed of even such minor misconduct as picking up others' lost property (Xz 18/81–84). (He does not explain what relevance this claim has to actual, nonideal conditions.) A passage in a late stratum of the *Analects* considers the objection—attributed to Zǎi Wǒ, a disciple

Confucius frequently criticizes—that a single year of mourning should be sufficient, since the three-year ritual has bad consequences. (Zǎi Wǒ's worry is not that it reduces general welfare but that it causes gentlemen to fall out of practice in ceremonies and music.) The text acerbically dismisses the idea that a year's mourning is enough:

> "As to the gentleman in mourning, in eating he finds no sweetness, in hearing music no joy, in dwelling no comfort. So he does not eat rice or wear embroidered clothes. Now if you are comfortable eating rice and wearing embroidered clothes, then do so." Zǎi Wǒ went out. The Master said, "Such is Zǎi Wǒ's lack of benevolence! Only when a child is three years old does it leave its parents' arms. As to the three-year mourning, it is the mourning custom throughout the world. Did Zǎi Wǒ receive three years' care from his parents?" (LY 17.21)

From this passage we can extract three potential lines of argument for the three-year mourning ritual. First, the gentleman mourns for three years because to do otherwise would leave him uneasy with grief and thus unable to enjoy his normal diet, clothing, and dwelling. Second, the three-year ritual should be observed because it is a universal custom. Third, the ritual acknowledges the three years of care we received from our parents as infants.

The Mohists' treatment of the distinction between custom and morality suggests how they would answer the second of these arguments. They would note that the three-year ritual is not, in fact, a universal custom and then explain that, even if it were, a practice can be customary without being right. A variation of the third argument is explicitly addressed in the "Dialogues." Gōng Mèngzǐ, the text's spokesman for the Rú, explains that the three-year mourning symbolizes children's attachment to their parents, as young children are deeply upset by separation from their mother or father. The Mohist response is caustic:

> Our Master Mòzǐ said, "Now an infant knows only to be attached to its parents and that's all. Unable to find its parents, it cries without cease. What is the reason for this? It's the height of ignorance. That being so, then how is the knowledge of the Rú any better than an infant's?!" (Mz 48/44–46)

The sarcasm perhaps obscures the philosophical point. Even if we grant that we owe a distinctive debt to our parents and feel special grief over losing them, these facts pin down no particular form of conduct as the appropriate way to acknowledge our special relationship and emotions. To suggest it is inherently appropriate to model our conduct, even symbolically, on the behavior of infants, who are incapable of acting any other way, is in a sense to reduce oneself to their cognitive and emotional level.

The first of the three lines of argument raises a more interesting question, which I suggest captures the main ethical significance of the Ruist defense of the three-year mourning ritual: what role, if any, should emotions play in determining ethical norms? The *Analects* passage seems to imply that a properly cultivated gentleman mourns his parents for three years because in a sense his emotions leave him unable to do otherwise. The ritual is merely an outward codification of his natural emotional responses. An extreme version of this line of argument might claim that the ritual is justified simply because it is a spontaneous expression of natural emotions. This claim would be implausible, of course, since obviously not all spontaneous expressions of emotion are morally permissible, let alone obligatory. (Suppose a person's spontaneous response to people who disagreed with her was to slap them.) Moreover, it is preposterous to claim that the specific, elaborate rituals advocated by the Rú represent the typical, morally decent person's spontaneous response to the death of a parent. However, we can easily imagine a more plausible way to develop this basic Ruist idea. Most of us will agree that certain distinctive emotions, such as grief over the loss of close kin, are an inescapable part of life. One could argue that the appropriate expression of these emotions is a crucial component of the good life or of human welfare. One could then argue that the three-year mourning ritual—or some other proposed norm—is justified on the grounds that it is a uniquely appropriate or satisfying way of expressing these characteristic human emotions. This is roughly the approach that Xúnzǐ takes. He contends that the ancient sage-kings established the three-year mourning ritual as the only appropriate, moderate, and orderly way of expressing mourners' grief and longing for the deceased (*Xz* 19/93–103).[16] Although mourners' pain persists after twenty-five months, he says, one must then return to normal life, as this period is a moderate mean between the extremes of immediately forgetting one's deceased parent and mourning indefinitely. Interestingly, Xúnzǐ thus accepts the Mohist proposal that the appropriate mourning ritual will be moderate, representing a mean between practices that are too plain and too elaborate. He simply disagrees about what counts as moderate.

The Mohists do not directly address this third line of argument, which could well have been proposed long after their essay on funerals was written. From what they do say, they would probably agree that bereavement is a fact of life that ethical norms must take into consideration. Moreover, the appropriate norms will be moderate ones that balance the expression of grief and respect with the need to move on. (As we have seen, their own rituals allow for three days of mourning, followed by regular sacrificial rituals expressing devotion to the deceased.) No doubt they would rightly reject as absurd Xúnzǐ's claim that twenty-five months is a "moderate" norm. More generally, they could agree that ethical norms must be compatible with characteristic human emotions but would probably argue that emotions alone do not determine what is ethically right or wrong, nor directly justify any particular style or type of ritual performance.[17] There is simply no compelling argument from the premise that people need to express certain emotions to the conclusion that some particular type of ritual performance is correct, a point that the *Zhuāngzǐ* will later drive home (Zz 6/65). Indeed, to the extent that typical human responses and needs do set rough constraints on justifiable ceremonial forms, the bizarrely protracted and burdensome funerary rituals the Mohists opposed were surely unjustified. For they hardly conform to—and might even suppress—most people's spontaneous psychological response to grief and their need to acknowledge loss while moving on.

In the Hàn dynasty, the rich burials and lengthy mourning practices the Mohists opposed gradually fell out of favor and more moderate funerals became customary. These remained, however, considerably more elaborate than the Mohists' proposed norms.

CONDEMNING MUSIC

A further, distinctive consequence of the Mohists' commitment to moderation in expenditure was the doctrine they called "condemning music." According to the surviving essay presenting it, this doctrine was not a blanket condemnation of musical entertainment or performance.[18] Indeed, "condemning music" is an unhappy label for it, one that probably undermined the Mohists' cause rhetorically. The text does not imply that they opposed, for instance, farmers singing work songs in the fields or families enjoying folk songs around the hearth. The chief target of their condemnation was the aristocratic practice of mounting grand musical shows at public expense—particularly when the taxpayers footing the bill were poor farmers and artisans barely able to provide for their families. A further object of Mohist criticism was the widely shared assumption in Warring States political thought that the regular performance of ceremonial music was a means of maintaining social order and thus an important function of government.

As the Mohists use the term, "music" (*yuè* 樂) typically refers not just to the performance of music but to an elaborate musical extravaganza held in a luxuriously decorated open-air theater. While aristocrats and officials sat in pavilions, dining on a sumptuous banquet, dance troupes would perform to the accompaniment of an orchestra comprising stringed instruments, woodwinds, and enormous sets of bells and drums. In some cases, commoners might be admitted to view the show. These productions were not merely a form of entertainment but also often part of state ceremonies. The performance of appropriate music was thought to have a transformative psychological effect that contributed to ethical cultivation and social order.[19] Sponsoring regular, proper musical performances was thus considered a requirement for orderly government, and the Mòzǐ reports that some rulers and ministers considered the construction of musical instruments a service to the state (Mz 32/7).

The Mohists argue that these extravagant musical productions are not among the duties of government and in fact are morally wrong. Their grounds are not that music—nor lavish shows, banquets, or theaters—is intrinsically bad. On the contrary, they acknowledge that the performances are delightful. The instruments sound pleasant, the decorations are beautiful, the food tastes delicious, and the pavilions are comfortable. Invoking their doctrine of the Three Models, however, the Mohists contend that such entertainment corresponds neither to the deeds of the sage-kings nor to the benefit of the people and thus is wrong (Mz 32/6–7). (They also invoke "documents of the former kings," citing cases in which rulers, the Lord on High, or Heaven punished excessive music and dancing.)

The problem, as they see it, is that government sponsorship of extravagant musical shows amounts to "robbing the people of their resources for food and clothing" (Mz 32/2–3) to provide aesthetic and sensual pleasures for the elite—and this in times when society was in disorder. For the huge cost of the shows, with their great bells, giant drums, and other instruments, was borne by struggling taxpayers. The Mohists support taxation—even heavy taxation—provided the funds are used to promote the welfare of all. The sage-kings, they claim, taxed people heavily to pay for boats and vehicles that benefited everyone (32/8–11). But musical shows do nothing to satisfy people's basic needs for food, clothing, and respite from labor (32/12–14). They use up resources and interfere with production by shifting people away from useful work. The orchestras and dance troupes recruit performers away from productive activities, such as planting and cultivating for the men or spinning and weaving for the women (32/18–23). The practice of regularly sponsoring such shows creates a parasitic class of entertainers who contribute no productive work to society (32/28–29). The shows are enjoyable only if shared with a large audience, but to attend them officials must leave their duties and commoners their labor. Were everyone to develop a fondness for musical shows, rulers and ministers would neglect to hear lawsuits and direct government affairs, leading to disorder;

officers and gentlemen would neglect to manage the bureaucracy and collect taxes, leaving the treasury and granaries empty; farmers would neglect their crops, so food would be insufficient; and women would neglect their textiles, so clothing would be unavailable (32/36–43).

As to the idea that musical performances contribute to social order, the Mohists ask,

> Now great states attack small states, great clans assault small clans, the strong oppress the weak, the majority tyrannize the few, the cunning deceive the ignorant, the noble are contemptuous of the common, bandits, robbers, and thieves spring up everywhere, and all this cannot be stopped. That being so, then for the sake of these problems let's strike the giant bells, beat the sounding drums, strum the zithers and lutes, blow the flutes and pipes, and wave the shields and axes in the war dance. Can the disorder in the world be put in order by this? (Mz 32/14–16)

Besides rejecting "music" as wasteful, then, the Mohists also reject optimistic views about the ethically or socially transformative effects of ritualized state ceremonies and music. This stance underscores their cultural and social differences from the aristocracy and the Rú. We can see how the idea that state-sponsored musical performances promote social harmony might seem persuasive to an elite subculture whose members identify with courtly mores and find a sense of peace and belonging in traditional ceremonial music. But the Mohists feel no deep identification with this subculture or its music, and so they press the equally understandable, commonsensical point that whatever salutary effects it may indeed have, the performance of music can hardly be expected to prevent war, crime, and exploitation. They thus conclude that, on balance, state sponsorship of lavish musical productions does not promote benefit and in fact tends to be harmful, as it diverts resources from basic needs and interferes with economic production and government administration. Since "music" neither promotes benefit nor corresponds to the deeds of the sage-kings, holding musical shows is wrong.

If the Mohists were correct in their contentions about the exorbitant cost of the shows, the financial burden to taxpayers, the economic circumstances of the typical commoner, and the state of social disorder—and perhaps in many instances they were—then we can hardly dispute their conclusion that mounting such shows at public expense was morally abhorrent. Still, the position they take in "Condemning Music"—"making music is wrong [*fēi* 非]"—goes beyond what their arguments justify. After all, by their own account, there is nothing wrong with music in itself. The problems lie in the exploitation, waste, and negligence associated with musical shows of a particular type, mounted in particular circumstances. Two natural counterarguments in favor of alternative, moderate forms of musical entertainment come to mind. First, although the Mohists acknowledge the enjoyment music brings and the beauty of the decorations at the shows, they nowhere allow that the aesthetic, emotional, or social goods associated with music constitute benefits. We can grant that these goods are less fundamental than food, clothing, and shelter, which should take priority. Nevertheless, most of us agree that they are beneficial and contribute to human welfare. Suppose a state were prosperous enough that it could reliably satisfy all its residents' subsistence needs. Why not allow musical shows in moderation, provided they do not create a heavy economic burden or interfere too much with work?

One reason for the Mohists' neglect of these other goods might be that musical shows were enjoyed primarily by a privileged minority. Their position might be motivated by an implicit conception of distributive justice that favors the interests of the less-advantaged majority over those of an elite minority.[20] Without question, given their commitment to promoting "the benefit of all the world," in some scenarios the Mohists would favor the interests of a disadvantaged majority over those of a privileged few. The emphasis in the second "Moderation in Use" essay on how the sage-kings cared about the people, along with the slogan that they refrained from "anything that added expense without adding to the people's benefit," also suggests that the Mohists give priority to the welfare of the common people over spending on nonessentials for the ruling class. But the chief explanatory factor behind their condemnation of elite entertainment is probably that they give priority to certain types of goods, not that they give priority to the interests of the disadvantaged. Their specific complaint is not that the interests of the poor should outweigh those of the privileged. It is that in seeking aesthetic, emotional, and sensual enjoyment, aristocrats and officials wrongfully deprive people of basic necessities (Mz 32/2–3). For the Mohists, basic material welfare outweighs all other goods: the first priority is to secure food, clothing, and shelter for all. Naturally, then, the subsistence needs of the disadvantaged take priority over the aesthetic, emotional, or sensual pleasures of the elite. The interests of the less well-off need not always trump those of the more well-off, however. As we have seen in previous chapters, the Mohists advocate redistribution of resources only to relieve the destitute, not to rectify inequality.

A second counterargument is that enjoying music and other entertainment in moderation need not interfere with economic production—and thus with providing for the welfare of all—and may even contribute to it. The Mohists themselves emphasize that people need regular respite from labor.[21] Common sense dictates that people work more effectively when they have sufficient rest and recreation. So why not allow inexpensive musical entertainment, in moderation, as part of the normal cycle of work and leisure?

Two passages in later strata of the Mòzǐ hint at possible responses to these arguments for musical entertainment in moderation. One of the "Dialogues" (Mz 48/33–40) depicts Mòzǐ observing that Ruist ceremonies and music are so time-consuming that, were people to observe all the mourning rituals and practice all the poetry, songs, and dances, gentlemen would have no time for governing, commoners none for work. In defense of Ruist practices, Gōng Mèngzǐ replies that one can attend to government or work when the state is disorderly or impoverished and engage in ceremony and music when it is well governed and wealthy. Mòzǐ responds that a state can be well governed and wealthy only if people continually attend to government and work. Slacking off when all is well is a recipe for disaster. As a rebuttal to Gōng Mèngzǐ, this response is cogent enough. Read as an elaboration of the Mohist stance on music, however, it seems to imply that the Mohists see no middle ground between constant diligence and rash negligence. They overlook the possibility that people could pursue both work and the arts, enjoying poetry and music in their leisure time.

This point is pressed in a late dialogue included among the "Summaries," the first seven books of the Mòzǐ. A Ruist named Chéng Fán points out that in ancient times, when tired from work, people at all levels of society, from rulers to ministers and officials to farmers, relaxed to accompaniment of music, their instruments ranging from the rulers' bronze bells and drums to the farmers' simple ceramic pipes (Mz 7/1–11). Chéng asks, doesn't the Mohist doctrine that the sage-kings made no music condemn everyone to unremitting labor and stress, which no living creature can sustain? Mòzǐ replies that beginning with Yáo and Shùn, down through Tāng and Wǔ to Chéng (a later Zhōu king), the music of the sage-kings grew increasingly elaborate while the effectiveness of their rule declined. Thus "the more elaborate the music, the less effective the government" (7/8). Still, Chéng insists, Mòzǐ must acknowledge that the sage-kings indeed enjoyed music, as he has just said so himself. Mòzǐ answers that the sage-kings sought to reduce excess; their music was so minimal as to amount to none. As a defense of the antimusic stance, this response is disappointing. It fails to address Chéng's initial question and hardly establishes a causal relation between music and ineffectual government. Yet the text seems to grudgingly concede Chéng's point: music has a role alongside work, and the sage-kings themselves enjoyed it. The official stance of this late text is thus not to forbid music but to discourage excess.

Readers today may be struck by the Mohists' insensitivity to the aesthetic value of music. What value they do attribute to music is instrumental: it produces enjoyment and helps people relax. Again, however, the Mohists' utilitarian focus was unremarkable in their time. Even Xúnzǐ, who presents the only explicit rejoinder to the Mohists on music in the Warring States literature, accepts their assumption that the value of music, if any, lies in its utility, which he too construes narrowly.[22] Xúnzǐ attacks Mòzǐ on the grounds that proper music is an indispensable means of maintaining social order, because it channels emotions in constructive, orderly ways and transforms people ethically by stirring up appropriate feelings and motivation. The inspiration for this argument could of course have been rhetorical. If Xúnzǐ were to establish that regular performances of court music, with all their elaborate trappings, have good consequences for society as a whole, he could justify elaborate musical shows on the Mohists' own grounds. Still, it is remarkable that he does not defend music by appeal to its inherent beauty, nor even the pleasure it brings.[23] Perhaps he should have, since the consequentialist arguments he offers are weak. Just as in his arguments against moderation, he fails to show that maintaining social order requires extravagant musical shows, rather than only moderate or economical performances. Nor does he show that music is more effective in promoting social order than other, more frugal means. Indeed, a lesson we might draw from Xúnzǐ's ineffective defense is that a genuinely compelling justification for the arts probably must appeal to their intrinsic value, not merely their instrumental value.

CRITIQUE OF RUISM

The Mohists critique Ruist views and practices mainly in two texts, "Gōng Mèng" (book 48) and "Condemning the Rú" (book 39). Although their remarks indicate familiarity with material eventually incorporated into the *Analects*, their discussions show no awareness of what interpreters today typically see as that text's major ethical themes, such as Confucius's "one thread" of empathetic consideration toward others (*shù* 恕) or the "negative golden rule" of not doing to others what one does not desire oneself.[24] Nor do the Mohists ever criticize a purported Ruist doctrine of "graded care" or "love with distinctions."[25] None of the Mohist criticisms concern what interpreters today consider the heart of Ruist ethical thought, such as its emphasis on devoted family relationships, benevolence, or moral cultivation through ceremonial propriety. Mohist opposition to Ruism is almost wholly unrelated to ethical theory and moral psychology. Rather, the Mohists focus on features of the early Ruist subculture that were conspicuous in their time but are strongly downplayed by sympathetic interpreters today.

The Mohists offer six main criticisms of the Rú. The unifying theme is that Ruism as they know it misguidedly interferes with promoting the benefit of the world. Ruist doctrines and practices either waste material resources, hinder their production, or squander opportunities to benefit people or improve social conditions.

A passage in the "Dialogues" summarizes four of the criticisms, claiming that the widespread adoption of the Ruist *dào* would lead to social catastrophe (Mz 48/49–58). First, the Rú are impious. They treat Heaven as insentient and the ghosts as inanimate, thus disrespecting and displeasing these spiritual beings. They incoherently practice sacrificial rituals while denying the existence of ghosts (48/40–42). Since they mismanage relations with the ghosts, spirits, and Heaven, they fail to fulfill humanity's proper role in the normative order of the cosmos. Second, they undertake rich, wasteful burials and onerous, protracted mourning rituals that leave mourners near death themselves from hunger and exhaustion. These practices waste resources and interfere with economic production. Third, they frivolously waste time on music and dance instead of productive activity. Their music corrupts people (39/13, 39/45), presumably by encouraging idleness. Fourth, they are fatalists, who take wealth, longevity, social order, and physical safety to be predestined, thus breeding indolence, poverty, and disorder. The gist of these criticisms is that the Ruist *dào* is useless and even harmful, and so by Mohist ethical standards it is immoral.

Beyond these points, the Mohists identify two further Ruist tendencies that in their view systematically neglect opportunities to benefit the world. First, the reflexive traditionalism of the Rú prevents them from taking the initiative to find novel ways to benefit society. The *Mòzǐ* twice rebuts the Ruist saying that a gentleman transmits but does not initiate.[26] The commonsense Mohist reply is that, to increase the total good, one transmits good things from the past while also initiating good things in the present (Mz 46/51–52). Indeed, the claim that the *dào* of the gentleman is to transmit but not initiate leads to a practical contradiction. Anything worth transmitting must have been initiated in the past. If the gentleman does not initiate, then the traditions we transmit were initiated by petty people. In transmitting them, then, the gentleman is actually following the *dào* of these petty people, not the *dào* of a gentleman (39/21).

The final criticism is that—perhaps because of their fatalism—the Rú content themselves with self-cultivation and do not strive to promote the public good. In the Mohists' view, they advocate passivity and even negligence.

The Ruist Gōng Mèngzǐ cites a saying that the gentleman is like a bell: unless struck, it remains silent (Mz 48/1–7). By contrast, the Mohists hold that officials must be prepared to speak out when necessary, such as to dissuade their ruler from potentially harmful actions. Holding one's tongue unless asked is tantamount to concealing information and withholding effort, thus neglecting opportunities to benefit one's ruler or parents. Such conduct is contrary to the relational virtues (39/28–31). In another exchange (48/9–14), Gōng Mèngzǐ contends that social and political activism is unnecessary. One should simply focus on developing one's qualifications and abilities. Competent people will naturally acquire a reputation, just as an able fortune-teller attracts a regular clientele without traveling around hawking his talents or a beautiful maiden attracts suitors without parading herself about. The Mohist response is that this stance neglects what we can do for others. A beautiful maiden always has plenty of suitors, but without the Mohists' proselytizing, few people have a chance to learn about the good. Moreover, activism beings greater rewards than self-improvement alone. A talented fortune-teller who works from home may earn a decent income, but one who goes out to seek clients will earn considerably more.

CONCLUDING REMARKS

This chapter concludes my discussion of Mohist thought by examining the four remaining doctrines in the Mohists' ten-point reform platform. I have attempted to show that the Mohist just war theory is principled and surprisingly nuanced, anticipating modern just war theories in several respects. In their economic doctrines, the Mohists present compelling arguments against wasteful and exploitative practices. Yet their positive proposals often outrun what their arguments can actually justify. They tend to posit a false dilemma between extravagance and parsimony without acknowledging intermediate positions. Their economic doctrines assume a restrictive conception of human welfare, in which the only goods that count are material wealth, population, and social harmony and stability. Given their social and historical circumstances, the defects in their arguments and their narrow conception of the good are understandable and perhaps largely excusable. The Mohist program is in effect a refugee ethic, born from an era of war and scarcity, that places material welfare and social stability above all else. In economic conditions as precarious as those the Mohists depict, frugality may well be justified and ensuring basic material welfare may trump the pursuit of other goods. Moreover, the focus on material welfare and social order that seems distinctive to us in fact reflects the terms of political discourse in the Mohists' time and to them may have been simply commonsensical.

Still, it is puzzling why they assume that a society that adopted Mohist economic policies would never become wealthy enough to relax its stance even slightly and allow moderate spending on nonessentials. It is frustrating that they are so reluctant to admit that music—and by extension, the arts and entertainment—has any significant value at all. The Mòzǐ never acknowledges that in more prosperous conditions music and other cultural activities should be permitted or encouraged, since they too are goods that contribute to well-being. Mohist economic doctrines thus tend to present an impoverished, unappealing conception of the good life, one ill suited for any circumstances other than war or scarcity. Despite the compelling motivation for their economic strictures—their admirable commitment to meeting the basic needs of all—it is difficult to avoid seeing their stance as that of a dour moral saint for whom nothing matters other than benevolence and righteousness, construed as a commitment to meeting everyone's subsistence needs. Although their official position is moderation, not parsimony, their assumption of perpetual economic hardship and their narrow conception of benefit would likely entail a severe, spartan lifestyle for most people. In this respect, the Mohist dào may indeed be too harsh.

There is some evidence that, late in the movement's development, the Mohists came to acknowledge a wider range of goods while still contending that economic conditions ruled out their pursuit. The Hàn-dynasty Shuō yuàn contains a passage—perhaps the writing of a late Warring States or Hàn Mohist writer—in which Mòzǐ seems to acknowledge the worth of beauty, pleasure, and other nonmaterial goods. Nonetheless, most people's economic circumstances are precarious enough that these amount to luxuries, which are not the sage's priority. Only when adequate food, clothing, and shelter are guaranteed can we consider pursuing gourmet flavors, visual beauty, and musical enjoyment. The duty of the sage is to pursue "the material [zhí 質] first and only then adornment [wén 文]."²⁷

The Mohists are sometimes accused of having a thin moral psychology and neglecting the nuances of moral motivation. As I explained in chapter 7, I think this charge is unsupported. Their texts provide a plausible, reasonably thorough account of how to lead people to conform to their conception of morality. Any motivational problems that do arise for the Mohist dào are attributable more to their singular focus on "the material" while perpetually deferring "adornment"—and thus continually setting aside or downplaying much of what people genuinely value. Such problems arise from their normative stance and their unremittingly pessimistic appraisal of society's economic circumstances, not from an inadequate understanding of moral psychology. (Alternatively, we might say they make the psychological error of dramatically underestimating how much people value "adornment" and overestimating the importance they attach to righteousness.) When the *Zhuāngzǐ* criticizes the Mohists for "going against the hearts of all under heaven" (Zz 33/24), it is referring to their severe, frugal lifestyle, not their core moral doctrines. Their economic doctrines, I suggest, presented the main obstacle to wider acceptance of their *dào*.

EPILOGUE

THE MOHISTS DESERVE credit for many major philosophical achievements, including China's first ethical and political theories, history's earliest form of consequentialism, a nuanced, intriguing moral psychology, and a fascinating, largely compelling semantic theory and epistemology.[1] Their pragmatic approach to language and knowledge and their externalist epistemology provide an intriguing contrast with the representative realism and internalism that have dominated the modern Western philosophical tradition. They take major steps toward a viable account of impartial, objectively justified moral norms. Their ethical theory has important defects, to be sure, but one of its strengths is that some of these defects could be remedied without abandoning the theory's basic framework. Both the Mohists' insights and their errors are of deep philosophical interest. Their arguments can be simplistic in places, and sometimes they avoid the hard questions that critics today might wish they had addressed. Yet they articulate numerous profound issues, take important, insightful positions on them, and defend these positions with interesting, forceful reasoning. All this is not to mention their impact as social and political reformers who raised moral awareness, sought to improve living conditions for the poor, opposed unjustified warfare, and helped to shape the emerging conception of a disciplined, meritocratic bureaucracy providing competent government administration.

Mohism never achieved a position of dominance or orthodoxy, but at its peak in the fourth and third centuries B.C.E., no school was more influential. This status is attested by no less an authority than Mencius, who laments that "the statements of Mò Dí and Yáng Zhū fill the world" (*Me* 6.9), and by the attention Xúnzǐ devotes to refuting Mohist economic doctrines. Though their importance is routinely slighted in Ruist-biased accounts of Chinese thought, the Mohists played a major part in articulating the conceptual framework of early Chinese epistemology, philosophy of language, logic, political theory, psychology, and ethics. Their ideas were a crucial stimulus for Mencius, Xúnzǐ, the Daoists, and the Legalists, all of whom either borrowed Mohist ideas or developed their own views partly in response to them. One sign of the Mohists' status is that later Warring States critics—as well as Hàn-dynasty texts—often pair them with the Rú as a bloc, referring to the two as Rú-Mò, the twin "moralizing" schools devoted to ideals of benevolence and righteousness. An amusing *Zhuāngzǐ* passage critical of Confucius depicts him explaining the gist of benevolence and righteousness in Mohist terms, as "inclusive care without partiality" (*Zz* 13/49–50). Ruism owes an unacknowledged debt to Mohism for its notion of comprehensive moral concern, as reflected, for instance, in Mencius's doctrines of benevolent government and of extending our natural concern for kin to reach everyone (*Me* 1.7). Xúnzǐ too follows the Mohists' lead by consistently offering consequentialist justifications for his ethical views, grounding them in the good of social order (*zhì* 治) so prominent in Mohism. His epistemology, ontology, and philosophy of language are all heavily indebted to the Mohists. A late passage in the *Xúnzǐ* even approvingly uses Mohist terminology, referring to the sage-king Yáo's "promoting the worthy" (*shàng xián* 尚賢) and his "comprehensive benefit and inclusive care" (*Xz* 25/18–19).[2] By the Hàn dynasty, in a memorial of 134 B.C.E., we find the Ruist Gōngsūn Hóng—a high-ranking imperial official—explaining benevolence in explicitly Mohist vocabulary, as "promoting benefit and eliminating harm, inclusively caring without partiality" (*HS* 58, 2616).

With few exceptions, Chinese thought after the Hàn turned away from the Mohists' epistemological, semantic, and logical interests to focus on moral metaphysics and moral psychology, thus bypassing what might have been their chief legacy. For this reason, Mohism is sometimes depicted as a dead-end splinter movement unrepresentative of the Chinese intellectual mainstream. Such a characterization is false and anachronistic, however. Much of what is plausible or intriguing in Mohist thought embodies concepts, assumptions, and problems that were elements of mainstream Warring States intellectual discourse.

Following the unification of China under the Qín dynasty (221–207 B.C.E.), the Mohist movement declined, eventually vanishing altogether by the middle of the Western Hàn (206 B.C.E.–24 C.E.). After Ruism won imperial favor in 136 B.C.E., Confucius came to be venerated as China's greatest sage. The thought and texts of Mòzǐ and his school fell into neglect and obscurity. Interest in Mohism revived only in the Qīng dynasty (1644–1911), when scholars stimulated by contact with the West went looking for untapped intellectual resources in their own tradition, particularly materials related to science and logic.

The decline and disappearance of Mohism in the Hàn was probably due to a conflux of factors, which jointly rendered the movement unappealing both as a political program and as a source of ethical guidance.[3] These factors almost certainly did *not* include rejection of the Mohists' core ethical and political doctrines, such as their consequentialism, their concern for the welfare of all, and their commitment to unified ethical norms enforced by a centralized, merit-based bureaucracy. Nor did Mohism die out because inclusive care was too idealistic or because Mohist philosophy was in some sense foreign to the spirit of early Chinese civilization.[4] On the contrary, probably a significant factor in the movement's decline was the widespread acceptance and appropriation—if only in a haphazard, unsystematic way—of its core ethical and political themes.[5] Ironically, the Mohists' success in promulgating their most important ethical and political ideas probably cost their movement its comparative appeal. For once these ideas had been absorbed into the intellectual mainstream, they no longer provided a reason to support or identify with Mohism instead of the Rú or other schools of thought. What remained as distinctive of the Mohist *dào* was a package of harsh, unappealing economic and cultural views—mainly, their severe parsimony and opposition to ceremony and music—which were unlikely to attract the influential supporters needed for the movement to thrive. The content of these views may have become less relevant as well, since political unification and improved economic circumstances probably ameliorated the military and economic problems the Mohists addressed.

Two Hàn-dynasty sources—the *Zhuāngzǐ* "All Under Heaven" essay and Sīmǎ Tán's famous review of the "six schools"—clearly indicate that the Mohists' consequentialism and doctrine of inclusive care were not a focus of controversy.[6] For these texts, what stands out about the Mohists are the same features that Xúnzǐ attacks: their ascetic, parsimonious lifestyle, their opposition to elite cultural practices, and their consequent failure (as critics see it) to properly acknowledge differences in social rank. The writer of "All Under Heaven," for instance, criticizes Mòzǐ for "going too far" in pursuit of parsimony and self-discipline. His chief complaints are that Mòzǐ "demolishes the ancient ceremonies and music"; stipulates the same burial guidelines for all, allowing no differences between the burial of an emperor and that of a mere officer; and advocates a "barren," difficult *dào* of unremitting self-sacrifice and altruistic labor. The Mohists' discipline and asceticism run "contrary to the hearts of all the world." Mòzǐ's intentions were right, says the writer, but his practice was wrong, though he was nevertheless "a talented man," "the finest in the world" (Zz 33/16–33). In his account of Mohism's strengths and weaknesses, Sīmǎ Tán mentions only the Mohists' economic doctrines, predictably complaining that their funerals acknowledge no distinctions in social status. Their way, he says, is "frugal and difficult to follow," though he praises them for their insight into ensuring economic sufficiency by "strengthening fundamentals and moderation in use." He remarks that times change and the Mohists' deeds cannot be followed universally, implying perhaps that he sees their *dào* as appropriate to their original social circumstances, though not his own.[7] For these Hàn writers, then, it is primarily the stringency of Mohist economic doctrines, combined with the rejection of entrenched elite customs—especially those devoted to public display of social status—that explains Mohism's lack of appeal in their day.[8] On both counts, Mohist positions clash directly with what Schwartz calls the "inertial power" of "deeply rooted cultural orientations."[9]

As to other areas of potential influence, the Mohists' simplistic, conservative folk religion would have been unappealing to Hàn literati, who had become fascinated with elaborate, naturalistic systems of correlative cosmology. The later Mohists' groundbreaking investigations in language, epistemology, metaphysics, and science were preserved only in dense, difficult texts that most readers would have found barely intelligible. Moreover, by the Hàn, these texts were probably already badly corrupt.

To these points we can add several observations about crucial changes in social and political circumstances under the Qín and then the Hàn dynasty. Besides inclusive care, the Mohists' signature doctrine had always been their opposition to warfare. With the unification of the empire, this doctrine became practically redundant, since wars among the Central States largely ceased. As Graham points out,[10] unification under a centralized regime also probably cost the Mohists—and other representatives of the middle classes—much of the limited political leverage they exerted in the smaller states of the pre-Qín era. As a subelite movement, Mohism had always been at a disadvantage in winning supporters among the powerful. But in the smaller, decentralized states of preimperial times, this disadvantage was offset to some extent by their usefulness to the aristocracy. Given the Mohists' expertise as defense tacticians, engineers, and craftsmen, rulers of smaller states would have found it prudent to employ them and heed at least bits of their economic and military advice. In a relatively small-scale political society, a disciplined, tightly organized band of middle-class reformers might naturally acquire a modicum of political clout. After unification, however, the Mohists' role in these small states, and thus their political influence, probably diminished and perhaps evaporated entirely. The changing political structure would have made it imperative for them to find patrons among the aristocracy, but their severe economic and cultural doctrines no doubt made this a Sisyphean task. Also, unlike the Rú, who through their role in rituals, ceremonies, and musical performances would automatically have been attached to royal courts and aristocratic houses, the Mohists seem to have been organized as quasi-independent paramilitary organizations, which as we saw in the story of Fù Tūn may even have enforced their own laws. With the establishment of a unified, centralized political order, it is unlikely that these extragovernmental organizations would have survived or been tolerated for long.[11] In a decentralized political setting in which the middle classes had more influence, the Mohist movement might have carried on indefinitely. Its eclipse no doubt reflects Hàn-dynasty social and political circumstances as much as it does the unattractiveness of the Mohist lifestyle.

By the Hàn, then, compared with the classical learning, ceremonies, music, and poetry of the Rú, the speculative metaphysics of the *yīn-yáng* theorists, and the romantic nature mysticism, poetry, and literary sophistication of the Daoists, the Mohists offered little to attract adherents, especially politically powerful ones. Though they originated much of the conceptual framework of early Chinese philosophy, the Mohists now found themselves advocating a *dào* perceived as unnecessarily austere and so at odds with prevailing conceptions of the good life that it stood little chance of inspiring a wide following. Unwilling or unable to modify their teachings or to develop new doctrines to cope with a changing social, economic, and intellectual setting, the Mohists faded away because their reformist social and economic platform had become unappealing and redundant.

GLOSSARY

ài 愛:	care
ài rén 愛人:	care about others
Bā 巴:	a minor ancient state in western China
běn 本:	root
biàn 辨:	distinguish, distinction
biàn 辯:	distinguish, discriminate, debate, dialectics
biàn-yìng 辯應:	discriminate and respond
biàn zhě 辯者:	dialecticians, disputers
biǎo 表:	standard, gnomon
bié 別:	difference, separation
Bì Yuán 畢沅:	Qing-dynasty scholar
cháng 常:	constant, regular
Chéng Fán 程繁:	Ruist figure
Chéng Yí 程頤:	Song-dynasty thinker
chū 出:	go out, issue
Chǔ 楚:	one of the seven major Warring States
Chǔ Líng Wáng 楚靈王:	King Líng of Chǔ
cí 慈:	parental kindness
cí guò 辭過:	avoiding excess
dàng 當:	fitting, on the mark
dào 道:	way
Dàodéjīng 道德經:	Daoist text traditionally associated with Lǎozǐ 老子
Dào zàng 道藏:	the Daoist Patrology collection
Dì 帝:	Shāng-dynasty god

dìng 定:	fix, settle
fǎ 法:	model, standard, law, emulate
Fǎ Jiā 法家:	"Legalism," or the "School of Standards"
fēi 非:	wrong, not-this
fēi gōng 非攻:	condemning aggression
fēi mìng 非命:	condemning fate
"Fēi Rú" 非儒:	"Condemning the Rú"
fēi yuè 非樂:	condemning music
Fù Tūn 腹䵍:	Mohist grand master
Gāo Xīn 高辛:	Hàn-dynasty emperor
gōng 攻:	attack, aggression
Gōng Mèngzǐ 公孟子:	Ruist opponent of Mòzǐ
Gōngsūn Hóng 公孫弘:	Hàn-dynasty official
hài 害:	harm
Hàn 漢:	dynasty name
Hán Fēi 韓非:	preimperial Chinese political thinker
Hánfēizǐ 韓非子:	preimperial political anthology associated with Hán Fēi
Hán Yù 韓愈:	Táng-dynasty scholar and poet
Huáinánzǐ 淮南子:	Hàn-dynasty philosophical text
huì 惠:	generosity
Huì Shī 惠施:	late fourth-century thinker
huò 惑:	confusion
Hú Shì 胡適:	modern scholar
jiān 兼:	inclusion, whole, aggregate
jiān ài 兼愛:	inclusive care
jiān xiāng ài jiāo xiāng lì 兼相愛交相利:	inclusively care about each other and in interaction benefit each other
Jié 桀:	one of the four tyrants
jié yòng 節用:	moderation in use
jié zàng 節葬:	moderation in burial
Jìn 晉:	an ancient state whose partition marked the onset of the Warring States era
Jīng 荊:	another name for the state of Chǔ
jīng 經:	classic; short saying
Jìn Wén Gōng 晉文公:	Duke Wén of Jìn
jì sì 祭祀:	sacrificial rituals
jūnzǐ 君子:	gentleman
jùzǐ 鉅子:	grand master
Kǒngzǐ 孔子:	Confucius

lèi 類:	kind
lǐ 禮:	ceremony, ritual, propriety, etiquette
lì 利:	benefit, welfare
Lì 厲:	one of the four tyrants
Lǔ 魯:	a minor ancient state in central China, possibly Mòzǐ's home state
luàn 亂:	disorder, chaos
Lùn héng 論衡:	Hàn-dynasty philosophical text
lún liè 倫列:	relation ranking
Luòyáng 洛陽:	capital of Zhōu dynasty
Lǔ Shèng 魯勝:	early commentator on the Mohist "Dialectics"
Lǔshì chūnqiū 呂氏春秋:	*The Annals of Lü Buwei*
Lǔ Yáng Wén Jūn 魯陽文君:	Lord Wén of Lǔ Yáng
Mèng Shèng 孟勝:	Mohist grand master
Mèngzǐ 孟子:	Mencius; Ruist thinker, ca. 372 B.C.E.–289 B.C.E.
Miáo 苗:	name of tribe defeated by King Yǔ
míng 名:	name, term
mìng 命:	fate, destiny
Míng 明:	dynasty, 1368–1644
míng guǐ 明鬼:	understanding ghosts
Mò biàn 墨辯:	Mohist "Dialectics"
Mò Dí 墨翟:	Mòzǐ's personal name
Mò jiā 墨家:	Mohist school
Mò zhě 墨者:	ancient term for Mohists
Mòzǐ 墨子:	founder of the Mohist movement
néng 能:	ability
níu 牛:	ox
piān 篇:	book, scroll
Qí 齊:	one of the seven major Warring States
qīn 親:	parents, relatives, to be close or dear to someone
Qín 秦:	dynasty, 221 B.C.E.–206 B.C.E.
qíng 情:	genuine, facts
Qīng 清:	dynasty, 1644–1911
Qín Gǔ Lí 禽滑釐:	leading disciple of Mòzǐ
Qínzǐ 禽子:	Master Qín, Qín Gǔ Lí
qǔ 取:	select, choose
rán 然:	so, thus
rén 人:	person, human, others
rén 仁:	benevolence, moral goodness, humaneness

rén zhě 仁者:	benevolent person
Rú 儒:	Erudite, scholar, Confucian
ruò 若:	like, as, similar
shàn 善:	good
Shāng 商:	dynasty, ca. 1600 B.C.E.–1046 B.C.E.
Shàng Dì 上帝:	the Lord on High
shàng tóng 尚同:	identifying upward
shàng xián 尚賢:	promoting the worthy
shě 舍:	reject
shì 士:	officer, scholar
shì 是:	right, this
shì-fēi 是非:	this versus not-this, right versus wrong
Shǐ jì 史記:	Hàn-dynasty *Records of the Grand Historian*
shǒu 守:	defend, defense
shù 恕:	empathetic consideration
Shùn 舜:	one of the six sage-kings
shuō 說:	explanation, persuasion, doctrine
Shuō yuàn 說苑:	Hàn-dynasty text
Sīmǎ Niú 司馬牛:	Confucian disciple
Sīmǎ Qiān 司馬遷:	Hàn-dynasty scholar-official
Sīmǎ Tán 司馬談:	Hàn-dynasty scholar-official
Sòng 宋:	dynasty, 960–1279
Sòng Xíng 宋鈃:	late third-century B.C.E. thinker
Sūn Xīngyǎn 孫星衍:	Qing-dynasty scholar
Sūn Yíràng 孫詒讓:	Qing-dynasty scholar
Táng 唐:	dynasty, 618–907
Tāng 湯:	one of the six sage-kings
Téng 滕:	a minor ancient state in central China
tì 悌:	fraternal love
tiān 天:	Heaven, nature, sky
tiān mìng 天命:	Heaven's mandate, fated by Heaven, natural destiny
tiān xià 天下:	the human, social world, the empire
tiān xià zhī lì 天下之利:	the benefit of all the world
tiān zhì 天志:	Heaven's intent
tóng 同:	same
tuī 推:	extend, push
tuī lèi 推類:	extending kinds
Wáng Chōng 王充:	Hàn-dynasty thinker
wèi 為:	for the sake of, on behalf of

wèi 偽:	artificial, fake
Wèi 衛:	one of the seven major Warring States
wèi bǐ yóu wèi jǐ 為彼猶為己:	for others as for oneself
wèi wǒ 為我:	for myself, for oneself
wén 文:	pattern, form, adornment
Wén 文:	one of the six sage-kings
Wú 吳:	an ancient state in southeastern China
wú 無:	absence, nonexistence
Wǔ 武:	one of the six sage-kings
wù 惡:	dislike, disregard, contempt
Wūmǎzǐ 巫馬子:	Mohist opponent
wú sī 無私:	impartial
xià 下:	lower, below
Xià 夏:	dynasty, ca. 2070 B.C.E.–1600 B.C.E.
xiāng ruò 相若:	mutually similar, identical
Xiàn Huì 獻惠:	king of Chǔ
xiào 孝:	filial piety, familial devotion
xiǎo rén 小人:	petty person
xíng 行:	conduct, practice, action
xìng 性:	innate nature
Xúnzǐ 荀子:	Ruist thinker, fl. 289 B.C.E.–238 B.C.E.
yán 言:	sayings, statements, pronouncements, teachings
Yáng Zhū 楊朱:	early Chinese figure known for ethical egoism
Yán Huí 顏回:	Confucius's favorite disciple
Yànzǐ 晏子:	later-generation teacher associated with Mohism
Yáo 堯:	one of the six sage-kings
yì 義:	righteous, moral, right, duty
yì 意:	intention, thought, point
yì 異:	different
Yín Wén 尹文:	late fourth-century thinker
yīn-yáng 陰陽:	shadow and light, the two fundamental poles
Yí Zhī 夷之:	a Mohist who appears in the *Mencius*
yòng 用:	use, utility
Yōu 幽:	one of the four tyrants
yóu 猶:	like, as, similar
yǒu 有:	present, exist
Yǒuzǐ 有子:	early Rú quoted in the *Analects*
Yǔ 禹:	one of the six sage-kings
yù 欲:	desire

yuán 原:	source
yuè 樂:	music
Yuè 越:	a minor ancient state in southern China
Yuè Wáng Gōujiàn 越王句踐:	King Gōujiàn of Yuè
Yú Yuè 俞樾:	Qing-dynasty scholar
Zǎi Wǒ 宰我:	disciple of Confucius
zēng 憎:	despise, detest
Zhèng 鄭:	a minor ancient state in central China
zhī 知:	know
zhí 質:	material, stuff
zhì 治:	order, govern
zhì 志:	intent, determination, commitment
zhōng 忠:	loyalty
Zhōng yōng 中庸:	*Doctrine of the Mean*
Zhōu 周:	dynasty, ca. 1045 B.C.E.–256 B.C.E.
Zhòu 紂:	one of the four tyrants
zhū 誅:	punish
Zhuāngzǐ 莊子:	Daoist anthology named after Zhuāng Zhōu 莊周
Zǐ Gòng 子貢:	disciple of Confucius
Zǐ Lù 子路:	disciple of Confucius
Zǐ Sī 子思:	Confucius's grandson
Zǐ Xià 子夏:	disciple of Confucius

NOTES

PREFACE

1. I have in mind texts such as *The Annals of Lü Buwei*, *Hánfēizǐ*, *Huáinánzǐ*, and *Lùn Héng*. (The first two of these precede the imperial era by a decade or two.) For instance, the *Annals* says that "Confucius and Mòzǐ desired to put the great *dào* into practice in the world but did not achieve it, though this was enough for them to achieve an eminent reputation" (13/7).
2. This claim is from Fukui Shigemasa, who noted Mohist-like formulations of ethical ideals in Ruist texts. See A. C. Graham, *Later Mohist Logic, Ethics and Science* (Hong Kong: Chinese University Press, 1978), 64–65n79.
3. For a detailed account of the textual history of the *Mòzǐ*, see ibid., 64–72.
4. Why was the *Mòzǐ* included in a collection of Daoist texts? A likely conjecture is that religious Daoists found Mohist beliefs about Heaven, spirits, and ghosts similar enough to their own that they included the *Mòzǐ* as part of their heritage.
5. See Tang Chun-I [Táng Jūnyì] 唐君毅, 中國哲學原論導論篇 [Origins of Chinese philosophy: Introduction] (Taipei: Xuésheng, 1986), 114–15. For a discussion of Táng's interpretation, see Chris Fraser, "Táng Jūnyì on Mencian and Mohist Conceptions of Mind," *Contemporary Confucians of the Chinese University* (New Asia Academic Bulletin 19, ed. Cheng-yi Chung, Hong Kong: New Asia College, 2006): 203–33.
6. Móu Zōngsān 牟宗三, 墨子 [Mòzǐ], in 國史上的偉大人物 [Great figures in Chinese history], ed. Zhāng Qíyún 張其昀 (Taipei: Zhōnghuá wénhuà, 1954), 121. Móu's view is repeated verbatim in Cài Rénhòu 蔡仁厚, 墨家哲學 [Mohist philosophy] (Taipei: Dōng dà, 1978) 83. Táng, *Introduction*, 109–10, states a similar view.
7. David Nivison, *The Ways of Confucianism*, ed. Bryan W. Van Norden (La Salle, Ill.: Open Court, 1996), 83, 130.
8. Benjamin Schwartz, *The World of Thought in Ancient China* (Cambridge, Mass.: Harvard University Press, 1985), 145; cf. 262.

9. David B. Wong, "Universalism vs. Love with Distinctions: An Ancient Debate Revived," *Journal of Chinese Philosophy* 16, no. 3–4 (1989): 263.
10. David B. Wong, "Mohism: The Founder, Mozi (Mo Tzu)," in *Encyclopedia of Chinese Philosophy*, ed. Antonio Cua (London: Routledge, 2002), 454. Schwartz, *World of Thought*, 147, presents a similar view.
11. Bryan W. Van Norden, "A Response to the Mohist Arguments in 'Impartial Caring,'" in *The Moral Circle and the Self: Chinese and Western Approaches*, ed. Kim-chong Chong, Sor-hoon Tan, and C. L. Ten (La Salle, Ill.: Open Court, 2003), 53.
12. Wing-tsit Chan, *A Source Book in Chinese Philosophy* (Princeton: Princeton University Press, 1963), 212.
13. Yi-pao Mei, *Mo-tse, the Neglected Rival of Confucius* (London: Probsthain, 1934), 193.
14. E. R. Hughes, *Chinese Philosophy in Classical Times* (London: Dent, 1942), also recognized some of the Mohists' contributions.
15. Chad Hansen, *A Daoist Theory of Chinese Thought* (Oxford: Oxford University Press, 1992), 97.
16. Ibid., 95.
17. Franklin Perkins, "Introduction: Reconsidering the *Mozi*," *Journal of Chinese Philosophy* 35, no. 3 (2008): 380.
18. Writers who take the Mohists to be committed to this claim include Nivison, *The Ways of Confucianism*, 133; Táng, *Introduction*, 115; Cài, *Mohist Philosophy*, 44; Wong, "Universalism," 251; JeeLoo Liu, *An Introduction to Chinese Philosophy* (Oxford: Blackwell, 2006), 110; and Bryan W. Van Norden, *Virtue Ethics and Consequentialism in Early Chinese Philosophy* (Cambridge: Cambridge University Press, 2007), 179.
19. Few writers have appreciated the consequences of the Mohist view of perception, reasoning, and action. The prominent exception is Hansen, *Daoist Theory*, 140–43.
20. The others are Mei, *Neglected Rival*; Augustinus A. Tseu, *The Moral Philosophy of Mo-Tze* (Taipei: China Printing, 1965); Graham, *Later Mohist*, which mainly concerns the "Dialectics"; and Scott Lowe, *Mo Tzu's Religious Blueprint for a Chinese Utopia* (Lewiston, N.Y.: Mellen Press, 1992), which is a Sinological dissertation, not a philosophical study.
21. Chris Fraser, "Mohist Canons," in *Stanford Encyclopedia of Philosophy*, http://plato.stanford.edu/archives/sum2009/entries/Mohist-canons/ (article published in 2005).

INTRODUCTION

1. Citations to the Mòzǐ give chapter and line numbers in the Harvard-Yenching concordance. These can be used to find passages through the "Additional Information" tab in the electronic text of the Mòzǐ online at Ctext.org, which also provides Mei's translation.
2. These customs are paraphrased from the Mòzǐ, book 25, "Moderation in Burial." Some may have been aristocratic rituals rarely practiced by commoners. In fairness, the Erudites themselves did not endorse human sacrifice.
3. The "Erudites," of course, are just the Rú 儒. The term "Rú" is often misleadingly translated as "Confucian," but its connotation is closer to "erudite," "literati," or

"scholar." Confucius was the most famous and influential of the Rú, but semantically "Rú" does not allude to him or his teachings. He was not the first Rú, and not all Rú were his followers. To avoid conflating Ruism as a whole with Confucius's thought, I will generally leave the word "Rú" untranslated.

4. See, for instance, LY 6.9, 11.17, 14.3, 15.7, 17.1, 18.6, 18.7.
5. "Mohism" is an English rendering of the Chinese Mò zhě 墨者 or Mò jiā 墨家, two terms for Mòzǐ's followers. The h in "Mohism" is phonetically redundant but conventionally included to clarify pronunciation of the vowels.
6. The classic study of social mobility in early China is Cho-yun Hsu, *Ancient China in Transition* (Stanford: Stanford University Press, 1965). For a more recent overview, see Mark Edward Lewis, "Warring States: Political History" in *The Cambridge History of Ancient China*, ed. Michael Loewe and Edward L. Shaughnessy, 587–650 (Cambridge: Cambridge University Press, 1999). For a summary of the Mohists' historical milieu, see Scott Lowe, *Mo Tzu's Religious Blueprint for a Chinese Utopia* (Lewiston, N.Y.: Mellen Press, 1992).
7. This point was first argued in Liáng Qǐchāo 梁啟超, 墨子學案 [A study of Mòzǐ] (Shànghǎi: Shāngwù, 1923). Mohist writings never mention Mòzǐ's being a government official. One passage depicts him dispatching a follower for employment in Sòng (Mz 49/64–71), implying that Mòzǐ did not live there. Book 50 depicts him rushing from Qí to dissuade the King of Chǔ from attacking Sòng. Passing through Sòng on his return, he is denied shelter by a gatekeeper, again implying that he was not from Sòng.
8. Zhāng Chúnyī 張純一, 墨子集解 [Collected explications of Mòzǐ] (Taipei: Wén shǐ zhé, 1982).
9. This idea is from Fāng Shòuchǔ 方授楚, 墨學源流 [Sources of Mohism] (Shànghǎi: Zhōnghuá, 1989).
10. A. C. Graham, trans., *Chuang-tzu: The Inner Chapters* (London: Allen and Unwin, 1981), 34.
11. Ibid., 19, suggests that for the Zhōu aristocracy both rén 仁 (benevolent) and rén 人 (person) originally implied noble status. In Mohist writings, however, any such class connotation has faded away.
12. Chén Qǐtiān 陳啟天, 增訂韓非子校釋 [Collated explications of the *Hánfēizǐ*, expanded and revised] (Taipei: Shāngwù, 1969), 478.
13. Chad Hansen, *A Daoist Theory of Chinese Thought* (Oxford: Oxford University Press, 1992), 97–98, rightly objects to the "style slander" directed at the *Mòzǐ*, which too often interferes with appreciating the depth or richness of Mohist arguments. (For an example, see Burton Watson, *Mo Tzu: Basic Writings* [New York: Columbia University Press, 1963], 11.) Still, the earliest sections of the *Mòzǐ* are remarkably plodding and repetitive, as we should expect if they indeed originated as oral compositions intended for repeated presentation. Later parts of the *Mòzǐ*, such as the "Dialogues" (books 46–49), the "Summaries" (books 4–7), and the "Lesser Selection" (book 45), have a more refined style.
14. This hypothesis about their religious beliefs is from Fung Yu-lan, *A Short History of Chinese Philosophy*, ed. Derk Bodde (New York: Macmillan, 1948), 52.

15. Graham, *Disputers of the Tao*, 35.
16. The *Hánfēizǐ* identifies three factions of Mohists. The *Zhuāngzǐ* mentions two of these and identifies three further groups. *The Annals of Lü Buwei* names roughly a dozen followers of Mòzǐ, three of whom hold the title *jùzǐ*. Altogether, early sources mention the names of some two to three dozen of Mòzǐ's first- and later-generation followers, some of whom might have been heads of other factions. For details, see, for instance, Cài Rénhòu 蔡仁厚, 墨家哲學 [Mohist philosophy] (Taipei: Dōng dà, 1978), 10–15, and the appendices in Sūn Yíràng 孫詒讓, 墨子閒詁 [Interspersed commentaries on Mòzǐ], 2 vols. (Běijīng: Zhōnghuá, 2001).
17. See *Mz* 9/13, 12/40, 25/49, and 5/1ff. Book 50 of the *Mòzǐ* is an anecdote about Mòzǐ successfully persuading the King of Chǔ to call off a planned invasion of Sòng by demonstrating the invincible defense tactics the Mohists had prepared to protect it.
18. For an overview, see Robin D. S. Yates, "The Mohists on Warfare: Technology, Technique, and Justification," *Journal of the American Academy of Religion* 47, no. 3 (1980): 549–603
19. See Erik W. Maeder, "Some Observations on the Composition of the 'Core Chapters' of the *Mozi*," *Early China* 17 (1992): 27–82, and Chris Fraser, "Thematic Relationships in MZ 8–10 and 11–13," *Warring States Papers* 1 (2010): 137–42.
20. Books 4–7 summarize Mohist doctrines on Heaven, political administration, economics, defense, and music. Book 3, "On Dyeing," is an anecdote about how people's environment, especially their associates, colors their character. The same anecdote appears in *LSCQ* 2/4; it may not be Mohist in origin. (The *Mòzǐ* version begins with what looks like a garbled attempt to splice the phrase "Our Master Mòzǐ states" onto an existing text.) Books 1 and 2 expound mainstream early Chinese views on self-cultivation and the value of worthy scholar-officials. Neither mentions Mòzǐ or characteristic Mohist doctrines. Their content might not be of Mohist origin, as they extol the ideal of the *jūnzǐ* (gentleman), a phrase other parts of the *Mòzǐ* almost always use to indicate social rank, not ethical status. This block of seven books is probably the latest part of the corpus. Book 3 mentions the fall of a king known to have died in 286 B.C.E. (D. C. Lau, *Lao Tzu: Tao Te Ching* [London: Penguin, 1963], 99).
21. One clue to their dates is that book 18, which falls within a relatively early stratum, must have been written after 431 B.C.E., since it mentions a war that occurred that year (Graham, *Disputers of the Tao*, 44). Another is that book 19, which falls within a middle stratum, was probably written before 334 B.C.E., because among belligerent contemporaneous states it mentions Yuè, which was absorbed by its enemy, Chǔ, that year.
22. For further discussion of stratification and other textual issues, including the nature and significance of the "Triads," see the supplement on "Texts and Authorship" in Chris Fraser, "Mohism," in *Stanford Encyclopedia of Philosophy*, http://plato.stanford.edu/archives/fall2009/entries/mohism (article published in 2002).
23. The label "state consequentialism" for Mohist ethics is from Philip J. Ivanhoe, *Confucian Moral Self-Cultivation* (Indianapolis: Hackett, 2000), 15, and Philip J. Ivanhoe and Bryan W. Van Norden, eds., *Readings in Classical Chinese Philosophy* (New York: Seven Bridges Press, 2000), 56. The Mohists are concerned specifically with beneficial con-

sequences for the state only in certain political and economic contexts, such as when discussing the importance of recruiting talented officers (*Mz* 8/1) or increasing the population (20/11–14). In general, their focus is the benefit of "all under heaven" (*tiān xià* 天下)—all the people of the world, considered as an aggregate or a community—not the benefit of a political entity such as the state. Benefit to the state is not mentioned in any of the major formulations of their consequentialism; see, for instance, *Mz* 15/1, 16/1, 26/36, 27/49, 28/35, 32/1–2, and 47/16–18.

24. *Shàng tóng*, the name of this doctrine, can be interpreted in two ways. One is to take *shàng* as a verb meaning "promote" or "exalt" and *tóng* (same, similar) as its object, yielding "promoting identity" or "exalting conformity." The other is to take *shàng* as an adverb and *tóng* as a verb, yielding "upward conforming" or "identifying upward." The first reading is supported by parallelism with *shàng xián* (promoting the worthy), the other major Mohist political doctrine. However, the discussion in the *shàng tóng* books uses the phrase *shàng tóng* specifically to refer to identifying with or conforming to superiors. Hence the second reading seems more justified.

25. "Consequentialism" refers to a family of ethical theories that give different explanations of the relevant consequences (such as happiness, pleasure, or well-being) and the primary focus of evaluation (such as actions, rules, or motives). The most familiar type of consequentialism is probably act utilitarianism, according to which acts are right or wrong to the extent that they contribute to happiness or its opposite. The classical utilitarianism of Bentham and Mill is often regarded as a brand of act utilitarianism. Another well-known type of consequentialism is rule utilitarianism, the view that acts are right just when they conform to rules that, if generally followed, would best promote general happiness. Consequentialism contrasts with the view that moral value is determined by character traits—the core idea in virtue ethics—and the view that some kinds of actions or rules have intrinsic moral value, independent of their consequences—the core idea in deontological ethics.

26. According to direct consequentialism, what is morally right or good is so because it directly produces better consequences than alternatives. Act utilitarianism is a form of direct consequentialism. Indirect consequentialism holds that what is right or good is so because it follows from something else—a set of rules or principles, for instance—that in turn is justified by good consequences. Rule utilitarianism is a form of indirect consequentialism. Instead of instructing us to seek directly to maximize happiness, it holds that right actions are those that conform to a set of rules that, if generally followed, would promote general happiness better than any alternative rules would.

27. An implicit conception of impartiality is reflected in the Confucian "negative golden rule": "What you yourself do not desire, do not do to others" (*LY* 12.2, 15.24, 5.12). However, the *Analects* does not develop this idea systematically.

28. *Dào* (way) refers to a way, style, or pattern of life or of performing some activity. It may include practices, institutions, and traditions, along with rules, techniques, styles, and attitudes. As a way of life, it also includes dispositions and habits, and thus virtues.

29. Chad Hansen explores such assumptions in "Punishment and Dignity in China," in *Individualism and Holism: Studies in Confucian and Taoist Values*, ed. Donald Munro, 359–83

(Michigan Monographs in Chinese Studies, no. 52) (Ann Arbor: Center for Chinese Studies, University of Michigan, 1985).
30. The Mohists' approach also prompts the interesting question of how a contemporary consequentialist might defend an individualistic form of consequentialism over their communitarian version.
31. For a helpful discussion of the characterization of ethical theories in terms of the priority of the right versus the good, see Charles Larmore, *The Morals of Modernity* (Cambridge: Cambridge University Press, 1996). Mohist ethics seems an interesting exception to Sidgwick's well-known generalization that ancient ethical theories tend to be attractive, or centered on the notion of the good, rather than imperative, or centered on the notion of what is right, as modern theories are (Henry Sidgwick, *The Methods of Ethics*, 7th ed. [Indianapolis: Hackett, 1981], 105). Indeed, I suspect that Mohist and Ruist ethics combine both attractive and imperative elements.
32. The first scholars to explicitly identify the role of model emulation in early Chinese ethics seem to have been Hu Shih 胡適, 中國哲學史大綱卷上 [Outline of the history of Chinese philosophy, vol. 1] (Shànghǎi: Commercial Press, 1919), and Donald Munro, *The Concept of Man in Early China* (Stanford: Stanford University Press, 1969).

1. ORDER, OBJECTIVITY, AND EFFICACY

1. Mothers, daughters, and sisters are not mentioned. Like most ancient Chinese thinkers, the Mohists marginalize the roles of women. The exception is women's economic role in bearing children and producing textiles, which contribute to the basic goods of population and wealth.
2. Chad Hansen, *A Daoist Theory of Chinese Thought* (Oxford: Oxford University Press, 1992), 108.
3. The *Analects* has traditionally been treated as a collection of the sayings of Confucius. Since parts of this collection likely date from long after Confucius's death, however, I treat it as simply a record of one branch of early Ruist thought. Besides bits of Confucius's own speech, it probably contains remarks by several generations of his followers, sometimes explicitly presented as such, sometimes placed into the mouth of his literary persona. For a stimulating, though speculative, theory about the development of the *Analects*, see E. Bruce Brooks and A. Taeko Brooks, *The Original Analects* (New York: Columbia University Press, 1998), along with John Makeham, review of *The Original Analects*, *China Review International* 6, no. 1 (1999), 1–33.
4. LY 6.27, 8.2, 8.8, 9.11, and 12.15. By contrast, some passages, such as 3.3, imply that benevolence is a precondition for proper performance of ceremony.
5. On the role of ceremonial propriety in government, see also LY 2.3, 3.19, 13.3, 13.4, 14.41, and 15.33.
6. For this reason, one can question whether the earliest Rú—the writers of much of the *Analects*—fully recognize the difference between etiquette or propriety, on the one hand, and moral right and wrong, on the other. A normative ethics that stresses ceremonial propriety to the extent the *Analects* does seems to fall short of constituting a moral theory.

1. ORDER, OBJECTIVITY, AND EFFICACY 249

7. Other passages in which the Mòzǐ alludes to ceremonial propriety in a positive light, as an appropriate guide to conduct, include 6/3, 48/41, 49/3, 49/63, and MB A9.
8. Generally, the Mohists avoid characterizing norms of conduct they endorse as "ceremonial propriety." This may be partly to differentiate themselves from the Rú, partly to distinguish their purportedly objectively justified norms from parochial etiquette. In contexts where one might refer to ceremonial propriety, as when describing burial rituals, their texts instead speak of *fǎ* 法 (models, standards); see, for example, Mz 25/83. The Mohists attach great importance to religious rituals that venerate Heaven, nature spirits, and ancestral ghosts, but they refer to these as *jì sì* 祭祀 (sacrificial ceremonies), not *lǐ* 禮 (ceremonial or ritual propriety).
9. Among the Ruist texts that have come down to us, the first such theory is found in the Xúnzǐ, from the middle of the third century B.C.E.
10. Hansen was the first to note the major conceptual breakthrough the Mohists make in drawing this distinction (*Daoist Theory*, 107).
11. Hansen underscores this point and its relation to the Mohists' critique of traditionalism (ibid., 99–100, 106–8).
12. Mohist texts regularly valorize six legendary sage-kings of high antiquity: Yáo, a mythical figure traditionally said to have reigned from 2356 B.C.E. to 2255 B.C.E.; Shùn, his successor, who supposedly ruled from 2255 B.C.E. to 2205 B.C.E.; Shùn's successor Yǔ, purportedly the founder of the Xià dynasty, reputed to have reigned from 2205 B.C.E. to 2197 B.C.E. and to have undertaken China's first large-scale flood-control projects; Tāng, founder of the Shāng dynasty, said to have reigned from 1766 B.C.E. to 1753 B.C.E.; Wǔ, founder of the Zhōu dynasty, who reigned from 1122 B.C.E. to 1115 B.C.E.; and Wǔ's father, Wén, king of the state of Zhōu. Mohist praise for the sage-kings is often paired with condemnation of four equally famous tyrants: Jié, last ruler of the Xià before he was overthrown by Tāng; Zhòu, last ruler of the Shāng, overthrown by Wǔ; and Yōu and Lì, two cruel rulers during the Zhōu dynasty.
13. The passage uses the word "all-inclusive" (*jiān* 兼), not "impartial" (*wú sī* 無私). Given the emphasis on the equal status of all, however, and the description of Heaven as impartial just a few lines earlier, I suggest that the care and benefit referred to are indeed impartial.
14. T. M. Scanlon calls this feature "the universality of reason judgments" (*What We Owe to Each Other* [Cambridge, Mass.: Harvard University Press, 1998], 73).
15. As James Griffin says, "To argue that pains are equally reason-generating considerations, no matter whose they are, is not to argue that pains matter equally in determining what an agent ought to do, no matter whose they are" (*Value Judgement* [Oxford: Clarendon Press, 1996], 77).
16. Fatalism should be distinguished from determinism, the view that every event has a cause and so is causally determined. Determinism does not entail that human agency is ineffectual.
17. For details, see Chris Fraser, "The Mohist Conception of Reality," in *Chinese Metaphysics and Its Problems*, ed. Chenyang Li and Franklin Perkins, 69–84 (Cambridge: Cambridge University Press, 2014).

18. A. C. Graham makes a similar observation: *Disputers of the Tao* (La Salle, Ill.: Open Court, 1989), 50.
19. The Mohist position may be too strong, as a coherent consequentialism might require only that certain courses of action usually or probably produce better results, not that they invariably do. However, the Mohists regard fatalism as sundering any regular causal connection between our conduct and its outcome, thus making good or bad consequences unpredictable. For instance, they see fatalism as detaching rewards and punishments from worthy or vicious conduct (*Mz* 35/30–36).
20. The Mohists do not consider the possibility that some people might be fated to be virtuous and industrious and thus to enjoy good outcomes, while others might be fated to be unworthy and idle and thus to encounter bad ones.
21. Van Norden suggests that Mohist criticisms of the Ruist view of fate are "a misinterpretation of the role of fate in the thought of Kongzi" (Bryan W. Van Norden, *Virtue Ethics and Consequentialism in Early Chinese Philosophy* [Cambridge: Cambridge University Press, 2007], 152). While the views the *Mòzǐ* attributes to the Rú might not be those of Confucius, the fatalistic doctrines attributed to Gōngmèngzǐ and others at *Mz* 48/28–29, 52–54, and 39/10–13 probably accurately represent the views of some Rú. Indeed, Gōngmèng's statement about fate at 48/28–29 is remarkably similar to the saying Zǐ Xià quotes at *LY* 12.5. The Mohists' main concern is not that the Rú themselves are indolent fatalists but that the doctrine of fatalism breeds widespread, harmful shirking (39/10–13). (Two passages, 39/13 and 39/45–46, do denounce the Rú for fatalistic negligence, but these ad hominem attacks do not appear as part of the Mohists' critical refutation of fatalism.)
22. A tension obtains in the early Ruist view of Heaven, however, because Heaven too is sometimes depicted as determining events for arbitrary or inscrutable reasons. Grieving the death of Yán Huí, Confucius laments, "Ah, Heaven is killing me! Heaven is killing me!" (*LY* 11.9). Another passage seems to equate Heaven with fate: in response to Sīmǎ Niú's worry that everyone but he has brothers, Zǐ Xià cites an adage that "as to life and death, there is fate; wealth and honor lie with Heaven" (*LY* 12.5).
23. For a detailed discussion, see Franklin Perkins, "The Mohist Criticism of the Confucian Use of Fate," *Journal of Chinese Philosophy* 35, no. 3 (2008): 421–36, and Edward Slingerland, "The Conception of *Ming* in Early Confucian Thought," *Philosophy East and West* 46, no. 4 (1996): 567–81.
24. Perkins, "Mohist Criticism," 429. I thank Perkins for discussions concerning the Mohist view of fate and for sharing with me his work in progress on the subject.
25. See also the discussion in Mark Csikszentmihalyi, *Material Virtue: Ethics and the Body in Early China* (Leiden: Brill, 2004), 43–44.
26. I rebut this view in Chris Fraser, "Mohism and Self-Interest," *Journal of Chinese Philosophy* 35, no. 3 (2008): 437–54.
27. The Mohists may be guilty of rhetorical excess here. Denying this causal connection removes some but not necessarily all motivation for the virtues. On the other hand, it is clear that they are thinking of the general populace, not members of a reflective, idealistic moral elite. In this sense, their claim is comparable to Mencius's view

that without stable economic resources, the common people cannot be expected to conduct themselves well (*Me* 1.7).

28. As we will see in chapter 3, this is a central concern of Mohist political theory as well. The system of rewards and punishments is an explicit expression of the unifying norms by which we achieve social order. If people lose confidence in the system, because it is unfairly administered or because they disagree with the underlying norms, social order disintegrates.

2. EPISTEMOLOGY AND LOGIC: DRAWING DISTINCTIONS

1. The various forms of knowledge are interrelated and to some extent can be characterized in terms of one another. Although there are various ways of linking them conceptually, however, they seem to refer to distinct capacities. For a collection of essays debating the relations between different types of knowledge, see John Bengson and Marc Moffett, *Knowing How: Essays on Knowledge, Mind, and Action* (Oxford: Oxford University Press, 2011).
2. For details concerning the epistemology of the "Dialectics," see Chris Fraser, "Mohist Canons," in *Stanford Encyclopedia of Philosophy*, http://plato.stanford.edu/archives/sum2009/entries/Mohist-canons/ (article published in 2005).
3. I use "term" here as in traditional logic, to refer to a common noun or a noun phrase that can serve as the subject or predicate of an assertion.
4. For a detailed discussion, see Chris Fraser, "Distinctions, Judgment, and Reasoning in Classical Chinese Thought," *History and Philosophy of Logic* 34, no. 1 (2013): 1–24.
5. The label "predicate attitude" is from Chad Hansen, "Term-Belief in Action," in *Epistemological Issues in Classical Chinese Philosophy*, ed. Hans Lenk and Gregor Paul, 45–68 (Albany: SUNY Press, 1993).
6. Donald Munro, *The Concept of Man in Early China* (Stanford: Stanford University Press, 1969), calls attention to this feature of early Chinese thought, which has been a central theme of Chad Hansen's work. For a detailed discussion, see Chris Fraser, "The School of Names," in *Stanford Encyclopedia of Philosophy*, http://plato.stanford.edu/archives/fall2005/entries/school-names/.
7. Hansen and Garrett have called attention to the role of distinctions and pattern recognition in early Chinese conceptions of knowledge and reasoning; see Chad Hansen, *A Daoist Theory of Chinese Thought* (Oxford: Oxford University Press, 1992), and Mary Garrett, "Classical Chinese Conceptions of Argumentation and Persuasion," *Argumentation and Advocacy* 29, no. 3 (1993): 105–15.
8. As Graham suggests, for early Chinese thinkers, "The crucial question . . . is not the Western philosopher's 'What is the truth?' but 'Where is the Way?'" (A. C. Graham, *Disputers of the Tao* [La Salle, Ill.: Open Court, 1989], 3). Hansen's interpretation of the classical discourse revolves around this theme (*Daoist Theory*).
9. The *Mòzǐ* refers several times to rules or guidelines as "models" (*fǎ*), such as at Mz 25/55.
10. Here perhaps I disagree slightly with Hui-chieh Loy, "Justification and Debate: Thoughts on Mohist Moral Epistemology," *Journal of Chinese Philosophy* 35, no. 3 (2008):

455–71, which suggests that the Three Models (discussed later in this chapter) are better interpreted as standards of justification than as decision-making procedures or guidelines for action. To be sure, the Three Models are introduced as criteria for distinguishing whether statements are *shì* or *fēi*. Moreover, models such as the set square and compass are used to check, or evaluate, whether things are square or round (*Mz* 27/63–67). However, the Mohists also imply that models are used to guide the performance of tasks (4/2–3). They refer to ethical norms such as inclusive care (15/11) and guidelines for diet, clothing, burials, and housing (21/5–19) as "models." So models probably combine evaluative and action-guiding functions.

11. Hansen highlights this contrast and stresses the pragmatic focus of Mohist epistemology (*Daoist Theory*, 104, 139).
12. Few philosophers today accept the JTB view in this simple form because of the well-known counterexamples given by Edmund L. Gettier, in "Is Justified True Belief Knowledge?" *Analysis* 23 (1963): 121–23. However, modified versions of the JTB account remain influential.
13. For a detailed discussion, see Chris Fraser, "Knowledge and Error in Early Chinese Thought," *Dao: A Journal of Comparative Philosophy* 10, no. 2 (2011): 127–48.
14. A widely used example is chicken sexing. Supposedly, chicken sexers can reliably sort newly hatched female chicks from visually indistinguishable male chicks even though they may be unable to give reasons for identifying a chick as male or female or may give reasons that are actually false. Suppose an expert chicken sexer holds the true belief that a particular chick is female but cannot give a true reason to justify this belief. Externalists hold—while internalists deny—that the sexer knows the chick is female.
15. First the center post is planted, and then the second post is planted a measured distance eastward along the line between the center post and the point on the horizon where the sun rises. The third post is then planted the same distance westward along the line between the first two posts and the point on the horizon where the sun sets. The line connecting the posts indicates east and west, while the line connecting the center post to any other point equidistant from the other two indicates north and south.
16. In the other two versions of the theory, the issue is specified as recognizing what is "genuine" (*qíng* 情) versus what is "fake" (*wèi* 偽) (*Mz* 36/2) and as "fixing" (*dìng* 定) distinctions (*biàn* 辯), such as that between sunrise and sunset (37/2).
17. Of the canonical list of six sage-kings, the Mohists tend to emphasize the latter four. They share with the Rú admiration for the Zhōu kings Wén and Wǔ but attempt to outdo the Rú by also highlighting Yǔ and Tāng, kings of the even more ancient Xià and Shāng dynasties.
18. Grammatical and terminological evidence suggests that several paragraphs in each book have been dislocated and reassembled in the wrong place, such that each of the three extant books contains material that originally belonged in the others. The introductory paragraphs of the second and third books may also be missing.
19. This is Graham's suggestion (*Disputers of the Tao*, 36), which I criticize in the supplement on texts and authorship in Chris Fraser, "Mohism," in *Stanford Encyclopedia of*

Philosophy, http://plato.stanford.edu/archives/fall2009/entries/mohism (article published in 2002).
20. The Mohists overlook the likely fatalist rejoinders that the tyrants' failure and sages' success were predestined, that fate is not a physical object, and that some people are fated to be diligent, others not.
21. One passage in the "Inclusive Care" books does depict Mòzǐ saying that if inclusive care could not be applied in practice—presumably with good consequences—he too would reject it (*Mz* 16/22).
22. I thank Dan Robins for this suggestion.
23. Hansen has consistently emphasized this feature of Mohist thought (*Daoist Theory*).
24. Loy reaches a similar conclusion ("Justification and Debate," 460).
25. This practical orientation led Hansen to propose that the Mohists' discussions of how to distinguish *shì* from *fēi* should be interpreted as addressing the pragmatic or normative issue of what *dào* to follow, not the semantic issue of whether various claims are true, and that early Chinese thinkers might not even have a concept of truth. I have previously argued that terms such as *shì* (this), *dàng* (fitting), and *rán* (so) play conceptual roles that overlap enough with the role of "true" that early texts can justifiably be said to employ a truthlike concept in evaluating the semantic status of utterances. Still, Hansen is surely correct that the Mohists' primary theoretical concern is with *dào*, since they contend that whether or not ghosts actually exist, the proper *dào* is to conduct ourselves as if they do. For a detailed discussion, see Chris Fraser, "Truth in Mohist Dialectics," *Journal of Chinese Philosophy* 39, no. 3 (2012): 351–68.
26. I thank Loy Hui-chieh for this observation.
27. For an extended discussion, see Fraser, "Distinctions."
28. Of course, grasping the logical relation between the premises and conclusion of a valid argument is also a form of pattern recognition.
29. See chapter 5 for a translation of this passage.
30. *Mz* 26/1; see also 9/32–34, 17/11–12, 49/25.
31. Several of the key points in this section, including the centrality of *biàn* to the Mohist conception of ethics and agency and the analogy between skill and the Mohist conception of action, were first introduced in Hansen's seminal discussion, *Daoist Theory*, 140–43.
32. Another form of moral deliberation, discussed in the "Dialectics," is distinguishing the greater of two benefits or lesser of two harms.
33. I owe this formulation to Dan Robins.
34. For a detailed discussion, see Chris Fraser, "Action and Agency in Early Chinese Thought," *Journal of Chinese Philosophy and Culture* 5 (2009): 217–39.
35. I take skills to be reliable abilities to discriminate and respond to things so as to succeed in performing certain tasks. Virtues I take to be stable dispositions to discriminate and respond to things in certain ways, partly by holding characteristic cognitive, evaluative, and emotional attitudes. Unlike skills, virtues are not tied to the performance of particular tasks, and they involve a standing responsiveness to certain sorts of reasons. The exercise of a skill is optional in a way that the exercise of a virtue is not. We can refrain from riding bicycles without losing our bike-riding

skills, but we cannot refrain from kind conduct and attitudes without losing the virtue of kindness.

3. POLITICAL THEORY: ORDER THROUGH SHARED NORMS

1. The Mohists see human beings as distinguished from animals by social order, grounded in observance of shared moral norms. Without an orderly society, humans live like animals. This view resonates with those of Mencius and Xúnzǐ, both of whom see righteousness as distinguishing humans from animals.
2. Hui-chieh Loy, "On a *Gedankenexperiment* in the *Mozi* Core Chapters," *Oriens Extremus* 45 (2005): 141–58, also makes this point.
3. As Hansen says, "*shì* and *fēi* are not merely assignments, but assignments with behavioral consequences—like pro and con attitudes" (Chad Hansen, *A Daoist Theory of Chinese Thought* [Oxford: Oxford University Press, 1992], 120).
4. See Loy, "*Gedankenexperiment*," 148.
5. Benjamin Schwartz, *The World of Thought in Ancient China* (Cambridge, Mass.: Harvard University Press, 1985), 142. For a similar view, see Lao Sze-kwang [Láo Sīguāng] 勞思光, 新編中國哲學史 [New edition of *History of Chinese Philosophy*], 3 vols. (Taipei: Sān mín, 1984), 1:298.
6. Mz 14/5ff., 17/1ff., 31/4.
7. The regular-practice condition is only implicit. But part of the point of Mòzǐ's rebuttal is that Wūmǎ's policy would tend to be self-defeating if followed by others, so of course it would be self-defeating if followed by everyone. I return to this point in chapter 5.
8. The main advocate of this emendation seems to be Yi-pao Mei, *The Ethical and Political Works of Motse* (London: Probsthain, 1929). In his 1894 commentary, Sūn suggests the text should read "Heaven" instead of "all under heaven" but stops short of emending it (Sūn Yíràng 孫詒讓, 墨子閒詁 [Interspersed commentaries on *Mòzǐ*], 2 vols. [Běijīng: Zhōnghuá, 2001], vol. 1). Watson agrees that *tiān* probably does the selecting but is doubtful about the emendation (Burton Watson, *Mo Tzu: Basic Writings* [New York: Columbia University Press, 1963], 35). Among more recent writers, Van Norden accepts the emendation, apparently because he regards the view that Heaven selects the leader as the only alternative to attributing a social contract theory to the Mohists (Bryan W. Van Norden, *Virtue Ethics and Consequentialism in Early Chinese Philosophy* [Cambridge: Cambridge University Press, 2007], 164–65). The proposed emendation is unjustified on philological grounds, since the text is intelligible as it stands, no variant readings exist, and most likely the wording *tiān xià* would be favored by the principle of preferring the more difficult reading. Most Chinese editions do not even mention the issue. See, for instance, Wú Yùjiāng 吳毓江, 墨子校注 [*Collated Annotations on Mòzǐ*] (Běijīng: Zhōnghuá, 1993).
9. Mz 9/53ff., 19/7ff., 28/27ff.
10. The one exception is at Mz 12/50–51, which refers to "the Lord on High, ghosts, and spirits" establishing states and installing leaders. However, the topic of the passage is not the origin of political authority. It is that the Lord and spirits instated leaders to

3. POLITICAL THEORY: ORDER THROUGH SHARED NORMS   255

   benefit the people, rather than to enjoy the perquisites of office. The parallel passage at 13/16–17 does not mention the Lord on High or the spirits.
11. I am drawing here on Jean Hampton's notion of "convention consent" (*Political Philosophy* [Boulder, Colo.: Westview Press, 1998]), by which spontaneous solutions to coordination problems can arise and receive people's tacit acknowledgment without a formal procedure or covenant and without even actually earning people's endorsement.
12. Comparisons with Hobbes are common in the literature. See, for example, Fung Yu-lan [Féng Yǒulán] 馮友蘭, 中國哲學史 [History of Chinese philosophy], expanded and revised edition (1944; repr., Taipei: Shāngwù, 1994), 1:133–36; Donald Jenner, "Mo Tzu and Hobbes: Preliminary Remarks on the Relation of Chinese and Western Politics," *Cogito* 2 (1984): 49–72; Lao, *History*, 1:297–98; Schwartz, *World of Thought*, 142–44; Hansen, *Daoist Theory*, 132–33; and Van Norden, *Virtue Ethics*, 163–66.
13. In order of increasing severity, these were tattooing the face, cutting off the nose, chopping off one or both feet, castration, and death. The Mohists warn that these punishments must be applied sparingly, in such a way that they contribute to order, not disorder (*Mz* 12/42–46).
14. This interpretation coheres with the remarks at *Mz* 13/17–22, which describe the importance of a unified *yì* that the common people genuinely endorse. In the passage about encouraging people to report care and benefit, however, people are depicted as being motivated not by their own concern for the community but the desire to be rewarded or praised by their leaders and to avoid censure and punishment (13/25–26).
15. This reading dovetails with Hansen's interpretation of the Mohist claim that Heaven itself follows consequentialist norms. Hansen sees the Mohist position as entailing the idea that benefit or welfare is a "natural urge" and thus can serve as the root of moral norms that most people will find it natural to follow (*Daoist Theory*, 121–24).
16. See Van Norden, *Virtue Ethics*, 163; Philip J. Ivanhoe, "Mohist Philosophy," in *Routledge Encyclopedia of Philosophy*, ed. Edward Craig, 6:451–55 (London: Routledge, 1998); and Philip J. Ivanhoe and Bryan W. Van Norden, eds., *Readings in Classical Chinese Philosophy* (New York: Seven Bridges Press, 2000), 56.
17. Erica Brindley, "Human Agency and the Ideal of *Shang Tong* (Upward Conformity) in Early Mohist Writings," *Journal of Chinese Philosophy* 34, no. 3 (2007): 409–25, discusses the interplay of these influences.
18. "Rule by law" is a label for a political system that maintains order by promulgating and enforcing laws. "Rule of law" refers to a system in which the law is the highest governing authority, such that no person stands above the law and the content of particular laws is determined according to procedures stipulated in the law (such as in a constitution). "Rule of man" refers to a system in which some person or persons stand above the law, as when a despot or an oligarchy dictates the content of the law. Rule of man is consistent with rule by law but not with rule of law.
19. For a contrasting interpretation, see Van Norden, *Virtue Ethics*, 166, which contends that for the Mohists political authority is ultimately conferred by Heaven. I find the evidence for this interpretation weak. Even the one passage that does refer to "the Lord on High" (*shàng dì*) creating states and installing leaders stresses that the

purpose of doing so was to promote benefit, implying that the justification for political authority lies in its good consequences (Mz 12/50–51).
20. Mz 27/3–5, 26/14–15, 28/9–10.
21. Interestingly, the text's description of how the sages employed the capable—by listening to their words, tracing their conduct, examining their capabilities, and assigning them posts accordingly (Mz 9/6)—closely resembles the management techniques later advocated by Hán Fēi, who was probably influenced by the Mohists.

4. HEAVEN: THE HIGHEST ETHICAL MODEL

1. Dì was a legacy of Shāng-dynasty religious beliefs, a high god the Mohists worshipped along with Heaven, ghosts, and spirits, who appears especially frequently in Mòzǐ passages that quote from Shāng or Zhōu texts. Dì is not identical to Heaven, but their roles overlap enough that in certain contexts it is unclear whether they are distinct entities. For example, one Mòzǐ passage seems to equate "following Dì's guidelines" with "taking Heaven's intent as a model" (Mz 28/70–71). Another cites ancient documents assigning roughly the same role to Dì and to Heaven as a cosmic authority that disapproves of music making (32/45–48). Some passages indicate that performing sacrifices to "Dì on high and the ghosts and spirits" is a way of showing respect for and earning approval and favors from Heaven (for instance, 26/20, 28/28–29). Other passages drop the reference to Dì and speak instead of performing sacrifices to "Heaven and the ghosts" (for example, 27/9).
2. Ivanhoe suggests that the Mohist relation to Heaven is transactional (Philip J. Ivanhoe, "Mohist Philosophy," in *Routledge Encyclopedia of Philosophy*, ed. Edward Craig [London: Routledge, 1998], sec. 4). Táng expresses a similar view (Táng Jūnyì 唐君毅, 中國哲學原論導論篇 [Origins of Chinese philosophy: Introduction] [Taipei: Xuéshēng, 1986], 201).
3. In principle, people can also be rewarded after death by receiving praise, veneration, and ancestral sacrifices or by being denounced and having their bloodline cut off, leaving no descendants to perform sacrifices for them. The deceased continue to be regarded as denizens of this natural world and members of the human social structure.
4. See also Mz 26/30–33, 27/35–39, 28/19–23.
5. Mz 4/16–22, 26/23–36, 27/42–63, 28/23–34.
6. Mz 4/9–11, 26/41–44, 27/73–74, 28/44–46, 72–73.
7. Mz 9/52, 27/22–26, 35–39, 39–41, 28/21–23.
8. Mz 26/14–22, 27/2–6, 28/9–18.
9. David B. Wong ("Chinese Ethics," in *Stanford Encyclopedia of Philosophy*, http://plato.stanford.edu/archives/spr2008/entries/ethics-chinese, sec. 3) suggests that the appeal to Heaven to support Mohist consequentialism may be circular, since in his view the main reason for taking Heaven to be noble and wise is just that it promotes the benefit of all. I suggest that the Mohist appeal to Heaven is almost transparently circular. However, the crux of the circularity is not that Heaven's wisdom and nobility simply amount to its benefiting all. It is that, as the highest cosmic authority, Heaven

is by definition noblest and wisest, and given the Mohist understanding of social order and the relation between order and righteousness, righteousness inherently requires that we conform to Heaven's intent. As I explain further later in this chapter, the appeal to Heaven does not constitute an independent argument for Mohist consequentialism so much as a way of articulating the Mohist view of impartially, objectively justified moral norms.

10. This debate was launched by Denis Ahern, "Is Mo Tzu a Utilitarian?" *Journal of Chinese Philosophy* 3, no. 2 (1976): 185–93, which notes evidence both for and against a consequentialist interpretation. Advocates of a divine will interpretation include David Soles, "Mo Tzu and the Foundations of Morality," *Journal of Chinese Philosophy* 26, no. 1 (1999): 37–48; Yong Li, "The Divine Command Theory of Mozi," *Asian Philosophy* 16, no. 3 (2006): 237–45; and Daniel Johnson, "Mozi's Moral Theory: Breaking the Hermeneutical Stalemate," *Philosophy East and West* 61, no. 2 (2011): 347–64. Advocates of a consequentialist reading include Dirck Vorenkamp, "Another Look at Utilitarianism in Mo-Tzu's Thought," *Journal of Chinese Philosophy* 19, no. 4 (1992): 423–43; Kristopher Duda, "Reconsidering Mo Tzu on the Foundations of Morality," *Asian Philosophy* 11, no. 1 (2001): 23–31; Chris Fraser, "Mohism," in *Stanford Encyclopedia of Philosophy*, http://plato.stanford.edu/archives/fall2009/entries/mohism (article published in 2002); Hui-chieh Loy, "The Moral Philosophy of the Mozi 'Core Chapters'" (PhD diss., University of California, Berkeley, 2006); and Bryan W. Van Norden, *Virtue Ethics and Consequentialism in Early Chinese Philosophy* (Cambridge: Cambridge University Press, 2007).
11. For a helpful discussion, see Shelly Kagan, *Normative Ethics* (Boulder, Colo.: Westview Press, 1997), 17–22, which introduces the terminology of "factors" versus "foundations."
12. Watson's unfortunate translation of this claim as "Heaven decides what is right for the Son of Heaven" (Burton Watson, *Mo Tzu: Basic Writings* [New York: Columbia University Press, 1963], 80) misleadingly implies that right and wrong are fixed by Heaven's decision. As Van Norden points out, the Chinese text has no such implication (*Virtue Ethics*, 147). A more accurate translation is "Heaven governs over the Son of Heaven."
13. Mz 4/9, 26/44, 27/73, 28/69, 72–73.
14. Duda correctly notes this point ("Reconsidering Mo Tzu," 27–28).
15. In Classical Chinese, the claim that righteousness "issues" (*chū* 出) from Heaven need not imply that Heaven creates it or determines its content. Compare the similar claim in the *Analects* that when the *dào* prevails in the world, "ceremonial propriety and music . . . issue from the Son of Heaven" rather than from the various lords (*LY* 16.2). The point is not that the Son of Heaven creates the ceremonies and music or determines their content but that he directs or presides over them. Analogously, righteousness may "issue from Heaven" in the sense that Heaven presides over the hierarchy of authority through which it is realized.
16. Van Norden reaches a similar conclusion (*Virtue Ethics*, 148).
17. Heaven is not said to desire righteousness only because it desires these goods—that is, Heaven's desire for righteousness is not reduced to its desire for the goods, making its desire for righteousness instrumental. The text's claim is epistemic: we

know Heaven desires righteousness because it desires these goods, which obtain if and only if righteousness does.
18. The texts do not imply that the factors that identify what is righteous are the relevant factors because Heaven desires or intends them. This view would be a divine will theory. Rather, they claim only that Heaven reliably desires righteousness. For similar reasons, I was mistaken to suggest in Fraser, "Mohism," that the role of Heaven in Mohist thought resembles that of the ideal observer in an ideal observer theory. The epistemic role of Heaven is similar to that of an ideal observer. But in an ideal observer theory, the foundational explanation of the factors that identify what is morally right is that they are what an ideal observer would endorse. Mohist texts do not offer a parallel explanation involving Heaven.
19. To my knowledge, the only writer to have articulated this aspect of the role of Heaven in Mohist ethics is Hansen (Chad Hansen, *A Daoist Theory of Chinese Thought* [Oxford: Oxford University Press, 1992], 114–15, 123–24).
20. There are fascinating parallels, along with significant differences, between features of Mohist ethics and the views of "theological" or "Anglican" proto-utilitarians such as Richard Cumberland (1631–1718) and John Gay (1699–1745). In arguing that "natural" norms require us to act for the common good, not only our own, both invoke a deity who desires the good of all. Unlike Cumberland and Gay, however, the Mohists appeal to the deity's intent specifically as a model of righteousness, not as a foundational justification or source of moral obligation. For an informative discussion of early utilitarianism, see Colin Heydt, "Utilitarianism Before Bentham," in *The Cambridge Companion to Utilitarianism*, ed. Ben Eggleston and Dale Miller, 16–37 (Cambridge: Cambridge University Press, 2014). (I thank an anonymous referee for calling my attention to these points.)
21. An obvious extension of Mohist ethics would be to take the interests of nonhuman animals into consideration as well. The Mohists do not take this step, however. In early Chinese thought, only the *Zhuāngzǐ* treats nonhuman animals as deserving ethical consideration.
22. Thomas Nagel, *The View from Nowhere* (Oxford: Oxford University Press, 1986), 162.
23. Ibid., 162–63.
24. Ibid., 183.
25. It is thus not quite accurate to suggest, as Van Norden does, that Mohist ethics forces us to adopt the "view from nowhere" or "ignores the validity of our particular perspectives and the value of the particular commitments and relationships that make us who we are" (*Virtue Ethics*, 198). The Mohists ask us to adopt norms that are justified from the standpoint of Heaven, but they do not demand that we adopt that standpoint ourselves. Their ethics emphasizes our relationships with those closest to us—our family members and political associates. However, they do tend to ignore objectively defensible reasons, arising from particular perspectives, that do not fall within the narrow values of the unified moral norms of Heaven. In this respect, they do not give particular perspectives their due.
26. This insight is due to writers such as Wilfred Sellars, *Empiricism and the Philosophy of Mind* (Cambridge, Mass.: Harvard University Press, 1997); Robert Brandom, *Making It*

Explicit (Cambridge, Mass.: Harvard University Press, 1994); and T. M. Scanlon, *What We Owe to Each Other* (Cambridge, Mass.: Harvard University Press, 1998). Brandom calls this an "I-thou" understanding of objectivity (*Making It Explicit*, 599).
27. The first of these claims is the basis for the central argument for inclusive care and other Mohist doctrines. The second is from the "Dialectics" (*MB* A8). It is reiterated in the "Greater Selection," which explains that while our parents are alive we are to devote special treatment to them, but after their deaths we are to act on behalf of "all the world" (EC9).
28. *MB* EC1.

5. ETHICS: THE BENEFIT OF ALL

1. Chris Fraser, "Mohist Canons," in *Stanford Encyclopedia of Philosophy*, http://plato.stanford.edu/archives/sum2009/entries/Mohist-canons/ (article published in 2005), sec. 3, and Chris Fraser, "The Ethics of the Mohist 'Dialogues,'" in *The "Mozi" as an Evolving Text: Different Voices in Early Chinese Thought*, ed. Carine Defoort and Nicolas Standaert, 175–204 (Leiden: Brill, 2013).
2. A major contribution to these topics is Dan Robins, "The Mohists and the Gentlemen of the World," *Journal of Chinese Philosophy* 35, no. 3 (2008): 385–402, on which this section draws.
3. See *Mz* 19/22–23, 31/43, 32/24–25.
4. See, for example, Wing-tsit Chan, *A Source Book in Chinese Philosophy* (Princeton: Princeton University Press, 1963), 211; Benjamin Schwartz, *The World of Thought in Ancient China* (Cambridge, Mass.: Harvard University Press, 1985), 14, 138; Philip J. Ivanhoe and Bryan W. Van Norden, *Readings in Classical Chinese Philosophy* (New York: Seven Bridges Press, 2000), 56; Philip J. Ivanhoe, "Mohist Philosophy," in *Routledge Encyclopedia of Philosophy*, ed. Edward Craig (London: Routledge, 1998), 6:451; Kwong-loi Shun, *Mencius and Early Chinese Thought* (Stanford: Stanford University Press, 1997), 29; Chad Hansen, *A Daoist Theory of Chinese Thought* (Oxford: Oxford University Press, 1992), 112; David B. Wong, "Mohism: The Founder, Mozi (Mo Tzu)," in *Encyclopedia of Chinese Philosophy*, ed. Antonio Cua, 453–61 (London: Routledge, 2002); David B. Wong, "Chinese Ethics," in *Stanford Encyclopedia of Philosophy*, http://plato.stanford.edu/archives/spr2008/entries/ethics-chinese; and Bryan W. Van Norden, *Virtue Ethics and Consequentialism in Early Chinese Philosophy* (Cambridge: Cambridge University Press, 2007), 179. A much-needed corrective is Robins, "Mohists and Gentlemen."
5. See Hansen, *Daoist Theory*, 106–8, and Wong, "Mohism," 454.
6. See Schwartz, *World of Thought*, 148; Ivanhoe and Van Norden, *Readings*, 56; and Chan, *Source Book*, 211.
7. See Wong, "Mohism," 453–54; Ivanhoe, "Mohist Philosophy," 451; Shun, *Mencius*, 30; and Chris Fraser, "Mohism," in *Stanford Encyclopedia of Philosophy*, http://plato.stanford.edu/archives/fall2009/entries/mohism (article published in 2002).
8. Contra Chan, *Source Book*, 211; Alice Lum, "Social Utilitarianism in the Philosophy of Mo Tzu," *Journal of Chinese Philosophy* 4, no. 2 (1977), 193–94; Tang Chun-I [Táng Jūnyì] 唐君毅, 中國哲學原論導論篇 [Origins of Chinese philosophy: Introduction] (Taipei:

Xuésheng, 1986), 229; Hansen, *Daoist Theory*, 112; JeeLoo Liu, *An Introduction to Chinese Philosophy* (Oxford: Blackwell, 2006), 110; and Van Norden, *Virtue Ethics*, 179. One relatively late Mohist text, "Condemning the Rú," mentions a doctrine corresponding roughly to "graded care." Instead of rejecting it, however, the text ridicules the Rú for failing to follow it consistently (Mz 39/1–4).

9. With rare exceptions (Mz 35/20), the Mohists usually do not evaluate people or their character as righteous or not.
10. Loy rightly emphasizes this point (Hui-chieh Loy, "Mozi," in *The Internet Encyclopedia of Philosophy*, 2007, http://www.iep.utm.edu/m/mozi.htm, sec. 4).
11. As Shun observes, the implication is that any plausible norm will be one whose general promulgation would be beneficial (*Mencius*, 33).
12. Hansen, *Daoist Theory*, 110, insightfully calls attention to the Mohist ideal of a "constant" *dào*. This ideal is only implicit, however. The Mohists' explicit position is that action is guided through statements, which must have good consequences when publicized and widely practiced. Statements that meet these conditions should be made constant or regular. A plausible inference is that the right *dào* will be constant, in that it can be publicized and regularly practiced by all.
13. Roughly this view is targeted in the opening line of the *Dàodéjīng*, which contends that although a *dào* can be taken as a guide, the result is not a "regular" or "constant" *dào*.
14. Mohist texts sometimes describe harmful conduct as unbenevolent when we might have expected them to say it is unrighteous. Sometimes they use the two concepts interchangeably or as a pair in ways that suggest their content overlaps; see Mz 17/1ff., 25/12, 28/38.
15. Mz 16/1, 15/1, 32/1.
16. For the suggestion that the Mohists treat the virtues as reducible to conduct, see Loy, "Mozi," sec. 4, and Hui-chieh Loy, "The Moral Philosophy of the Mozi 'Core Chapters'" (PhD diss., University of California, Berkeley, 2006), 217n5. For the claim that Mohist ethics is outer directed and unconcerned with motives, see Schwartz, *World of Thought*, 147, and Wong, "Mohism," 454.
17. See also Mz 15/1, 16/1, 26/36, 27/49, 28/35.
18. Other passages illustrating these goods include Mz 8/1, 12/75, 16/83, 26/12, 27/20, 35/1, and 46/27.
19. Mz 14/4, 15/2, 16/2, 26/36, 27/14, 28/36.
20. Mz 14/4, 15/4, 16/3, 16/84.
21. Mz 9/2, 11/22, 12/31, 13/6.
22. This is the converse of the description of disorder at Mz 11/4 and 12/4. Such mutual assistance is also among the results of inclusive care and following Heaven's intent (16/18, 27/16).
23. Mz 16/84, 25/39, 32/3.
24. See *Mz*, books 5, 20, and 21.
25. Insofar as the Mohists acknowledge only a single general good, "the benefit of all," Wong is correct in calling theirs a "monistic" view of value ("Mohism," 458). This

characterization is potentially misleading, however, since benefit for them is a complex good alluding to multiple sources of value.
26. The helpful concept of a "focal point" is from Shelly Kagan, "Evaluative Focal Points," in *Morality, Rules, and Consequences*, ed. Brad Hooker, Elinor Mason, and Dale Miller, 134–55 (Edinburgh: Edinburgh University Press, 2000).
27. The idea of treating *dào* as an evaluative focal point is from Chad Hansen, "Dào as a Naturalistic Focus," in *Ethics in Early China*, ed. Chris Fraser, Dan Robins, and Timothy O'Leary, 229–56 (Hong Kong: Hong Kong University Press, 2011). The label "*dào* consequentialism" is from Fraser, "Mohism."
28. Writers who interpret Mohist ethics this way include Táng, *Introduction*, 114–17; Schwartz, *World of Thought*, 148; David Nivison, *The Ways of Confucianism*, ed. Bryan W. Van Norden (La Salle, Ill.: Open Court, 1996), 94; Ivanhoe and Van Norden, *Readings*, 56; and Van Norden, *Virtue Ethics*, 179. Among the few who have acknowledged the importance of special relationships in Mohism are A. C. Graham, *Disputers of the Tao* (La Salle, Ill.: Open Court, 1989), 43; Hansen, *Daoist Theory*; and Dan Robins, "Mohist Care," *Philosophy East and West* 62, no. 1 (2012): 60–91.
29. As noted in chapter 1, the Mohist conception of social order is blatantly sexist: relationships between and with women are hardly even mentioned. Also conspicuously absent from this list is friendship between peers.
30. Van Norden, *Virtue Ethics*, 179.
31. To my knowledge, the first publication to call attention to this point was Fraser, "Mohism."
32. Wong thus seems to oversimplify in implying that for the Mohists "the moral duties of family relationships" derive from their role in "promoting the good of all" ("Mohism," 458).
33. Wong offers an interpretation along these lines ("Chinese Ethics," sec. 3), although perhaps his point is simply that because of their overarching consequentialism, the Mohists treat different sources of value as commensurable. Filial devotion and crime prevention are distinct goods, for instance, but since both are benefits, the Mohists assume that should they conflict in a particular case, we can weigh them against each other and choose the greater benefit.
34. See Wong, "Chinese Ethics," sec. 2.5.
35. My discussion draws partly on the account of this event in the *Zuǒ zhuàn*.
36. *LSCQ* 1/5. (Contra Knoblock and Riegel's translation, the text does not specify that Fù executed his son himself.)
37. Nivison, for instance, contends that Mohist ethics is heroically stringent (*The Ways of Confucianism*, 131).
38. For details, see Fraser, "Ethics of the Mohist 'Dialogues.'"
39. Roman Malek suggested this interpretation to me.
40. What would the Mohist response be to poverty in societies other than our own? If our state is prosperous while foreign states are impoverished, are we to donate our surplus resources to them? Because of how the Mohists see our interactions with others as structured by a hierarchy of social and political relations, they would probably

regard poverty in foreign states mainly as a diplomatic issue. Our state should act as a good neighbor to other states, providing charitable assistance when needed, but individual residents of a prosperous state are not expected to intervene directly to relieve poverty in foreign lands. The exception would be members of the later Mohist sects described in the *Zhuāngzǐ*, who expressly sought to emulate the global altruism of the sage-king Yǔ.

41. The "Dialectics" shifts to a broader, psychological criterion of benefit: benefit is "what one is pleased to obtain" (*MB* A26). This criterion would allow the Mohists to expand their conception of benefit to include a wider range of goods. However, it is even more open to the critical challenge sketched here, since different people might be pleased by a diverse plurality of goods.
42. *Mz* 28/49–50. The passage is translated in the introduction.
43. *Mz* 28/34–43, 19/10–19.
44. This sketch is too simplistic, of course. Contemporary consequentialists offer more sophisticated accounts of human welfare than the Mohists, along with proposals to account for goods such as dignity or autonomy. However, I suggest that a suitably elaborated version of this line of argument offers a powerful criticism even of highly sophisticated versions of consequentialism.
45. For a seminal argument along these lines, see Susan Wolf, "Moral Saints," *Journal of Philosophy* 79, no. 8 (1982): 419–39.
46. Prudential value refers to what is in agents' self-interest, given their goals and ends, moral value to what is justified by moral considerations. The two sometimes diverge, as when the action that seems fairest or most honest runs against our material self-interest. In such cases, moral value is generally thought to take priority. Most important, the censure directed at immoral conduct is considerably more severe than that associated with imprudent behavior.
47. *Mz* 10/47, 13/58, 19/63, 25/86, 28/71.
48. This point is from Robins, "Mohists and Gentlemen."

6. INCLUSIVE CARE: FOR OTHERS AS FOR ONESELF

1. See, for example, Fung Yu-lan, *A Short History of Chinese Philosophy*, ed. Derk Bodde (New York: Macmillan, 1948), 53; Wing-tsit Chan, *A Source Book in Chinese Philosophy* (Princeton: Princeton University Press, 1963), 211; or A. C. Graham, *Disputers of the Tao* (La Salle, Ill.: Open Court, 1989), 41.
2. See, for instance, Cài Rénhòu 蔡仁厚, 墨家哲學 [Mohist philosophy] (Taipei: Dōng dà, 1978), 44; Eric Hutton, "Moral Connoisseurship in Mengzi," in *Essays on the Moral Philosophy of Mengzi*, ed. Xiusheng Liu and Philip J. Ivanhoe (Indianapolis: Hackett, 2002)," 179; JeeLoo Liu, *An Introduction to Chinese Philosophy* (Oxford: Blackwell, 2006), 110; David Nivison, *The Ways of Confucianism*, ed. Bryan W. Van Norden (La Salle, Ill.: Open Court, 1996), 133; Bryan W. Van Norden, *Virtue Ethics and Consequentialism in Early Chinese Philosophy* (Cambridge: Cambridge University Press, 2007), 179; and David B. Wong, "Universalism vs. Love with Distinctions: An Ancient Debate Revived," *Journal of Chinese Philosophy* 16, no. 3–4 (1989): 251.

6. INCLUSIVE CARE: FOR OTHERS AS FOR ONESELF   263

3. For example, a popular introductory ethics textbook describes morality as requiring "the impartial consideration of each individual's interests" and suggests that "the conscientious moral agent is someone who is concerned impartially with the interests of everyone affected by what he or she does" (James Rachels, *The Elements of Moral Philosophy*, 3rd ed. [Boston: McGraw-Hill, 1999], 15–19).
4. For *ài* as parental love, see *Mz* 27/39 and *MB* EC7; as sexual affection, *MB* NO15; as fondness for attractive appearance, *Mz* 9/36; as concern about wasted expenses, *Mz* 31/103; as concern about livestock, *MB* A7; as concern about political subjects, *Mz* 28/22.
5. For "care and benefit," see *Mz* 9/54, 13/23, 16/65, and 18/23. For the latter three formulations, see 9/55, 16/5, 27/45, and 4/11.
6. An interesting contrast holds between the Mohist stance and the Kantian principle of treating humanity as an end in itself, not merely as a means to one's own ends. The Kantian principle is grounded in respect for the dignity of each individual as an autonomous, rational agent. It is thus individualist and reflects the assumption that human beings are distinguished by their capacity for rational agency. The Mohist view is nonindividualist, grounded in a commitment to the welfare of humanity as a whole, of which each individual is a part. It appeals mainly to people's capacity for learning and following an impartially justified social *dào*, not a supposedly innate, autonomous capacity for reasoning.
7. The conceptual links between care and benefit should answer the worry among contemporary Ruist writers that for the Mohists inclusive care might have only instrumental value, rather than being itself inherently morally right or justified. Inclusive care is not simply a means of promoting the welfare of all. It is the attitude of an agent who is committed to everyone's welfare and thus to following "the *dào* of benevolence and righteousness." For the Ruist criticism, see, for example, Tang Chun-I [Táng Jūnyì] 唐君毅, 中國哲學原論導論篇 [Origins of Chinese philosophy: Introduction] (Taipei: Xuéshēng, 1986), 113; Chan, *Source Book*, 211; and Lao Sze-kwang [Láo Sīguāng] 勞思光, 新編中國哲學史 [New edition of *History of Chinese Philosophy*], 3 vols. (Taipei: Sān mín, 1984), 1:291–96. These writers seem to misconstrue consequentialism as the view that morality is a means of obtaining nonmoral goods. As they understand it, consequentialism does not really qualify as a moral theory at all, for it transforms what we normally think of as morality into an aspect of prudential rationality.
8. The fragment reads, "The [instance of] caring about others that is caring about Jill arises from consideration of Jill's benefit" (*MB* EC2).
9. Discussions with Dan Robins in 2001 helped to clarify this important point.
10. This point is underscored by the explanation to canon A8 in the "Dialectics" (*MB* A8). The canon states that righteousness is benefit. The explanation adds, "In intent, one takes all the world as one's portion and in ability one is able to benefit it. It is not necessarily applied." That is, to be righteous, a person must commit to benefiting all the world and be capable of acting on this commitment. The person need not actually benefit everyone, however, as the chance to do so may not arise.
11. On the differences between the three "Inclusive Care" essays, see Chris Fraser, "Doctrinal Developments in MZ 14–16," *Warring States Papers* 1 (2010): 132–36, and the

nuanced discussions in Carine Defoort, "The Growing Scope of '*Jiān* 兼': Differences Between Chapters 14, 15 and 16 of the *Mozi*," *Oriens Extremus* 45 (2005): 119–40, and Hui-chieh Loy, "The Moral Philosophy of the Mozi 'Core Chapters'" (PhD diss., University of California, Berkeley, 2006).

12. Ascribing all forms of disorder to a single cause is typical Mohist hyperbole. Elsewhere the Mohists similarly attribute disorder to the ruler's failure to promote worthy officials (book 8), to people's failure to understand that ghosts and spirits reward the worthy and punish wrongdoing (book 31), and to the prevalence of fatalism among the populace (book 35).

13. Dan Robins helped me to see this point. See Chris Fraser, "Mohism and Self-Interest," *Journal of Chinese Philosophy* 35, no. 3 (2008): 448; Dan Robins, "Mohist Care," *Philosophy East and West* 62, no. 1 (2012): 60–91.

14. To be "for" (*wèi* 為) others is to be committed to them as ends, as when a father seeks to obtain something for his son's benefit (*MB* EC7) or an official has responsibility for those he serves (*MB* A19). The formulation "for others as for oneself" might have been partly a response to Yáng Zhū, figurehead for a brand of ethical egoism. The Yangist slogan was to be "for oneself" (*wèi wǒ* 為我).

15. Defoort ("Growing Scope") and Loy ("Moral Philosophy") both call attention to this pattern.

16. In the third essay, the link between inclusive care and the virtues is drawn in the essay's conclusion (*Mz* 16/84), rather than in the Argument from Consequences.

17. I credit this observation to Defoort, "Growing Scope." *Jiān ài* begins to be used only in relatively late strata of the "Triads"—it occurs once in "Inclusive Care III" and several times in "Heaven's Intent III"—and is then used several times in the "Dialogues," "Dialectics," and "Summaries."

18. "Identifying Upward" indicates that when social disorder prevails, people refuse to share surplus labor and resources (*Mz* 11/4, 12/4). The implication is that in an orderly society, people see to the needs of their circle and then share surplus goods or labor with outsiders.

19. I advanced this claim in Chris Fraser, "Mohism," in *Stanford Encyclopedia of Philosophy*, http://plato.stanford.edu/archives/fall2009/entries/mohism (article published in 2002), sec. 7. Loy reaches similar conclusions ("Moral Philosophy").

20. For examples of *qīn* used to refer to emotional closeness, see *Mz* 8/9, 35/26, 36/19, and 49/90. In a widely discussed exchange with the Mohist Yí Zhī, Mencius rejects equal care for all on the grounds that a person could not feel the same level of endearment (*qīn*) toward a neighbor's child as toward a relative's (*Me* 5.5). The criticism conflates equal care with equal endearment, which the Mohists do not advocate.

21. Robins's interpretation is similar: "Mohist care is fundamentally a normative attitude" ("Mohist Care," 76). "To be for someone is . . . to accord normative significance to her well-being" (80).

22. See Fraser, "Mohism and Self-Interest," 448. See also Robins's discussion of the conditional nature of inclusive care ("Mohist Care," 73–76). As he remarks, inclusive care

is not addressed to the situation of "an individual agent in a world of people who do not care" (74).
23. This label and that for the "Ruler" argument are from Bryan W. Van Norden, "A Response to the Mohist Arguments in 'Impartial Caring,'" in *The Moral Circle and the Self: Chinese and Western Approaches*, ed. Kim-chong Chong, Sor-hoon Tan, and C. L. Ten, 41–58 (La Salle, Ill.: Open Court, 2003).
24. Chad Hansen (*A Daoist Theory of Chinese Thought* [Oxford: Oxford University Press, 1992], 112), Van Norden (*Virtue Ethics*, 188), and Loy ("Moral Philosophy," 283-84) all mention the possible false dilemma and consider the objection that people's first choice might be a caretaker who is biased in favor of his family and friends, including the soldier's family, not one who cares all-inclusively about everyone. I will not dwell on this objection, since the gist of my criticism is that the argument's aims are limited—it attempts to show only that inclusive care "can be used," not that it is preferable to any competing norm—and even if we accept the Mohists' hypothetical premises, which rule out such a favorably biased caretaker, the argument's conclusion is very weak.
25. Hansen takes the Caretaker to be an argument against Ruist "partial moral concern" that shows it to be collectively self-defeating—that is, practiced collectively, it leads to a worse outcome, by its own lights, than if it were not practiced (*Daoist Theory*, 112-13). He construes the Caretaker as aimed at justifying inclusive care as a public *dào* on grounds accepted by its opponents, thereby overcoming the problem of moral reform—the challenge of justifying new moral norms to an audience convinced that their traditional practices are correct. Van Norden interprets both the Caretaker and the Ruler as normative arguments on behalf of inclusive care against either a Ruist or a Yangist (ethical-egoist) position (*Virtue Ethics*, 184). The Caretaker in particular he sees as a failed attempt to "demonstrate to the partialist that he should be an impartialist" (183). Neither writer mentions the objections to which the arguments are replies. Loy too takes them to be normative arguments on behalf of inclusive care ("Moral Philosophy," 280). On the interpretation presented here, these discussions, despite their merits, are largely beside the point, as they take the arguments out of context. My own 2002 treatment of the arguments explains their context but frames them inaccurately and misleadingly treats them as attempts to justify inclusive care (Fraser, "Mohism," sec. 7). Fraser, "Mohism and Self-Interest," ties the arguments more tightly to the associated objections and summarizes their aim as showing that inclusive care is compatible with shared values such as one's family's welfare (451). This reading converges with Robins's more recent treatment ("Mohist Care," 73).
26. Van Norden dismisses the argument too quickly, as he assumes it is aimed at justifying inclusive care over a partialistic Ruist doctrine (*Virtue Ethics*, 193). The text is clear that the aim is only to show that inclusive care is compatible with filial devotion.
27. This is the modicum of truth in Mencius's complaint that inclusive care amounts to denying one's father (*Me* 6.9).
28. Yi-pao Mei, *Mo-tse, the Neglected Rival of Confucius* (London: Probsthain, 1934), 193.
29. I owe this idea to a conversation with Roman Malek.

7. MOTIVATION: CHANGING PEOPLE IN A GENERATION

1. See, for instance, David Nivison, *The Ways of Confucianism*, ed. Bryan W. Van Norden (La Salle, Ill.: Open Court, 1996), 96; Kwong-loi Shun, "Mo Tzu," in *The Cambridge Dictionary of Philosophy*, ed. Robert Audi (Cambridge: Cambridge University Press, 1995), 515; Philip J. Ivanhoe, "Mohist Philosophy," in *Routledge Encyclopedia of Philosophy*, ed. Edward Craig (London: Routledge, 1998), 6:451–55; and Bryan W. Van Norden, *Virtue Ethics and Consequentialism in Early Chinese Philosophy* (Cambridge: Cambridge University Press, 2007), 309.
2. See Chad Hansen, *A Daoist Theory of Chinese Thought* (Oxford: Oxford University Press, 1992), 108. This and other points cited in the following are developments of seminal ideas introduced in Hansen's work, especially his discussion of the structure of "*dào* ethics" and the Mohist conception of agency (140–43).
3. For an example of this assumption, see Nivison, *The Ways of Confucianism*, 131.
4. See, for instance, ibid., 133; Tang Chun-I [Táng Jūnyì] 唐君毅, 中國哲學原論導論篇 [Origins of Chinese philosophy: Introduction] (Taipei: Xuéshēng, 1986), 115; Cài Rénhòu 蔡仁厚, 墨家哲學 [Mohist philosophy] (Taipei: Dōng dà, 1978), 44; David B. Wong, "Universalism vs. Love with Distinctions: An Ancient Debate Revived," *Journal of Chinese Philosophy* 16, no. 3–4 (1989), 251; JeeLoo Liu, *An Introduction to Chinese Philosophy* (Oxford: Blackwell, 2006), 110; and Van Norden, *Virtue Ethics*, 179.
5. Arguably, the belief-desire model is itself an extension or generalization of the practical syllogism.
6. Chris Fraser, "Action and Agency in Early Chinese Thought," *Journal of Chinese Philosophy and Culture* 5 (2009): 217–39.
7. Although they do not explicitly discuss such positive and negative responses in detail, the Mohists seem to refer to them in general by the paired terms *qǔ* 取 (select) and *shě* 舍 (reject) (for instance, at *Mz* 39/22).
8. Hansen, *Daoist Theory*, 120.
9. See, for example, *Mz* 10/47. Similar phrasing appears in the concluding paragraph of most books in the "Triads."
10. Proponents of this view include Thomas Nagel, *The Possibility of Altruism* (Princeton: Princeton University Press, 1970), 27–32; Christine Korsgaard, "Skepticism about Practical Reason," *Journal of Philosophy* 83, no. 1 (1986): 5–25; and T. M. Scanlon, *What We Owe to Each Other* (Cambridge, Mass.: Harvard University Press, 1998), 33–36.
11. In this respect, the Mohist position seems to converge with what Shafer-Landau calls "motivational judgment internalism," the view that if an agent judges an action to be right, the agent is thereby (defeasibly) motivated to perform it (Russ Shafer-Landau, *Moral Realism: A Defense* [Oxford: Oxford University Press, 2003], 142–45).
12. Here I am construing Humeanism as the view that beliefs and desires are mutually independent types of states, that desires are necessary for motivation, and that beliefs are not sufficient to motivate. Anti-Humeanism I construe as the view that beliefs—or in the Mohists' case, states with a theoretical role overlapping that of beliefs—can be sufficient to motivate.

13. Shun sees the breakup of families in the Mohist state of nature as evidence that the Mohists think people lack affection for kin (Kwong-loi Shun, *Mencius and Early Chinese Thought* [Stanford: Stanford University Press, 1997], 34). But to explain the breakups, they need assume only that people's commitment to conflicting norms can overpower their affection for kin, not that they lack affection.
14. Hence I think the Mohists would reject the distinction Nivison draws between doing something one recognizes as morally right and doing it "with the inner *feeling* that it just is the thing to do" (*The Ways of Confucianism*, 131; emphasis in original). For them, the conviction that something is *shì* or *yì* probably carries with it the sort of feeling he alludes to. Nivison faults the Mohists for neglecting "the problem of my ability to feel the way I would have to to be genuinely moved" to do what is right (ibid., 96). The role of *shì-fēi* attitudes renders this criticism question-begging: to have the appropriate *shì-fēi* attitudes is precisely to be "genuinely moved."
15. In contemporary ethics, Griffin has articulated a related position, arguing that cognitive recognition and affective reaction are inextricably intertwined (James Griffin, *Value Judgement* [Oxford: Clarendon Press, 1996], 20–36).
16. The Mohists are thus unlikely to advocate guiding action by "dispassionate intellect," as Wong suggests they do (David B. Wong, "Mohism: The Founder, Mozi [Mo Tzu]," in *Encyclopedia of Chinese Philosophy*, ed. Antonio Cua [London: Routledge, 2002], 453), for they draw no clear distinction between intellect and the passions. The passage Wong cites as emphasizing intellect over emotions—translated in chapter 5—in fact advocates guiding conduct by objective norms of benevolence and righteousness rather than personal emotions and preferences, because the latter are too easily biased (*Mz* 47/19–20). Intellect is not mentioned.
17. This brief account should be sufficient to rebut Nivison's claim that the Mohists have no explanation of akrasia beyond "sheer perversity" on the agent's part (*The Ways of Confucianism*, 84).
18. For the claim that the Mohists advocate a "wholly outer-directed" ethics and are unconcerned with whether agents act from the right motives, see Wong, "Mohism," 454, and Benjamin Schwartz, *The World of Thought in Ancient China* (Cambridge, Mass.: Harvard University Press, 1985), 147.
19. I thank Hui-chieh Loy for suggesting I include this observation.
20. See, for instance, *Mz* 46/12–15, 48/84, and 49/36–38. For a more detailed discussion, see Chris Fraser, "The Ethics of the Mohist 'Dialogues,'" in *The "Mozi" as an Evolving Text: Different Voices in Early Chinese Thought*, ed. Carine Defoort and Nicolas Standaert, 175–204 (Leiden: Brill, 2013).
21. A practitioner of inclusive care is depicted engaging in a bit of self-coaching at *Mz* 16/26–27, for instance.
22. Nivison holds that for the Mohists, there is "*no problem of inner psychic restructuring or nurturing needed* to make a person morally perfect" (*The Ways of Confucianism*, 83; emphasis in original). Similarly, Wong suggests that for them "no transformation of human character is needed to act on the right values" (David B. Wong, "Chinese Ethics," in *Stanford Encyclopedia of Philosophy*, http://plato.stanford.edu/archives

/spr2008/entries/ethics-chinese, sec. 3). I suggest that, on the contrary, the Mohists' emphasis on education and practice indicates that they consider a process of nurturing or transformation crucial to ensuring correct performance of the *dào*. They seek to transform how people distinguish *shì-fēi*, the norms they follow in acting on these attitudes, and the reliability with which they do so.

23. According to Nivison, the Mohists' assumption that people will respond to normative arguments by modifying their attitudes and conduct commits them to a form of voluntarism, namely the view that agents have direct, voluntary control over their motivational states (*The Ways of Confucianism*, 130; see also 83, 93). This interpretation is shared by Ivanhoe ("Mohist Philosophy," sec. 2) and Slingerland (Edward Slingerland, *Effortless Action* [New York: Oxford University Press, 2003], 128–29). In fact, voluntarism is probably inconsistent with the role the Mohists assign to normative argumentation. Were they voluntarists, the Mohists could not assume that cogent arguments are a reliable means of influencing what people deem *shì* or *fēi* and how they act. For if people's *shì-fēi* attitudes were under their voluntary control, they could at will ignore the force of any argument. Nivison's view seems premised on the assumption that the Mohist reform program is aimed primarily at changing people's affections (*The Ways of Confucianism*, 130), which he seems to regard as the only reliable source of morally worthy motivation (99, 142–45). I am arguing that the Mohists are instead concerned mainly with changing people's *shì-fēi* attitudes and associated patterns of conduct. Note that in calling for people to "examine" their doctrines, the Mohists implicitly allow that conversion to their *dào* may take time and psychological effort.
24. On this point, see also Hansen, *Daoist Theory*, 99–100.
25. This section thus rebuts the view that the Mohists take self-interest to be people's predominant source of motivation. For versions of this view, see Nivison, *The Ways of Confucianism*, 83; Schwartz, *World of Thought*, 145; Ivanhoe, "Mohist Philosophy," sec. 4; and Shun, *Mencius*, 35. For a detailed discussion, see Chris Fraser, "Mohism and Self-Interest," *Journal of Chinese Philosophy* 35, no. 3 (2008): 437–54.
26. Passages such as these also refute skepticism about whether the Mohists ascribe to people any sort of morally worthy motivation. Nivison, *The Ways of Confucianism*, 83, and Ivanhoe, "Mohist Philosophy," sec. 4, for example, seem to maintain that for the Mohists there is no such thing as virtuous motivation. Contemporary New Confucian writers have expressed similar views (Cài Rénhòu 蔡仁厚, 墨家哲學 [Mohist philosophy] [Taipei: Dōng dà, 1978], 83).
27. Thus I suggest that the Mohists' claims about reciprocity answer Shun's worry that, because they do not regard their *dào* as "the realization of certain inclinations that human beings already share," they may have difficulty explaining how people can come to practice it (*Mencius*, 34–35). A tendency toward reciprocity is a shared inclination that is realized in the practice of the Mohist *dào*.
28. As this section indicates, the Mohist reform project does not require wholesale changes in people's motivation but mainly seeks to build on existing motivation, particularly people's commitment to righteousness and to values such as social order, filial devotion, and self-interest. The widely repeated claim that the Mohists see

human nature as "extremely plastic" (Ivanhoe, "Mohist Philosophy," 451) or "highly malleable" (Van Norden, *Virtue Ethics*, 195) is thus unsustainable.

8. WAR AND ECONOMICS

1. Bryan W. Van Norden, *Virtue Ethics and Consequentialism in Early Chinese Philosophy* (Cambridge: Cambridge University Press, 2007), 176, makes this observation.
2. Contemporary just war theory typically proposes six criteria that must jointly be satisfied to justify going to war: just cause, such as self-defense or the defense of innocents; right intention, or fighting specifically for a just cause; probability of success, as war can be justified only if there is a reasonable chance of achieving its aims; proportionality, or not causing harm that outweighs the expected goods reflected in the just cause; last resort, or waging war only when all feasible peaceful alternatives have been exhausted; and proper authority, or having the legitimate political authority to wage war. As we will see, Mohist texts allude to the first three of these and arguably imply the next two. Only the sixth is absent from their remarks about war, although I suggest their requirement of divine sanction fills a similar role.
3. As Wong and Loy emphasize (Benjamin Wong and Hui-chieh Loy, "War and Ghosts in Mozi's Political Philosophy," *Philosophy East and West* 54, no. 3 [2004], 354–55).
4. Wong and Loy raise this concern (ibid., 347).
5. Van Els calls this criterion an "impossible test," crediting the phrase to Michael Nylan (Paul van Els, "How to End Wars with Words: Three Argumentative Strategies by Mozi and His Followers," in *The "Mozi" as an Evolving Text: Different Voices in Early Chinese Thought*, ed. Carine Defoort and Nicolas Standaert [Leiden: Brill, 2013], 91).
6. For an expanded treatment of just war theory in the *Mòzǐ*, see Chris Fraser, "The Mozi and Just War Theory in Pre-Han Thought" (unpublished manuscript).
7. This shortcoming has been widely noted. See, for instance, Hui-chieh Loy, "Mozi," in *The Internet Encyclopedia of Philosophy*, 2007, http://www.iep.utm.edu/m/mozi.htm, sec. 10; Van Norden, *Virtue Ethics*, 174; and Dan Robins, "The Mohists and the Gentlemen of the World," *Journal of Chinese Philosophy* 35, no. 3 (2008): 394.
8. I credit this observation to Robins ("Mohists and Gentlemen," 391–92).
9. This observation too is Robins's (ibid., 394).
10. Moreover, as Robins notes (ibid., 394), Xúnzǐ exaggerates the degree of austerity the Mohists advocate. He also wrongly claims they require the ruler to labor side by side with the people, undermining their difference in status (Xz 10/55–56).
11. The relevant discussions are at Xz 6/5, 10/55–56, 11/60, and 17/51–52.
12. Robins underscores this point ("Mohists and Gentlemen," 394).
13. Xz 6/5, 10/55–56, 11/60, 17/51–52.
14. I say "some" of the aristocracy, because a passage in *Mencius* indicates that prolonged mourning was controversial: officials in the state of Téng believed the three-year mourning ritual contravened established practice (*Me* 5.2).
15. Wu Hung, "The Art and Architecture of the Warring States Period," in *The Cambridge History of Ancient China*, ed. Michael Loewe and Edward L. Shaughnessy (Cambridge: Cambridge University Press, 1999), 712.

16. In the context of Xúnzǐ's general theory of ritual, the three-year mourning is justified because of its purported effectiveness in preserving social order by providing a means for orderly expression of potentially disruptive emotions.
17. Recall the passage from the "Dialogues," discussed in chapter 5, that advocates acting from benevolence and righteousness, rather than from potentially biased emotions (*Mz* 47/19–20).
18. This point is widely recognized. See, for example, Chad Hansen, *A Daoist Theory of Chinese Thought* (Oxford: Oxford University Press, 1992), 136; Whalen Lai, "The Public Good That Does the Public Good: A New Reading of Mohism," *Asian Philosophy* 3, no. 2 (1993): 137; Van Norden, *Virtue Ethics*, 173; and Robins, "Mohists and Gentlemen," 390.
19. The major statement of this view is book 20 of the *Xúnzǐ*, "Discourse on Music." Related views can be found in the *Analects* and in book 5 of *The Annals of Lü Buwei*, among other texts. For detailed studies of the role of music in early Chinese thought, see Scott Cook, "Unity and Diversity in the Musical Thought of Warring States China" (PhD diss., University of Michigan, 1995), and "Xun Zi on Ritual and Music," *Monumenta Serica* 45 (1997): 1–38.
20. Loy suggests an interpretation along these lines ("Mozi," sec. 10).
21. *Mz* 32/12–13, 9/51, 37/11.
22. See book 20 of the *Xúnzǐ*. Another pre-Hàn text, book 5 of *The Annals of Lü Buwei*, briefly mentions "scholars of the age" who "condemn music" and in response seems to imply that music satisfies an unalterable desire that people have by nature (*LSCQ* 5/2). The argument is not spelled out explicitly, however. In its criticism of Mòzǐ, the *Zhuāngzǐ* "All Under Heaven" essay similarly implies that human beings have an inherent tendency to sing and make music (*Zz* 33/22–23), but this text too does not mention the aesthetic value of music.
23. For a detailed discussion, see Robins, "Mohists and Gentlemen." As Robins remarks, given Xúnzǐ's obvious fondness for music, he may well have thought it intrinsically valuable, but this point has no role in his arguments against the Mohists.
24. *LY* 4.15, 5.12, 12.2, 15.24. See also 6.30.
25. Such a doctrine is mentioned in the *Mòzǐ* only in book 46, where it is attributed to Wūmǎzǐ, who was not a Ruist. "Condemning the Rú" mentions the doctrine that kin of different degrees should receive differential treatment (*Mz* 39/1). Instead of rejecting it, the text ridicules the Rú for failing to interpret it consistently.
26. *Mz* 39/19–21, 46/49–52. For the Ruist version, see *LY* 7.1.
27. See Fung Yu-lan [Féng Yǒulán] 馮友蘭, 中國哲學史 [History of Chinese philosophy], expanded and revised edition (1944; repr., Taipei: Shāngwù, 1994), 1:137–38.

EPILOGUE

1. For a discussion of Mohist semantic theory and philosophy of language, see Chris Fraser, "Mohist Canons," in *Stanford Encyclopedia of Philosophy*, http://plato.stanford.edu/archives/sum2009/entries/Mohist-canons/ (article published in 2005).
2. The Mohist slogan "promote the worthy and employ the capable" appears numerous times throughout the *Xúnzǐ*, such as at 9/22–23, 10/82, and 12/12, among other passages.

3. The following account is conjectural, as historical information on the Mohists in the Hàn is sparse. For a detailed study of Mohism in Hàn thought, see Michael Nylan, "Kongzi and Mozi, the Classicists (Ru 儒) and the Mohists (Mo 墨) in Classical-Era Thinking," *Oriens Extremus* 48 (2009), 1–20.
4. For the claim that Mohism was too idealistic, see Wing-tsit Chan, *A Source Book in Chinese Philosophy* (Princeton: Princeton University Press, 1963), 212. For the suggestion that Mohism was foreign to Chinese culture, see A. C. Graham, *Disputers of the Tao* (La Salle, Ill.: Open Court, 1989), 43. Wong too attributes the eclipse of Mohism to the Mohist philosophical style's being "more typical of the Western tradition" (David B. Wong, "Mohism: The Founder, Mozi [Mo Tzu]," in *Encyclopedia of Chinese Philosophy*, ed. Antonio Cua [London: Routledge, 2002], 460). Claims that Mohism is in some sense "non-Chinese" overlook the extent to which the Mohists' conceptual framework, their style of reasoning, and their theoretical concerns were absorbed and developed by most later thinkers, such as Xúnzǐ, the writers of *The Annals of Lü Buwei*, the writers of key *Zhuāngzǐ* texts such as the "Essay on Evening Things Out" and "Autumn Waters," the Legalists, and figures such as Sòng Xíng, Yín Wén, and Huì Shī. Even Mencius, supposedly the paradigmatically Chinese thinker, borrows concepts and argument techniques from the Mohists (see, for example, *Me* 1.7, 7.1).
5. An interesting example of such appropriation comes from the first chapter of the *Shǐ jì*, the records of the five mythical emperors, which uses a cluster of Mohist-sounding phrases to praise Emperor Gāo Xīn, saying that he benefited all, followed the moral norms of Heaven, moderated expenditures, guided the people while benefiting and instructing them, and respectfully served the ghosts and spirits (*SJ* 1, 13). (I thank Nicolas Standaert for this reference.) For other fascinating examples, see Joachim Gentz, "Mohist Traces in the Early *Chunqiu Fanlu* Chapters," *Oriens Extremus* 48 (2009): 55–70.
6. A passage in one Hàn source does remark that Mohist inclusive care fails "to distinguish near relations from distant" (*HS* 30, 1737–38). Even in this passage, however, the Mohists' asceticism, frugality, and opposition to ceremony are treated more prominently. The one-line biography of Mòzǐ in the *Shǐ jì* states that he was "good at defense" and "practiced moderation in use" but does not mention Mohist ethical doctrines (*SJ* 74, 2349–50).
7. *SJ* 130, 3290–91.
8. Writing in the next century, Wáng Chōng also attributes the decline of Mohism to its norms' being "difficult to follow" (*LH* 83/358/22).
9. Benjamin Schwartz, *The World of Thought in Ancient China* (Cambridge, Mass.: Harvard University Press, 1985), 172.
10. Graham, *Disputers of the Tao*, 34.
11. Schwartz, *World of Thought*, 169.

BIBLIOGRAPHY

Ahern, Denis. "Is Mo Tzu a Utilitarian?" *Journal of Chinese Philosophy* 3, no. 2 (1976): 185–93.
Bengson, John, and Marc Moffett, eds. *Knowing How: Essays on Knowledge, Mind, and Action*. Oxford: Oxford University Press, 2011.
Brandom, Robert. *Making It Explicit*. Cambridge, Mass.: Harvard University Press, 1994.
Brindley, Erica. "Human Agency and the Ideal of *Shang Tong* (Upward Conformity) in Early Mohist Writings." *Journal of Chinese Philosophy* 34, no. 3 (2007): 409–25.
Brooks, E. Bruce, and A. Taeko Brooks. *The Original Analects*. New York: Columbia University Press, 1998.
Cài Rénhòu 蔡仁厚. 墨家哲學 [Mohist philosophy]. Taipei: Dōng dà, 1978.
Chan, Wing-tsit. *A Source Book in Chinese Philosophy*. Princeton: Princeton University Press, 1963.
Chén Qǐtiān 陳啓天. 增訂韓非子校釋 [Collated explications of the *Hánfēizǐ*, expanded and revised]. Taipei: Shāngwù, 1969.
Cook, Scott. "Unity and Diversity in the Musical Thought of Warring States China." PhD diss., University of Michigan, 1995.
——. "Xun Zi on Ritual and Music." *Monumenta Serica* 45 (1997): 1–38.
Csikszentmihalyi, Mark. *Material Virtue: Ethics and the Body in Early China*. Leiden: Brill, 2004.
Cuī Qīngtián 崔清田. 显学重光：近现代的先秦墨家研究 [Eminent scholars return to the light: Modern and recent research on pre-Qin Mohism]. Shěnyáng: Liáoníng jiàoyù, 1997.
Defoort, Carine. "The Growing Scope of '*Jian* 兼': Differences Between Chapters 14, 15 and 16 of the *Mozi*." *Oriens Extremus* 45 (2005): 119–40.
Defoort, Carine, and Nicolas Standaert, eds. *The "Mozi" as an Evolving Text: Different Voices in Early Chinese Thought*. Leiden: Brill, 2013.
Desmet, Karen. "The Growth of Compounds in the Core Chapters of the *Mozi*." *Oriens Extremus* 45 (2005): 99–118.

———. "MZ 39: An Anomaly in the Mohist Ethical 'Core Chapters'?" Paper presented at the seventeenth conference of the Warring States Working Group, University of Leiden, 2003.
Ding, Weixiang. "Mengzi's Inheritance, Criticism, and Overcoming of Mohist Thought." *Journal of Chinese Philosophy* 35, no. 3 (2008): 403–19.
Duda, Kristopher. "Reconsidering Mo Tzu on the Foundations of Morality." *Asian Philosophy* 11, no. 1 (2001): 23–31.
Durrant, Stephen W. "A Consideration of Differences in the Grammar of the Mo Tzu 'Essays' and 'Dialogues.'" *Monumenta Serica* 33 (1977–1978): 248–67.
Fāng Shòuchǔ 方授楚. 墨學源流 [Sources of Mohism]. Shànghǎi: Zhōnghuá, 1989.
Forke, Alfred. *Me Ti*. Berlin: Vereinig, 1922.
Fraser, Chris. "Action and Agency in Early Chinese Thought." *Journal of Chinese Philosophy and Culture* 5 (2009): 217–39.
———. "Distinctions, Judgment, and Reasoning in Classical Chinese Thought." *History and Philosophy of Logic* 34, no. 1 (2013): 1–24.
———. "Doctrinal Developments in MZ 14–16." *Warring States Papers* 1 (2010): 132–36.
———. "The Ethics of the Mohist 'Dialogues.'" In Defoort and Standaert, *The "Mozi,"* 175–204.
———. "Introduction: *Later Mohist Logic, Ethics and Science* after 25 Years." In Graham, *Later Mohist Logic*, xvii–xxxiv.
———. "Is MZ 17 a Fragment of MZ 26?" *Warring States Papers* 1 (2010): 122–25.
———. "Knowledge and Error in Early Chinese Thought." *Dao: A Journal of Comparative Philosophy* 10, no. 2 (2011): 127–48.
———. "Language and Ontology in Early Chinese Thought." *Philosophy East and West* 57, no. 4 (2007): 420–56.
———. "Mohism." In *Stanford Encyclopedia of Philosophy*. Article published 2002. http://plato.stanford.edu/archives/fall2009/entries/mohism.
———. "Mohism and Motivation." In *Ethics in Early China*, edited by Chris Fraser, Dan Robins, and Timothy O'Leary, 73–90. Hong Kong: Hong Kong University Press, 2011.
———. "Mohism and Self-Interest." *Journal of Chinese Philosophy* 35, no. 3 (2008): 437–54.
———. "Mohist Canons." In *Stanford Encyclopedia of Philosophy*. http://plato.stanford.edu/archives/sum2009/entries/Mohist-canons/. Article published 2005.
———. "The Mohist Conception of Reality." In *Chinese Metaphysics and Its Problems*, edited by Chenyang Li and Franklin Perkins, 69–84. Cambridge: Cambridge University Press, 2014.
———. "The *Mozi* and Just War Theory in Pre-Han Thought." Unpublished manuscript.
———. "The School of Names." In *Stanford Encyclopedia of Philosophy*. http://plato.stanford.edu/archives/fall2005/entries/school-names/.
———. "Táng Jūnyì on Mencian and Mohist Conceptions of Mind." *Contemporary Confucians of the Chinese University* (New Asia Academic Bulletin 19, edited by Cheng-yi Chung, Hong Kong: New Asia College, 2006): 203–33.
———. "Thematic Relationships in MZ 8–10 and 11–13." *Warring States Papers* 1 (2010): 137–42.
———. "Truth in Moist Dialectics." *Journal of Chinese Philosophy* 39, no. 3 (2012): 351–68.
Fung Yu-lan [Féng Yǒulán] 馮友蘭. 中國哲學史 [History of Chinese philosophy]. Expanded and revised edition. Vol. 1. 1944. Reprint, Taipei: Shāngwù, 1994.

———. *A Short History of Chinese Philosophy*. Edited by Derk Bodde. New York: Macmillan, 1948.
Garrett, Mary. "Classical Chinese Conceptions of Argumentation and Persuasion." *Argumentation and Advocacy* 29, no. 3 (1993): 105–15.
Geaney, Jane. "A Critique of A. C. Graham's Reconstruction of the 'Neo-Mohist Canons.'" *Journal of the American Oriental Society* 119, no. 1 (1999): 1–11.
———. *On the Epistemology of the Senses in Early Chinese Thought*. Society for Asian and Comparative Philosophy 19. Honolulu: University of Hawai'i Press, 2002.
Gentz, Joachim. "Mohist Traces in the Early *Chunqiu Fanlu* Chapters." *Oriens Extremus* 48 (2009): 55–70.
Gettier, Edmund L. "Is Justified True Belief Knowledge?" *Analysis* 23 (1963): 121–23.
Graham, A. C., trans. *Chuang-tzu: The Inner Chapters*. London: Allen and Unwin, 1981.
———. *Disputers of the Tao*. La Salle, Ill.: Open Court, 1989.
———. *Divisions in Early Mohism Reflected in the Core Chapters of Mo-tzu*. Singapore: Institute of East Asian Philosophies, 1985.
———. *Later Mohist Logic, Ethics and Science*. Hong Kong: Chinese University Press, 1978.
Griffin, James. *Value Judgement*. Oxford: Clarendon Press, 1996.
Hampton, Jean. *Political Philosophy*. Boulder, Colo.: Westview Press, 1998.
Hansen, Chad. "Chinese Language, Chinese Philosophy, and 'Truth.'" *Journal of Asian Studies* 44, no. 3 (1985): 491–519.
———. "*Dào* as a Naturalistic Focus." In *Ethics in Early China*, edited by Chris Fraser, Dan Robins, and Timothy O'Leary, 229–56. Hong Kong: Hong Kong University Press, 2011.
———. *A Daoist Theory of Chinese Thought*. Oxford: Oxford University Press, 1992.
———. *Language and Logic in Ancient China*. Ann Arbor: University of Michigan Press, 1983.
———. "Punishment and Dignity in China." In *Individualism and Holism: Studies in Confucian and Taoist Values*, edited by Donald Munro, 359–83. Michigan Monographs in Chinese Studies, no. 52. Ann Arbor: Center for Chinese Studies, University of Michigan, 1985.
———. "Term-Belief in Action." In *Epistemological Issues in Classical Chinese Philosophy*, edited by Hans Lenk and Gregor Paul, 45–68. Albany: SUNY Press, 1993.
Harbsmeier, Christoph. *Language and Logic*, vol. 7, part 1 of *Science and Civilisation in China*, by Joseph Needham. Cambridge: Cambridge University Press, 1998.
———. Review of *Later Mohist Logic, Ethics and Science*, by A. C. Graham. *Bulletin of the School of Oriental and African Studies* 43, no. 3 (1980): 617–19.
Heydt, Colin. "Utilitarianism Before Bentham." In *The Cambridge Companion to Utilitarianism*, edited by Ben Eggleston and Dale Miller, 16–37. Cambridge: Cambridge University Press, 2014.
Hsu Cho-yun. *Ancient China in Transition*. Stanford: Stanford University Press, 1965.
Hughes, E. R. *Chinese Philosophy in Classical Times*. London: Dent, 1942.
Hu Shih [胡適]. *The Development of the Logical Method in Ancient China*. Shanghai: Commercial Press, 1922.
———. 中國哲學史大綱卷上 [Outline of the history of Chinese philosophy, vol. 1]. Shànghǎi: Commercial Press, 1919.
Hutton, Eric. "Moral Connoisseurship in Mengzi." In *Essays on the Moral Philosophy of Mengzi*, edited by Xiusheng Liu and Philip J. Ivanhoe, 163–86. Indianapolis: Hackett, 2002.
Ivanhoe, Philip J. *Confucian Moral Self-Cultivation*. Indianapolis: Hackett, 2000.

———. "Mohist Philosophy." In *Routledge Encyclopedia of Philosophy*, edited by Edward Craig, 6:451–55. London: Routledge, 1998.

Ivanhoe, Philip J., and Bryan W. Van Norden, eds. *Readings in Classical Chinese Philosophy*. New York: Seven Bridges Press, 2000.

Jenner, Donald. "Mo Tzu and Hobbes: Preliminary Remarks on the Relation of Chinese and Western Politics." *Cogito* 2 (1984): 49–72.

Jochim, Christian. "Ethical Analysis of an Ancient Debate: Moists versus Confucians." *Journal of Religious Ethics* 8, no. 1 (1980): 135–47.

Johnson, Daniel. "Mozi's Moral Theory: Breaking the Hermeneutical Stalemate." *Philosophy East and West* 61, no. 2 (2011): 347–64.

Johnston, Ian. *The Mozi*. Hong Kong: Chinese University Press, 2010.

Kagan, Shelly. "Evaluative Focal Points." In *Morality, Rules, and Consequences*, edited by Brad Hooker, Elinor Mason, and Dale Miller, 134–55. Edinburgh: Edinburgh University Press, 2000.

———. *Normative Ethics*. Boulder, Colo.: Westview Press, 1997.

Knoblock, John. *Xunzi: A Translation and Study of the Complete Works*. 3 vols. Stanford: Stanford University Press, 1988–1994.

Knoblock, John, and Jeffrey Riegel. *Mozi: A Study and Translation of the Ethical and Political Writings*. Berkeley: Institute of East Asian Studies, University of California, 2013.

Korsgaard, Christine. "Skepticism about Practical Reason." *Journal of Philosophy* 83, no. 1 (1986): 5–25.

Lai, Whalen. "The Public Good That Does the Public Good: A New Reading of Mohism." *Asian Philosophy* 3, no. 2 (1993): 125–41.

Lao Sze-kwang [Láo Sīguāng] 勞思光. 新編中國哲學史 [New edition of *History of Chinese Philosophy*]. 3 vols. Taipei: Sān mín, 1984.

Larmore, Charles. *The Morals of Modernity*. Cambridge: Cambridge University Press, 1996.

Lau, D. C. *Lao Tzu: Tao Te Ching*. London: Penguin, 1963.

Lewis, Mark Edward. "Warring States: Political History." In Loewe and Shaughnessy, *Cambridge History*, 587–650.

Lǐ Díshēng 李滌生. 荀子集釋 [Collected explications of *Xúnzǐ*]. Taipei: Xuéshēng, 1979.

Lǐ Shēnglóng 李生龍 and Lǐ Zhènxīng 李振興. 新譯墨子讀本 [Newly paraphrased *Mòzǐ* reader]. Taipei: Sān mín, 1996.

Li, Yong. "The Divine Command Theory of Mozi." *Asian Philosophy* 16, no. 3 (2006): 237–45.

Liáng Qǐchāo 梁啟超. 墨子學案 [A study of *Mòzǐ*]. Shànghǎi: Shāngwù, 1923.

Liu, JeeLoo. *An Introduction to Chinese Philosophy*. Oxford: Blackwell, 2006.

Loewe, Michael, and Edward L. Shaughnessy, eds. *The Cambridge History of Ancient China*. Cambridge: Cambridge University Press, 1999.

Lowe, Scott. *Mo Tzu's Religious Blueprint for a Chinese Utopia*. Lewiston, N.Y.: Mellen Press, 1992.

Loy, Hui-chieh. "Justification and Debate: Thoughts on Mohist Moral Epistemology." *Journal of Chinese Philosophy* 35, no. 3 (2008): 455–71.

———. "The Moral Philosophy of the Mozi 'Core Chapters.'" PhD diss., University of California, Berkeley, 2006.

———. "Mozi." In *The Internet Encyclopedia of Philosophy*, 2007. http://www.iep.utm.edu/m/mozi.htm.

———. "On the Argument for *Jian'ai*." *Dao: A Journal of Comparative Philosophy* 12, no. 4 (2013): 487–504.

———. "On a *Gedankenexperiment* in the *Mozi* Core Chapters." *Oriens Extremus* 45 (2005): 141–58.

Lu, Xiufen. "Understanding Mozi's Foundations of Morality: A Comparative Perspective." *Asian Philosophy* 16, no. 2 (2006): 123–34.

Luán Tiáo-fǔ 欒調甫. 墨子研究論文集 [Anthology of Mòzǐ research]. Běijīng: Rénmín, 1957.

Lum, Alice. "Social Utilitarianism in the Philosophy of Mo Tzu." *Journal of Chinese Philosophy* 4, no. 2 (1977): 187–207.

Maeder, Erik W. "Some Observations on the Composition of the 'Core Chapters' of the *Mozi*." *Early China* 17 (1992): 27–82.

Makeham, John. Review of *The Original Analects*, by E. Bruce Brooks and A. Taeko Brooks. *China Review International* 6, no. 1 (1999): 1–33.

Mei, Yi-pao, trans. *The Ethical and Political Works of Motse*. London: Probsthain, 1929.

———. *Mo-tse, the Neglected Rival of Confucius*. London: Probsthain, 1934.

Móu Zōngsān 牟宗三. 墨子 [*Mòzǐ*]. In 國史上的偉大人物 [Great figures in Chinese history], edited by Zhāng Qíyún 張其昀. Taipei: Zhōnghuá wénhuà, 1954.

Munro, Donald. *The Concept of Man in Early China*. Stanford: Stanford University Press, 1969.

Nagel, Thomas. *The Possibility of Altruism*. Princeton: Princeton University Press, 1970.

———. *The View from Nowhere*. Oxford: Oxford University Press, 1986.

Nivison, David. *The Ways of Confucianism*. Edited by Bryan W. Van Norden. La Salle, Ill.: Open Court, 1996.

Nylan, Michael. "Kongzi and Mozi, the Classicists (Ru 儒) and the Mohists (Mo 墨) in Classical-Era Thinking." *Oriens Extremus* 48 (2009): 1–20.

Perkins, Franklin. "Introduction: Reconsidering the *Mozi*." *Journal of Chinese Philosophy* 35, no. 3 (2008): 379–83.

———. "The Mohist Criticism of the Confucian Use of Fate." *Journal of Chinese Philosophy* 35, no. 3 (2008): 421–36.

Plato. *Euthyphro*. Translated by G. M. A. Grube. In *Plato: Complete Works*, edited by John M. Cooper, 1–16. Indianapolis: Hackett, 1997.

Puett, Michael. *To Become a God: Cosmology, Sacrifice, and Self-Divinization in Early China*. Cambridge, Mass.: Harvard University Asia Center, 2002.

Rachels, James. *The Elements of Moral Philosophy*. 3rd ed. Boston: McGraw-Hill, 1999.

Rawls, John. *A Theory of Justice*. Rev. ed. Cambridge, Mass.: Belknap Press, 1999.

Robins, Dan. "Mohist Care." *Philosophy East and West* 62, no. 1 (2012): 60–91.

———. "The Mohists and the Gentlemen of the World." *Journal of Chinese Philosophy* 35, no. 3 (2008): 385–402.

Scanlon, T. M. *What We Owe to Each Other*. Cambridge, Mass.: Harvard University Press, 1998.

Schwartz, Benjamin. *The World of Thought in Ancient China*. Cambridge, Mass.: Harvard University Press, 1985.

Sellars, Wilfred. *Empiricism and the Philosophy of Mind*. Cambridge, Mass.: Harvard University Press, 1997.

Shafer-Landau, Russ. *Moral Realism: A Defense*. Oxford: Oxford University Press, 2003.

Shun, Kwong-loi. *Mencius and Early Chinese Thought*. Stanford: Stanford University Press, 1997.

———. "Mo Tzu." In *The Cambridge Dictionary of Philosophy*, edited by Robert Audi, 515. Cambridge: Cambridge University Press, 1995.

Sidgwick, Henry. *The Methods of Ethics*. 7th ed. Indianapolis: Hackett, 1981.

Slingerland, Edward. "The Conception of *Ming* in Early Confucian Thought." *Philosophy East and West* 46, no. 4 (1996): 567–81.

———. *Effortless Action*. New York: Oxford University Press, 2003.

Soles, David. "Mo Tzu and the Foundations of Morality." *Journal of Chinese Philosophy* 26, no. 1 (1999): 37–48.

Sūn Yíràng 孫詒讓. 墨子閒詁 [Interspersed commentaries on *Mòzǐ*]. 2 vols. Běijīng: Zhōnghuá, 2001.

Sūn Zhōngyuán 孫中原. 墨學通論 [A comprehensive study of Mohism]. Shěnyáng: Liáoníng jiàoyù, 1993.

Tán Jièfǔ 譚戒甫. 墨辯發微 [A detailed study of the Mohist dialectics]. Běijīng: Zhōnghuá, 1964.

Tán Yǔquán 譚宇權. 墨子思想評論 [A critical study of Mòzǐ's thought]. Taipei: Wénjīn, 1991.

Tang Chun-I [Táng Jūnyì] 唐君毅. 中國哲學原論導論篇 [Origins of Chinese philosophy: Introduction]. Taipei: Xuéshēng, 1986.

———. 中國哲學原論原道篇弌 [Origins of Chinese philosophy: Origins of Dao]. Vol. 1. Taipei: Xuéshēng, 1986.

Taylor, Rodney L. "Religion and Utilitarianism: Mo Tzu on Spirits and Funerals." *Philosophy East and West* 29, no. 3 (1979): 337–46.

Tseu, Augustinus A. *The Moral Philosophy of Mo-Tze*. Taipei: China Printing, 1965.

van Els, Paul. "How to End Wars with Words: Three Argumentative Strategies by Mozi and His Followers." In Defoort and Standaert, *The "Mozi,"* 69–94.

Van Norden, Bryan W. "A Response to the Mohist Arguments in 'Impartial Caring.'" In *The Moral Circle and the Self: Chinese and Western Approaches*, edited by Kim-chong Chong, Sor-hoon Tan, and C. L. Ten, 41–58. La Salle, Ill.: Open Court, 2003.

———. *Virtue Ethics and Consequentialism in Early Chinese Philosophy*. Cambridge: Cambridge University Press, 2007.

Vorenkamp, Dirck. "Another Look at Utilitarianism in Mo-Tzu's Thought." *Journal of Chinese Philosophy* 19, no. 4 (1992): 423–43.

Wáng Zànyuán 王讚源. 墨子 [*Mòzǐ*]. Taipei: Dōng dà, 1996.

Watanabe Takashi. *Kodai Chūgoku shisō no kenkyū*. Tokyo: Sōbunsha, 1973.

Watson, Burton, trans. *Mo Tzu: Basic Writings*. New York: Columbia University Press, 1963.

Williams, Bernard. *Moral Luck*. Cambridge: Cambridge University Press, 1981.

Wolf, Susan. "Moral Saints." *Journal of Philosophy* 79, no. 8 (1982): 419–39.

Wong, Benjamin, and Hui-chieh Loy. "War and Ghosts in Mozi's Political Philosophy." *Philosophy East and West* 54, no. 3 (2004): 343–63.

Wong, David B. "Chinese Ethics." In *Stanford Encyclopedia of Philosophy*. http://plato.stanford.edu/archives/spr2008/entries/ethics-chinese.
———. "Mohism: The Founder, Mozi (Mo Tzu)." In *Encyclopedia of Chinese Philosophy*, edited by Antonio Cua, 453–61. London: Routledge, 2002.
———. "Universalism vs. Love with Distinctions: An Ancient Debate Revived." *Journal of Chinese Philosophy* 16, no. 3-4 (1989): 251–72.
Wu Hung. "The Art and Architecture of the Warring States Period." In Loewe and Shaughnessy, *Cambridge History*, 651–744.
Wú Jìn'ān 吳進安. 墨家哲學 [Mohist philosophy]. Taipei: Wǔnán, 2003.
Wú Yùjiāng 吳毓江. 墨子校注 [Collated annotations on *Mòzǐ*]. Běijīng: Zhōnghuá, 1993.
Xú Fùguān 徐復觀. 中國人性論史 [History of Chinese theories of people's nature]. Taipei: Shāngwù, 1969.
Xú Xīyàn 徐希燕. 墨学研究 [Research on Mohism]. Běijīng: Shāngwù, 2001.
Yáng Jùnguāng 楊俊光. 墨子新論 [A new study of *Mòzǐ*]. Nánjīng: Jiāngsū jiàoyù, 1991.
Yates, Robin D. S. "The Mohists on Warfare: Technology, Technique, and Justification." *Journal of the American Academy of Religion* 47, no. 3 (1980): 549–603.
Zhāng Chúnyī 張純一. 墨子集解 [Collected explications of *Mòzǐ*]. Taipei: Wén shǐ zhé, 1982.
Zhang Qianfa. "Human Dignity in Classical Chinese Philosophy: Reinterpreting Mohism." *Journal of Chinese Philosophy* 34, no. 2 (2007): 239–55.
Zhōng Yǒulián 鐘友聯. 墨子的哲學方法 [*Mòzǐ*'s philosophical method]. Taipei: Dōng dà, 1986.

INDEX

action: and consequentialism, 141–42, 143; discrimination-and-response model of, 23, 76, 190, 191, 196; and education, 195–96; and epistemology, 50; and ethics, 154, 157; and Heaven, 123, 125; and identifying upward, 90–91; and inclusive care, 161, 170, 171, 175, 183; models for, ix, 23, 24, 27, 39, 53, 55, 63, 69; and motivation, 75, 185–87, 189–95, 201; and reasoning, 74–76; and righteousness, 78, 190; and *shì-fēi* distinctions, 52, 53, 79–80; statements guiding, 52–53, 134; Western concepts of, 23, 75. *See also* conduct

activism, moral, 3, 4–5, 15, 48, 149, 229

aesthetic value: Mohist indifference to, 10, 155, 227, 230; of music, 227, 270n22; and pluralism, 101; vs. utility, 214, 216, 223, 225

agency: and fatalism, 40–48; of ghosts, 107; of Heaven, 109, 114; human, 40–48, 108; and reasoning, 74–76; Western concepts of, 74, 75

akrasia (weakness of will), 194, 269n17

Analects, 44, 136, 227, 247n27; on ceremonial propriety, 32, 33, 248n6, 257n15; and Confucius, 8, 248n3; on funeral rites, 219–20, 221; and individualism, 31; on motivation, 186; on music, 257n15, 270n19; on social status, 9; and special relationships, 146, 147

Annals of Lü Buwei: and funeral rites, 219; and influence of Mohism, 271n4; on Mohism, 11, 12, 102, 243n1, 246n16; on music, 270n19, 270n22; on reasoning, 73; and special relationships, 148

Aristotle, 23, 24, 189–90

audience, of Mohists, 130–33; elite as, 131, 149, 191; and ethics, 149, 150, 151, 156, 187; and inclusive care, 162

"Avoiding Excess," 212–13

behaviorism, 24, 194

belief-desire model, 75, 76, 186, 189, 190, 194, 266n5

benefit (*lì*): and assessment of ethics, 152–57; and care, 158, 160–62, 191, 200, 263n7; and consequentialism, 121, 138, 142, 262n44; criteria for, 262n41; economic, 152, 214, 217, 218; vs. harm (*hài*), 123–24, 125, 138, 142, 154, 157, 165, 169, 181, 206–7; and Heaven, 114, 127; inclusive care as, 162–69, 173, 174, 182, 183; and models, 53, 64–66, 67,

benefit (*continued*)
69, 140; and Mohist audience, 130; vs. music, 223, 224, 230; and righteousness, 133–34, 263n10; and Ruism, 229; and special relationships, 146–49; and the state, 90, 94, 102; three kinds of, 16, 41–43, 66, 67, 71, 91, 96, 98, 102, 112–14, 120, 125, 128, 136, 138–41; and warfare, 206–7

benefit of all the world (*tiān xià zhī lì*), 19, 102, 129–57, 234; and benevolence, 127, 135–36, 137, 150; components of, 140; and consequentialism, 122, 143; difficulty of, 149; and divine will theory, 118, 119; economic, 100, 212, 219, 225; and education, 197; and Heaven, 104, 112, 113, 125, 126, 127, 256n9; and inclusive care, 158, 161, 165, 166, 170, 172, 175, 180–81, 182; and models, 53; and morality, 21, 123–24; and motivation, 199, 200; and righteousness, 150, 263n10; and Ruism, 228; vs. special relationships, 143–49; vs. the state, 247n23; and warfare, 204, 206–10

benevolence (*rén*), 135–38; and benefit to all, 127, 135–36, 137, 150; and ceremonial propriety, 32, 34; and consequentialism, 138, 142, 143; difficulty of, 150; of elite, 133, 136, 245n11; and emotions, 267n16, 270n17; in ethics, 129, 151, 152, 155, 156–57; and fate, 62; and funeral rites, 218, 219; of Heaven, 67, 105, 106, 108–11; as Heaven's intent, 114, 115, 137; and inclusive care, 164–66, 183; and models, 9, 18, 35, 41, 70, 71, 72; and motivation, 135, 136, 191, 197, 199; vs. nonessentials, 230; and righteousness, 137, 260n14; and ritual, 248n4; in Ruism, 227, 233; of rulers, 2, 35, 88; and special relationships, 146

Bentham, Jeremy, 19, 247n25

Bì Yuán, x

biàn. *See* distinctions, drawing

biǎo (markers), 62–63, 64. *See also* models

bureaucracy, 31, 136, 150, 160, 199; as audience, 131, 191; meritocratic, 10, 17, 18, 20, 96, 211, 232, 234; and Ruism, 229. *See also* officers; state, the

ceremonial propriety (*lǐ*), 45, 128, 249n8, 257n15; vs. customs, 33–34; and objective standards, 32–33; and Ruism, 10, 32, 33, 132, 227, 248n6. *See also* ritual

Chan Wing-tsit, xi

Chéng (sage-king), 226

Chéng Fán, 226

Chéng Yí, x

Christianity, x

Chǔ, state of, 6, 7, 204, 215, 245n7, 246n17, 246n21

cí. *See* kindness, parental

communitarianism, x, 21, 172; in ethics, 132–33, 138, 151, 155; and Heaven, 126–27; vs. individualism, 17, 31, 97, 102, 141, 155, 187, 248n30; influence of, 20; and unified norms, 31, 87

conceptualism, Enlightenment, xiii

condemning aggression (*fēi gōng*), 18, 130, 131, 203, 204–11

"Condemning Aggression" (books 17–19), 14, 130, 206, 207, 208

condemning fatalism (*fēi mìng*), 18

"Condemning Fatalism" (books 35–37), 46, 62

condemning music (*fēi yuè*), 18

"Condemning Music" (book 32), 224

"Condemning the Rú" (Fēi Rú; book 39), 13, 132, 217, 227, 260n8, 270n25

conduct (*xíng*): benevolent, 135, 136, 137; and fatalism, 41, 44, 45, 64; of Heaven, 36, 104, 106, 110, 111, 113, 115, 119, 121; and inclusive care, 150, 160, 162, 164, 166, 168, 170, 171, 177, 178, 181, 183; individual, 141; justification for, 127, 162; and language, 52; models for, 5, 10, 16, 21, 24, 32–33, 39, 54, 71, 78, 79, 81–82, 83, 117, 119, 124, 141, 165; and motivation, 192, 197; and relational virtues, 145, 149; rewards and punishments for,

40, 46–48, 90, 92, 94, 99; righteous, 133, 134, 135; and social roles, 29, 38, 53, 90, 95; and statements, 63, 87–89, 177, 178. *See also* action

Confucianism. *See* Ruism

Confucius (Kǒngzǐ): and *Analects*, 8, 248n3; ascent of, 233–34; and ceremonial propriety, 32; and fatalism, 45; on funeral rites, 220; and Heaven, 44, 250n22; and Mohism, 43, 233; and Mòzǐ, ix, xii, 7, 8, 19; Mòzǐ on, 13; and the Rú, 4, 245n3; and special relationships, 147

consequentialism: act, 141–42, 247n26; on benefit, 121, 122, 138, 142, 143, 262n44; communitarian, 21; *dào*, 138, 141–43; direct vs. indirect, 247n26; and divine will theory, 117, 118, 119, 120; ethics of, 129, 153, 154–57; and fatalism, 41, 42, 48, 250n19; and frugality, 138–39, 141, 142; and Heaven, 104, 105, 121–22, 125, 126, 138, 139, 142, 255n15, 256n9; and hierarchy, 91, 95–96, 121–22; and impartiality, 38–39, 121; and inclusive care, 142, 162–69, 172, 180, 181, 182, 183, 184; individualistic, 248n30; and models, 68, 121, 122, 141, 142, 143; Mohist, xii, 17, 19, 138–39, 232–34, 247n25; and music, 227; and political theory, 86; and promoting the worthy, 142; and rewards and punishments, 93–94; and righteousness, 121, 122, 138; rule, 141, 247n26; and special relationships, 147; state, 17; and value, 261n33, 263n7; and warfare, 209

Cumberland, Richard, 258n20

dào (the Way), 4, 7, 247n28; and ceremonial propriety, 33; and consequentialism, 138, 141–43; constant (*cháng*), 102, 172, 207, 260nn12–13; difficulty of, 149; and distinctions, 63–64, 89, 123; and divine will theory, 118; and ethics, 130, 132, 133; and fatalism, 42, 64; and Heaven, 44, 108, 110, 112, 128; and individual, 31, 263n6; and models, 34, 54, 69, 79;

Mohist, 21, 107, 109, 130, 132, 135, 148, 185, 187–89, 202, 253n25

Dào Zàng, x

Dàodéjīng, 4, 20, 103

Daoism, 10, 31, 50, 87, 103; difficulty of, 152; and Mohism, xii, 20, 155, 233, 236, 243n4

Development of the Logical Method in Ancient China (Hú Shì), xi

Dì (Shàng Dì; Lord on High), 105, 116, 218, 223, 254n10, 255n19, 256n1. *See also* Heaven

dialecticians (*biàn zhě*), 7

dialectics, Mohist. *See* distinctions, drawing

"Dialectics" (Mò biàn; books 40–45), 12, 13, 73, 253n32, 259n27; on benefit, 262n41, 263n10; and consequentialism, 142; on ethics, 129, 130, 140; on Heaven, 128; on inclusive care, 160, 171, 264n17; on knowledge, 58, 60, 62; on models, 54; on relation ranking, 145

"Dialogues" (books 46–50), 8, 13, 134, 270n17; audience for, 150–51; on causal pluralism, 108–9; and consequentialism, 142; on epistemology, 50, 62; on ethics, 129, 147, 151, 153, 155; on frugality, 213, 219, 220, 226; on ghosts, 46; on inclusive care, 264n17; on individual, 31, 187; on Ruism, 132, 228; on self-interest, 80, 81

Dié Bí, 108

discrimination-and-response model, 194

disorder (*luàn*), 15, 27–31, 264n18; causes of, 28–29, 73, 264n12; and ceremonial propriety, 32; and diversity of norms, 79–80, 82–83, 87, 100; and fatalism, 42, 45, 66; and frugality, 212, 215, 218, 223, 224; and knowledge, 60–61; and leaders, 53, 84, 86, 88, 98, 101; and self-interest, 80–81; and the state, 78, 92; in state of nature, 30, 78–84, 86, 93, 96, 99, 101–2, 191–92, 199, 267n13; warfare as, 27–28, 206, 209. *See also* order, sociopolitical distinctions, drawing (*biàn*; dialectics), ix, x, xii, 20, 50; and action, 52, 53, 79–80; and *dào*, 63–64, 89, 123; and divine will theory, 118; education in, 195–96; graphs for, 51; and Heaven, 123, 125; and knowledge, 57, 58, 60, 61; and models, 53, 54–56, 69, 74–75; in Mohist religion, 109; and motivation, 190, 193–94, 195, 199; normative, 51–53, 63; and reasoning, 70, 73–75; in relationships, 227; and sage-kings, 64; and *shì-fēi*, 51–53; skills for, 22–24, 57, 60–61, 75–76, 89, 193, 194, 253n35; in social status, 211–12; and Three Models, 62, 63–64

divine will theory, 117–21

economic issues, 1, 5, 6, 203–4, 211–27; and benefit, 100, 152, 212, 214, 217, 218, 219, 225; and decline of Mohism, 234–36; Mencius on, 250n27; narrowness of Mohism on, 229–31. *See also* frugality; moderation

education, moral, 10, 16, 17, 22, 23, 53, 268n22; and identifying upward, 87; and motivation, 195–96; and promoting the worthy, 99, 100; techniques for, 197–98; and Three Models, 63; and unified norms, 69, 87, 94, 102; Xúnzǐ on, 57

emotions, 24, 151, 267nn14–16, 270n17; and benefit, 214, 225; and funeral rites, 220–21, 222; and inclusive care, 158, 159, 161, 164, 168, 171, 175, 189; and motivation, 192–93, 201; and music, 227; in relationships, 143, 145, 220

epistemology, 20, 22–23, 48, 49–76, 232, 233, 235; and drawing distinctions, 49–53; and ethics, 74–76; and fatalism, 41, 58, 62, 64, 65, 67, 68; and inclusive care, 161; and logic, 69–73; and models, 55–57; and Three Models, 62–69; Western vs. Chinese, 49–50. *See also* knowledge

Erudites (Confucians), 3–4, 8–9. *See also* Ruism

ethics, Mohist, xii–xiii, 8, 19–20, 129–57, 232–34; assessment of, 152–56; audience for, 149, 150, 151, 156, 187; communitarian, 132–33, 138, 151, 155, 187; and conception of value, 112, 123, 124–25, 130, 153, 154–55, 157; consequentialist, 129, 153, 154–57; and *dào*, 130, 132, 133; deontological, 121, 247n25; difficulty of, 149–52, 185, 188; and epistemology, 74–76; and government, 132, 150, 187; Heaven in, 104, 129, 152, 154, 156–57; historical context of, 129; and models, 31, 34; motivation for, 136–37; in relationships, 129, 130, 153, 157; righteousness in, 129, 133–35, 151, 156–57; vs. tradition, 132, 228, 249n11; virtue, 104, 247n25

Euthyphro (Plato), 59

externalism, epistemic, 61, 232

fǎ. *See* models

fatalism, 203, 253n20; and agency, 40–48; condemning (*fēi mìng*), 18, 46, 62; and consequentialism, 41, 42, 48, 250n19; vs. determinism, 249n16; and epistemology, 41, 58, 62, 64, 65, 67, 68; and models, 65, 67, 68, 197; and Mohist audience, 130; and order, 41, 42, 45, 137, 264n12; and rewards and punishments, 46, 99, 250n19; in Ruism, 43, 44–45, 46, 48, 132, 228, 250n21; and Three Models, 62, 64

fate (*mìng*): and Heaven, 107, 109; and human efficacy, 40–48; and models, 40, 65–68, 197; and wealth, 40, 44, 58, 62

fēi gōng. *See* condemning aggression

fēi mìng (condemning fatalism), 18

filiality (*xiào*), 3, 71, 268n28; and benevolence, 135–36, 137; and consequentialism, 142, 143; and ethics, 130, 132; and funeral rites, 217, 219; and Heaven, 106, 113; and inclusive care, xi, xii, 161, 163, 165, 171, 174, 179–80, 182, 189, 196, 265n26; and order, 28, 140; and relationships, 144, 146, 147; and ritual, 219, 221–22; and value, 261n33 frugality: and consequentialism, 138–39, 141, 142; criticism of, 229, 269n10, 271n6; and decline of Mohism, 231, 234, 235; difficulty of, 152, 235; and disorder, 212, 215, 218, 223, 224; and Heaven, 126; and motivation, 197, 202; and Ruism, 131, 132; and wealth, 3, 140. *See also* moderation

Fù Tūn, 148, 149, 236

funeral rites, 10, 17, 81; and ceremonial propriety, 33; and decline of Mohism, 234, 235; moderation in, 18, 141, 142, 203, 211, 216–22; and prolonged mourning, x, 3, 8, 18, 33, 71, 132, 138–39, 197, 211, 216–21, 226, 228, 269n14, 270n16; and Rú, 45, 217, 219–21

Gāo Xīn, Emperor, 271n5

Gay, John, 258n20

gentlemen (*jūnzǐ*), 9, 32, 133, 224, 246n20; as audience for Mohism, 131, 149; and Ruism, 228, 229

ghosts and spirits, 18, 203, 253n25; and consequentialism, 138, 142; and Daoism, 243n4; and disorder, 137, 264n12; and ethics, 154; and Heaven, 104, 112, 113, 116; and models, 65, 66, 67, 68–69; and Mohist audience, 130; in Mohist religion, 105–9; rewards and punishments by, 40–41, 46; and Ruism, 132, 228; sacrifices to, 68, 105–7, 112, 116, 132, 140, 155, 218, 219, 221, 228, 249n8, 256n1, 256n3; and warfare, 205, 206–7, 208

"Gōng Mèng," 227

Gōng Mèngzǐ, 220, 226, 250n21

Gōujiàn, King of Yuè, 173

Graham, A. C., xii, 9, 10, 235

grand master (*jùzǐ*), 11, 102, 148

"Greater Selection," 161, 259n27

Hàn dynasty, ix, 4, 204, 222, 233–34, 235, 236

Hán Fēi, 93, 94, 103, 256n21

Hán Yù, x

Hánfēizǐ, 10, 11, 12, 67, 243n1, 246n16

Hansen, Chad, xii, 31

Heaven (*tiān*), 10, 16, 17, 104–28, 256n1; and benefit of all the world, 104, 112, 113, 125, 126, 127, 256n9; benevolence of, 67, 105, 106, 108–11; and causal pluralism, 108–10; and consequentialism, 104, 105, 121–22, 125, 126, 138, 139, 142, 255n15, 256n9; and *dào*, 44, 108, 110, 112, 128; and Daoism, 243n4; and divine will theory, 117–21; in ethics, 104, 129, 152, 154, 156–57; and evil, 104, 107–10; and fatalism, 43, 48; and hierarchy, 95, 96, 104, 105, 106, 116, 117; and identifying upward, 89, 90; impartiality of, 37–39, 67, 104, 105, 111, 115, 122–27, 257n9; vs. Judeo-Christianity, 105–6, 108; as model, 36–39, 84, 102, 104–28; in Mohist religion, 105–7, 115, 122, 124; and Moral Exemplar argument, 115–16, 117, 119, 121; and morality, 21, 81–82, 102, 104, 105, 110–14; and music, 223; objectivity of, 104, 105, 110, 111, 115, 122–27, 257n9; and Orderly Government argument, 116, 117, 119, 120, 121; and promoting the worthy, 97; rewards and punishments by, 40–41; and Ruism, 44, 128, 132, 228, 250n22; sacrifices to, 140, 249n8; and selection of leader, 84–86; and social contract, 254n8; and the state, 92, 95, 255n19; and warfare, 205, 206, 208–9

Heaven, mandate of (*tiān mìng*), 43, 92, 95, 127, 208–9, 210

Heaven's intent (*tiān zhì*), 110–27, 203; benevolence as, 114, 115, 137; and divine will theory, 120–21; and inclusive care, 113, 162, 184, 264n17; and models, 54–56, 64, 65, 67, 110–15, 122–23, 257n9, 258n25; in Mohist religon, 106, 109; obedience to, 114–17, 120–21; righteousness as, 112–16, 122–127, 257n9; and warfare, 209–10

"Heaven's Intent" (books 26–28), 9, 18, 67, 96, 112–20, 127, 206, 264n17

Herodotus, 33
Hobbes, Thomas, 78, 86, 89
Hú Shì, x, xi, 248n32
Huáinánzǐ, 8, 11, 12, 243n1
Huì Shī, 271n4
Hume, David, 23, 24, 189, 192, 266n12

identifying upward (*shàng tóng*), 17, 77, 99, 203, 247n24; and authoritarianism, 101, 102, 103; in government, 87–96; and inclusive care, 173–74; and motivation, 198, 200–201
"Identifying Upward" (books 11–13), 9, 84, 90, 118, 264n18; political theory of, 86, 92–93, 95–96
impartiality, 32–39, 232, 249n13, 263n3; and consequentialism, 38–39, 121; difficulty of, 188; and equal moral status, 180, 181, 182; in ethics, 129, 130, 151, 152, 153, 156–57; and funeral rites, 219; of Heaven, 37–39, 104, 105, 111, 115, 122–27, 257n9; and inclusive care, 158, 175, 180, 181, 183, 189; in Ruism, 247n27
inclusive care (*jiān ài*), ix–x, 17–19, 29, 158–84, 203, 259n27; as attitude, 159, 162, 166, 170, 181, 182; as benefit, 158, 160–69; and benefit of all the world, 158, 161, 165, 166, 170, 172, 175, 180–81, 182; Caretaker argument for, 176–77, 178, 180, 200, 265nn24–25; and conduct, 150, 160, 162, 164, 166, 168, 170, 171, 177, 178, 181, 183; and consequentialism, 142, 153, 162–69, 172, 180, 181, 182, 183, 184; vs. contempt (*wù*), 160; development of concept of, 162–69; difficulty of, 149, 150, 158–59, 163, 164, 166, 168, 169, 170, 173–76, 177, 188, 234; and education, 196, 197; and emotions, 158, 159, 161, 164, 168, 171, 175, 189; and false dilemma, 178, 181, 265n24; and filiality, xi, xii, 161, 163, 165, 171, 174, 179–80, 182, 189, 196, 265n26, 271n6; formulations of, 169–72; and Heaven's intent, 113, 162, 184, 264n17; and impartiality, 158, 175, 180, 181, 183, 189; Mencius on, xi, 264n20, 265n27; and models, 66, 138, 158; and Mohist audience, 130–31; and motivation, 200, 202; objections to, 159, 162, 172–80; for poor and weak, 168–69, 170; and reciprocity, 173, 174, 179, 187–88; religious view of, 184; Ruism on, 131–32, 178, 233, 263n7, 265n25; Ruler argument for, 177–78, 180, 200, 265n25; and social relationships, 102, 143, 145, 146, 159, 162–72, 182, 183, 188–89, 264n20; and the state, 160, 169, 170, 174–75, 176, 177, 188; strong, 170–72, 180–82; terms for, xiv, 19, 169, 171, 180; and Three Models, 65, 71, 162, 175, 176; translation of, 159, 167; use (*yòng*) of, 176–79, 200, 253n21
"Inclusive Care" (books 14–16), 9, 14, 28, 73, 130, 162, 163, 169–73, 176, 183, 264n17
individual, 24, 176, 196, 263n6; and ethics, 130, 132, 155, 156; and impartiality, 38, 39; and morality, 21–22; and motivation, 77, 97, 195, 202; self-interest of, 80–81; vs. society, 31, 77, 97, 102, 187; and utility, 214
individualism: vs. communitarianism, 17, 31, 97, 102, 141, 155, 187, 248n30; vs. unified norms, 86–87
internalism: epistemic, 61; motivational judgment, 266n11
Ivanhoe, Philip J., xiv

jiān ài. See inclusive care
Jié (tyrant), 37, 208, 209
jié yòng. See under moderation
jié zàng. See under moderation
Johnston, Ian, xiv
JTB (justified true belief), 60, 61, 252nn12–14
jūnzǐ. See gentlemen
just war theory, 204, 229, 269n2
justification, 22, 33, 50, 74, 139, 186; for conduct, 127, 162; in ethics, 152, 153;

and Heaven, 111, 124, 126, 127, 258n20, 258n25; impartial, 20, 38–39, 127; of inclusive care, 162–69, 178, 180; and knowledge, 60, 61; and models, 53, 55, 56; and Moral Exemplar argument, 116; and Three Models, 252n10
jùzǐ (grand master), 11, 102, 148

Kant, Immanuel, 21, 24, 75, 263n6
kindness, parental (*cí*), 28, 29, 135, 144, 163, 171, 173, 182
kinds (*lèi*): distinguishing between, 22, 50, 51–52, 57, 59, 74, 190, 194–95; extending (*tuī lèi*), 70–71
kinship (*qīn*), xii–xiii, 29, 38, 97, 107, 136; and inclusive care, 143, 159, 171, 177, 178, 180, 182, 189, 271n6; Ruism on, 227, 270n25; and special relationships, 147, 149. *See also* filiality
Knoblock, John, xiv
knowledge (*zhī*): 57–61, 232; education for, 196; and models, 53, 55, 56, 59, 61; and motivation, 193, 194, 195; and reasoning, 74, 75; skills as, 22–24, 57, 60–61, 75–76, 89, 193, 194, 253n35; and Three Models, 62; types of, 49–50, 251n1; Western views of, 61

language, 20, 50, 74, 232, 233, 235; and models, 53, 55, 69; and the state, 52–53
law, rule of, 87, 94, 255n18
Legalism, 20, 93, 233, 271n4
lèi. See kinds
Lì (tyrant), 37, 249n12
lǐ. See ceremonial propriety
lì. See benefit
Liáng Qǐchāo, x
Líng, King of Chǔ, 173
literacy, 6, 9, 65
Locke, John, 78
logic, 48, 55, 69–76, 161, 233
loyalty (*zhōng*), 29, 106, 132, 144, 147, 149, 189, 205

Lǔ, state of, 8, 215
Lǔ Shèng, ix
Lǔ Yáng, state of, 209, 210
luàn. See disorder
Lùn Héng, 243n1

markers (*biǎo*; models), 62–63, 64
mathematics, Mohist, 75
Mei Yi-Pao, xi–xii, xiv, 182
Mencius (*Mèngzǐ*), ix, 31, 33, 250n27, 254n1, 269n14; on fate, 44, 45; on inclusive care, xi, 264n20, 265n27; and Mohism, x–xi, 12, 20, 24, 43, 157, 232, 233, 271n4; on motivation, 185, 186; on special relationships, 145, 146, 147
Mèng Shèng, 102, 148, 149
military affairs, 213, 218; Mohist expertise in, 11–14, 204, 235, 236. *See also* warfare
militias, Mohist, 12, 149, 151
Mill, John Stuart, 19, 247n25
mind, philosophy of, xi, xiii, 50
míng. See name
mìng. See fate
míng guǐ. See understanding ghosts
models (standards; *fǎ*), 15–24; for action, ix, 23, 24, 27, 39, 53, 55, 63, 69; and benefit, 53, 64–66, 67, 69, 140; vs. ceremonial propriety, 249n8; and consequentialism, 68, 121, 122, 141, 142, 143; constant (*cháng*), 122, 125, 134; vs. customs, 81, 82; and distinctions, 53, 54–56, 69, 74–75; and divine will theory, 118, 119, 120; for education, 57, 196; emulation of, 53, 87–88, 89, 142, 196, 197, 198, 201, 248n32; and ethics, 148, 151; and fate, 40, 65–68, 197; Heaven as, 36–39, 84, 102, 104–28; and Heaven's intent, 54–56, 64, 65, 67, 110–15, 122–23, 257n9, 258n25; and identifying upward, 87–96; and inclusive care, 66, 138, 158; and knowledge, 53, 55, 56, 59, 61; and laws, 94; in Mohist religion, 105; and motivation, 190, 197–98, 199, 201; objectivity

models (continued)
in, 5, 27, 32, 34–39, 48, 53, 56, 232; and perceptual evidence, 64–66, 67, 69; and reasoning, 70, 71, 74; and rewards and punishments, 47–48, 66, 251n28; and sage-kings, 64–68; and the state, 31, 35, 66, 92–93; unified, 15–16, 30–31, 32, 78–87, 92–93, 99, 133–34, 140, 187, 199, 201, 234, 251n28

"Models and Standards," 34–35, 38, 115, 118, 119

moderation: in burial (*jié zàng*), 18, 203, 216–22; and critique of Ruism, 228; and decline of Mohism, 235; economic, 211–27; in music, 211, 225–27, 230; in use (*jié yòng*), 18, 203, 211–22. *See also* frugality

"Moderation in Burial" (book 25), 81, 219, 244n2

"Moderation in Use" (books 20–21), 212, 225

Mohism: decline of, ix–x, 231, 234–36; doctrines of, ix, 17–19; factions in, 11, 12, 13, 246n16; influence of, 19–20, 232–33; origins of, 1–5; as reform movement, 18–19, 185, 186, 187–89, 232, 235–36; as religion, 105–9, 115, 122, 124, 151–52, 184, 235; significance of, 19–24; themes in, 15–17

morality: and benefit of all the world, 21, 123–24; vs. customs, 33–34, 142, 218–19, 220; and Heaven, 21, 81–82, 102, 104, 105, 110–14, 122–27; and impartiality, 38–39; and inclusive care, 159, 183, 184; Mohist influence on, 20–21; and Mohist religion, 105, 106–7; and motivation, 24; of Mòzǐ, 8; nature of, 122–27, 183–84; objective standards of, 5, 27, 32–39, 48; public vs. private, 31, 102; and *shì-fēi*, 51–53, 63; unified, 15, 81–82; and warfare, 206. *See also* benevolence; ethics, Mohist; models; righteousness

motivation, xi, 23–25, 185–202, 266n12; and action, 75, 185–87, 189–95, 201; and benevolence, 135, 136, 191, 197, 199; and distinctions, 50–51, 79–80, 123, 190–99, 201; and education, 195–96; and emotions, 192–93, 201; and fatalism, 41; and identifying upward, 198, 200–201; impartial, 39, 153; and individual, 77, 97, 195, 200, 202; and models, 190, 197–99, 201; and moderation, 227, 230–31; and peer pressure, 201, 202; and political authority, 83, 91, 99–100; psychology of, 158, 186, 189, 194, 230–31; and reciprocity, 200, 201, 202, 268n27; and rewards and punishments, 46–48, 92, 93, 99–100, 198, 200, 216, 255n14; and righteousness, 191, 192, 193–94, 197, 198–99, 202; and self-interest, 174, 200, 201, 202, 268n25, 268n28; sources of, 185, 187, 198–201; techniques for, 197–98; and voluntarism, 268n23; for warfare, 207–8

Móu Zōngsān, xi

Mòzǐ, 4, 28, 44, 186; abridged text of, x; appreciation of, x, xi–xii; commentary on, ix; dating of, 246n21; on Mòzǐ, 7–8; oral composition of, 9–10, 245n13; organization of, 12–15; prejudice against, x–xi; prose style of, 10; translations of, xiv

Mòzǐ (Mò Dí), 4, 5, 7–12, 232, 245n7; as author of *Mòzǐ*, 13, 14–15; on condemning aggression, 204; and Confucius, ix, xii, 7, 8, 19; on ghosts, 46; life of, 7–8; and Mencius, x–xi; name of, 8; and Ruism, ix, x, 8–9; and warfare, 205

music (*yuè*), 66, 257n15; aesthetic value of, 227, 270n22; condemning, 3, 10, 18, 33, 66, 126, 132, 153, 203, 216, 222–27; and decline of Mohism, 234, 236; moderation in, 211, 225–27, 230; and Ruism, 33, 152, 220, 228, 257n15, 270n19; *Xúnzǐ* on, 270nn22–23

Nagel, Thomas, 125
name (*míng*), 50, 51, 57, 58
Nivison, David, xi

objectivity, 92, 133, 151; of Heaven, 104, 105, 110, 111, 115, 122–27, 257n9; in moral standards, 5, 27, 32–39, 48, 53, 56, 232

officers (*shì*; teachers, administrators), 7, 10, 156, 198, 199, 211; as audience, 191; and inclusive care, 174, 177; and moderation, 215, 224

"On Dyeing" (book 3), 246n20

order, sociopolitical (*zhì*), 27–31, 48, 77–103; and authoritarianism, 100–103; as benefit for all, 139–40; and benevolence, 136, 137; breakdown of, 2–5, 6–7; causes of, 15–17, 73; and ceremonial propriety, 32–33; and consequentialism, 121, 122, 138; and divine will theory, 119, 120; and ethics, 132, 133, 153, 155, 156, 187; and fatalism, 41, 42, 45, 137, 264n12; and Heaven, 40, 107, 108, 110, 128; as Heaven's intent, 112–17, 257n9; and hierarchy, 91, 95–96, 104–6, 116–19, 121–22, 132; and identifying upward, 87, 89, 91; and inclusive care, 163–64, 166; and influence of Mohism, 20, 233; and moderation, 18, 214, 215, 216, 218, 229, 230, 270n16; and Mohist conception of value, 78, 83–84, 91, 94, 101–2; in Mohist religion, 105, 107; and motivation, 185, 196, 199, 268n28; and music, 222, 223, 224, 227; and objective standards, 5, 35–36; and political theory, 29–30; and promoting the worthy, 96, 98; and relationships, 29, 30, 143–44, 147; and rewards and punishments, 46, 251n28; and Ruism, 3, 4, 10, 228; and unified norms, 22, 53, 79–80, 82–83, 86–87, 103, 254n1; and warfare, 209; and women, 261n29

Perkins, Franklin, xii, 45
Plato, 59–60, 98
politics, 77–103, 232, 233; and decline of Mohism, 236; and ethics, 129, 141, 156; and inclusive care, 174, 188; and models, 31, 34, 127; and Mohist audience, 130; Mohist influence on, 20, 22; and motivation, 198, 199; and order vs. disorder, 29–30, 43; and Three Models, 63

population, 1, 6; as benefit, 16, 41, 42, 66, 67, 91, 96, 98, 102, 113, 125, 136, 138, 139, 140; and ethics, 153, 155, 156; and fate, 40, 42, 62; and moderation, 214, 218, 229

poverty, 1–2, 261n40; and ethics, 130, 139; and fate, 40, 42, 43, 44, 66, 228; and frugality, 212, 215, 218, 222, 225; and inclusive care, 166, 168–69, 170; relief of, 4, 5, 87, 185, 232

practical syllogism model, 186, 189, 194

promoting the worthy (*shàng xián*), 96–100, 203, 247n24; in bureaucracy, 10, 17, 18; and consequentialism, 142; and identifying upward, 77, 88; and order, 95, 264n12; Xúnzǐ on, 233, 270n2

"Promoting the Worthy" (books 8–10), 30, 95, 97–100, 160, 197, 249n23, 258n21

psychology, xiii, 20, 23, 48, 232, 233; behaviorist, 24, 194; and demanding ethics, 188; and epistemology, 50; of motivation, 186, 189, 194, 230–31; and music, 223; Ruism on, 227

Qí, state of, 7, 215, 245n7
qīn. See kinship
Qín dynasty, 7, 233–34, 235
Qín Gǔ Lí (Master Qín), 14
Qīng dynasty, x, 234

reasoning, 69–76; analogical, 9, 13, 35, 54, 56, 59, 63, 71, 73, 74, 98, 110–11, 135–36, 190, 194, 218; deductive, 74, 190; Western, 74

reciprocity: in ethics, 140, 144; and Heaven, 114; in inclusive care, 102, 166–69, 173–74, 179, 181, 187–88; and motivation, 200, 201, 202, 268n27 relational virtues, 99, 143–49; difficulty of, 150, 188; in ethics, 140, 153, 157; and fatalism, 46, 47; and funeral rites, 218; and Heaven, 113, 125; and inclusive care, 160–64, 166, 168–72, 182, 189; and motivation, 199–200; and Ruism, 229. *See also* filiality

relationships, social: vs. benefit to all, 143–49; and ceremonial propriety, 32; emotions in, 143, 145, 220; in ethics, 129, 130, 153, 157; and Heaven's intent, 113, 258n25; hierarchical, 102–3; and impartiality, 38, 39; and inclusive care, 102, 143, 145, 146, 159, 162–72, 182, 183, 188–89, 264n20; and order, 29, 30, 143–44, 147; and politics, 261n40; ranking of (*lún liè*), 145, 183; and rewards and punishments, 46, 47; in Ruism, 131–32. *See also* filiality; social status

rén. *See* benevolence

Republic, The (Plato), 98

rewards and punishments: and consequentialism, 93–94; and fatalism, 46, 99, 250n19; and Heaven, 40–41, 95, 106, 108, 110, 111, 114, 116; and identifying upward, 89, 90–91; and models, 47–48, 66, 251n28; in Mohist religion, 105, 107, 109; and motivation, 46–48, 92, 93, 99–100, 198, 200, 216, 255n14; and order, 46, 251n28; and the state, 87, 92–93, 94, 140

Riegel, Jeffrey, xiv

righteousness, moral (*yì*), 21, 233, 254n1; and action, 78, 190; and benefit, 127, 133–34, 150, 263n10; vs. benevolence, 137, 260n14; and ceremonial propriety, 32, 34; and consequentialism, 121, 122, 138; vs. customs, 81, 132, 133; difficulty of, 149, 150, 188; and divine will theory, 117–21; and emotions, 267n16, 270n17; in ethics, 129, 133–35, 151, 155, 156–57; and fatalism, 41, 42; and frugality, 219, 230, 231; and Heaven, 104, 110, 116–19, 257n15, 257n17, 258n18, 258n20; as Heaven's intent, 112–16, 122–27, 257n9; and identifying upward, 89, 91; and inclusive care, 164, 165, 166, 180, 183, 184; and models, 31, 56; and Moral Exemplar argument, 116; and motivation, 191–94, 197, 198–99, 202, 268n28; and order, 27, 28; and promoting the worthy, 97, 99–100; and reasoning, 72–73; and relational virtues, 143, 144, 145, 146, 148; and rewards and punishments, 46–47; and the state, 92–93, 95–96; unified, 30, 78–87, 89, 91, 92–93, 95, 99–103; and warfare, 61, 205, 207

ritual, 10, 236; vs. ceremonial propriety, 249n8; demands of, 152; extravagant, 3, 216, 224; and filiality, 219, 221–22; in Mohist ethics, 132, 155; Ruism on, 18, 19, 217, 228; sacrificial, 68, 105–7, 112, 116, 132, 140, 155, 218, 219, 221, 228, 249n8, 256n1, 256n3. *See also* funeral rites

Rousseau, Jean-Jacques, 78

Ruism (the Rú), 244n3, 247n27; ascent of, 233–34; and ceremonial propriety, 10, 32, 33, 132, 227, 248n6; difficulty of, 152; and fatalism, 43, 44–45, 46, 48, 250n21; and funeral rites, 45, 217, 219–21; and Heaven, 44, 128, 132, 228, 250n22; on inclusive care, 131–32, 178, 233, 263n7, 265n25; on kinship, 227, 270n25; and Mohism, ix–x, xii, 8–9, 19, 20, 31, 50, 131, 155, 233, 236, 252n17; Mohist critique of, 13, 142, 203, 204, 227–29; on music, 224, 226; and special relationships, 145–49; and the state, 32, 87, 229

sagehood, 8, 21, 163; in Mohist ethics, 130, 150–51, 152, 155

sage-kings, 15, 64–68, 233, 249n12, 252n17; and consequentialism, 141, 142; and divine will theory, 118; and education, 197, 198; and fatalism, 18, 46; and Heaven, 16, 36, 37, 97, 106, 114, 116; and inclusive care, 162, 166, 175, 176; and moderation, 33, 212, 217–19, 221, 223–26; in Mohist ethics, 132, 149, 155, 156; and the state, 64, 66, 85, 97, 191; and Three Models, 65, 133; and warfare, 205, 208, 209, 210. *See also* Shùn; Tāng; Wén; Wǔ; Yáo; Yǔ

Schwartz, Benjamin, xi, 80, 235

self-cultivation, 130, 150, 228, 246n20

self-interest: and motivation, 200, 201, 202, 268n25, 268n28; and prudential value, 262n46; and warfare, 207, 209

self-sacrifice, 11, 149, 150, 166, 179, 234–35

Shāng dynasty, 43, 64, 208, 249n12, 252n17

shàng tóng. *See* identifying upward

shàng xián. *See* promoting the worthy

Shǐ jì (Records of the grand historian), 211, 271nn5–6

shì-fēi (this/not-this), 20, 50–53, 167, 267n14; and action, 52, 53, 79–80; and authoritarianism, 101, 102; and desire (*yù*) vs. detestation (*wù*), 191; education in, 53, 195–96, 268n22; and Heaven, 123, 125; and identifying upward, 87–88, 89, 90; and models, 54, 55, 56, 61, 67, 69, 74; in Mohist religion, 109; and motivation, 190–95, 197, 198–99, 201; and reasoning, 70, 71, 75; and Three Models, 62, 63–64, 252n10; vs. truth, 64, 253n25; and unified norms, 79–82, 133, 191–92; and voluntarism, 268n23

Shùn (sage-king), 64, 147, 218, 226, 249n12

Shuō yuàn, 230

Sīmǎ Niú, 250n22

Sīmǎ Tán, 234

slavery, 154, 205, 217

social roles, 16, 30; and conduct, 29, 38, 53, 90, 95; hierarchical, 102–3

social status, 1, 6, 10; and benevolence, 136, 245n11; and decline of Mohism, 234–36; distinctions in, 211–12; elite, 31, 33, 98, 130, 131, 136, 211, 223, 224, 234, 235, 250n27; and ethics, 130, 150; hierarchical, 91, 95–96, 102, 104–6, 116–19, 121–22, 132; mobility in, 97, 100; and moderation, 33, 215, 216–17, 223, 224, 225; and Mohist audience, 31, 131; vs. moral status, 180–82; of Mòzǐ, 8–9; and promoting the worthy, 97, 98, 100; and wealth, 96, 97, 100, 115; Xúnzǐ on, 269n10

Socrates, 19, 31, 59–60

Sòng, state of, 204, 245n7, 246n17

Sòng Xíng, 271n4

state, the: authoritarian, 100–103; and benefit of all, 38, 247n23; ethics in, 132, 134, 150, 155, 187; and fatalism, 42; and funeral rites, 217, 218, 219; and Heaven, 95, 112, 116, 117, 119, 120, 121, 255n19; hierarchical, 30, 84, 87, 88, 94, 95–96, 98–99, 211; and identifying upward, 87–96; and inclusive care, 160, 169, 170, 174–75, 176, 177, 188; and language, 52–53; and models, 31, 35, 66, 92–93; moderation in, 100, 212, 215–16; and Mohism, 4, 20, 22, 232, 233, 234; and music, 216, 222, 223, 224, 226; and order, 77–103; origins of, 78–87; and promoting the worthy, 96–100; public support for, 90–92, 94, 100; and relational virtues, 143–44; and Ruism, 32, 229; and sage-kings, 64, 66, 85, 97, 191; selection of leader for, 83–86, 93; and unified norms, 15, 82–83, 86–87, 133–34, 140, 199; and warfare, 205–6, 207

statements (*yán*), 133, 143; action-guiding, 52–53, 134; and conduct, 63, 87–89, 177, 178; constant (*cháng*), 122, 125, 134, 260n12; and Heaven's intent, 122, 123; and identifying upward, 87, 88, 89; and motivation, 192, 197, 201; and Three Models, 62–63, 64

Sturgeon, Donald, xiv

"Summaries" (books 4–7), 12, 226, 246n20, 264n17

Sūn Xīngyǎn, x
Sūn Yíràng, x

Tāng (sage-king), 37, 64, 175, 208, 226, 249n12, 252n17
Táng Jūnyì, xi
Theaetetus (Plato), 60
Three Models (root, source, use), 62–69, 133; and consequentialism, 142; documents as source in, 65, 66, 162, 175, 223; and funeral rites, 217; and inclusive care, 65, 71, 162, 175, 176; and justification, 252n10; and music, 223
"Three Roots," 97
tiān. See Heaven
tiān mìng. See Heaven, mandate of
tiān xià zhī lì. See benefit of all the world
tiān zhì. See Heaven's intent
"Triads," 13, 14, 30, 31, 50; audience for, 131, 150, 151, 191; chronology of, 15; and ethical demands, 149; on ethics, 129, 140, 149, 151, 153, 155; on Heaven, 115; on inclusive care, 160, 163, 171, 264n17; on Ruism, 132; on Three Models, 62, 65

understanding ghosts (*míng guǐ*), 18
"Understanding Ghosts" (book 31), 65, 68
utilitarianism, Western, 17, 19, 247n25, 258n20
utility (*yòng*): vs. aesthetic value, 214, 216, 223, 225; and moderation, 212–13; of music, 227

value, Mohist conception of, 10, 20–22, 25, 131, 132, 261n33, 262n46; in ethics, 112, 123, 124–25, 130, 153, 154–55, 156, 157; historical context for, 156; and order, 78, 83–84, 91, 94, 101–2; and special relationships, 146
"Valuing Morality," 14
Van Norden, Bryan, xi, xiv
virtue theory, 121

Wáng Chōng, 271n8
warfare, 2–6, 10, 15, 17, 204–11; aggressive (*gōng*), 34, 160, 193, 196, 205–8, 232; vs. benefit, 204, 206–10; and decline of Mohism, 235, 236; defensive, 204–5, 211; vs. diplomatic relations, 205, 207; as disorder, 27–28, 61, 140, 206, 209; and frugality, 212, 229, 230; and Heaven, 205–10; and just war theory, 204, 229, 269n2; Mohist expertise in, 11–14, 204, 235, 236; and motivation, 185, 199, 202; proportionality in, 210; punitive (*zhū*), 206, 208–11; reasoning against, 71–72
Warring States era, 6–7, 20
Watson, Burton, xiv
wealth: as benefit, 41–43, 66, 67, 71, 91, 98, 102, 112–14, 120, 128, 136, 139, 140; and critique of Ruism, 228; distribution of, 77, 100; in ethics, 153, 155, 156; and fate, 40, 44, 58, 62; and frugality, 214, 215, 218, 229; and inclusive care, 166, 168, 169; and social status, 96, 97, 100, 115
Wén (sage-king), 37, 43, 64, 175, 249n12, 252n17
Wén, Duke of Jìn, 173
Wén, Lord of Lǔ Yáng, 209
Western philosophy, 23, 74, 75, 232, 234; epistemology in, 49–50, 61; utilitarian, 17, 19, 247n25, 258n20
women, 213, 248n1, 261n29
Wong, David, xi
Wǔ (sage-king), 37, 43, 64, 175, 208, 226, 249n12, 252n17
Wú, state of, 6
Wūmǎzǐ, 8, 82, 102, 254n7, 270n25; on inclusive care, 171, 172; on righteousness, 134–35; on self-interest, 80, 81

Xià dynasty, 64, 208, 249n12, 252n17
Xiàn Huì, King (Chǔ), 8
xiào. See filiality

xíng. See conduct
xìng. See human nature
Xúnzǐ, ix, 57, 103, 110, 185, 254n1, 270n2; on frugality, 211, 215–16, 219, 221–22, 227, 269n10; and Mohism, 12, 20, 43, 233, 234, 271n4; on ritual, 270n16
Xúnzǐ, 249n9; and epistemology, 50; and individualism, 31; on Mohist ethics, 155; on motivation, 186; on music, 270nn22–23; on reasoning, 73

yán. See statements
Yán Huí, 44, 250n22
Yáng Zhū, 232, 264n14
Yángchéng, Lord of, 148, 149
Yangism, 265n25
Yáo (sage-king), 64, 218, 226, 233, 249n12
yì. See righteousness, moral
Yí Zhī, 264n20
Yín Wén, 271n4
yīn-yáng theory, 236
yòng. See utility
Yōu (tyrant), 37, 249n12
Yǒuzǐ, 136

Yǔ (sage-king), 11, 37, 64, 149, 175, 218, 249n12, 252n17, 262n40; and warfare, 208, 209
yuè. See music
Yuè, state of, 6, 246n21

Zǎi Wǒ, 219–20
Zhèng, state of, 209–10
zhī. See knowledge
zhì. See order, sociopolitical
zhōng. See loyalty
Zhòu (tyrant), 37, 43, 208, 209, 249n12
Zhōu dynasty, 4, 6–7, 10, 64, 249n12, 252n17; and ceremonial propriety, 33; and Heaven, 43, 44
Zhuāngzǐ, 4, 31, 103, 128, 204, 258n21; "All Under Heaven," 11, 211, 234, 270n22; and epistemology, 50, 67, 73; on frugality, 211, 222, 231; and Mohism, 12, 20, 233, 234, 271n4; on Mohist ethics, 149, 150, 155; on Mohist factions, 11, 246n16, 262n40
Zǐ Lù, 45
Zǐ Xià, 250nn21–22

GPSR Authorized Representative: Easy Access System Europe, Mustamäe tee 50, 10621 Tallinn, Estonia, gpsr.requests@easproject.com

www.ingramcontent.com/pod-product-compliance
Lightning Source LLC
Chambersburg PA
CBHW051350290426
44108CB00015B/1955